Palgrave Series in Islamic Theology,
Law, and History

Series editor
Khaled Abou El Fadl
School of Law
University of California
Los Angeles
CA, USA

This ground-breaking series, edited by one of the most influential scholars of Islamic law, presents a cumulative and progressive set of original studies that substantially raise the bar for rigorous scholarship in the field of Islamic Studies. By relying on original sources and challenging common scholarly stereotypes and inherited wisdoms, the volumes of the series attest to the exacting and demanding methodological and pedagogical standards necessary for contemporary studies of Islam. These volumes are chosen not only for their disciplined methodology, exhaustive research, or academic authoritativeness, but for their ability to make critical interventions in the process of understanding the world of Islam as it was, is, and is likely to become. They make central and even pivotal contributions to understanding the experience of the lived and living Islam, and the ways that this rich and creative Islamic tradition has been created and uncreated, or constructed, deconstructed, and reconstructed. In short, the volumes of this series are chosen for their great relevance to the many realities that shaped the ways that Muslims understand, represent, and practice their religion, and ultimately, to understanding the worlds that Muslims helped to shape, and in turn, the worlds that helped shaped Muslims.

More information about this series at
http://www.springer.com/series/14659

Joseph J. Kaminski

The Contemporary Islamic Governed State

A Reconceptualization

Joseph J. Kaminski
International University of Sarajevo
Sarajevo, Bosnia and Herzegovina

Palgrave Series in Islamic Theology, Law, and History
ISBN 978-3-319-86056-5   ISBN 978-3-319-57012-9 (eBook)
DOI 10.1007/978-3-319-57012-9

© The Editor(s) (if applicable) and The Author(s) 2017
Softcover reprint of the hardcover 1st edition 2017
This work is subject to copyright. All rights are solely and exclusively licensed by the Publisher, whether the whole or part of the material is concerned, specifically the rights of translation, reprinting, reuse of illustrations, recitation, broadcasting, reproduction on microfilms or in any other physical way, and transmission or information storage and retrieval, electronic adaptation, computer software, or by similar or dissimilar methodology now known or hereafter developed.
The use of general descriptive names, registered names, trademarks, service marks, etc. in this publication does not imply, even in the absence of a specific statement, that such names are exempt from the relevant protective laws and regulations and therefore free for general use.
The publisher, the authors and the editors are safe to assume that the advice and information in this book are believed to be true and accurate at the date of publication. Neither the publisher nor the authors or the editors give a warranty, express or implied, with respect to the material contained herein or for any errors or omissions that may have been made. The publisher remains neutral with regard to jurisdictional claims in published maps and institutional affiliations.

Cover credit: © Oleg Boldyrev/Alamy Stock Photo

Printed on acid-free paper

This Palgrave Macmillan imprint is published by Springer Nature
The registered company is Springer International Publishing AG
The registered company address is: Gewerbestrasse 11, 6330 Cham, Switzerland

This book is dedicated to my late grandfather, John Victor Penrod [1932–2009], who taught me the values of hard work, discipline, and intellectual curiosity.

Series Editor's Preface

The volume that I have the honor of introducing in the Palgrave Series on Islamic Theology, Law, and History is a distinctively thoughtful and, I daresay, intellectually prodigious contribution to contemporary scholarly discourses on Islam and governance. Since the end of the age of empires and the rise of nation-states, the subject of Islam and government has been the focus of much attention. Of the many writings in this field, Joseph Kaminski's contribution is necessary, comprehensive, pressing, and superlative. This volume provides readers with a learned and cautious exploration of the major intellectual orientations within the Islamic classical heritage on what may be described as Islamic politics. However, Kaminski does not analyze the classical Islamic discourses on power, justice, and government in an historical vacuum. One of the most important contributions of this book is that it situates and links classical Islamic political thought with its proper historical lineage in Greek and Persian thought. However, Kaminski does not treat the classical normative orientations of the Islamic tradition as determinative for modern Muslims. Unlike many studies that limit themselves to an historical exploration of pre-modern Islamic thought without investigating the ways that contemporary Muslims have negotiated their own intellectual heritage, with notable mastery and finesse, Kaminski gives equal weight to the classical heritage as well as the lived experience of modern Muslims. Consequently, readers will receive a deeply informed introduction to the classical discourses on governance and politics as well as insightful case studies of the ways that the Islamic intellectual heritage was negotiated by modern Muslims in Turkey, Egypt, Tunisia, and Malaysia. Most significantly, Kaminski does not limit himself to a descriptive survey of the continuities and disruptions between the Muslim past and present. Kaminski's project is far more ambitious. He attempts a reconceptualization of what Islamic governance means in the modern age and, in this regard, his arguments are provocative and compelling. Notably, Kaminski is equally comfortable and adept at navigating the intellectual terrain of Islamic thought as he is with Western political theory. In analyzing what the right to self-determination means for modern Muslims, Kaminski takes readers on an intellectual journey from Michel Foucault and Ernesto Laclau to Robert Dahl's *Polyarchy* in arguing for a substantial difference between what he describes as an Islamic state as opposed to an Islamic governed state. Perhaps most provocatively, Kaminski argues that while democracy is a necessary and wise form of rule for an Islamic governed state, the same cannot be said about liberalism. Moreover, Kaminski contends that while democracy is compatible with the values of Islamic governance, liberalism is not. Whether readers are ultimately persuaded by the author's approach or not, it is undeniable that Kaminski has made an emphatically pressing and cogent contribution to contemporary discourses on Islamic political thought, liberalism, and democracy. In my view, no serious student of Islamic political thought or Islamic politics can afford to ignore Kaminski's challenging and inspiring contribution to the field. With this, I take distinct pride in introducing this inspired and sorely needed scholarly voice to readers interested not just in Islam and governance and politics, but also the role of religion and religiously inspired traditions in modern polities.

March 2017

Khaled Abou El Fadl
Alfi Distinguished Professor of Islamic Law
UCLA School of Law

Acknowledgements

I first would like to thank the series editor, Khaled Abou El Fadl, for believing in this manuscript. It truly is an honor to be a part of this very prestigious series. I would also like to thank Amy Invernizzi and Phil Getz at Palgrave for all of their help during the publishing process. Second, I would like to thank my late dissertation advisor, Michael A. Weinstein, for sharing his wisdom with me over the years—it was truly a privilege to have spent 5 years under your aegis while I was at Purdue. I hope that you would have been proud of my efforts in this work. I would also like to extend my deepest gratitude to Stephen Eric Bronner and the late Marshall Berman for their years of unwavering support, mentorship, and professional guidance—you both most certainly taught me to think outside the box and not be afraid to take risks. Regarding this particular book, I would like to thank Fred Dallmayr, Zillur R. Khan, Saqib Sheikh, and Robert Oprisko for your invaluable advice.

Next, I would like to thank the following individuals who I feel most directly inspired my intellectual and professional development over these years: Richard Ossana, Ralph Holden, Pam Miller, Harry Targ, William McBride, S. Laurel Weldon, Bert Rockman, Jay McCann, Richard Wolin, Joan Tronto, David Palazzo, Barry Murdaco, Justin Mueller, Christopher Kulseza, Marco Morini, Peter Plenta, Jared Bell, Nathan Munier, Emil Knezovic, Ali Çaksu, Aliye Fatima Mataraci, and Mesut Idriz.

Finally, I would like to thank my amazing wife, Maryam Golzardi, and her father, Mohammad Reza Golzardi, for the long intellectual conversations about Islam and politics we had over tea in Sarajevo. I would also like to extend my warmest affections to my parents Debbie and Joseph William Kaminski, my sister Holly, my wonderful nieces Giana and Liliana, my cousins Eric and Lindsay, and my saintly grandmother, Suzanne Penrod, for their years of continued emotional support while I was living away from home in New Jersey, New York City, and Sarajevo; you guys have always been there for me and I love you all dearly.

Contents

1 Introduction: Determining the Basis for Political Discourse for the Next Generation   1

Part I   Historical Context and Theoretical Framework

2 The Trajectory of the Development of Islamic Thought—A Comparison Between Two Earlier and Two Later Scholars   31

3 The Ontological Framing of this Model of a Contemporary Islamic Governed State   71

4 Considering Leadership and Laws in a Contemporary Islamic Governed State   105

5 Considering Bureaucracy and Democracy in a Contemporary Islamic Governed State   137

6 The Importance of Involving Women in the Political Apparatus of a Contemporary Islamic Governed State   169

7 The Importance of Economic Justice in a Contemporary Islamic Governed State ... 189

Part II Case Studies in the Contemporary Muslim World

8 The Case of Turkey: Soft Power and Economic Growth ... 211

9 The Case of Egypt: Revolution, Counterrevolution, and a Return to Brutal Dictatorship ... 231

10 The Case of Tunisia: Pragmatism and Cooperation ... 249

11 The Case of Malaysia: Prioritizing Economic Growth and Modernization ... 265

12 Conclusion: Creating a New Discourse ... 279

Bibliography ... 295

Index ... 325

List of Figures and Tables

Fig. 3.1 "Do you favor or oppose making sharia law, or Islamic law, the official law of the land in our country?"   90

Table 2.1 Synopsis of *Mu'tazilah*, *Ash'arī/Māturīdī*, and *Ḥanbalī/Atharī* approaches to Islamic theology   37

Table 4.1 Leadership styles and corresponding attributes   108

CHAPTER 1

Introduction: Determining the Basis for Political Discourse for the Next Generation

In regard to Tunisia's nascent Islamist movement during the 1990s, John Voll commented that "the battle at present is not over specific programs or particular policies; it is to determine the basis for political discourse for the next generation" (1997: 14). This general theme can be broadened to include the rest of Muslim world even today. Addressing Voll's question in relation to the broader Muslim world is at the heart of what this project is about. Despite the enormous range of opinions held by contemporary scholars of the Muslim world, some common points can be drawn from their works.

One of these points is the undeniable growth of Islam. Islam is expected to continue to grow significantly over the next two decades. In 2011, the Pew Research Center's Forum on Religion & Public Life predicted that the world's Muslim population would increase by about 35% in the next 20 years, rising from approximately 1.6 billion in 2010 to around 2.2 billion by 2030 (*Pew Research Center: Forum on Religion & Public Life* 2011). The twenty-first century scholarly consensus also overwhelmingly accepts the general idea that Islam is experiencing an awakening and is taken more seriously in this current generation than it was in previous recent generations (Lapidus 2002; Roy 2004; Esposito 2010).

In 2006, a collection of lectures delivered by the highly regarded late Saudi Sheikh Muḥammad Ibn Ṣāliḥ al-ʿUthaymīn was compiled into a book by one of his students titled, *The Islamic Awakening: Important Guidelines*. One of the main points of the book was to promote the argument that the Muslim world was in the midst of an Islamic awakening the likes of which has not been seen in centuries. More specifically, Sheikh'Uthaymīn's point throughout the complied collection of lectures was that the younger generations were taking a leading role in Islam's most recent awakening. Over the past few decades, the *ummah* or global community of Muslim believers has been returning to Islam and the teachings of the *Qur'ān* in a more serious manner all across the Muslim diaspora. There is no reason to think this trend will be changing anytime soon. Around the same time as 'Uthaymīn's complied lectures were published as a book, Oliver Roy (2004) postulated that a new, globalized Islam has emerged, and that for better or for worse, this globalized Islam will continue to evolve and remain salient in the foreseeable future.

As we stand a little over a decade later, Roy's hypothesis appears to be quite accurate. Neither the Arab Revolutions of 2011 nor certain more recent transnational terrorist organizations like *Al-Shabāb* or ISIS existed when Roy originally published his book.[1] Islam remains a powerful force that will continue to reshape the world in the foreseeable future. In the words of Andrew March, "No single one of Islam's political commitments is unique to Islam, but no other religious tradition displays all of them together, from political solidarity to a theory of righteous warfare" (2015: 174). Mohammad Iqbal in his 1930 Presidential Address to the All-India Muslim League made the point that Islam does not separate the spiritual from the material in the same way European ideologies do.

> Islam does not bifurcate the unity of man into an irreconcilable duality of spirit and matter. In Islam God and the universe, spirit and matter, Church and State, are organic to each other. Man is not the citizen of a profane world to be renounced in the interest of a world of spirit situated elsewhere. To Islam, matter is spirit realizing itself in space and time. (Iqbal, quoted by Hay and De Bary, et al. (Ed.) 1988: 764)

More recently, the popular Kuwaiti public motivational speaker, Tariq al-Suwaidan made a similar point asserting that "Islam is not a religion. It's a way of life that teaches us about our relationship with God, with the universe, and our relationship with ethics with the economy and our political system" (al-Suwaidan, quoted in Mok 2014: *online*). This is true within both the *Sunni* and *Shī'ah* discourses. This project is situated within a growing canon of literature that looks at the relationship between modern Western conceptualizations of politics and Islam. The literature on this topic suggests that the relationship between the two is complex and needs to be further analyzed.

What this Work Seeks to Actually Do

This work engages with what has become the almost taboo normative discourse surrounding the intersection of politics and Islam. Unlike many other recent works on Islam and governance, this work will directly engage with *the elephant in the room* that is *Sharī'ah* while formulating a general discursive framework for an Islamic governed state. Rather than taking the easy route and downplaying the role of *Sharī'ah* or making efforts to hide and/or sanitize it, this work accepts *Sharī'ah* as an inalienable part of any genuinely Islamic governed state. What *Sharī'ah* actually means and how it is implemented is the issue at hand. The forthcoming chapters will directly address these questions in greater detail.

The main issue this manuscript tackles can be traced back to Voll's aforementioned quotation about "determining the basis for political discourse for the next generation" that served as the introductory quotation to this chapter. *Discourses* can be understood as "systems of thoughts composed of ideas, attitudes, courses of action, beliefs and practices that systematically construct the subjects and the worlds of which they speak" (Lessa 2006: 285). The notion of discourse at a sociological level was first described in detail by Michel Foucault in his iconic *L'Archéologie du savoir* as an abstract construct that was "constituted by a set of sequences of signs in so far as they are enouncements [*énoncés*][2]" (1969: 141). An *énoncé* is often translated into English as a statement or proclamation. *Énoncés* allow for one to assign meaning to a word or set of words. For Foucault, a *discursive formation* was defined by repeating sequences, patterns, or regularities that ultimately produce a specific discourse. Cynthia Hardy later expanded upon Foucault's point by arguing that the meanings of any specific discourse are "created, supported, and contested through the production, dissemination, and consumption of texts; and emanate from interactions between the social groups and the complex societal structures in which the discourse is embedded" (2001: 28). This is to suggest that specific discourses are shaped by both endogenous and exogenous factors.

The late Argentine philosopher Ernesto Laclau also wrote extensively on the notion of discourse, albeit from a much different vantage point than Foucault. On the core assumption of a discursive approach to reality, Laclau commented that "The basic hypothesis of a discursive approach is that the very possibility of perception, thought and action depends on the structuration of a certain meaningful field which pre-exists any factual immediacy" (2007: 541). In Laclau's assessment, the main contributions of discourse theory within the realm of politics generally have been related to conceptualizations of power and hegemony.

> Discourse for us is a kind of link between social elements where each of the elements, considered in isolation, is not necessarily linked to the other. For us [Laclau and Chantal Mouffe], as you know, there is no 'natural' or 'necessary' relationship between elements that precedes the act of linking itself. Therefore, linking them involves some kind of intervention. This intervention is exactly what we call hegemony. So discourse theory and hegemony are names for two sides of the same perspective. (Laclau, interviewed in Hansen and Sonnichsen 2014: 256–257)

Laclau's appropriation of the notion of discourse differed from Foucault's. Foucault's understanding of discourse was more directly connected to "the social" and structures of politics. It differed from Laclau's efforts to explain *discourse* as a more general ontological phenomenon. Laclau argued that for Foucault, "all distinctions were ontic, and his different analyses sought to differentiate ever more areas of ontic differences" (Laclau, interviewed in Hansen and Sonnichsen 2014: 261). For Laclau and Mouffe, discourse "has an ontological dimension which is not at all present in Foucault's analysis," whereas for Foucault, "discourse is simply a regional area of the social" which he "never had a conception of the ontic/ontological distinction" for as did Laclau and Mouffe (Laclau, interviewed in Hansen and Sonnichsen 2014: 261).

The *ontic* versus the *ontological* in regard to Islamic governance is an important distinction to make from the outset here. The contemporary British public intellectual Ziauddin Sardar makes it clear that once Islam is denigrated into being just another political ideology, it risks losing its sense of humanity and ultimately becoming something very corrosive.

> But once Islam, as an ideology, becomes a programme of action of a vested group, it looses [sic: read loses] its humanity and becomes a battlefield

1 INTRODUCTION: DETERMINING THE BASIS FOR POLITICAL DISCOURSE ... 5

where morality, reason and justice are readily sacrificed at the altar of emotions. Moreover, the step from a totalistic ideology to a totalitarian order where every human situation is open to state arbitration is a small one. The transformation of Islam into a state-based political ideology not only deprives it of all its moral and ethical content, it also debunks most of Muslim history as un-Islamic. (Sardar 2003: 30)

Sardar's concern is one that is taken seriously in this work as well. I believe by focusing on the "ontic" rather than the "ontological," i.e., offering a discursive framework for an "Islamic *governed* state" (governed being the key word) which focuses primarily on the epistemic moorings of governance, rather than the more ontologically pervasive notion of an "Islamic state," one has a much greater possibility of avoiding the pitfalls of authoritarianism and an all-consuming ideology that, a priori, dictates even the more insignificant personal details of daily life. Compulsory *ḥijāb* wearing mandated by law (even for non-Muslims), bans on females driving automobiles, virginity/sexual purity tests, and an overzealous *muṭawwi'īn* or *komiteh* are all by-products of an all-consuming ideology that spends more time worrying about controlling bodies than controlling corrupt political actors or inefficient governance.[3] Of course there is an undeniable biconditional relationship between the way the state operates and the mores and norms it ultimately projects. However, by focusing on governance and not getting bogged down in unwieldy debates regarding the minutia of individual morality, there remains more flexibility in the later construction of categories that exist outside the purview of the purely political; theorizing in this more ontically restricted manner preserves the possibility for the emergence of an authentic civil society that is not completely under the auspices of a totalizing state-sanctioned dogma.

Foucault (1970) utilized the concept of discursive formations in his own analyses surrounding theoretical frameworks about political institutions, economic institutions, and even the way natural history was analyzed. He argued that all meanings attached to words, ideas, or concepts (or discourses) were inextricably linked to power relations. "Whether it is our concepts of madness, illness, crime, 'normal' sexual behavior, the individual, or political agency, for Foucault, the meanings that humans attach to these aspects of reality, in other words, interpretations, are indissociable from power" (Krishna 2009: 63). The classic contemporary example illustrating this point is that of labeling an individual or group as "freedom fighters" or "terrorists." While each term may refer to the same entity, they carry with them radically different emotional attachments and political ramifications.

Laclau claimed that due to the impossibility of a closed totality (i.e., in this particular case, the fact that short of divine intervention, there will never be a fully defined, unchanging, and "complete" Islamic political discourse), all of the humanity is in a constant struggle with each other for power. One of the most important of these power struggles perhaps lies in being able to define and ultimately control a specific discourse or set of competing/alternative discourses.

> ...the impossibility of a closed totality unties the connection between signifier and signified. In that sense there is a proliferation of 'floating signifiers' in society, and political competition can be seen as attempts by rival political forces to partially fix those signifiers to particular signifying configurations. (Laclau 2007: 545)

Power exists among multiple actors both within and outside a discourse that can never fully be quantified or readily reduced back to one specific source. Power is anywhere and everywhere, so to speak. It is in constant flux, contingent upon multiple factors—some obvious and some completely undetected, hidden, and/or even ignored.

I believe that a discursive approach to Islamic governance ought to first focus on offering a set of coherent axioms or "guideposts" before formulating more specific, localized theories, and ultimately specific policies and programs. The limited serious scholarly efforts at defining a more general discourse, or even competing discourses, toward Islamic governance are why we still see a wide range of governing practices lumped under a banner so expansive that it actually means almost nothing. Entities ranging from the pragmatic and moderately conservative, such as the national-based Islamic political parties that operate within the confines of secular constitutions in places like Tunisia, Malaysia, Indonesia, and Turkey, to the theo-democratic regime in Iran, to the absolute monarchy acting as "Custodian of the 2 Holy Mosques" in Saudi Arabia, all the way to the truly grotesque like ISIS and the *Tālibān*, all get lumped together under the increasingly meaningless monikers of "Islamism" or "political Islam" one way or another.

If more scholarly efforts are not made to offer coherent theories of Islamic governance or "Islamism-in-practice," the entire concept will eventually lose all meaning. Ultimately, as can already be seen today, it will continue to be more rigidly defined by Western political powers and the neoliberal global media apparatus in a way that *all* of the aforementioned groups located somewhere within the current rubric of "Islamism" would object to. This leaves the entire construct of Islamic governance in a very precarious position; its meanings and parameters are literally being more clearly defined by those openly opposed and hostile to the notion of it altogether, than those agnostic or supportive of it. This means the average global citizen's general idea of "Islamic governance" is being framed more and more from the likes of Donald Trump or Pamela Geller and Robert Spencer's *American Freedom Defense Initiative*, rather than by actual scholars of Islam or Islamic political philosophy. As forces hostile to Islam further monopolize the "idea-market" on what Islamic governance means, it will become increasingly difficult to wrestle the power to define the discourse on this topic away from such entities. This is another reason why I believe a project like this is important and timely right now; it might be too late in 5 or 10 years.

While earlier figures such as Abul ala Maududi, Hasan al Banna, Ayatollah Khomeini, and Alija Izetbegović primarily addressed "the need for" or "the importance of" Islamic government in their own unique and insightful ways, this work seeks to go beyond the nauseating rhetoric of *al-Islām huwa-'l-ḥāl* or "Islam is the Solution" that sadly often has become an idle *cliché* at best and an excuse for horrific violence at worst. In one of his numerous recent public lectures, in four and a half minutes Sheikh Hamza Yusuf made multiple powerful and salient points. The crux of his argument was that notion of Islamic governance (at least as it currently stands) lacks any real content or meaning. He rightfully makes the point that there exist only a handful of *ḥudūd* or divinely mandated punishments. According to Yusuf, there are actually only 4 such punishments that are agreed upon and 13 that to this day remain hotly debated among scholars. He goes on to argue that considering all of the complexities of governance and administration in the contemporary world, no state today can operate based on such a minimalistic jurisprudential framework alone.

> ...religion actually has very little to do with the running of a state. Building roads has nothing to do with what *madhhab* you follow. "You know, oh that's a Hanifi road." "No, that's a *madhhab*." Right, a *madhhab* means a road in Arabic, but *madhhab* is a school, is a metaphor taken from

the real *madhhab* which is a road. No, a road is; you can build it from stone, you can build it from asphalt, you can build it from concrete—and that's just what you want—is honesty, you want vetting, you want transparency—those are secular ideals as well, right? A post office is not an Islamic concept, right? [...] Seriously, think about it—the vast majority of government just does not relate to religion; it just relates to common decency. (Yusuf lecture 2013: *online*)

Toward the end of his lecture, he makes the point that if Muslims living in the eight century in places like Syria or Palestine were transplanted into a contemporary Scandinavian state like Norway, they would be amazed with the quality of governance and social justice.

While I agree with many Yusuf's more general points, especially those regarding the reality that one cannot simply turn to a jurisprudential ruling from 10 centuries ago to adequately confront many of today's most pressing administrative and security issues, I still firmly believe that based on empirical evidence that will be shown in the later chapters, a very large number of Muslims do want *Sharī'ah*, at minimum, as a *source* for laws. I also believe that many Muslims living in OIC member states would like to live in a state that operates within Islam's laudable ethical, jurisprudential, economic, and social frameworks.

Rather than cheerleading for an Islamic governed state, this work seeks to articulate a practical discursive framework for actually making this happen in a way that results in a viable and equitable state. In many ways, this work is an effort to address Yusuf's comments about the lack of content in today's iteration of "an Islamic state" by trying to offer concrete ways to help bring the quality of governance of a place like Norway to a Muslim state that is underpinned by *Sharī'ah* values—values that were originally meant to be impartial and fair rather than arbitrary, unduly harsh, and just another tool of repression for a corrupt political ruling elite.

Ayatollah Khomeini's thought offered perhaps the most sophisticated model of the more practical institutional elements in an "Islamic state" most clearly seen in his articulation of *velāyat-e faqīh*, or the guardianship of the jurist, in which the leading Islamic jurist (*faqīh*) provides guardianship (*velāyat*) over both the people and the nation. Despite his model's successful implementation following the 1979 Iranian Revolution, it did not adequately address many of the real-world questions that contemporary political scientists grapple with today.

Khomeini's writings on Islamic governance did not go much into detail about the role of democracy, women's rights, public administration, and economic justice in their contemporary context based on existing empirical data and published scholarly research. While he did make allusions to some of these points, for example, noting that the previous economic order had divided people into oppressors and the oppressed—by in large—he glossed over them in favor selling to his reader the importance of an Islamic government and why it had yet to be established. It is highly unlikely that Khomeini looked at the writings of empirically oriented academics who wrote earlier in the twentieth century like Seymour Lipset, Max Weber, Anthony Downs, or Robert Dahl for empirical and theoretical guidance while articulating his vision of an Islamic governed state. This work does.

Ultimately, this work *only* looks to establish a normative discursive framework surrounding essential elements that must be grappled with prior to efforts by other scholars or political actors to construct more specific policies and legislative institutions. There is no reason to talk about how many chambers of parliament or parliamentarians any specific state ought to have before engaging in a discussion on what the mind-set of the individual parliamentarian ought to look like and what values ought to guide his or her decision-making processes; there is no point in talking about the specific legalistic functions of an Islamic governed state's leader without discussing the personality qualities and values that are necessary to successfully lead in the first place. While specific policies and legislative institutions might be the façade that is most readily seen by the public, the discursive framework or theoretical normative foundations of an Islamic governed state must be first seriously considered.

One can use an architectural analogy to better understand what this work attempts to do; when building a house, there is no point in articulating concise final dimensions for a roof or for the windows of a house that still does not have the actual final dimensions of the concrete foundation determined. This work will not place the *final coat of paint* on the house that is the ideal Islamic governed state. This project is not even an effort to establish the final measured concrete foundation for the house that is the ideal Islamic governed state—this work only hopes to act as a shovel that can break the ground of Islamic governance that has become ossified so that the *real* digging can actually begin.

Islam and Governance—A Brief Overview of Last 20 Years

The general contemporary scholarly consensus over the past two decades is that democracy cannot be conceived of in the same manner in the Muslim world as it is in the West (Bulliet 1994; Voll 1997; Abou El Fadl 2004; Esposito 2004; Dallmayr 2010). These sentiments have echoed even more loudly following the disastrous aftermath of the US coalition-led efforts to *democratize* Iraq following the removal of Saddam Hussein in (2003). In 2005, Eric Davis argued that among ordinary Iraqis, the memory of a democratic and cosmopolitan past—one that was brutally suppressed under the long rule of Saddam Hussein—was still present within the collective national ethos. Based on this, Davis saw the potential for a peaceful and prosperous co existence among the various ethnic groups living in Iraq following Saddam's removal:

> Since 2003, some Sunni and Shi'ite clerics have harked back to the ecumenical tradition of the 1920 Revolution by meeting to denounce the efforts of radical Islamists and ex-Baathists to reimpose sectarianism on Iraq. In these significant ways, the history of modern Iraq offers no support for the politics of religious radicalism, but instead underlines the prospect that Iraq's two major Muslim communities can find common ground for cooperation and even mutual acceptance in the pursuit of national goals. (2005: 60)

Sadly, Davis' optimistic prognostication has proven thus far to be woefully inaccurate. Once in power, Iraq's largely secular *Shī'ah* political leadership, led by Nouri al-Maliki, almost immediately began to purge the government of *Sunni* politicians, the Kurds were marginalized and rampant corruption and sectarianism ruled the day. In an effort to not upset anyone, the post-Saddam constitution was left incredibly vague. It also sets up a situation in which Kurds living in the north and *Shī'ah* living in the south could form their own oil-rich entities, while the Sunnis would be left in the oil-dry central part of the country. A general sense of hopelessness and resentment festered among ordinary Iraqi citizens that ultimately led to the rise of extremism, ISIS, and chaos.

Ten years after Davis' article, Iraq can only be described as one of the most epic foreign policy and nation building disasters in USA's history. The US credibility in the Middle East has yet to recover. The tragic case of Iraq shows that different approaches are needed when considering Muslim states transitioning away from autocratic or tyrannical modes of governance. This book argues that an alternative path should be considered: a path that incorporates an inclusive and accommodating interpretation of Islam into the governing model of the state; a path that looks more toward ancient, rather than Enlightenment philosophies for inspiration; and ultimately, a path that is developed organically based on local customs and values. A model is needed that engages with some of the institutional elements commonly found in Western constructs of liberal democracy when appropriate, but remains rooted in a social contract that is based on the *Qur'ān* and the *Sunnah* of the Prophet (ﷺ).[4]

The question of Islam and its compatibility with democracy has been examined in great detail in the past, but has recently taken on new salience. Khaled Abou El Fadl claims that there are serious issues in regard to the compatibility of Islam and Western models of liberal democracy from the very outset. One of these issues relates to where the sources of the themselves originate and how this impacts governance. European Enlightenment scholars have argued that one of the most undeniable fundamental guiding principles of the Enlightenment was the notion that laws were created *by* men, *for* men (Gay 1969; Bronner 1995, 1999; Himmelfarb 2004). In the words of Max Horkheimer and Theodor Adorno, "The program of the Enlightenment was the disenchantment of the world; the dissolution of myths and the substitution of knowledge for fancy" (2002: 3). The revelation was no longer a valid source of laws within the new Enlightenment discourse—secularism was the widely held battle cry among the Enlightenment's more radical figures such as Diderot and Voltaire. In the words of Harvey Cox, secularism could best be understood as, "the liberation of man from religious and metaphysical tutelage, the turning of his attention away from other worlds and toward this one" (1966: 17). This stands in stark contrast to the basic Islamic worldview which does place primacy on revelation as a primary source of laws. This point will be much further elaborated upon in Chaps. 2 and 3.

Abou El Fadl believes that even though within the Islamic worldview the most central, moral, and ethical laws ultimately derive God, this does not preclude the operationalization of democracy *within* an Islamic framework. He comments that; "My answer begins from the premise that democracy and Islam are defined in the first instance by their underlying moral values and attitudinal commitments of their adherents—not by the way those values and commitments have been applied" (2004: 4). Within the Islamic discourse lie the practical possibilities of legitimate democratic practices; "democracy—by assigning equal rights of free speech, association, and suffrage to all—offers the greatest potential for promoting justice and protecting human dignity without making God responsible for injustice or the degradation of human beings" (2004: 6). Based on this belief, he concludes that democratic governance best articulates a vision of justice that is the most compatible with the values espoused by the *Qur'ān*.

He also believes in the possibility of a governing structure where God remains the ultimate Sovereign *and* where democratic practices within an Islamic framework establish worldly standards for fairness and justice. "Islamic political thought contains a range of interpretive possibilities. And once again, some of these possibilities resonate more strongly with democratic principles" (2004: 12). Within the range of possibilities are democratic solutions in regard to problems surrounding the rule of law. Abou El Fadl argues that "there has always been a complex relationship between Shari'a law as articulated by the jurists and the administrative practices of the state" (2004: 14). He believes that future scholarship surrounding the laws in the Muslim world must account for historical change, especially those changes in regard to things like human rights; Muslims must seriously commit to recognizing human rights as a universal value that is inexorable from the central tenets of Islam. Abou El Fadl insists that the law of the state is separate from the *Sharī'ah*, even if the *Sharī'ah* influences the laws and that *Sharī'ah* interpretations will always subject to human agency. For example, he mentioned that while it is accepted that a thief's hands should be cut off based on *Sharī'ah*, it is still the role of legal scholars and judges to define what constitutes "a thief"? Abou El Fadl argued that even "cut off" can be interpreted in numerous ways and not simply in its most literal sense.

Based on all of this, he concluded that *Sharī'ah* should be a guide for crafting laws or *a source for laws*, but not the laws of the state themselves. The work that contemporary scholars need to pursue is how to apply *Sharī'ah* to contemporary administrative practices. This book looks at the *Qur'ān*, the *Sunnah* of the Prophet (ﷺ), and some of the most widely accepted *'aḥādīth*, and integrates these values into a modern administrative and governing framework. It justifies why this framework fits within the purview of Islam by referencing primary Islamic sources and historical examples.

Fred Dallmayr's *The Promise of Democracy: Political Agency and Transformation* has an entire chapter that focuses specifically on the relationship between Islam and democracy. Dallmayr asks, "can democracy be religious, and if so, how can it be religious? How can we bring religion into modern democratic politics, and how can modern democracy be reconciled with religion?" (2010: 155). Dallmayr argues that rather than resisting religion altogether, "it is time to recuperate the genuine meaning of Islam" as a summons to freedom, justice, and service to the God who, throughout the *Qur'ān*, is called "all merciful and compassionate (*rahman-i-raheem*)" (2010: 156–157). For Dallmayr, democracy does not have to be rigidly secular. Existing religious institutions must renounce their despotic element and instead embrace what he calls, "a more humanistic general vocabulary" that includes language about human rights, individual freedoms, and social justice. When considering Islam and its relationship (and often clash) with the prevailing secular norms and standards of modernity at the global level, Dallmayr forcefully recommends:

> ...it is time, not to abandon Islam in favour of some doctrinaire secularism or laïcism (which does not have sufficient tools to resist the idols of the market), but to reinvigorate the "salt" of Islamic faith so that it can become a beacon of light for Muslims and the world around them. (2010: 156)

What Dallmayr calls for is precisely what my project offers, an effort to engage a religious discourse that broadens its range to accommodate widely held contemporary global norms while remaining in accord with the core premises of the religion itself—or getting back to "the 'salt' of Islamic faith" once again. Dallmayr looks to find a way to "re-enchant" modernity in a way that stands at odds with Weber and Adorno's assertions that the enlightenment and modernity in general are little more than an enduring process of disenchantment.

John Voll believes that, as the state of research currently stands, the broader philosophical aspects undergirding an Islamic political discourse are what currently need to be focused upon rather than micro-level issues such as specific codes or policies. He believed that this could be done.

In regard to Tunisia's Islamist movement in the 1990s, Voll noted that it provided "a clearly comprehensive vocabulary and set of conceptualizations for later use in promulgating specific policies and programs" (Voll, in Entelis (Ed.) 1997: 14). Other Islamic-oriented groups also have the potential to shape the discourse that will be foundational to articulating more specific future policies and programs. This project articulates some foundational premises for crafting institutions within an Islamic discourse. It is from these broader theoretical constructs that more specific policies and programs can be ultimately developed tailored to the needs of individual states.

Voll is adamant that Western efforts at bringing secular democracy have failed and have only ushered in a new type of oppressive authoritarianism; efforts to *Westernize* North Africa in the past century have pretty much been an unmitigated disaster. This should not be all that surprising considering the vastly different historical circumstances surrounding the way secularism took hold between the West and the Muslim world. Secularism in the West was more of a bottom-up process driven largely by civil society, while in the Muslim world secularism was a top-down process first imposed by colonizers and then by the local elites and autocrats that inherited the mantle of authority from those colonizers following their departure (Nasr 2010b). Nader Hashemi aptly comments that

> In the past 200 years, the Muslim world's experience with secularism has been largely negative. It is important to appreciate that in Europe secularism was an indigenous and gradual process evolving in conjunction with socio-economic and political developments while supported by intellectual arguments – and, critically, by religious groups – that eventually sank deep roots within its political culture. By contrast, the Muslim experience has been marked by the perception of secularism as an alien ideology imposed from the outside, first by colonial and imperial invaders, then by local elites who came to power during the post-colonial period. (2014: 444)

Voll goes on to argue that where Westernization has failed Islam can succeed. The way to bridge the seemingly irreconcilable gap between the elites and the poor masses is via an authentic organically developed local discourse. Islamic conceptualizations of ideas, identities, and concepts are not dependent upon past major events that happened in Europe or the USA such as the French Revolution or the American Revolution. "Islam provides a broad set of concepts for discourse that can go beyond the old

European and North American models" (Voll, in Entelis (Ed.) 1997: 10). Voll's argument is precisely what I also propose in this project, a mode of politics that is not dependent upon the Enlightenment for the framing of its basic values and principles that is also grounded in a recognizable local discourse that at its very core transcends class distinctions.

John Esposito's work also engages with the question of democracy and its compatibility to Islam. Like Abou El Fadl, Dallmayr, and Voll, Esposito also recognized the inherent compatibilities between Islam and democratic modes of governance, but not necessarily in the Western liberal way. Often those in the West like to assume democracy is synonymous with "liberal democracy." Esposito (2004) rightfully makes the important point that democracy can take on many forms: liberal forms, socialist forms, or even a blend of religious elements and democracy. He referenced former Iranian president Mohammed Khatami who argued that Iran was an example of a state that followed the third option, a blend of religious elements and democratic elements. Like Voll, Esposito argues that even reformist efforts within the Muslim world should not simply uncritically adapt Western modes of democracy into their political framework. Esposito reminds his audience that "reformist efforts toward political liberalization, electoral politics, and democratization within the Muslim world do not imply the uncritical acceptance of western democratic forms" (1997: 97). Even the reformers must recognize the complexity in creating a model of governance that is effective and meets the standards of fairness and integrity within the Islamic discourse.

In the end, Esposito argues that one of the biggest challenges in transforming politics in the Muslim world ultimately lies in opening the discourse to a diverse set of voices. This means wrestling power from the elites that often have acted with impunity. He makes the point that too often reformers of any type are perceived as threats by the orthodoxy and that too often their voices are silenced by a repressive state apparatus. In his words, "the most important challenge for Islamic reformers will be the transfer of their reformulations from the elite few to the institutions and peoples of Islam" (2004: 100). He concludes that this requires institutional change and a new way of looking at pedagogy, and the way the teachers themselves are taught to teach. Many of Esposito's concerns parallel the central concerns of my project. I agree that the voices of reform must come from a diverse set of voices, especially those working within the Islamic framework that is not connected to any particular source of power or political influence. Scholars and policy makers alike must be free to express their ideas without the threat of imprisonment or worse.

CARPE DIEM!—WHY *NOW* IS THE TIME FOR SCHOLARS TO OFFER NEW IDEAS

While each individual uprising that was a part of the various 2011 Arab Revolutions was unique in their own ways, all of these individual revolutions shared a common underlying thread; oppressive and repressive autocratic governments that placed Western interests over their own citizens' needs could no longer suffice. While democratization and individual rights have been important leitmotifs in all of the Arab Revolutions, they have not replaced the importance of Islam as a way of life—slogans referring to Allah, the *Qur'ān* and the *Sunnah* of the Prophet (ﷺ), were common in all of these revolutions.

Historically in the West, mass publics have viewed the role of intellectuals with a great deal of suspicion. The iconic American historian Richard Hofstadter (1963) famously argued that as the Cold War started, the overall disdain toward intellectuals felt by Americans had risen to a new level. Many Americans felt that the so-called experts were nothing more than opportunists who sought to advance their own ends at the expense of others. These *professional intellectuals* were often viewed as out of touch elites whose national loyalties could not be trusted by a nation that as of 1950 had only 6% of its population in possession of a bachelor's degree (Chronicle of Higher Education 2011: *online*). The average American citizen was fearful of intellectuals crafting philosophy and public policy that could potentially fundamentally alter their daily lives that they had grown comfortable with and accustomed to. Intellectuals and academics were viewed by many as Soviet sympathizers who wanted to redistribute the nation's new found wealth and ultimately transform the USA into an authoritarian communist state.

The situation is quite different now in the Muslim world. There are millions of Muslims that are *not* comfortable with the status quo. Considering all of the major social upheavals and regional wars that have occurred over the past decade, it is clear that this particular part of the world is in need of new ideas to help spark debate and discussion. Before any lasting positive political or social change can be implemented, scholars first need to offer ideas that are accessible to both the political actors and mass publics who ultimately hold the final responsibility for transforming governing structures and society. This project aims to offer a unique and intellectually rigorous contribution that is not teeming with insider jargon or overly complex formal models that only someone in possession of a Ph.D. with a quantitative background in the social sciences can grasp. This project targets a diverse audience that not only includes academics interested in this issue, but also policy makers, students, and people outside academia who have a general interest in Islam and politics.

The ultimate goal of this project is to contribute to a living, breathing discourse that is still evolving and finding itself. There were some very interesting books and articles in the 1980s and 1990s on Islam and contemporary governance. Along with the works mentioned in the introductory paragraphs, other excellent works in the recent decades that have explored this topic included Leonard Binder's *Islamic* Liberalism (1988), Timothy Sisk's *Islam and Democracy: Religion, Politics, and Power in the Middle East* (1994), and John P. Entelis edited volume titled *Islam, Democracy and the State in North Africa* (1997).

There have also been a few more recent works address this topic such as Muqtedar Khan's edited volume, *Islamic Democratic Discourse: Theory, Debates, and Philosophical Perspectives* (2005), Nader Hashemi's *Islam, Secularism, and Liberal Democracy* (2009), and Wael Hallaq's *The Impossible State: Islam, Politics, and Modernity's Moral Predicament* (2013). It is important to remember that most of these works were products of a closed and largely unchallenged authoritarian discourse that dominated the Muslim world that does really not exist today, a discourse in which generally secular authoritarian regimes were almost completely unaccountable to their oppressed societies. The 2011 Arab Revolutions, despite their many shortcomings, have at the least shown that alternative visions are possible and that autocratic regimes in the Muslim world can no longer rule without any accountability. Now is the time to begin making serious efforts toward articulating alternative visions of politics in these states.

Despite the recent hijacking of the ideals of Arab Revolutions by various militant groups and dictators, the initial intellectual trajectory of these revolutions was *against* extremism and violence. The call among moderate voices was for the construction of a new society, a society that remained Islamic, but was still modern. Following the death of 9/11 mastermind Osama Bin Laden, Radwan Sayyid, a professor of Islamic studies at the Lebanese University in Beirut commented that; "The problem now is not how you can destroy something, how you can resist something, it's how can you build something new—a new state, a new authority, a new relationship between the public and leadership, a new civil society" (Shadid and Kirkpatrick 2011: *online*). Technology has advanced to the point where Muslims even in some of the most remote parts of the world still have access to information and means of communication that previously were unavailable even to those living in the West.

Beginning in the 1970s and 1980s, cheap and readily accessible new media technologies such as VHS and audio cassettes emerged as popular means for communicating information outside the control of the state monopolized communications apparatus (Salvatore 2013). During the 1990s, new and independent newspapers such as *Al-Jazeera* attracted young critical columnists along with young independent minded audiences.

> The launch of *Al-Jazeera* in 1996 represented a watershed in the longer trajectory, for the plain reason that the new TV channel started to broadcast all the news that the state-owned TVs did not provide and, most critically, to frame them via the widespread public perception of the fading legitimacy of Arab governments. (Salvatore 2013: 219)

The twenty-first century saw the emergence of the Internet and social media as the next step in the information evolution. Both popular magazine and academic articles have recently been published that explained how influential social media was in facilitating mass mobilization against the Mubarak regime. This all happened not just over a period of weeks or months, but over an entire decade (Burris 2011; Eltantawy and Wiest 2011; Salvatore 2013).

The dire circumstances that surround much of the Muslim world and the developing world in general are a second major reason why this project is important. In Ali Allawi's critically acclaimed book, *The Crisis of Islamic Civilization* (2009), Allawi, the former Minister of Finance in the Iraqi Transitional Government, commented that the lack of existential self-determination was a major part crisis surrounding contemporary Islamic civilization:

> The crisis in Islamic civilization arises partly from the fact that it has been thwarted from demarcating its own pathways into contemporary life. The western mould of modernity has been superimposed on its worldview, and

Islam has been unable to relate to the modern world except through this awkward and often painfully alien framework. (2009: 9)

Along with the often suffocating imposition of Western notions of modernity and liberty by the former colonial powers, the world is now also dominated by powerful non-state actors. Multinational corporations and transnational terrorist organizations continue to grapple for control over the domestic and international affairs of many Islamic countries. Following the publication of Allawi's book, a new, even more frightening non-state actor has taken a foothold in the Muslim world: the fanatical terrorist group commonly referred to as ISIS (Islamic State of Iraq and Syria) in the West, or *ad-Dawlah al Islāmiyah fi 'l- Irāq wa-sh-Shām* in the Arab world. Today, all Muslim nations need leadership that is stronger than ever to resist the temptations of groups who seek to plunder and pillage their resources in the name of either unfettered capitalism or religious extremism. The amount of wealth, technology, and opportunities in this twenty-first century world is far superior now to any other time in history. Well-designed economic policies that emphasize fairness while promoting investment and growth could easily create new and viable opportunities for mass publics that have been suffering for far too long. Major innovations in medicine, transportation, and communications technologies all give rise to possibilities that in the past were inconceivable.

The process of transforming governmental institutions, recalcitrant power structures, and social relations between the dominant and the dominated will not happen overnight. Aristotle reminds us all that; "For one swallow does not make a summer, nor does one day; and so too one day, or a short time, does not make a man blessed or happy" (*Nicomachean Ethics*, Book I, Chapter 7: 1098a). The establishment of good governing practices that are seen as legitimate by the people is an essential first step towards altering the totality of social relations in the Muslim world today.

Going Back to Get to the Future

Before one can properly discuss the development of a modern Islamic political framework, one must be aware of the history of the development of Islamic thought. Shortly after the death of the Prophet Muhammad (ﷺ), scholars began writing within what one can call *the Islamic framework*. This means that while all their various writings differed—often to very large degrees—they all still shared certain foundational beliefs such as the oneness of God and the Prophethood of Mohammed (ﷺ) as being the seal of the Prophets. These foundational beliefs were in many ways ensconced within and inextricable from their writings that focused on a wide array of topics that included not only theology, but also subjects like history, metaphysics, ethics, astronomy, biology, and other countless other academic disciplines. Each scholar is in some way representative of the era in which he wrote.

The argument in Chap. 2 is that historical conditions, and the more specific life circumstances of individual scholars, have had a major impact on the type of Islamic scholarship produced. My hypothesis is that during eras in which Islamic civilization was in ascendency, the ideas offered by Islam's scholars were fundamentally different than the ideas offered by Islam's scholars during eras in which Muslims were persecuted or where there was rampant political corruption.

During periods of prosperity, the scholarly discourse tended to be more permissive. There was a greater focus upon the mystical experience and inward applications of spirituality when it came to purely theological questions. Islamic writing in general was more philosophical and less theological, in the traditional sense of the word. Earlier writers showed a deep interest in social and political questions and sought to address them from within an Islamic ontological perspective. Diversity in opinions and legal decisions made by individual interpretation, or *ijtihād*, were common and encouraged.

During periods of persecution, the discourse shifts inward. Islamic philosophy during these periods primarily focused on ritualistic purity and literalism. The scope of Islamic writing contracted and became more theologically oriented; it was less philosophical in the traditional sense of the word. Diversity in opinions and legal decisions made via *ijtihād* were often discouraged. Orthodoxy and orthopraxy became the dominant themes of Islamic scholarship.

Today's Muslim scholars and academics hold views that run the gamut of the theological spectrum. At one end are very conservative, classically trained scholars such as Rabee al-Madkhali and Saleh Al-Fawzan in Saudi Arabia who rely heavily on *'aḥādīth* as a source of authority and are highly critical of anything that can be considered as innovation (*bid'ah*). As for some of their more controversial views, Al-Madkhali espouses a twenty-first century Islamic reiteration of the Medieval Christian *Divine Right of Kings* doctrine, opposing all forms of political engagement that challenge the Saudi Monarchy, and Al-Fawzan has been quoted as staunchly supporting slavery. On the other end are Western-educated scholars who consider themselves to be "Quranists" (*Qur'āniyyūn*) who reject *'aḥādīth* altogether, a position well outside the mainstream of Islam today. Examples include Edip Yüksel, who spent over 4 years imprisoned in Turkey for his radical views, and Irshad Manji, a LGBT rights advocate who describes herself as a *Muslim refusnik* that refuses "to join an army of automatons in the name of Allah" (Manji, quoted in Brown 2014: *online*). The twenty-first century has also seen both attacks on the central premises of Islam by those opposed to Islam in general and a re-emergence of the religion into relevance for those who previously were only tacit followers.

The concluding argument of Chap. 2 suggests that Islam is re-entering a period of ascendency, not only in terms of highly diverse scholarly output, but also due to the various emerging moderate Islamist political movements and grassroots social activist circles. Based on the availability of information and overall interest in the topic of Islam and its function in the contemporary world, now is an ideal time to return to questions of political organization and Islam in a more meaningful and scholarly way.

Plato, Aristotle, and Ancient Greek Scholarship

Continuing with the theme, *going back to get to the future*, Chaps. 3 through 7 will regularly make references to ancient Greek thought. The many similarities between ancient Greek and Islamic thought should be clear in these chapters. The most important difference between Islamic/Greek conceptions of the state and Enlightenment conceptions of the state hinge upon the prioritization of which approach posits as its most fundamental values. Virtue, the harmonization of individual interests with societal interests, and personal moral development are essential within the Greek and Islamic discourses. This stands in stark contrast to Enlightenment thought which prioritizes individual liberties and rights and has little concern with questions of personal morality. Enlightenment-based arguments focus more on what Isaiah Berlin (2004) would call in the 1960s, the aspects of negative liberty or the liberty from government intrusion. The emphasis on negative liberty generally seen in modern secular democratic societies radically differs from the vision of government that the ancients postulated.

Unlike their Enlightenment counterparts, the ancients argued that an effective government should aim to perfect the soul and create moral citizens, even if this is at the expense of certain individual liberties. In Plato's *Timaeus*, it is posited that the physical world was created by a divine creator who sought to create a good and orderly world based on the ideal forms of the eternal world. Slavoj Žižek argues that; "For Plato, the natural world is the product of a divine craftsman who looked to the world of eternal being for his model of the good and then created a natural order" (2014: 9). The general Islamic discourse also sees the natural world as the creation of an all good, divine creator that creates man in God's own eternal image. *The Oneness of Allah*, the most fundamental concept in Islam, was actually referenced by the Greek Neo-Platonist, Plotinus, during the third century CE, centuries before Islam came into being. Plotinus argued that there is one ultimate transcendent being that is completely indivisible and unlike any other substance in the universe (Taylor 1994). As in Islam, *the Transcendent One*, for Plotinus, is the source of all that is and ultimately will ever be.

In Isaiah Berlin's parlance, the Islamic conceptualization of the state would equate closer to positive liberty, or having the power and resources to pursue self-mastery, thus taking precedence over negative liberty, which as discussed earlier, is generally understood as the freedom from government interference. Berlin concluded that effective states find a harmonious balance between positive and negative liberty. Post-Enlightenment liberal thinkers have generally prioritized negative liberty over positive liberty. From an Islamic worldview, the ancients had the right ideas about the importance of virtuous citizens and piety, but they, as Aristotle admits, lacked a formal foundational ethical system to define what "the good" is. As will later be shown, within the Islamic discourse, this system has been articulated. This difference in the prioritization of fundamental values cannot be downplayed and is at the heart of the schism between the Muslim world and the West today.

To fully appreciate Islamic political thought and philosophy, one must be aware of other global philosophical developments that are congruent with and/or have directly influenced Islamic philosophy. On the importance of Muslim scholars being familiar with non-Islamic thought, the Persian philosopher, Seyyed Hossein Nasr argues; "Students should be encouraged to know something of this rich intellectual background and not be presented with a picture of the Islamic tradition as a monolithic structure amenable only to one level of interpretation" (2010a: 169). Considering that Islamic scholars preserved the writings of Aristotle and Plato, it is not surprising that these two thinkers are frequently encountered in earlier rationalist Islamic thought. To appropriately understand Al-Fārābī and Ibn Rushd, one must be well versed in the writings of Plato, Aristotle, and Plotinus. On the other hand, in order to understand why someone like Al-Ghazālī was so averse to the ancient Greeks (and Al-Fārābī and Ibn Rushd for that matter), it would obviously be helpful to understand ancient Greek thought.

All civilizations are situated upon multiple axes. "Any civilization has an inner and outer aspect: an inner aspect of beliefs, ideas, and values which inform the outer aspect of institutions, laws, government, and culture" (Allawi 2009: xvi). Islamic civilization is no exception. Along with exploring the philosophical relationship between the ancient Greeks and a modern Islamic conception of statecraft, Chaps. 3–7 will look at some of the foundational building blocks to crafting a modern Islamic governed state. The role of leadership, bureaucracy, democracy, women's rights, and economic justice will be discussed in a normative manner that connects modern ideas of governance to an Islamic worldview. The broader motif of Chaps. 3–7 is that the "inner aspects" of Islamic beliefs and values can, and ultimately must, shape the "outer aspect" of government and institutions.

Case Studies and Application

Chapters 8–11 will look at a few examples of individual states currently existing in the Muslim world. It will apply the general theoretical framework offered in the first half of the book to each case and evaluate what elements these individual cases have been successful or unsuccessful at incorporating into their own state. Each of these case study chapters will end with a "what is to be learned from this case" concluding section. The states to be examined are Turkey, Egypt, Tunisia, and Malaysia. These cases represent a good cross section of the Muslim world. While each case represents a very different cultural tradition, nonetheless, they all have (or in the case of Egypt, *recently had*) strong Islamic political elements within their current political discourses.

The purpose of these chapters is not to give a comparative taxonomy of the political systems and/or the contemporary sociopolitical realities facing all of these countries. There already exists excellent recent works that do precisely this.[5] These brief case study chapters will offer some political history and general contemporary political analysis; however, the focus will be primarily on exploring the elements within these states that are the most worth considering in relation to the general discursive framework presented in Part I of this book.

Notes

1. This work will refrain from using the popular catch-phrase "the Arab Spring" that was largely the creation of Western media outlets and amounts to little more than another orientalist designation seeking to divide "things *Oriental* into manageable parts" (Said 1978: 72). In the words of Everette E. Dennis on the moniker, *the Arab Spring*, "No matter its origin, it was contentious almost from the start, which was inevitable since it was used to grossly generalize tumultuous events, each with distinct characteristics in different countries with divergent cultural conditions" (Dennis, referenced in Abusharif 2014: 1).
2. I translated this from the original text in French which stated: "[*le discours est*] *constitué par un ensemble de sequences de signes, en tant qu'elles sont des énoncés.*"
3. *Muṭawwiʿīn* is the name for the official vice police who found in Saudi Arabia, Afghanistan, and Indonesia's conservative *Ache* province (among other places). They regularly intervene when they witness unmarried people of the opposite sex commingling, alcohol consumption, gambling, or other public activities deemed un-Islamic. In Iran, these vice police are known as *komiteh*. Komiteh were originally committees that partook in the 1979 Iranian Revolution. They were also involved in purges against dissident leftists and Kurds in Iran during the 1980s. In 1991, they were incorporated into the police force and today serve a similar role as *muṭawwiʿīn* in *Sunni* states; however, their reach is broader in scope, also rooting out political dissent unlike their *muṭawwiʿīn* counterparts.
4. When referencing Islam's Prophet, the complimentary phrase, or *aṣ-ṣalātu ʿala -n-nabī*, "ﷺ" will be used any time I mention his name in my own words. In English, this commonly is translated as "may God honor him and grant him peace." There have been numerous scholarly rulings on this particular subject—the general consensus is that it is very important to mention the *ṣalāwat* anytime the Prophet's name is invoked in speech or writing. The former Saudi Grand Mufti, Abdul ʿAzīz ibn Bāz, issued a *fatwā* on this matter. To support his ruling, he referenced the thirteenth century hadith specialist, Ibn Al-Salah, who stated, "A person must keep writing the form of sending Salat and taslim i.e. 'peace and blessing be upon the Messenger of Allah' in full form upon mentioning him. A person must not be weary of repeating it, because it is one of the greatest

benefits which the Hadith students and writers may overlook" (Ibn Al-Salah, quoted by Ibn Baz, 2014: 398).

5. One recommended example of a recent work that offers an excellent comparative taxonomy of the contemporary political systems and sociopolitical realities facing Turkey, Malaysia, Pakistan, Bangladesh, Mali, Indonesia, and Senegal, is Paul Kubicek's *Political Islam and Democracy in the Muslim World* (Boulder, CO, Lynne Rienner Publishers 2015).

References

Abou El Fadl, Khaled. 2004. Islam and the challenge of democracy. In *Islam and the challenge of democracy*, ed. K. Abou El Fadl, J. Cohen, and D. Chasman, 3–48. Princeton, NJ: Princeton University Press.

Abusharif, Ibrahim N. 2014. Parsing 'Arab Spring:' Media coverage of the Arab Revolutions. Northwestern University in Qatar Occasional Paper Series.

al-'Uthaymīn, Muḥammad Ibn Ṣāliḥ. 2006. *The great Islamic awakening* trans. and ed. Faisalibn Muhammed. Birmingham, UK: Al Hidaayah Publishing.

Allawi, Ali A. 2009. *The crisis of Islamic civilization*. New Haven, CT: Yale University Press.

Aristotle. 2001. *The basic works of Aristotle*. ed. J. McKeon. New York: The Modern Library.

Berlin, Isaiah. 2004. *Liberty*. New York: Oxford.

Binder, Leonard. 1988. *Islamic liberalism: A critique of development ideologies*. Chicago, IL: University of Chicago Press.

Bronner, Stephen E. 1995. The great divide: The Enlightenment and its critics. *New Politics* 5 (3): 65–86.

Bronner, Stephen E. 1999. *Ideas in action: Political tradition in the 20th century*. New York: Rowman & Littlefield.

Bulliet, Richard. 1994. *Islam: The view from the edge*. New York: Columbia University Press.

Burris, Greg. 2011. Lawrence of e-rabia. Facebook and the new Arab revolt. *Jadaliyya*. http://www.jadaliyya.com/pages/index/2884/Lawrence- Accessed 14 Dec 2016.

Chronicle for Higher Education. 2011. Adults with degree, by county. http://chronicle.com/article/Adults-With-College-Degrees-in/125995/ Accessed 18 Mar 2015.

Cox, Harvey. 1966. *The secular city: Secularization and the urbanization in theological perspective*. New York: Macmillan.

Dallmayr, Fred. 2010. *The promise of democracy: Political agency and transformation*. Albany, NY: SUNY Press.

Davis, Eric. 2005. The new Iraq: The uses of historical memory. *Journal of Democracy* 16 (3): 54–68.

Eltantawy, Nahed, and Julie Wiest. 2011. Social media in the Egyptian revolution: Reconsidering resource mobilization theory. *International Journal of Communication* 5: 1207–1224.
Entilis, John (ed.). 1997. *Islam, democracy, and the state in North Africa*. Bloomington, IN: Indiana University Press.
Esposito, John. 2004. Practice and theory, In *Islam and the challenge of democracy*, ed. K. Abou Fadl, J. Cohen, and D. Chasman, 93–100. Princeton, NJ: Princeton University Press.
Esposito, John. 2010. *The future of Islam*. New York: Oxford University Press.
Foucault, Michel. 1969. *L'Archéologie du savoir*. Paris: Éditions Gallimard.
Foucault, Michel. 1970. *The order of things*. New York: Pantheon.
Gay, Peter. 1969. *The Enlightenment: An interpretation—Volume II: The science of freedom*. New York: Knopf.
Hallaq, Wael. 2013. *The impossible state: Islam, modernity, and modernity's moral predicament*. New York: Columbia University Press.
Hansen, Allan D., and André Sonnichsen. 2014. Discourse, the political and the ontological dimension: An interview with Ernesto Laclau. *Distinktion: Scandinavian Journal of Social Theory* 15 (3): 255–262.
Hardy, Cynthia. 2001. Researching organizational discourse. *International Studies in Management and Organization* 31 (3): 25–47.
Hashemi, Nader. 2009. *Islam, secularism, and liberal democracy: Toward a democratic theory for Islamic societies*. New York: Oxford University.
Hashemi, Nader. 2014. Rethinking religion and legitimacy across the Islam-West divide. *Philosophy and Social Criticism* 40 (4–5): 439–447.
Himmelfarb, Gertrude. 2004. *The roads to modernity: The British, French, and American Enlightenments*. New York: Knopf.
Hofstadter, Richard. 1963. *Anti-intellectualism and American life*. New York: Vintage.
Horkheimer, Max, and Theodor Adorno. 2002. *Dialectic of Enlightenment*. New York: Continuum.
Hay, Stephen N., William T. De Bary, et al. 1988. *Sources of Indian tradition*, vol. 2. New York: Columbia University.
Ibn Baz, Abdul Aziz bin Abdullah. 2014. The obligation of invoking peace and blessings on the Prophet in a complete form. In *Fatwas of Ibn Baz*, compiled online by Kingdom of Saudi Arabia's Portal of the General Presidency of Scholarly Research and 'Ifta. http://www.alifta.net/Fatawa/FatawaChapters. aspx?languagename=en&View=Page&PageID=139&PageNo=1&BookID=14 Accessed 3 May 2015.
Khan, Muqtedar M. A. (ed.). 2005. *Islamic democratic discourse: theory, debates, and philosophical perspectives*. Lanham, MD: Lexington Books.
Krishna, Sankaran. 2009. *Globalization and postcolonialism: Hegemony and resistance in the twenty-first century*. New York: Rowan and Littlefield.

Kubicek, Paul. 2015. *Political Islam and democracy in the Muslim world*. Boulder, CO: Lynne Rienner.
Laclau, Ernesto. 2007. Discourses. In *Contemporary political philosophy*, ed. R. Gooden, P. Petit, and T. Pogge, vol. II, 541–547. Malden, MA: Blackwell Publishing.
Lapidus, Ira. 2002. *A history of Islamic societies*. Cambridge, UK: Cambridge University Press.
Lessa, Iara. 2006. Discursive struggles within social welfare: Restaging teen motherhood. *The British Journal of Social Work* 36 (2): 283–298.
March, Andrew. 2015. Political Islam: Theory. *Annual Review of Political Science* 18: 103–123.
Mok, Opalyn. 2014. Islam not a religion but way of life, says Kuwaiti writer, Feb 25. *The Malaymail Online*. http://www.themalaymailonline.com/malaysia/article/islam-not-a-religion-but-way-of-life-says-kuwaiti-writer#sthash.LBRy8RUC.dpuf Accessed 26 July 2015.
Nasr, Sayeed Hossein. 2010a. *Islam in the modern world*. New York: Harper One.
Nasr, Vali. 2010b. *The rise of Islamic capitalism: Why the new Muslim middle class is key to defeating extremism*. New York: Free Press.
Pew Research Center: Forum on Religious & Public Life. 2011. The future of the world's global Muslim population: Projections from 2010–2030. Project Directed by Brian Grim and Mehtab Kerim. January 2011. http://www.pewforum.org/files/2011/01/FutureGlobalMuslimPopulation-WebPDF-Feb10.pdf Accessed on 4 Mar 2014.
Roy, Oliver. 2004. *Globalized Islam: The search for a new ummah*. New York: Columbia University Press.
Salvatore, Armando. 2013. New media, the 'Arab spring', and the metamorphosis of the public sphere: Beyond western assumptions of collective agency and democratic politics. *Constellations* 20 (2): 217–228.
Sardar, Ziauddin. 2003. Rethinking Islam. In *Islam, postmodernism and other futures: A Ziauddin Sardar reader*, ed. Sohail Inayatullah, and Gail Boxwell 27–34. London: Pluto Press.
Shadid, Anthony and David Kirkpatrick. 2011. In Arab world, Bin Laden's legacy is confused, May 2. *New York Times*. http://www.nytimes.com/2011/05/03/world/middleeast/03arab.html Accessed on 14 Dec 2016.
Sisk, Timothy. 1994. *Islam and democracy: Religion, politics, and power in the Middle East*. Washington, D.C.: United States Institute of Peace.
Taylor, Thomas, trans. 1994. *Collected writings of Plotinus*. Somerset, UK: Prometheus Trust.
Voll, John. 1997. Sultans, saints, and presidents: The Islamic community and the state in North Africa. In *Islam, democracy, and the state in North Africa*, ed. J. Entilis, et al., 1–17. Bloomington, IN: Indiana University Press.

Yusuf, Hamza. 2013. Islamic state and shari'a law are fantasies [Lecture]. Part of the Deen Intensive Foundation Lecture Series: 2013 Videos and Resources, *Introduction to logic.* https://www.youtube.com/watch?v=qraC3-VPi94 Accessed 19 Feb 2015.

Žižek, Slavoj. 2014. *Absolute recoil: Towards a foundation of a new dialectical materialism.* London, UK: Verso.

PART I

Historical Context and Theoretical Framework

CHAPTER 2

The Trajectory of the Development of Islamic Thought—A Comparison Between Two Earlier and Two Later Scholars

Introduction

Islam's Golden Age began roughly around the time *al-Khilāfah al-'Abbāsīyah* (the Abbasid Caliphate) assumed the mantle authority from *al-Khilāfah al-'Umawiyya* (the Umayyad Caliphate) in 750 CE. It lasted until the beginning of the Crusades, culminating with the sack of Baghdad in 1258 CE by Genghis Khan's grandson, Hulagu, and the Mongols. During Islam's Golden Age, Muslim scholars wrote on numerous issues and considered many different ideas. Greek philosophy, especially the ideas of Aristotle and Plato, were of central importance in the writings of earlier Islamic scholars such as Al-Fārābī, Ibn Sīnā [Avicenna], Ibn Rushd [Averroes] Abu Bakr al-Rāzī, Ibn Bājja [Avempace], and Al-Kindī.

The trajectory of these Golden Age scholars' writings was especially broad. Not only did they engage in political philosophy, but they also were deeply interested in metaphysics, ethics, biology, and medicine. Charles Butterworth published an article in 1996 actually titled, "*Averroës*, Precursor of the Enlightenment?" The early Islamic philosophers even were concerned about things that only very recently have been seriously explored by contemporary scholars such as pollution and waste disposal. They offered diverse opinions and arguments that some would consider heretical. These scholars' focus was much less on ritualistic purity and orthopraxy.

I hypothesize that historical conditions, both at the micro- and macro-levels, played a major role in determining the trajectory of Islamic thought. During the good times, scholarly writings tended to be more philosophical in the traditional sense of the word and less doctrinaire. Such writings were deeply curious about the intellectual continuities between the Islam and the ancient Greeks. Writers who wrote after the decline of the Islamic Golden Age tended to be more doctrinaire and concerned with ritualistic purity. I also contend that writers during the Islam's Golden Age were more interested in political philosophy than the later scholars due to necessity. As the Islamic world entered its decline, there was not as much interest in politics, since Islam's core religious practices were perceived as being in a state of disarray. As a result, Islamic scholars tended to focus on Islam's theological and orthopraxic aspects more than anything else.

To further illustrate this point, this chapter will compare Al-Fārābī and Ibn Rushd—both whom lived during the Islamic Golden Age, to Ibn Taymiyyah and Mohammad ibn 'Abd al-Wahhāb—both of whom lived following the sack of Baghdad in 1258 CE. I decided to focus on these particular four scholars because they are all the representatives of the *Sunni* tradition who were interested in the issues that could be considered both philosophical and theological in nature. The line between philosophy and theology is often blurred in Islamic scholarship. According to Oliver Leaman:

> One of the notable features of Islamic philosophy is the close relationship which exists between philosophy and theology. Although some of those philosophers who were very much influenced by Aristotle came to be rather dismissive of much of what comes under the label of theology or *kalam*, there was a persistent tendency for philosophers to use philosophy to help make sense of some of the main controversies in theology, and vice versa. (1996: 1)

The specific scholars looked at in this section all had a deep interest in the social relevance of Islam in their own times and addressed these concerns in their own unique ways. These are also four of the more famous scholars within the Islamic intellectual discourse; these were not just scholars popular among their own tribe only. Their thinking and writings have permeated the entire Muslim world, have been translated into numerous languages, and have also made their way into Western thought.

It is important to make the point here that this chapter is not trying to provide the reader with a deep critical exegesis of the more esoteric aspects of the ideas of the scholars discussed—there already exists an enormous body of literature that does this far better than I could in this one chapter. Doing this would also go well beyond the scope of this project. This particular chapter will provide the reader with a general understanding of the philosophical dispositions of each scholar investigated, and it will provide some insight into the life circumstances of each scholar discussed.

The purpose of this chapter is to support the overall conclusion is that, in general, Islamic political and philosophical trends are deeply impacted by historical realities and intellectual trends of the time. Understanding historical circumstances is important, especially when considering a new model for Islamic governance. This is to suggest that certain preconditions may need to be met before any serious efforts at reform can actually happen. To borrow from Karl Marx's lexicon, a certain level of *consciousness* is needed before any legitimate and lasting "revolution" could be seriously considered. Previously unthinkable uprisings in some of the world's most repressive authoritarian regimes is a signal that perhaps we are at the right historical moment for such theorizing to actually have legitimate real-time importance. Islamic political culture is capable of being transparent, just, and efficient. This should be the goal for any contemporary Islamic governed state.

Peripateticism Within the Early Islamic Philosophical Discourse

The early period of Islamic philosophy dated from roughly the early ninth-century CE to approximately the twelfth-century CE has come to be widely known as the *Peripatetic Arabic School*. A few of the more famous thinkers commonly identified with this particular discourse included Al-Kindī, Al-Fārābī, Ibn Sīnā, and Ibn Rushd. According to Leaman:

> Peripateticism or *mashsha'i* philosophy is very much based on Greek thought and in particular neo-Platonism. This started around the time of al-Kindi and is said to have come to an end with Ibn Rushd who represented the height of peripatetic thought in Andalus, the Islamic Empire in the Iberian Peninsula. (2015: xi)

Peripateticism dates back to Aristotle. "Peripatetic" is the transliteration of the ancient Greek word περιπατητικός (*peripatêtikos*), which roughly means "of walking" or "given to walking about" (Liddell et al. 1996). This approach to philosophy was informal and people working within this tradition freely inquired on various philosophical and scientific topics. The Peripatetic approach to scholarship was radically different from how philosophy is generally practiced today in academic institutions. The various sub-fields and categories that were later created by academics were of little interest to the early scholars who viewed the universe in a much more holistic way.[1] Most of the writers of the Islamic Peripatetic period were deeply interested in Islamic mysticism and saw it as being compatible with what contemporary scholars would consider the "hard sciences". Baghdad was the center of the Muslim world in regard to education and learning during this time. Muslim scholars from all over the world came to Baghdad to study logic, science, philosophy and theology.

Many of the Peripatetic Islamic scholars viewed the universe as a single, enormous divine procession. According to Ibn Sīnā:

> The origination of the universe is described as an eternal procession, or emanation. It is impossible that any change, whether it be an act of willing, intention, or capacity, should supervene upon it without prejudice to its immutability and perfection; and even a new relationship to an entity previously nonexistent, much as the creation of the world at a given moment, would involve change in its essence. (1960: 380)

This philosophical position implies that at the center of all that is exists an entity from which the universe proceeds. The Peripatetics were not Cartesian dualists by any means. For the Islamic Peripatetics, the physical and spiritual worlds were not looked at as separate and distinct entities as they are often conceived of as today by most people in the West. They viewed the physical and spiritual all as part of a larger process. In Western parlance, this would mimic the "Great Chain of Being" argument that has been around since the time of Plato.

The great chain of being idea was reevaluated by Arthur Lovejoy in the first half of the twentieth century. According to his classic work, *The Great Chain of Being: A Study of the History of an Idea*;

> Everything except God has in it some measure of privation, There are in the first place, in its generic nature or potentialities, which in a given state

of its existence, are not realized; and there are superior levels of being by virtue of specific degree of privation characteristic of it, it is constitutionally incapable of attaining. (1964: 59)

Lovejoy argued that the chain originates with God, and then keeps going on and on. This conceptualization of the universe was considered axiomatic up until the eighteenth century. He contended that from early in the Middle Ages up until around the late eighteenth century, many philosophers and scientists accepted a conception of the universe as a "Great Chain of Being." Each entity on the chain has a maximum potentiality which is then trumped by another entity and so on. Following God, are angels, demons, and other spiritual beings. Spirit is unchanging and permanent. At the bottom of the chain, as articulated by Lovejoy, are stones, clay, and other things that only possess the quality of physical existence. Such a worldview holds that everything is ultimately connected at some level. The categories that would later be introduced by Kant in his, *Critique of Pure Reason*, would be viewed as unnecessary by medieval thinkers.

Ethics were deeply imbued within the Islamic peripatetic discourse much like they also were for the Greeks. "The vain philosopher is not virtuous; he is ruled by his appetites and inclinations. Through time, he loses what he had learned and recedes into ignorance" (Azadpur 2011: 41). Philosophy is not something that can simply be learned via repetition. It must reach the depths of the soul. The vain philosopher, or *sophist*, "is not yet aware of the purposes for which philosophy is pursued" (Azadpur 2011: 41). For the peripatetic scholars, to pursue philosophy for anything other than knowledge and Allah's pleasure was ignoble. The *sophist* philosophizes for fame, fortune, and glory, whereas the *philosopher* philosophizes for the sake of philosophy alone.

A Brief Look at Some of the Major Schools *Kalām* Within the *Sunni* Discourse

Many different approaches to understanding the *Qur'ān* and the world, in general, emerged shortly after Islam's emergence. *'Ilm al-kalām* or "the science of discourse" is the Islamic philosophy of seeking theological principles through dialectic. It is often also called Islamic scholastic theology. Problems dealt with via *kalām*, such as the issues of the divine decree and predestination (*al-qaḍā' wa al-qadr*), free will (*ikhtīyār*), and divine justice (*al-ʿadl al-Ilāhī*), were the issues of primary importance among Muslims during the first half of the second century following the *Hijrah*. Among the most prominent approaches to *kalām* within the *Sunni* tradition were the *Muʿtazilah*, *Ashʿarī*, and *Māturīdī*. The *Atharīyyah* and the followers of Ahmed ibn Ḥanbal rejected *kalām* altogether (Table 2.1).

The *Muʿtazilah* approach to Islamic theology emerged in Basra and Baghdad during the eighth–tenth-centuries CE. The early *ʿAbbāsids* were deeply influenced by Muʿtazilite thought. The *ʿAbbāsids* stressed the value of knowledge. The *ʿAbbāsid* Caliph, Al-Ma'mun, who reigned from 813–833 CE, was sympathetic towards the Muʿtazilism. He was also highly critical of the traditionists whom he saw as potentially usurping power. At one time, the traditionists, who would later come to dominate the discourse, were actually viewed as the troublemakers by the ruling elites. "The traditionists were a threat. Al-Ma'mūn saw them as sowing seeds of destruction, menacing for who they were, for what they had come to be within the social fabric, and for the kinds of activities they were carrying out" (Nawas 1996: 705). In response to the traditionist threat, Al-Ma'mūn organized the *Miḥnah*—a policy of religious persecution against those who opposed the Muʿtazilite doctrine that the *Qur'ān* was created. This policy, that in many ways mirrored the later European medieval inquisitions, lasted for a period 15 years between 833 and 848 CE. Victims of the *Miḥnah* often were traditionists who were powerful and had influence. As a part of the *Miḥnah*, those suspected of engaging in sedition were required to pledge absolute loyalty oath (*bayʿah*) to Al-Ma'mūn.

The Muʿtazilites argued that the *Qur'ān* was created by God and could not be eternal because only God himself is eternal. They also privileged the role of reason to the extent that some critics claimed the Muʿtazilites were actually skirting around the essential role of revelation. The Muʿtazilites also believed in complete human free will. This stood in opposition to their contemporaries, the Jabarites who believed firmly that all human agencies derived from God alone. One of the leading proponents of this fatalistic position was the much reviled Jahm ibn Ṣafwān who "maintained that there is no difference between things that happen in the world in general and the actions of human beings; they are all continuously and directly created by God" (Mohamed referenced in Leaman (Eds.) 2006: 204). A couple centuries later, the Ashʿarites would take an intermediate position on this particular issue.

Table 2.1 Synopsis of *Muʿtazilah*, *Ashʿarī/Māturīdī*, and *Ḥanbalī/Atharī* approaches to Islamic theology

	Muʿtazilah	*Ashʿarī & Māturīdī*	*Ḥanbalī/Atharī*
Founded	Eighth century C.E in Iraq	Eighth–Tenth century	Ninth century
Nature of Quran	*Qurʾān* is created	*Qurʾān* is uncreated	*Qurʾān* is uncreated
Free will vs. determinism	Total free will	Partial determinism	Partial determinism
Reason versus revelation	Privilege of reason; recognizes Aristotelian logic and metaphysics as valid	Privilege of revelation; did/does not recognize Aristotelian logic and metaphysics as valid	Privilege of revelation; did/does not recognize Aristotelian logic and metaphysics as valid
Emphasis on ʾ*Aḥādīth*	Less than other schools	Strong	Strongest
Disposition towards outside ideas	More open	Conservative	Very conservative
Notable figures	Ahmad ibn Abi Duʾad, Abu Al-Hasan al-Ashari (early), Abu al-Hudhayl al ʿAllaf, Ibrahim an-Nazzam, Abd al-Jabbar ibn Ahmad	Abu Al-Hasan al-Ashari (late), Al-Ghazali, Ibn Khaldun, al-Nawawi, al-Qurtubi, Ibn Hajar al Asqalani	Ibn Hanbal, Khwaja ʿAbdullah al-Ansari, Ibn Taymiyyah, Mohammad ibn ʿAbd al-Wahhab, Salih al-Fawzan

The Muʿtazilites respected *'aḥādīth*, but were also deeply concerned with the possibility of inauthentic *'aḥādīth* sullying the discourse. According to Woodward and Martin, "The *Muʿtazilia* also accepted the authority of the two sacred texts, but made human reason (ʿaql) the warrant for determining what the text of the Qur'an and Hadith meant in particular circumstances" (1997: 15). For the *Muʿtazilah*, what is obligatory in terms of faith is due to reason; if something is unreasonable, then it does not have to be followed simply due to historical precedent (Arabi 2001; Woodward et al. 1997). The debate over the role of reason and revelation continue to be hotly debated among the *ʿUlamā* (religious scholars and authority figures) even today.

The theological counterparts to the *Muʿtazilah* were the Ashʿarites. The Ashʿarites (*al-Ashʿariyya*) believed that the *Qurʾān* is eternal and is uncreated. Abū l-Ḥasan al-Ashʿarī (873–935 CE) was the founder of what would become known as the *Ashʿarī* school of theology. Ashʿarī was at first a Muʿtazilite but then he joined the traditionist camp. "He brings along with him his rationalist weapons and places them in the service of traditionalism" (Makdisi 1962: 39). Ashʿarī refuted the Muʿtazilite doctrine that the *Qurʾān* was created. He also disagreed with the Muʿtazilite views that the eyes of human beings will never see God in the afterlife, and that we are the sole authors of our actions.

The Ashʿarites rejected the Muʿtazilite position that God is somehow constrained by any objective notion of justice and fairness.

> The Ashʿarites were subjectivists, in the sense that they emphasised the dependence of everything, even the meaning of ethical statements, on the will and decision of God. Their opponents, the Muʿtazilites, argued on the contrary that God is constrained in his actions by objective standards of justice. (Leaman 1996: 1)

The Muʿtazalite position is actually similar to the *Shīʿah* position on this matter that argues God cannot be unjust because his nature is to be just. According to Syed Hossein Nasr; "For Him [Allah] to be unjust would violate His own Nature, which is impossible. Intelligence can judge the justness or unjustness of an act and this judgment is not completely suspended in favor of a pure voluntarism on the part of God" (Nasr, in Tabatabae'i 1975: 13). Simply put, for Muʿtazilites, God is constrained by the rules of logic and traditional notions of justice within the *Muʿtazilah* school of thought, while God is not constrained by the rules of logic and traditional notions of justice within the *Ashʿarī* conceptualization of the universe. For the Ashʿarites, the notion of justice is not fixed. This is to suggest God can deem an action just at one time and deem it unjust at another if he so chose to. Nasr goes on to argue that;

> We might say that in the exoteric formulation of Sunni theology, especially as contained in Ash'arism, there is an emphasis upon the will of God. Whatever God wills is just, precisely because it is willed by God; and intelligence ('aql) is in a sense subordinated to this will and to the "voluntarism" which characterizes this form of theology. (1975: 12)

Despite these metaphysical differences on what God could do if he wanted to, both schools firmly believed that the *Qur'ān* was God's final decree to mankind, and that its law and resolutions were immutable.

Another key difference between the Ashʿarites and the Muʿtazilites were their respective positions on human agency and free will. As mentioned above, the Ashʿarites took an intermediate position between the Muʿtazilites (total free will) and the Jabarites (no free will). The Ashʿarites "sought a middle position by claiming that humans act autonomously (by their own will) but they acquire (*kasb*) the power to act from God at the moment the act occurs, thus preserving God's omnipotence" (Woodward et al. 1997: 25). This is very important, not only for metaphysical clarity, but for jurisprudential reasons as well. The Ashʿarite position on human agency preserved God's omnipotence, but at the same time, made humans accountable for their actions. One could not commit a sin and then claim that it was God's will, and that they were not responsible for their actions.

The Ashʿarite position on free will is very common in the Muslim world today. A very common utterance Muslims use whenever making a statement about something they intend on doing in the future is "*ʾInshāʾallāh*" which translates to "God willing". For example, if one is saying goodbye to a friend, they will commonly say something like, "I will see you again soon, *ʾInshāʾallāh*." This statement attests to the individual Muslim's recognition that regardless of their personal intent, ultimately it is Allah who will allow or disallow their action. Its origins lie within the *Qur'ān* itself, hence within the Ashʿarite worldview, giving their position even more credence and legitimacy; "And say not of anything: Lo! I shall do that tomorrow, except if Allah will. And remember thy Lord when thou forgettest, and say: It may be that my Lord guideth me unto a nearer way of truth than this" (*Qur'ān* 18: 23–24).[2] Some scholars have even gone as far as stating that this utterance is obligatory (*farḍ*) on all Muslims.[3]

What has come to be known as the *Māturīdī* approach to Islamic theology was founded by Muhammad Abū Mansūr al-Māturīdī (853–944 CE) around the same time the *Ash'arī* school came into prominence. Both approaches hold many similar beliefs. "Al Maturidi, followed in Abu Hanifa's footsteps, and presented the notion that God was the creator of man's acts, although man possessed his own capacity and will to act" (Shah 2006: 640). Like the Ash'arites, early Māturīdīs believed in partial determinism. Both are the representatives of the occasionalist approach to causation—a philosophical approach to causality which rejects the idea that created substances can be the efficient causes of events; rather, all events are caused directly by God. They also believed that the *Qur'ān* is eternal. They do differ on some minor points. For example, they have differing positions on both the nature of belief and the place of human reason.

The Māturīdīs believed that one's faith (*'īmān*) remained the same throughout their lifetime—it did not increase nor decrease. Only one's piety (*taqwā*) fluctuated. The Ash'arites claimed that belief does, in fact, increase and decrease. Māturīdīs also believe that humans have the capacity to come to certain ethical conclusions about what is right and wrong on their own without revelation, while Ash'arites do not think unaided reason can come to these conclusions. Their main difference, however, was in regard to the some of the attributes of Allah (Lucas 2006). For example, Māturīdīs believe that Allah's voice cannot be heard in the same way humans hear other sounds. Ash'arites do believe Allah's voice can be heard and often point to the example of the Prophet Moses' conversation with the God on Mount Sinai. Each school made efforts to base their arguments on references to *Qur'ān* and *'ahādīth*. Despite these and a few other minor differences in some of the more esoteric elements of Islamic creed (*'aqīdah*), for practical purposes, the Ash'arites and Māturīdīs are very similar. For the sake of this discussion, I placed the Māturīdīs in the same category as the Ash'arites in my brief taxonomy of theological schools listed above.

The third main *Sunni* Islamic theological approach to emerge during the Peripatetic era was the *Atharī/Ḥanbalī* approach. While it is important to note that "Hanbalism" technically is a *madhhab* and that it is possible for one who follows the *Ḥanbalī madhhab* to also be an Ashʿarite or *Māturīdī* in ʿ*aqīdah*, very rarely will one who follows the *Ḥanbalī* legalistic approach identify as anything other than *Atharī* in ʿ*aqīdah*. Those who follow the *Atharī* approach to ʿ*aqīdah* reject *kalām* altogether. The word "*athar*" in Arabic literally translates to "remnants". In the Islamic context, it is used to describe what is narrated from the Prophet (ﷺ) and his companions.

Those who identify as *Atharī* in ʿ*aqīdah* seek to emulate the earliest Muslims as closely as possible. Athari's reject *bāṭin* or hidden/esoteric (*Ṣūfī*) interpretations of the *Qurʾān* and God's divine attributes. Instead they understand the *Qurʾān* in a *ẓāhir* or literal/apparent manner. Atharis are vehemently opposed to engaging in *taʾwīl* or allegorical interpretations of the *Qurʾān* and anthropomorphic understandings of God's divine attributes.[4] The *Atharī* position on God's divine attributes perhaps is most aptly summed up by Ibn Ḥanbal's famous commentary on the matter. Ibn Qudamah reported that Ibn Ḥanbal commented; "His Attributes proceed from Him and are His own, we do not go beyond the Qur'an or the traditions from the Prophet and his Companions; nor do we know the how of these, save by the acknowledgement of the Apostle and the confirmation of the Qur'an"[5] (Ibn Ḥanbal, cited in Ibn Qudamah 1962: 9). They believe that the ʿ*aḥādīth* should have the ultimate authority in matters of belief and law, and they forbid the rational disputation of religious principles even if it verifies the truth of their own beliefs. Ibn Taymiyyah would later declare *kalām* and logic as unlawful. He tried to dissuade Muslims from the heretical beliefs of the Sufis, philosophers, speculative theologians, the *Shīʿah*, and other similar "deviant" groups (Hallaq 1993).

The *Ḥanbalī* approach to Islamic jurisprudence (*fiqh*) is recognized as being more conservative that other Sunni legalistic schools. *Aḥmad bin Muḥammad bin Ḥanbal Abū ʿAbd Allāh al-Shaybānī* (780–855 CE), or as he is more commonly referred to as today, Ibn Ḥanbal, was a well-educated scholar who sought to encourage moderation and piety among his followers. Unlike other founders of schools of Islamic jurisprudence, he was not technically a jurist. He took a similar position as the Ashʿarites in regard to the question surrounding free will and determinism. Like his later followers, Ibn Ḥanbal's opposition to the Caliph's position on the creation or uncreation of the *Qurʾān* resulted in severe physical punishment and torture. He was imprisoned and was flogged mercilessly until he was unconscious by the Caliph Al-Muʿtaṣim (Al-Maʾmūn's successor) for his belief that the *Qurʾān* was uncreated.

Ibn Ḥanbal's admirers followed his activities closely, even observing his eating habits as an example of his overall disposition. "He ate inexpensive yet filling food and did not resort to long voluntary fasts. His efforts to find a middle path that is situated between hedonism and self-mortification led him to a third behavioral pattern" (Hurvitz 2000: 53). The *Ḥanbāli* existential position was one of reflective contemplation. According to Hurvitz; "There are a number of indications that piety and mild asceticism had a powerful hold over the Hanbali moral imagination" (2000: 54). The followers of Ibn Ḥanbal, and what would later become the *Ḥanbāli* School of Islamic jurisprudence, followed what Hurvitz called a, "mildly ascetic lifestyle."

Despite Ibn Ḥanbal's conservatism, he was most certainly not of the *Khawārij*. As a matter of fact, he was very critical of this group that sought to label sinners as disbelievers. People who emulate this practice today are commonly referred to as "takfīrīs." Ibn Ḥanbal held the position that "even a Muslim guilty of a grave sin may not be excluded from the community except on the authority of a hadith account, which must be interpreted with restrictive literalism" (Abou Rauf 2007: 204). Things such as the non-observance of prayer, consumption of fermented alcohol, and the spreading of falsehoods against Islam were the only things that could *possibly* account for the accusation of *kufr*, or disbelief. As the Middle Ages went on, Perapatetism in the Muslim world was eventually abandoned for a more textually centered discourse. The punishments the early traditionists were subjected to by sympathizers of the Muʿtazilites also helped galvanize opposition to *Muʿtazilah* doctrine by the eleventh and twelfth centuries.

The Muʿtazilites, Ashʿarites/Māturīdīs, and Atharīs/Ḥanbalīs continued to grapple for acceptance throughout the eleventh and twelfth centuries. In the end, the Muʿtazilite position was defeated, and the *Ashʿarī/Māturīdī* and even more conservative *Atharī/Ḥanbalī* positions won out. George Makdisi argued that the Ashʿarites "march on as the dominant, largest, school of theology, carrying the banner of orthodoxy, straight through the centuries and down to modern times [1960's CE]" (1962: 39–40). However, over the past few decades, the *Ḥanbalī/Atharī* approach has grown in influence across the Muslim world. Its growth has been supported via large charitable endowments from the wealthy Gulf States that have included projects such as *masjīds*, libraries, and other similar institutions in developing countries such as

Afghanistan, Pakistan, and Bosnia and Herzegovina. These same actors have also engaged in similar activities in western Europe and the USA.

It is important to note that despite the fact that the Muʿtazilite position has significantly less support than the other theological approaches in the Muslim world today, there still are those who consider themselves to be situated within the Muʿtazilite intellectual tradition even if they do not accept all of its doctrines. During the twentieth century, some scholars have tried to bring Muʿtazilism back into the contemporary mainstream Islamic discourse. One such example was that of the twentieth-century Indonesian scholar and self-described "neo-Mutazilite", Harun Nasution who argued that; "The doctrines of dynamism, human freedom and accountability, rationalism and naturalism taught by the Muʿtazila contributed significantly to the development of philosophy and the religious and secular sciences during the Classical Period of Islamic civilization" (1997: 192). Nasution was opposed to occasionalism; he believed that occasionalism's denial of the existence of secondary, or created, causes hindered scientific enquiry and contributed to the decline of Islamic scientific advances and ultimately Islamic civilization in general.

Al-Fārābī: The Second Teacher

Abū Naṣr Muḥammad ibn Muḥammad Fārābī, commonly known as Al-Fārābī (872–950 CE), was among the earliest Peripatetic Islamic scholars. He remains one of the most influential figures of this era. He is widely known as "the second teacher" (after Aristotle, who is considered the first teacher) and is described by Majid Fakhry (2002) as the founder of Islamic Neo-Platonism. Al-Fārābī's understanding of political life was deeply connected with philosophy and what later would be called sociology. His method did not rely solely on divine revelation in order to grasp the rules of discourse. He sought to use empirical evidence coupled with a basic understanding of the human psyche to guide his philosophy. He had no reservations about looking towards the Ancients for guidance and understanding.

Al-Fārābī's *Book of Religion* describes a supreme ruler that emulates the Prophet Mohammed (ﷺ) in terms of leadership. This view is more clearly articulated in *The Political Regime*;

> The supreme ruler without qualification is he who does not need anyone to rule him in anything whatever, but has actually acquired the sciences and every kind of knowledge, and has no need of a man to guide

him in anything. He is able to comprehend well each one of the particular things that he ought to do. He is able to guide well all other to everything in which he instructs them, to employ all those who do any of the acts for which they are equipped, and to determine, define, and direct these acts towards happiness. (Al-Fārābī's cited in Lerner and Madhi (Eds.), 2011: 36)

Such a leader's soul is in union with the active intellect; he both rules and inspires at the same time. Through his rule, he moves people from sadness to happiness: from the darkness into the light.

Al-Fārābī goes on to argue that religion is dependent on philosophy and not the other way around.

> Therefore, all virtuous laws are subordinate to the universals of practical philosophy. The theoretical opinions that are in religion have their demonstrative proofs in theoretical philosophy and are taken in religion without demonstrative proofs. Therefore, the two parts of which religion consists [the theoretical and the practical] are subordinate to philosophy. (2001a: 97)

He believed that truth is most commonly ascertained by the individual via primary knowledge and demonstration. He also argued that the theoretical part of religion is that which the individual is not able to physically do when he understands it, such as divine grace and the process of creation, whereas the practical part of religion is that what the individual is physically capable of doing when he understands it, such as prayer and almsgiving. According to Butterworth:

> It [*Book of Religion*] begins with a description of a supreme ruler whose goals are similar to those of the Prophet and an analysis of his prescriptions. The reasons for everything done by this supreme ruler are traced back to philosophy so incessantly that religion appears to depend on philosophy, theoretical as well as practical. (1992: 31)

Like Plato, Al-Fārābī was of the opinion that an ideal government should be ruled by a philosopher king, except that for Al-Fārābī, the ruler must also be competent in understanding both the *Qur'ān* and the *Sunnah*. "In addition to Plato's qualifications, the first ruler (ra'is) possesses the Islamic qualifications of eloquence and soundness of bodily organs, which the jurists traditionally ascribed to the Caliph" (Fakhry 2002: 152).

Also like Plato, Al-Fārābī firmly believed that the philosopher and the intellectual were meant to be public figures; the true philosopher for Plato and Al-Fārābī could not remain a private individual. It was incumbent upon the true philosopher to assume public responsibilities (Watt 1995). Al-Fārābī's picture of political leadership had two key elements.

The first element was that the ruler had familiarity with what he called the universal rules. This can be understood as familiarity with the *Qur'ān* and *Sunnah*. The second element of political leadership involved the ruler regularly engaging in virtuous actions and behaviors even outside political life. Al-Fārābī saw no separation been between the public and the private life of an ideal leader—the political leader for Al-Fārābī is always at some level a public figure, even in his private life. The model of political leadership offered in the forthcoming chapters echoes Al-Fārābī's concern on this particular issue. The ideal ruler is driven by duty and justice, not personal gain or power. True rulers are quite skeptical of power, for in their wisdom they recognize the corrupting ability inherent within power itself.

At the beginning of Chap. 5 in the *Enumeration of the Sciences,* Al-Fārābī artfully used the metaphor of the good physician to understand the qualities that the good leader possesses;

> Indeed, a physician becomes a perfect healer only by means of two faculties. One is the faculty for the universals and the rules he acquires from medical books. The other is the faculty he attains by lengthy involvement in practicing medicine on the sick and by skill in it from long experience with, and observation of, individual bodies. (2001b: 77)

His main point is that understanding the book or the universals is not enough. The great political leader, like the great physician, must have intimate experience "practicing" his craft. It is through the repeated interactions with various "patients," all with unique conditions and ailments, that the doctor becomes an expert. We also see the difference spelled out between the *great leader* and the *great Imam* in this example—the great Imam does not require the same political training or worldly experience that the political leader does. This means that being a great religious scholar or pious person alone is not enough to automatically qualify one for a position of political leadership.

Al-Fārābī also wrote extensively on metaphysical topics. He held the Muʿtazilite position that the *Qur'ān* was created. He would later be severely castigated by Ash'arite scholars for holding this view. In spite of his critics, Al-Fārābī is credited with making the first attempt at offering a coherent explanation of the how the world works within an Islamic philosophical discourse (Fakhry 2002). He was also deeply interested in logic. According to Nicholas Rescher;

> More important, I believe, is that al-Farabi does not view logic as a matter of books and documents but as a *living oral tradition* of logical specialization and expertise. From this standpoint of logic viewed as a living discipline of specialized expertise channeled through a continuous oral tradition transmitted from a master to the scholars who "read" the canonical texts under his guidance, it is quite possible that al-Farabi answers the question of "How Greek logic reached the Arabs?" not only correctly, but comprehensively as well. (1963: 131)

In his works on logic, Al-Fārābī rigorously explored some of the basic constructs of grammar that would later be studied by linguists. He believed that the grammarian's aim was to determine the relationship between terms according to the rules of composition, whereas the logician's aim was to determine the relation of concepts according to the rules of prediction (Fakhry 1983). He readily acknowledged the significance of the contributions from the ancient Greeks on grammar and logic. Ancient Greek thought heavily influenced all aspects of Al-Fārābī's thinking—not just his political and ethical works.

Al-Fārābī lived during what has been considered by most scholars as the Islamic Golden Age. During this era, philosophers from all over the world regularly gathered in prosperous and elegant cities like Baghdad to engage in the most intellectually advanced discussions of their time. According to Muhsin Mahdi; "Al-Farabi was well versed in the Neo-Platonic philosophical tradition and the Christian Neo-Platonic theological tradition" (2001: 2). Relatively little is known about the personal biographical life details of Al-Fārābī. Majid Fakhry argued that he had a playful and eccentric personality;

> His personal character and demeanor are hinted at in anecdotes about his association with the Hamdani prince Saif ul-Daula [...] He is said to have had a great regard for al-Farabi, but was exasperated on occasion by his outlandish attire and boorish manners, as well as by the fact that, despite his asceticism and modesty, he frequently indulged in a certain degree of showmanship in the presence of his patron. (1983: 108)

Al-Fārābī wrote in an era and place where intellectual thought flourished. Ideas were openly debated, even among scholars of different religions. He was even interested in the fine arts. He had such a deep interest in music that he even wrote on its technical aspects. His best-known work on music known in English as the *Great Book of Music* (*Kitāb al-mūsīqā al-kabīr*), still survives today along with a few of his shorter treatises on melody. Al-Fārābī did not only write on music; he even played it. According to the renowned *Shāfi'ī* biographer, Ibn Khallikan, Al-Fārābī's music actually moved his audience to tears. The social environment within which Al-Fārābī was situated greatly impacted the way his discourse progressed. His ability to have the opportunity to play music and engage with Christian and Platonic ideas in a free and open manner is emblematic of the general proclivity towards new ideas and critical thought during his time. From a historical perspective, Al-Fārābī's writings occurred at the height of the Islamic Golden Age. The *'Abbāsid* Dynasty was in its glory during his lifetime time.

Ibn Rushd: The Symbiosis of Reason and Faith

'Abū l-Walīd Muḥammad Ibn 'Aḥmad Ibn Rushd (1126–1198 CE), commonly known as Ibn Rushd, and commonly referred to as Averroes in the West, is among the most well known of all medieval Islamic scholars. He was born into a powerful family of scholars and jurists in Córdoba and lived a life of privilege. Along with the Islamic sciences and philosophy, he was also trained in medicine. He followed in his grandfather's footsteps, becoming chief judge (*qāḍī*) of Córdoba under the Almoravid Dynasty (*Al-Murābiṭūn*) that stretched across the western Maghreb and Al-Andalus during the eleventh century. Ibn Rushd succeeded the renowned Islamic philosopher Ibn Tufayl as personal physician to the caliphs Abū Ya'qūb Yūsuf in 1182 and his son Abū Yūsuf Ya'qūb in 1184.

His thinking and scholarly contributions remain very relevant today. Ibn Rushd goes even further in making connections between philosophy and religion than did Al-Fārābī. Both peripatetic scholars appropriated the works of Aristotle and Plato differently in their writings; Ibn Rushd was critical of Al-Fārābī's efforts to synthesize the ideas of Plato and Aristotle. Ibn Rushd saw the thinkers as being too different to combine into one coherent doctrine. Ibn Rushd's ontology was also far more Aristotelian than Al-Fārābī's—Ibn Rushd believed essence and existence were essentially one. This overall view is significantly different from Plato's theory of ideas. Plato's theory of ideas posited that ideas precede particulars and that particulars are completely separate from essences which exist in their own abstract state, independent of minds. Aristotle's theory argues that particulars come first and that essences are "arrived at by a process of abstraction" (Fakhry 2001: 8).

While Al-Fārābī's work was more heavily steeped in political philosophy, Ibn Rushd was the medieval scholar who most specifically connected religion and philosophy. "Ibn Rushd is the only Muslim philosopher to dedicate a whole treatise to the connection between philosophy (science) and religion, which is the pressing issue in Arab-Muslim world in facing the challenge of the modem age" (Najjar 2004: 206). He strongly believed that no conflict existed between religion and philosophy—they should be understood as different ways of reaching the same truth. Along with believing that the universe was eternal and he also believed that the human soul is divided into two parts: one individual part and one divine part. Each individual soul is mortal, but all humans share one and the same divine soul. For Ibn Rushd, the *knowledge of truth* is derived from either religion or philosophy. The knowledge of truths derived from religion is based on faith and cannot be empirically tested— or to borrow from the lexicon of Karl Popper (1959), are *unfalsifiable*. This type of knowledge was seen as generally innate, and required little or no real training to understand. The type of second knowledge comes from philosophy. This type of knowledge, especially during the time in which Ibn Rushd lived, was generally inaccessible to the masses and was reserved for an elite few who had the intellectual capacity and financial resources to undertake its study.

Ibn Rushd's philosophy still shapes social and political ideas today. "His philosophy is thought to be indispensable for the revival of Islamic intellectual civilization, and social and political development within the context of the twentieth and twenty-first centuries" (Najjar 2004: 202). Similar to Al-Fārābī, and unlike later Islamic scholars, Ibn Rushd saw no incompatibilities between Greek thought and Islam. "For Averroes the Aristotelian rationalism through which he understood the world was discordant neither with Islam nor with his understanding of the nature of religious belief" (Taylor 2009: 234). He appropriated Plato's political philosophy with some Aristotelian modifications under his own terms and believed that Greek ideas also had relevance for an Islamic governed state as well. Following the ideas of Plato, Ibn Rushd was convinced that if the philosopher cannot rule, at the least, he must try to influence policy in the direction of the ideal state. During his own lifetime, he utilized Platonic ideas in his analysis of the shortcomings of the Almoravid state (Clancy-Smith 2001). His general line of argumentation was very similar to what Ibn Khaldun would argue two centuries later. He claimed that the sedentary lifestyle of the Almoravid dynasty lead to decadence and weakness, thus facilitating in the empire's downfall.

Ibn Rushd believed that philosophy was something to be taken quite seriously. He sincerely believed that Aristotle's work could not be improved in any significant manner. Unlike most contemporary students of Aristotle, Ibn Rushd "was persuaded that Truth had been almost entirely discovered by Aristotle in the past and that only minor adjustments and improvements could be made" (Genequand 1986: 2). His view on the centrality of logic put him in a far different position than later scholars like Ibn Taymiyyah who rejected syllogistic logic altogether. According to Richard C. Taylor;

> Consequently, in the case of religious law, Averroes asserts that, where there is difference between its apparent sense and the conclusion of a demonstrative syllogism, religious law must be interpreted to be in accord with the necessary truth achieved in demonstration. (2009: 230)

Ibn Rushd believed that religious laws and doctrines ultimately were subservient to Aristotelian logic. Since Islam was the ultimate truth for Ibn Rushd, demonstrative truths could never actually be in conflict with scripture—there could only be apparent conflict. In cases of apparent conflict between demonstrative truths and scripture, Ibn Rushd believed that scripture in these cases ought to be understood allegorically rather than literally. For Ibn Rushd, the ideal mode for understanding God was through logic and reason.

> Averroes clearly asserts the primacy of philosophical consideration (*i'tibār*) through intellectual syllogistic *qiyās 'aqlī* of a demonstrative sort (*burhānī*) as the proper type of reflection (*al-nazar*) for reaching the most perfect knowledge of God, the Artisan of all beings. (Taylor 2009: 231)

Ibn Rushd insinuated that those who were incapable of using philosophy and logic to understand God resorted to *taqlīd* (blind imitation) and literalist interpretations of the *Qur'ān*. For Ibn Rushd, philosophical inquiry was among the highest and most noble forms of worship.

Ibn Rushd's position on the excellence of philosophy can best be encapsulated in a fascinating passage that was discovered by Taylor that previously was missing in the Latin translation of Al-Fārābī's *Tafsīr mā ba'd aṭ-Ṭabī'at* that stated;

> The sharī'ah specific to the philosophers (ash-sharī'ah alkhāṣṣah bi-l-ḥukamā') is the investigation of all beings, since the Creator is not worshipped by a worship more noble than the knowledge of those things that He produced which lead to the knowledge in truth of His essence—may He be exalted! That [investigation philosophers undertake] is the most noble of the works belonging to Him and the most favored of them that we do in God's presence. How great is it that one perform this service which is the most noble of services and one take it on with this compliant obedience which is the most sublime of obediences! (Al-Farabi, quoted in Taylor 2012: 283)

In both Al-Fārābī and Ibn Rushd's purview, philosophers are the ones who best glorify God since they do so via their own God given logic and rational faculties, rather than through *taqlīd*. "According to Averroes, the rationality of philosophy, and of metaphysics in particular, constitutes the fullest form of the apprehension of created beings and of the Creator without thereby diminishing in any way the value of religious law" (Taylor 2009: 233). This is not to suggest that Ibn Rushd believed that turning to the *Qur'ān* to understand God was invalid. Ibn Rushd took his own personal faith very seriously; he was quite sensitive to attacks on his religious views (Nasr 1996). Ibn Rushd was open to the idea that there were multiple ways to comprehend God's presence.

In the eleventh century, Al-Ghazālī published his iconic traditionist manifesto, *The Incoherence of the Philosophers* (*Tahāfut al-Falāsifah*), that was primarily written in condemnation of the ideas of Al-Fārābī and Ibn Sīnā, and in defense of the belief in a temporary, finite, and created earth along with the Ash'arite theory of causation that has come to be known as occasionalism. Al-Ghazālī did not parse words when describing how he felt about those Islamic scholars who embraced Greek metaphysics;

> When I perceived this vein of folly throbbing within these dimwits, I took it upon myself to write this book in refutation of the ancient philosophers, to show the incoherence of their belief and the contradiction of their word in matters relating to metaphysics; to uncover the dangers of their doctrine and its shortcomings, which in truth ascertainable are objects of laughter for the rational and a less for the intelligent.... (2002: 3)

Ibn Rushd took it upon *himself* to offer the first major rebuttal of Al-Ghazālī. His *Tahāfut al-Tahāfut* contained 16 different sections, called "discussions" refuting Al-Ghazālī's metaphysical critiques, and four different "discussions" subsumed under the natural sciences. Near the very end of the first discussion ("concerning the eternity of the world"), Ibn Rushd articulates the reason for his refutation of Al-Ghazālī;

> We have not committed ourselves to anything more than to upsetting their theories, and to showing the faults in the consequence of their proofs so as to demonstrate their incoherence. We do not seek to attack from any definite point of view, and we shall not transgress the aim of this book, nor give full proofs for the temporal production of the world, for our intention is merely to refute their alleged knowledge of its eternity. (1954: 68).

This was an especially bold move considering the popularity of Al-Ghazālī and the waning popularity of those who embraced Hellenistic thought. Following its publication, Ibn Rushd's critique against Al-Ghazālī was not all that successful in the Muslim world (Ahmad 1994). In the fifteenth century at the behest of Fatih Sultan Mehmed II (Mehmed the Conqueror), the Turkic scholar, Mustafa Ibn Yusuf al-Bursawi, wrote a refutation of Ibn Rushd's arguments in *Tahāfut al-Tahāfut* and defended Al-Ghazālī's views.[6] However, the *Tahāfut al-Tahāfut* was embraced by later European and Jewish Averroists throughout the Middle Ages and into the European Renaissance.

Despite his affinity for Greek philosophy and metaphysics, Ibn Rushd was the religious authority of his day in Córdoba. According to Nasr;

> …ibn Rushd was the chief *qadi*, or judge of Cordova (Spanish Cordoba), which means that he was himself the embodiment of authority in Islamic law even if he were to be seen later by many in Europe as the arch rationalist and the very symbol of the rebellion of reason against faith. (1996: 26–27)

This is another example of the radically different historical circumstances surrounding earlier and later scholars. First, it is important to remember Córdoba, located on the Iberian Peninsula, had an entirely different intellectual temperament than Mesopotamia or the Arabia. Córdoba had a long tradition of Muslims, Christians, and Jews coexisting in relative peace and prosperity (Goodman 1999; Menocal 2002). A scholar/jurist openly embracing Greek logic and metaphysics during the eleventh or twelfth centuries in the same places where Ibn Taymiyyah and Mohammad ibn 'Abd al-Wahhāb were later dominant would never have been allowed to assume such a position of authority. Ibn Rushd's liberalizing interpretations were even controversial among his own contemporaries (Glick 1979). At the end of Ibn Rushd's life, as the Muslim world began its inward intellectual turn, many people began rejecting his writings because of perceived heresies. He was eventually exiled to Lucena, a primarily Jewish village outside of Córdoba, for a short period, and many of his writings were subsequently banned and his books burned. He died in Córdoba shortly after his brief 2-year period of exile.

Orthodoxy and the Inward Turn Following 1258 CE

As the previous sections showed, the writings of Al-Fārābī and Ibn Rushd were deeply influenced by the Greeks. By the time, Ibn Rushd died at the end of the twelfth-century CE, the Muslim world was quickly transitioning into a declining phase.[7] Even towards the end of Ibn Rushd's lifetime, the Peripatetic approach of the earlier Islamic scholars already began quickly falling out of favor. Serious political inquiry was no longer of interest to most Islamic thinkers following the thirteenth century. Following the fall of Baghdad, such concerns did not re-emerge until the middle of the nineteenth century with the writings of Jamal al-Din al-Afghani (1837–1897). According to Butterworth;

> Apart from Ibn Khaldun and perhaps Mulla Sadra, political reflection in the Arabic or Islamic tradition languished during the next six and a half centuries. Philosophical speculation was focused on metaphysical questions and issues of personal morality. When it did turn to politics, it usually took the form of particular advice to rulers and was directed to questions that would help them preserve their own reign. (1992: 33)

As mentioned in the introduction of this chapter, the earlier philosophers who were once revered would soon be openly critiqued and castigated by Ibn Taymiyyah and Mohammad ibn 'Abd al-Wahhāb. Eventually, the most conservative Sunni *madhhab* would come to dominate the region that is now Saudi Arabia, and it has an undeniably strong influence on thinking throughout the Muslim world today even among those who do not fully accept its doctrines.

Following the sacking of Baghdad in 1258 CE, the Muslim world was a far different place than it had been only a few generations earlier. At one level, an institutionalization or "normalization" of Islamic beliefs began. For Richard Bulliet, "[t]he variegated forms of Islam that dotted the Middle East and North Africa prior to the twelfth-century [CE] have passed away, leaving little trace except in old manuscripts" (1994: 186). Bulliet notes that one of the reasons for the decline of pluralism was due to the emergence of a new universalizing type of scholarship that sought to encourage compliance with a broader, more general doctrine of what he calls "the Great Tradition." This was often done at the expense of the smaller, local traditions, which became increasingly marginalized. Eventually, many of these local, non-literary traditions became disappeared altogether.

Second, during this period, many parts of the Muslim world were either at war or under the control of despotic governments.

> During this period, [around 1300 CE] Iraq, Iran, and Khurasan continued to smolder under the despotic control of the Tatars, Baghdad was not restored to the Muslims until its Tatar ruler embraced Islam. The Abbasid Caliph of Egypt himself led an expedition against Iraq and Baibers too made several efforts to regain that country, but none of their efforts proved successful. Memluks, however, held the reins of government over Egypt, Sudan, Syria, and Hejaz. [...] In its structure [the Memluk Sultanate] and organization, it was a military oligarchy without a constitution, a codified law or a consultative body. (Nadwi 2005: 11)

The people living in this increasingly fragmented Islamic world were now left confused and fearful. There was no real continuity of leadership to speak of, and the constant threat of invasion must have taken a tremendous psychological toll on the people living in these areas.

A third explanation for the decline of Islamic civilization is offered by Tunisian scholar Hichem Djait. According to Djait, Islam was at its strongest when it "was characterized by a high sense of religious and cultural homogeneity and historical consciousness" (Djait, quoted in Abu Rabi 1996: 33). Djait is not talking about cultural homogeneity in the way Bulliet is; in fact, he posits a radically different, "intellectually inclusive" understanding of cultural homogeneity. Djait contended that at its height, Islam was unified by the fact that all of its various movements were generally interested in all areas of scholarship. In the words of Djait,

Islam "pursued all the forms of learning with fierce vigor: history, geography, law, scholastic theology, philosophy, medicine, and mathematics" (1989: 119). However, he also notes that even prior to the European invasions, Islam began to move away from its broad scholastic interests and retreated into "a solitary existence or to an exclusive dialogue with the past" (Djait, quoted in Abu Rabi 1996: 34). This "exclusive dialogue with the past" was facilitated by certain prominent figures within the *Ash'arī* and *Atharī/Ḥanbalī* movements who discouraged the study of foreign philosophy and ideas for guidance.

Despite the emphasis on religious orthopraxy during the *Ash'arī* and *Atharī/Ḥanbalī* periods of prominence, science still flourished in the Muslim world. For example, Ibn al-Haytham and Abū Rayhān al-Bīrūnī were among the most important medieval scholars who used the scientific method in their approach to natural science, and they were both Ash'arites. Nonetheless, in general, there was a deep-seeded sense of skepticism towards non-Islamic sources by both *Ash'arī* and *Atharī* traditionists from the tenth century onward. Even up until today, Islam "has not been able to forge a coherent alliance between knowledge and action, or philosophy and movement" (Djait, quoted in Abu Rabi 1996: 35). If Islam wants to return to its glory days, theory and practice must come together. Contemporary Muslim scholars ought to familiarize themselves with Western philosophy and critical theory. Philosophizing without any real steps towards concrete political action is just empty talk.

All three explanations for the decline of Islamic civilization are worth considering. Each has some explanatory power, but none offer complete accounts on their own. Based on historical realities, at one level scholars did have to make a choice; Do they focus their energies and writings on topics related to Islamic ritual and orthopraxy, or do they take an even more dangerous route, potentially aligning themselves with a particular political movement or ideology that might, in the end, get them in trouble with the ruling authorities? As will be shown in the next sections, even scholars who stuck to a more conservative religious discourse were oppressed and jailed by the ruling authorities. On the other hand, as Djait noted, scholars began to move away from openness to scholarly inquiry and new approaches well before the actual Fall of Baghdad, which did not happen until the middle of the thirteenth century. By the time of Al-Ghazālī writings in the early twelfth century, the writing was on the wall for the way Islamic scholarship would develop over the next few centuries.

IBN TAYMIYYAH: THE CONSERVATIVE REFORMER OF THE THIRTEENTH CENTURY

In the midst of all of the *fitnah* transpiring throughout the Islamic world, in 661 AH (1263 CE), *Taqī ad-Dīn Ahmad ibn Taymiyyah* was born. In his early years, the world he lived in was constantly under attack from invading forces. Ibn Taymiyyah's family fled Iraq when he was only 7 years old due to the omnipresent fear of Mongol and Tatar invasions. The family ultimately settled in Damascus, where Ibn Taymiyyah spent his formative years. According to the biography of Ibn Taymiyyah authored by the highly regarded Indian Islamic scholar, Abul Hasan Ali Hasani Nadwi, "[e]verywhere he saw people terror stricken and panicked, running for their lives in utter confusion and disorder" (2005: 8). Despite all this confusion, Ibn Taymiyyah remained deeply interested in Islam and was deeply unsettled by the growing sectarianism and heretical practices that were becoming increasingly common in a world that was spinning out of control. By his early twenties, Ibn Taymiyyah was already delivering lectures to prominent contemporary scholars much older and more powerful than himself. His first major address to the prominent scholars made a strong impression. His first speech to a scholarly audience "was a speech so impressive and forceful, sparkling and majestic that the historian Ibn Kathir lists it as 'an astonishing event' in the annals of the year 683 A.H" (Nadwi 2005: 24). It was through his speeches that Ibn Taymiyyah began to develop his own philosophical disposition and attitudes towards other movements within Islam.

In regard to the burning question surrounding the creation or uncreation of the *Qur'ān*, Ibn Taymiyyah's position was somewhat complex. Jon Hoover argues in his critically acclaimed work that Ibn Taymiyyah believed that "God in His perfection has been speaking from eternity by His will and power when He wills and that God's speech subsists in His essence" (2004: 296). God's concretized speech is not eternal, meaning that technically the *Qur'ān*, as a physical artifact, also is not eternal. However, the *Qur'ān* also was not something created in the typical sense one conceives of something that is created since something that is created is disjointed or disconnected from God. Based on this reasoning, Ibn Taymiyyah concluded that the *Salaf*, along with Ahmad bin Ḥanbal, believed that the *Qur'ān* was uncreated because it always existed somewhere within God's essence (Hoover 2004). God's revelation of the *Qur'ān* to the Prophet Mohammed (ﷺ) was a revelation of something that had always existed within God's essence, in an *other-worldly* form, but during the period of revelation that occurred in the seventh-century CE, materialized in a corporeal, *worldly* form.

Ibn Taymiyyah was opposed to all sects created following the assassination of the fourth Sunni Caliph, Ali ibn Abi Talib. Ibn Taymiyyah openly labeled those *Khawārij*, *Shīʿah*, *Muʿtazilah*, *Murjiʿah*, Jahmites, and even Ashʿarites, a group with which he clearly had some philosophical similarities to, as heretics. Ibn Taymiyyah saw all of these movements as corrupting and misleading; they offered their own philosophical explanations of the world and existence in a way that Ibn Taymiyyah felt was contradictory to the *Qurʾān*. For Ibn Taymiyyah, *falāsifah* was unnecessary, and the only way to prevent error on the part of the believer was via unconditional submission to the authority of the earlier scholars and companions of the Prohpet (ﷺ). Ibn Taymiyyah saw modernizing or reformist movements as efforts to undermine the original ideas of the *Qurʾān*.

Ibn Taymiyyah opposed the works and ideas of Aristotelian philosophers who believed that concepts that are not self-evident can be known only through definition. He went on to argue that real essences are ultimately arbitrary and are merely assertions of the speaker based on their own subjective experience. Wael Hallaq argues that;

> Ibn Taymiyya's conception of the nominal sciences stood squarely in opposition to the philosophical doctrine of real essences and its metaphysical ramifications. The realism of this doctrine was bound to lead to a theory of universals that not only involved metaphysical assumptions unacceptable to such theologians as Ibn Taymiyya, but also resulted in conclusions about God and His existence that these theologians found even more objectionable. (1993: xx)

Ibn Taymiyyah's view on essences hints at a type of postmodern skepticism about the meanings of words, almost making Ibn Taymiyyah an Islamist Jacques Derrida. Like Derrida, Ibn Taymiyyah argued that meaning itself is not given; rather, it exists within a complex network of other things and concepts. "In literally dozens of treatises, Ibn Taymiyya untiringly asserts time and again that universals can never exist in the external world; they can only exist in the mind and nowhere else" (Hallaq 1993: xxii). Unlike Derrida, however, Ibn Taymiyyah most certainly believed that there is an ultimate foundational source (God's will) for an understanding of how history and logic unfold. However, this is something that only Allah would fully know, and that humans could only understand through Islamic sources and no other system of logic. Ibn Taymiyyah sought to bring Islam back to what he felt were its essential principles. While he was interested in sociopolitical issues, the reality was that there was not much room for political dissent in the despotic world he lived in. As a result, he focused more heavily on deeply metaphysical and theological issues. As will be shown a little later, this too ultimately put Ibn Taymiyyah on the wrong side of the ruling elites.

During the period of Ibn Taymiyyah, Muslims began to engage in practices that are by most Islamic standards today considered *shirk*. In regard to some of the practices of his contemporary Muslims living in Damascus, an adult Ibn Taymiyyah comments that "So credulous and superstitious they are [...] that when the enemy advanced against Damascus, they gathered around the tombs of their saints whom they expected to beat off danger" (Ibn Taymiyyah, quoted in Nadwi 2005: 75). Also during this time, numerous shrines dedicated to saints were being erected. According to Nadwi;

> ...certain indiscreet schools of mysticism in Islam had, for intellectual as well as development reasons, absorbed the Neo-Platonic and Hindu doctrines of initiation into the Divine mysteries. These mystical-ascetic attitudes had become so mixed up with Islamic beliefs and doctrines that it was difficult to distinguish one from the other. (2005: 5)

Ibn Taymiyyah was not *ipso facto* opposed to all movements within Islam. He did reserve some respect for Sufism. Ibn Taymiyyah was not as concerned with Ṣūfī spiritual practices as much as he was with false Ṣūfī inspired doctrines that were becoming more widely accepted.

> Some people accept everything of Sufism, it's right as well as wrong; others rejected it totally, both what is right and what is right, as some scholars of Kalām and fiqh do. The right attitude towards Sufism or any other thing is to accept what is in agreement with the Qur'ān and the *Sunnah*, and reject what does not agree. (Ibn Taymiyyah, quoted in Rafiabadi 2009: *online*)

The individual towards whom Ibn Taymiyyah was most critical was *Manṣūr al-Ḥallāj*. Al-Ḥallāj was an eccentric Ṣūfī scholar who had a rather unorthodox interpretation of Islam and monotheism in general. Al-Ḥallāj believed in a type of reincarnation in the vein of the way Christian viewed the resurrection of Jesus Christ. He also believed in the Christian version of the crucifixion of Jesus, which is at odds with all standard Islamic interpretations of the events surrounding Christ's death. Ultimately, Al-Ḥallāj was executed rather gruesomely for heresy in 922 CE. For Ibn Taymiyyah, such heretical views were wholly unacceptable and needed to be removed from the Islamic discourse as quickly as possible.

Ibn Taymiyyah is often identified as a foundational figure in contemporary Islamic extremist movements. However, if one looks carefully at the ideas of Ibn Taymiyyah, it is highly questionable as to whether these extremists are appropriately using Ibn Taymiyyah's words. Many contemporary extremists quote both *Khawārij* and Ibn Taymiyyah to justify their own actions. It is important to remember that Ibn Taymiyyah also was vehemently opposed to the *Khawārij*. Johannes Jansen notes that "it is ironic that this ancient *Khawarij* Movement is the very object of wrath of Ibn Taymiyyah whom the modern extremists quote extensively" (1987: 392). The life of Ibn Taymiyyah was marked by numerous conflicts and tribulations both at personal and societal levels. In the world in which Ibn Taymiyyah lived in, as mentioned above, violence and war were the norms. Mongol invasions were common during his lifetime. As much as Ibn Taymiyyah hated the *Khawārij*, he reserved even more animosity towards the invading Mongols. Jansen goes on to argue that Ibn Taymiyyah "is in his explicit aim to convince his readers that the Mongols 'who invade Syria again and again' are even worse than these Khawarij" (1988: 393). For Ibn Taymiyyah, it was incumbent upon all good Muslims to fight the infidel invaders; the Mongols represented a direct challenge to the Islamic world.

At a personal level, Ibn Taymiyyah was also persecuted for his beliefs. He is known to have spent at least three different jail terms during his adult life. Donald Little (1975) explored the personal life of Ibn Taymiyyah and found that some of his contemporaries thought he was mentally unstable. A passage from Ibn Battuta's *Rihla* on Ibn Taymiyyah mentioned that "[a]mong the chief Hanbali *fuqaha* in Damascus was Taqi al-Din ibn Taymiyyah who, although he enjoyed great prestige and could discourse on the scholarly disciplines, had a screw loose" (Ibn Battuta, quoted in Little 1975: 95). Some have speculated that Ibn Taymiyyah's "having a screw loose" referred to his short temper. However, when considering his difficult life circumstances, it is not inconceivable that he very well may have suffered severe psychological and emotional trauma. It also seems likely that his imprisonment only exacerbated his idiosyncrasies.

Ibn Taymiyyah was never married, which was somewhat uncommon (though not unheard of) at the time, especially in the case of very devout

Muslims. It is widely accepted that marriage is considered a major part of one's life purpose in Islam. One *Ṣaḥīḥ* rated *ḥadīth* from *Sunan an-Nasāʾī* reports; "the Prophet(ﷺ) said: "Whoever among you can afford it, let him get married, for it is more effective in lowering the gaze and guarding chastity..." (*Sunan an-Nasāʾī*, #3209). Ibn Taymiyyah also spent numerous brief stints in prison for preaching ideas that the state did not sanction. During his last prison sentence, the local authorities in Damascus even confiscated his writing materials (Nadwi 2005; Little 1975). In desperation while in prison near the end of his life, Ibn Taymiyyah resorted to using pieces of charcoal to write notes on scraps of paper.

During the twentieth century and even today, especially during times of great suffering and repression, it should not be surprising that Ibn Taymiyyah is so popular. "Ibn Taymiyyah is frequently ranked among those jurists of the highest caliber (mujtahid) for his sparkling intellect and inclusive writings, while he is religiously oriented social and political activism have inspired modern Muslims recognition of Ibn Taymiyyah as a revivalist of his age (mujaddid)" (Hassan 2010: 350–351). Throughout his extended period of persecution, Ibn Taymiyyah still was very well respected by Islamic scholars and theologians who ultimately had no power to stop the state from doing as it pleased with him. Ibn Taymiyyah died in prison at the age of 67. During his prison stay, he radically transformed the culture within the prison. He shifted his intellectual focus to direct Qur'anic exegesis, and his writings shifted their focus to ritualistic orthodoxy concerning practices like prayer and ritual worship; perhaps this was the focus of his interest because he realized it was the only thing he really had control of that the state could not take away.

Mohammad ibn ʿAbd al-Wahhāb: An Eighteenth-Century Conservative Ḥanbalī Response to Bidʿah in the Islamic Discourse

The movement founded by *Mohammad ibn ʿAbd al-Wahhāb* derived in many ways from the earlier works of fellow *Ḥanbalī* inspired scholar Ibn Taymiyyah (Fakhry 1983; Al-Fahad 2004; Delong-Bas 2004).

> In addition to their literalist adherence to the text of the Qur'an and the Traditions, the Wahhābis have in common with Ibn Taymiyyah the emphasis on ritual observance and the condemnation of the cult of the saints and similar excesses common with the *Sufi* orders. (Fakhry 1983: 318)

Mohammad ibn ʿAbd al-Wahhāb was born into a family that was well connected to the ruling princes in central Arabia (Voll 1975). His intellectual abilities have been hotly debated among contemporary scholars. According to Khaled Abou El Fadl (2007), he was not considered overly brilliant by his contemporary teachers; he was noted as being defiant, combative, and even arrogant. However, Natalia Delong-Bas (2004) argues that he was both a well-trained jurist and a prolific scholar, and that misguided *fatwās* attributed to his scholarship have sullied his reputation. While there will probably always be a debate about his true intentions and intellectual capacity, the reality is that he was influential during his own lifetime and remains very influential today.

Early in his intellectual development, Mohammad ibn ʿAbd al-Wahhāb was fully aware that the *Qurʾān* was a blueprint for legal decisions, and not an all-encompassing book of legal codes. According to Delong-Bas on the relation between the *Qurʾān* and formal law;

> The Qurʾan as God's word is a statement of God's will for all of humanity. Although it contains some legal prescriptions, it is not a law book. Rather, the Qurʾan provides moral and ethical guidance and values that human beings are supposed to apply to their personal and public life. (2004: 10)

Periodically scholars well versed in the *Qurʾān* would need to contribute new laws as the times change. Mohammad ibn ʿAbd al-Wahhāb sought to tighten in the ropes of the religion that was slowly losing its original direction.

At a very early age, ʿAbd al-Wahhāb was taught by his teacher, the respected *aḥādīth* scholar Muhammed Hayyat al-Sindhi, to reject heretical practices such as tomb worship. During his own lifetime, many Sufi's would build shrines and monuments to those whom they considered to be saints. This was completely unacceptable to ʿAbd al-Wahhāb who viewed the practice as *shirke-al-akbar* (major disbelief). "To worship the righteous and their tombs is a breach of faith. Since *tawhid* is to practice what one holds to be true, one cannot, at the same time, believe in the absolute power of God and venerate any other power" (Haj 2002: 356). The elimination of the practice of the veneration of saints was one of the fundamental principles that defined Mohammad ibn ʿAbd al-Wahhāb's legacy. Incorporating religious rituals and beliefs from other religions was one of the major signs of the deterioration of Islam for reformers living during the eighteenth century. ʿAbd al-Wahhāb and his followers set out to re-establish what they felt were the basic fundamental principles of Islam.

Ibn Taymiyyah gave equal treatment to both Islamic law and theology. He insisted that proper beliefs were the cause of correct behaviors. His work focused primarily on theology and law. His legal and theological positions were based strictly on the *Qur'ān* and the *'aḥādīth*. The *Ḥanbalī* legal school gives greater prominence to the *'aḥādīth* as a legal source than do the other three Sunni *maḏāhib* (Ali 2002). 'Abd al-Wahhāb emphasized *'aḥādīth* study. Christopher Melchert argued that Ahmed ibn Ḥanbal, "never depreciates the Qur'an, but clearly relies mainly on the hadith" (2004: 27). He felt that the content of the *ḥadīth* itself was as important as the chain of translation of the *ḥadīth* and encouraged those studying *'aḥādīth* to evaluate carefully whether a particular *ḥadīth* was in conflict with something stated directly in the *Qur'ān*. If there was a conflict between a particular *ḥadīth* and verse of the *Qur'ān*, then obviously, the *Qur'ān* must take preference.

As previously mentioned, the *Ḥanbalī madhhab* is also considered the most conservative of the four Sunni *maḏāhib*. One of the major misconceptions about what is commonly referred to as "Wahhabism" is that it is situated within the *Ḥanbalī* legal school. This is not technically correct; contemporary Wahhabism is not simply a radicalized version of *Ḥanbalī* legal jurisprudence. Contemporary *Wahhābī* jurisprudence actually deviates from the traditional *Ḥanbalī* legal discourse. According to Muhammed al-Atawneh:

> Moreover, Wahhābī jurisprudence breaks from the classical Ḥanbalī legal epistemology of Ibn Taymiyya and his disciples. This is manifested especially in: (1) limiting the practice of *ijtihād* to qualified scholars; (2) endorsing *taqlīd* for those unqualified to investigate the sacred texts; and (3) identifying public interest (*maṣlaḥa*) in accordance with the five objectives (*maqāṣid*) of the Sharī'a. (2011: 329)

The contemporary Saudi legal system incorporates elements of all four Sunni *maḏāhib* in its legal framework, although *Ḥanbalī* jurisprudence is most widely utilized. "Saudi support for inter-*madhhab* interpretation appears as early as the establishment of the modern Saudi legal system" (al-Atawneh 2011: 339). Ultimately, Saudi jurists recognized that regardless of one's *madhhab*, they still were adhering to the *Qur'ān* and *Sunnah*, and therefore were valid.

As mentioned above, despite similarities between the thought of Ibn Taymiyyah and Mohammad ibn 'Abd al-Wahhāb, there are also important critical differences. For example, Ibn Taymiyyah and the traditional *Ḥanbalī* legal approach allowed for the practice *ijtihād*, or independent reasoning. *Ijtihād* remained popular until around the tenth-century CE when the *'Ulamā'* decided that *ijtihād* should no longer be practiced; all future legal decisions were to be based solely only previously rendered decisions by the 4 main *madāhib*. While the tenth century began to see the move away from *ijtihād*, it wasn't until the sack of Baghdad in 1258 CE that the Iraqi *'Ulamā'* formally closed the doors on *ijtihād* (Ramadan 2006). Hisham Ramadan compares the decision-making process in regard to *fiqh* to how precedent works in the American legal system, albeit, in a most extreme sense. According to Ramadan;

> The rough equivalent of this phenomenon in American law would be the promulgation of a statue that restricted all judges to render decision solely via *stare decisis*, that is, adherence to decided cases, under a system of government where the legislative body is defunct and therefore incapable of issuing a new law in response to current needs. (2006: 21–22)

Ramadan goes on to argue that the abandonment of *ijtihād* in favor of *taqlīd* has had a very detrimental impact on Islamic civilization. Mohammad ibn 'Abd al-Wahhāb did not endorse *ijtihād* because of its potential hazards and misuses. Despite the ruling on *ijtihād*, Mohammad ibn 'Abd al-Wahhāb did not endorse blind *taqlīd* because "blind taqlīd may lead to heresy (kufr), sinfulness (fisq) or polytheism (shirk)" (al-Atawneh 2011: 338). Despite the acceptance of the other mainstream Sunni *madāhib*, the *Ḥanbalī* legal approach remains the most favored by contemporary Wahhābis.

> Note that for contemporary Wahhābīs, the Ḥanbalī *madhhab* is generally favored as a method of argumentation, especially in cases of legal disagreement, because the Ḥanbalīs, perhaps more than the other three Sunni *madhhabs*, remain closest to the original sources: the Qur'ān, the Sunna and the traditions agreed upon by the Companions of the Prophet. (al-Atawneh 2011: 342)

Most of the work and life of Mohammad ibn 'Abd al-Wahhāb was dedicated to rescuing Islam from heretical deviation. Like Ibn Taymiyyah,

ʿAbd al-Wahhāb wrote in a time when Islam was going through turmoil. Unlike Ibn Taymiyyah's era, much of the turmoil facing Islam came from internal rather than external sources. According to Abdul-Aziz Al-Fahad, during the eighteenth century;

> Arabian politics at the time were chaotic and bloody, and violence and conflict were endemic. Among the sedentary populations, or *Hadar*, neither tribal organization nor central authority existed. Almost every town and village was ruled independently by local chiefs, and even within such small locales independent and warring neighborhoods often could be found. (2004: 489)

Infidel invasions, while still a threat, did not possess the same salience that they did during the Crusades; rather the threat facing Islam in the eighteenth century is the Arabian Peninsula was from local tribal conflicts, distorted views, and heretical teachings that were regularly being transmitted on an even wider scale than during Ibn Taymiyyah's time.

The conflict between the declining Ottoman state [*Osmanlı Devleti*] and the followers of Mohammad ibn ʿAbd al-Wahhāb would continue into nineteenth century. Despite the fact that the Ottoman Empire was undeniably Muslim, its members were still viewed as foreigners and potentially dangerous by the local Arab populations that inhabited what today is contemporary Saudi Arabia (Al-Fahad 2004). For centuries, the Ottoman state had persecuted the Arab populations living in the Arabian Peninsula who never fully accepted Ottoman authority over their lands. In 1805, Wahhābi supporters briefly controlled the holy city of Mecca until the Ottomans finally reclaimed the city. The end result for the Saʿudi Imam and leader of the Wahhābi Movement was not pretty. "The Egyptians launched their campaigns to destroy the Wahhābis in 1811; by 1818, the Wahhābi capital, Dirʾiyyah, was in ruins and the Saʾudi Imam was taken to Istanbul where he was executed" (Al-Fahad 2004: 496). Regional conflicts between various local power brokers would continue into the twentieth century before ʿAbd al ʿAziz ibn ʿAbd al-Rahman (later King ʿAbd al ʿAziz) would finally establish Saudi Arabia as a state.

Although during his own life Mohammad ibn ʿAbd al-Wahhāb helped legitimize the authority of the people who would eventually make up the Saudi monarchy, it would be wrong to insinuate that at a deep philosophical level ʿAbd al-Wahhāb was simply a royalist with no interest in the mass public. According to Delong-Bas;

Most prominently, Ibn Abd' al Wahhab emphasized the legal principle of public welfare or interest (*maslahah*) as a guiding factor in the interpretation of Islamic law because this principle established the right and responsibility of the Muslim leadership to consider the welfare of the people as being of greater importance than strict and literal adherence to ritual. (2004: 284)

Based on all the evidence, 'Abd al-Wahhāb and the Saudi royalty worked together to consolidate each other's power; however, he was more concerned with maintaining veracity of Islam than he was with political orders or governance in any worldly sense.

Conclusion

This chapter showed that the style of scholarship produced in the Muslim world hinged on some key factors. During periods of persecution, the openness to analytic and political Greek or European thought generally declined; Islamic scholars turned inward and focused solely upon Islamic sources for guidance. However, one can still look at both early and later writings and see the possibilities for a new and uniquely Islamic form of governance. I would like to suggest that, as Sheikh al-'Uthaymīn said before, Islam is experiencing a genuine intellectual and philosophical resurgence. According to Richard Bulliet; "We are living in a crucial period of Islamic history, arguably the most intellectually and spiritually vigorous of the last thousand years" (1994: 4). Bulliet's observations were made nearly a decade before the Arab uprisings in 2011.

This chapter also showed that the geopolitical circumstances on the ground ultimately shift the discourse. Perhaps now, in an era in where Islamic oriented groups are finally beginning to have real access to political systems, there will emerge more scholars who operate within the general Islamic discourse interested in exploring the connections between Islam and politics like Al-Fārābī and Ibn Rushd. Muslim scholars did not really begin to dissect and theorize the modern "Islamic state" until the twentieth century due to the simple fact that institutions as they are conceived today, were not developed in any meaningful way prior to the twentieth century in the Muslim world, nor was the Muslim world organized in accordance to the Westphalian nation-state model. The time is ripe for political philosophers and theorists to offer new approaches to governance for states that for so long were weakened by colonialism or were run by dictators. The latter, more conservative scholars, focused primarily on ritualistic purity and orthopraxy; rich discussions on topics such as the qualities required of the just leader or administrative procedures and organization were largely absent from the writings of later scholars. Serious discussions on such topics are long overdue. There is not much writing by the later more theologically oriented scholars on modes of political leadership or political discourse in general. Al-Ghazālī and Ibn Taymiyyah's hostility towards ancient thought had more to do with its system of logic/metaphysics and its ultimate influence on Islamic religious doctrines, than with any other aspect of Greek thinking. I have *not* uncovered anything in my readings of Ibn Taymiyyah that suggests he was opposed to the creation of political institutions that may have borrowed elements from other philosophical traditions.

Ibn Rushd argued in his *Tahāfut al-Tahāfut* that Al-Ghazālī's real problem with Hellenistic philosophy was its pagan metaphysics rather than it approaches to mathematics, the natural sciences, or politics. More recent scholars have even argued that Al-Ghazālī's real goal in his *Tahāfut al-Falāsifa* was to simply defend the possibility of divine intervention against *Muʿtazilah* and *Shīʿah* thinkers that he felt elevated Greek theories of causality to the level of divine infallibility (Griffel 2007). There have also been recent movements within Islam that have sought a return to the rationalism of the past. One such example is what has been called Neo-Modernist Islamic Movement represented by people like Harun Nasution, Mohammed Arkoun, and Nasr Hamid Abu Zayd. These thinkers have made efforts to revitalize the rationalism embodied in earlier Muʿtazilism even if they did not all identify as Muʿtazilites.

The next chapter will argue that even some of the much more conservative scholars, such as Ayatollah Khomeini, had no reservations towards and even deep admiration of, Neo-Platonic and Aristotelian models of statecraft. This shows that even within the most theologically conservative worldviews, at least in regard to political and economic issues, there is room for considering different strands of thought from different civilizations.

Notes

1. The analytic disjunction between the physical sciences and philosophy during the Enlightenment era is credited to the thinking of Immanuel Kant in his, *Critique of Pure Reason* (Adorno 2001). It was not until the mid-twentieth century that critical theorists, most specifically Theodor Adorno, recognized the flaws inherent in such rigid positivist categorizations and instead sought to reconnect the two discourses via dialectical constellations. In the words of Frankfurt School scholar, Martin Jay, a constellation can be thought of as, "a juxtaposed rather than integrated cluster of changing elements that resist reduction to a common denominator, essential core, or generative first principle" (1984: 14–15).
2. All Quran references in this manuscript are quoted from, *The Meaning of the Glorious Qur'an*, translated by Mohammed Pickthall, (New York: Alavi Foundation, 2001), unless otherwise noted. All citations referring directly a verse in the *Qur'ān* will be labeled (*Qur'ān: sūrah #: āyah#*).
3. It is noted that the Prophet Mohammed's (ﷺ) paternal cousin declared the utterance of "*Inshā'allāh*" to be obligatory when making a statement on intention. According to Ahmad, "Ibn-e-Abbaas (RA) reported that a man said, "O Messenger of Allaah, whatever Allaah and you will." He (PBUH) said, "Are you making me equal to Allaah?" [Say instead:] "What Allaah alone wills" (*Musnad Ahmad Bin Ḥanbal* 2012: 1: 283).
4. *Bilā kayfā wa lā tashbīh* is a concept associated with al-Ashʿarī and Ibn Ḥanbal that means "without asking how or making comparison." *Bilā kayfā wa lā tashbīh* is a way articulate how God is beyond human comprehension and that all we can do is accept what the *Qur'ān* says and not further speculate upon its meanings, especially in a way that seeks to anthropomorphize them. Doing so diminishes the majesty and power of God. This concept is often invoked in conversations about God's divine attributes and the idea of "God's Throne" or "God's hands."
5. Abu Hanifa on the attributes of Allah commented similarly that "All His qualities are different from those of creatures. He knoweth, but not in the way of our knowledge; He is mighty, but not in the way of our power; He seeth, but not in the way of our seeing; He speaketh, but not in the way of our speaking; He heareth, but not in the way of our hearing. We speak by means of organs and letters, Allah speaks without instruments and letters.

Letters are created by the speech of Allah is uncreated" (Abu Hanifa, cited in Shah 2012: 573).
6. Often scholars refer to al-Bursawi's refutation of Ibn Rushd's work as the *Tahāfut al-Tahāfut al-Tahāfut*.
7. For a more detailed discussion on the trajectory of the rise and decline of empires, Ibn Khaldun's *Muqaddimah* (1377) is an invaluable Islamic source that has experienced a recent resurgence in popularity in the last few decades, especially in the West.

References

Abou El Fadl, Khaled. 2007. *The great theft: Wrestling Islam from the extremists*. New York: Harper Collins.
Abou Rauf, Feisal. 2007. What is Sunni Islam? In *Voices of Islam: Voices of tradition*, vol. 1, ed. V. Cornell, 185–216. Westport, CT: Praeger.
Abu Rabi, Ibrahim M. 1996. *Intellectual origins of Islamic resurgence in the modern Arab world*. Albany, NY: SUNY Press.
Adorno, T.W. 2001. *Kant's critique of pure reason*, ed. Rolf Teidemann. Redwood City, CA: Stanford University Press.
Ahmad, Jamil. 1994. Ibn Rushd. *Monthly Renaissance* 4 (9). http://www.monthly-renaissance.com/issue/content.aspx?id=744. Accessed 29 Oct 2016.
al-Atawneh, Muhammed. 2011. Wahhābi legal theory as reflected in modern official Saudi *Fatwā*s: *ijtihād, taqlīd*, sources, and methodology. *Islamic Law and Society* 18: 327–355.
al-Fahad, Abdul-Aziz H. 2004. From exclusivism to accommodation: Doctrinal and legal evolution of Wahhabism. *New York University Law Review* 79 (2): 486–519.
Al-Farabi. 2001a. Book of religion. In *Alfarabi, the political writings: "Selected aphorisms" and other texts*, ed. Charles Butterworth, 87–113. Ithaca, NY: Cornell University Press.
Al-Farabi. 2001b. Enumeration of the sciences. In *Alfarabi, the political writings: "Selected aphorisms" and other texts*, ed. Charles Butterworth, 76–84. Ithaca, NY: Cornell University Press.
Al-Farabi, 2011. The political regime. In *Medieval political philosophy*, 2nd ed., eds. R. Lerner and M. Mahdi, 31–57. Ithaca, NY: Cornell University Press.
Al-Ghazali. 2002. *The incoherence of the philosophers*, 2nd ed trans. and ed. Michael Mamura. Provo, Utah: BYU Islamic Transition Series.
Azadpur, Mohammad. 2011. *Reason unbound: On spiritual practice in Islamic peripatetic philosophy*. Albany, NY: SUNY Press.
Bulliet, Richard. 1994. *Islam: The view from the edge*. New York: Columbia University Press.

Butterworth, Charles. 1996. Averroës, precursor of the enlightenment? *ALIF: Journal of Comparative Poetics* 16: 6–18.
Butterworth, Charles. 1992. Political Islam: The origins. *Annals of the American Academy of Political and Social Science* 524: 26–37.
Clancy-Smith, Julia Ann. 2001. *North Africa, Islam, and the Mediterranean world: From the Almoravids to the Algerian war*. London: Frank Cass.
Delong-Bas, Natalia. 2004. *Wahhābī Islam: From revival and reform to global jihad*. New York: Oxford University Press.
Djait, Hichem. 1989. *Europe and Islam: Cultures and modernity*. Berkeley, CA: University of California Press.
Fakhry, Majid. 1983. *A history of Islamic philosophy*. New York: Columbia University Press.
Fakhry, Majid. 2001. *Averroes (Ibn Rushd) his life, works and influence*. London: Oneworld Publications.
Fakhry, Majid. 2002. *Al-Farabi: Founder of Islamic neoplatonism: His life and works*. New York: Oxford Press.
Genequand, Charles. 1986. Ibn Rushd's metaphysics. In *Islamic philosophy and theology: Text and studies*, vol. 1, ed. Hans Daiber. Leiden: E.J. Brill Publishers.
Glick, Thomas F. 1979. *Islamic and Christian Spain in the early middle ages*. Princeton, NJ: Princeton University Press.
Goodman, Len. 1999. *Jewish and Islamic philosophy: Crosspollinations in the classic age*. New Brunswick, NJ: Rutgers University Press.
Griffel, Frank. 2007. Al-Ghazālī. In *The Stanford encyclopedia of philosophy*, ed. Edward Zalta. http://plato.stanford.edu/archives/fall2007/entries/al-ghazali/. Accessed 15 July 2015.
Haj, Samira. 2002. Reordering Islamic orthodoxy: Muhammed ibn 'Abdul Wahhāb. *The Muslim World* 92 (3): 333–370.
Hallaq, Wael. 1993. *Ibn Taymiyya against the Greek logicians*. New York: Oxford University Press.
Hassan, Mona. 2010. Modern interpretations and misinterpretations of a medieval scholar: Apprehending the political thought of Ibn Taymiyyah. In *Ibn Taymiyyah and his times*, ed. Yossef Rapoport and Shahab Ahmed, 338–366. New York: Oxford Press.
Hoover, Jon. 2004. Perpetual creativity in the perfection of God: Ibn Taymiyya's hadith commentary on God's creation of this world. *Journal of Islamic Studies* 15 (3): 287–329.
Hurvitz, Nimrod. 2000. Schools of law and historical context: Re-examining the formation of the Hanbali *Madhhab*. *Islamic Law and Society* 7 (1): 37–64.
Jay, Martin. 1984. *Adorno*. Cambridge, MA: Harvard Press.
Jansen, Johannes. 1987. Ibn Taymiyyah and the thirteenth century: A formative period of modern Muslim radicalism. *Qaderni di Studi Arabi. Gli Arabi nella Sroria: Tanti Popoli una Sola Civilta* 5 (6): 391–396.

Leaman, Oliver. 2015. Introduction. In *The encyclopedia of Islamic philosophy* (reprint edition), ed. Oliver Leaman, xi–xvi. London: Bloomsbury.
Leaman, Oliver. 1996. Ghazali and the Ash`arites. *Asian Philosophy* 6 (1): 17–27.
Liddell, H., R. Scott, S. Jones, and R. Mackenzie. 1996. *A Greek-English lexicon*, 9th ed. New York: Oxford Press.
Little, Donald. 1975. Did Ibn Taymiyyah have a screw loose? *Studia Islamica* 41: 93–111.
Lovejoy, Arthur. 1964. *The great chain of being: a study of the history of an idea*. Cambridge, MA: Harvard Press.
Lucas, Scott C. 2006. Sunni theological schools. In *Medieval Islamic civilization: An encyclopedia*, vol. 1, ed. Joseph Meri, 809. New York: Routledge.
Mahdi, Muhsin. 2001. *Al-Farabi and the foundation of Islamic political philosophy*. Chicago: University of Chicago Press.
Makdisi, George. 1962. Ash'ari and the Asharites and Islamic history I. *Studia Islamica* 17: 37–80.
Melchert, Christopher. 2004. Ahmad Ibn Hanibal and the Qur'an. *Journal of Qur'anic Studies* 6 (2): 22–34.
Menocal, Maria Rosa. 2002. *The ornament of the world: How Muslims, Jews, and Christians created a culture of tolerance in medieval Spain*. New York: Little, Brown, and Company.
Mohamed, Yasien. 2006. Fate. In *The Qur'an: an encyclopedia*, ed. Oliver Leaman, 203–207. London: Routledge.
Musnad Ahmad Ibn Hanbal (3 vols.). 2012. Compiled by Ahmad Ibn Hanbal, trans. Nassirudin al-Khattab. Houston, TX: Dar-us-Salaam Publishers.
Nadwi, Abul Hasan A.H. 2005. *Shaikh-ul-Islam Ibn Taimiyah life and achievements*. London: UK Islamic Academy.
Najjar, Fauzi. 2004. Ibn Rushd (Averroes) and the Egyptian enlightenment movement. *British Journal of Middle Eastern Studies* 31 (2): 195–213.
Nasr, Vali. 1996. *Mawdudi and the making of Islamic revivalism*. New York: Oxford University Press.
Nasution, Harun. 1997. *Kaum Mu'tazilah dan pandangan rasionalanya* [The Mu'tazila and rational philosophy]. In *Defenders of reason in Islam: Mu'tazilism from medieval school to modern symbol*, trans. Mark Woodward, Richard Martin, and Dwi Atmaja, 180–193. London: Oneworld Publications.
Nawas, John A. 1996. The Miḥna of 218 A.H./833 A.D. revisited: An empirical study. *Journal of the American Oriental Society* 116 (4): 698–708.
Popper, Karl. 1959. *The logic of scientific discovery*. New York: Basic Books.
Qudamah, Ibn. 1962. *Censure of speculative theology: An edition and translation of Ibn Qudama's Tahrim an-nazar fi kutub ahl-al-kalam wit introduction and notes*, ed. George Makdisi. London: Luzac and Company.
Ramadan, Hisham. 2006. *Understanding Islamic law: From classical to contemporary*. New York: Altamira Press.

Rushd, Ibn. 1954. *Al tahafut al-tahafut*, vols. 1 and 2, trans. Simon Van Den Bergh. Cambridge: EJW Gibb Memorial Trust.
Sunan an-Nasā'ī (6 vols.). 2007. Compiled by Ahmad an-*Nasa'i*, trans. Nasiruddin al-Khattab. Houston, TX: Dar-us-Salaam Press.
Tabatabae'i, Muhammad Husayn. 1975. *Shi'ite Islam*, trans. and ed. Seyyed Hossein Nasr. Albany, NY: SUNY Press.
Taylor, Richard C. 2012. Averroes on the Sharī'ah of the philosophers. In *The Judeo-Christian-Islamic heritage: Philosophical & theological perspectives*, ed. Richard C. Taylor and Irfan A. Omar, 283–304. Milwaukee, WI: Marquette University Press.
Taylor, Richard C. 2009. Ibn Rushd/Averroes and Islamic rationalism. *Medieval Encounters* 15: 225–235.
Qur'ān. 2001. *The meaning of the glorious Qur'an*, trans. Mohammed Pickthall. New York: Alavi Foundation.
Rafiabadi, Hamid Naseem. 2009. *The intellectual legacy of Ibn Taymiyyah*. New Dehli: Sarup Book Publishers.
Rescher, Nicholas. 1963. Al-Farabi on logical tradition. *Journal of the History of Ideas* 24 (1): 127–132.
Shah, M. 2006. Later developments. In *Medieval Islamic civilization: An encyclopedia*, vol. 1, ed. Joseph Meri, 640. New York: Routledge.
Shah, Zulfiqar. 2012. *Anthropomorphic depictions of god: The concept of God in Judaic, Christian and Islamic traditions—Representing the unrepresentable*. Herndon, VA: International Institute of Islamic Thought (IIIT).
Sina, Ibn. 1960. *Al-Ilahiyat (theology)*, ed. M.Y. Moussa, S. Dunya, and S. Zayed. Cairo: Organisme General des Imprimeries Gouvernementales.
Voll, John. 1975. *Muḥammad Ḥayyā al-Sindī and Muḥammad ibn Abd al-Wahhab:* An analysis of an intellectual group in eighteenth-century Madīna. *Bulletin of Oriental and African Studies* 38: 32–39.
Watt, John. 1995. From Themistius to al-Farabi: Platonic political philosophy and Aristotle's rhetoric in the East. *Rhetorica: A Journal of the History of Rhetoric* 13 (1): 17–41.
Woodward, Mark, Richard Martin, and Dwi Atmaja. 1997. *Defenders of reason in Islam: Mu'tazilism from medieval school to modern symbol*. New York: Oxford Press.

CHAPTER 3

The Ontological Framing of this Model of a Contemporary Islamic Governed State

Introduction

Geraldine Brooks in her controversial internationally best-selling work, *Nine Parts of Desire: Unveiling the World of Islamic Women*, interviewed a young, unnamed Turkish architecture student who commented that; "You know, of course, that there are two types of Islam—American Islam and Muhammad's Islam [...]. In American Islam, religion is separate from politics, because it suits the superpowers interests" (1995: 19). This very telling comment to Brooks is emblematic of the larger debate that has dominated the Muslim world over the past few decades: Is there really an *American Islam*—one that is divorced from the political organization and praxis—and *Muhammad's* (ﷺ) *Islam*—one that is inherently political? Can religious values be reconciled with modern political institutions that often seem to be at odds with each other? The West has chosen the secular route, but can, or should, the same be done in the Muslim world? Should Islam divorce itself from its inherently political nature or should it embrace the idea of merging religious values and political institutions? If one believes the answer to the latter question is that Islam should embrace the idea of incorporating religious values within the framework of political institutions, the next question then becomes, how can this to be done in a feasible and efficient way that remains within the fold of Islam?

Wael Hallaq recently has argued that *Sharīʿah* was "a thorn in the side of colonialism in the Muslim world" due to its moral and egalitarian outlook which stood squarely at odds with colonialism's amorality and inequality (2013: 167). Despite his reservations about the prospects of a functional "Islamic state" in today's world, Hallaq still believes that the moral system embodied in historical *Sharī'ah* remains an invaluable source of capital that can sustain both an internal (domestic) and external (foreign policy and international relations) course of action for politics in the Muslim world. The real question at hand is how to articulate these aforementioned courses of action in a pragmatic and realistic way.

The former course mentioned by Hallaq is of primary interest in this work. In regard to the internal, or domestic, course of action that can be taken by states that seek ground themselves in Islamic values, he comments;

> First, in line with the central domain of the moral and its imperatives, Muslims can now begin—especially in light of the "Arab Spring"—to articulate and construct nascent forms of governance that would be in due course amenable to further and more robust development along the same lines. This would require nonconformist thinking and native imagination, because the social units that would make up the larger sociopolitical order must be rethought in terms of local communities that need, among other things, to be reenchanted. Historical moral resources would provide a blueprint for a definition of what it means to engage with economics, education, private and public spheres and, most of all, the environment and the natural order. (2013: 168)

Hallaq goes on to argue that indigenous considerations of the particular community in question need to dialectically engage with elements constitutive of the modern nation-state and its incumbent tendencies toward liberalizing universalizing values. It is also necessary to reshape Western liberalism's universalizing tendencies so that it is more receptive of Islam's moral considerations. Both of these elements are central to operationalizing the internal mode of action for Hallaq.

While I cannot really offer any ways in this work to reshape the Western world's predilection toward universalizing liberalism, I will make an effort to address some of the critical domains of politics and political life that Hallaq references in a way that engages with elements constitutive of the modern nation-state while remaining within Islam's ontological and epistemic frameworks.

The foundational basis of the model of an Islamic governed state (or Islamic governance) that is being expressed in these forthcoming pages can be attributed to the ideas and writings of the Tunisian intellectual Rachid al-Ghannouchi who described an Islamic government as one in which:

1. Supreme legislative authority is for the Shari'ah that is the revealed law of Islam, which transcends all laws. Within this context, it is the responsibility of scholars to deduce detailed laws and regulations to be used as guidelines by judges. The head of the Islamic state is the leader of the executive body entrusted with the responsibility of implementing such laws and regulations.
2. Political power belongs to the community (*ummah*), which should adopt a form of *shura*, which is a system of mandatory consultation. (2007: 273)

These two principles will undergird this entire endeavor. Ghannouchi's description of *Sharī'ah* as being the source of legislative authority in an Islamic governed state should not be understood as a cryptic call for a small cabal of high-ranking clerics sitting together in some medieval candlelight *madrasah* with Qur'ans in one hand and quill pens furiously scribbling immutable decrees on pieces of parchment in the other. What Ghannouchi is aiming at is a general jurisprudential praxis that keeps in the forefront the importance of *Sharī'ah* as being the authentic primary wellspring from which all subsequent laws should be vetted and evaluated in relation to. Those laws and policies that are clearly outside the fold of Islam are to be categorically rejected, while those laws and policies that are less clear in this regard are to be further deliberated upon until a consensus (*ijmā'*) emerges with the spirit of the *Sharī'ah* and a concern for the public good (*al maṣlaḥa*) in mind. Policy makers, academics, religious scholars, and politicians ought to collaborate when articulating more specific programs of action, while the principle of where legislative authority truly derives should remain omnipresent in all jurisprudential, policy making, and governing activities.

The second proposition offered by Ghannouchi—namely that political power belongs to the community—should be understood as a call for a civically engaged and educated civil society that serves as a check and balance on the actions of legislators. This is not a call for some type of unrealistic Athenian direct democracy; rather, it is a call for a society whose members do not merely sit on the sidelines as passive subjects completely detached from their government. The system of mandatory consultation envisioned by Ghannouchi must include a diverse set of voices and opinions even if these opinions are in contradistinction to the opinions held by the state and those in power.

Despite its obvious shortcomings, this work will be grounded in the Westphalian nation-state model for pragmatic reasons. At this point in history, there are no realistic alternative models; decentralized medieval feudalism, Ottoman-styled empires, and *legitimate* caliphates—despite the brutal efforts of transnational terrorist organizations like ISIS—do not appear to be making a comeback anytime soon. In an effort to keep this project as practical as possible, I feel that the Westphalian nation-state model is the best framework to conceptualize this particular model of a contemporary Islamic governed state.

The ideas discussed in these next few chapters will set the foundations for constructing a contemporary Islamic governed state. From these foundations, more specific policies can be developed in the future tailored to each individual state's specific needs. I will specifically look at some of the elements that are present in various contemporary political systems in the West and within the Muslim world. Even some of the most conservative Islamic thinkers in recent decades like Sayyid Qutb believed that learning about the arts and sciences from non-Muslim societies was acceptable. Qutb felt that Muslim societies should always seek knowledge and guidance from those knowledgeable, especially in regards to issues not directly related to fundamental religious beliefs. On this matter, he comments;

> If a proper atmosphere is not provided under which these sciences and arts develop in a Muslim society, the whole society will be considered sinful; but as long as these conditions are not attained, it is permitted from a Muslim to learn them from a Muslim or non-Muslim and to gain experience under his direction, without any distinction of religion. (2007: 109)

The much more moderate former Bosnian president Alija Izetbegović echoed this sentiment in a lecture given at an OIC conference in Iran on December 1997, while he was still president. Much to the surprise of his audience, he stated;

> Islam is the best but we [Muslims] are not the best... The West is neither corrupted nor degenerate... It is strong, well-educated and organized. Their schools are better than ours. Their cities are cleaner than ours... The level of respect for human rights in the West is higher and the care for the poor and less capable is better organized. The Westerners are usually responsible and accurate in their words... Instead of hating the West, let us... proclaim cooperation instead of confrontation. (Izetbegović, quoted in Gallagher 2003: 73)

There will be multiple references throughout these next few chapters to modern and contemporary Western thinkers when appropriate to build on a point. However, I believe pre-Enlightenment political philosophy is more useful to engage with when discussing the ontological framing of a contemporary Islamic governed state. Why I believe this is the case will be explained throughout these next few chapters. Finally, it is important to mention that this project does not seek to explain *how* any particular regime comes to power; regimes can come about via numerous ways, ranging from fair and free democratically contested elections to undemocratic military coups. This project is concerned with the philosophical underpinnings of an effective and functioning Islamic governed state, and not how any particular regime comes into power.

WHY *NOT* THE ENLIGHTENMENT OR LIBERALISM?

Nader Hashemi's, *Islam, Secularism, and Liberal Democracy: Toward a Democratic Theory for Muslim Societies*, as the title suggests, sought to show how a Muslim society can come to embrace liberal democracy. His work is well researched and quite interesting; however, it is fundamentally at odds what is being argued in this particular project. He believes that Muslim societies with strong Islamic underpinnings can eventually come to embrace liberal democracy. The caveat is that these societies have to renounce many aspects of their Islamic character.

> I have argued that political development does not require the privatization or marginalization of religion from the public sphere, but in order for religious groups to make a lasting contribution to democratic consolidation, a reinterpretation of religious ideas with respect to individual rights and the moral bases of legitimate political authority is needed. In short, the contribution religious groups can make to the development of democracy is

often a function of their ability to undertake some form of doctrinal reformulation in this direction. (Hashemi 2009: 173)

Based on Hashemi's proposition, a liberal-democratic state in the Muslim world should be allowed to have religious political parties and/or groups; however, these religious parties and/or groups need to *undertake some form of doctrinal reformulation*, which means abandoning certain elements that are understood as constitutive of the Islamic religious value system itself. Even if we assume somehow this can be done, I do not think a few doctrinal changes—or the abrogation of a few *āyāt* of the *Qur'ān* that are unsavory to the liberal palate—are enough to make a society grounded in Islamic values compatible with liberal democracy. Stylistic changes to certain specific religious practices and beliefs are only the tip of the iceberg when considering the deep incompatibilities between Islam and liberalism.

While Hashemi does not really go into detail clarifying which specific doctrines need to be purged from the Islamic discourse—as quoted above—he does mention that Muslim groups need to rethink their positions on "religious ideas with respect to individual rights and the moral bases of legitimate political authority." Doing this would literally mean making Islam, *not* Islam as will be explained in this chapter—the real incompatibilities between the Islam and liberalism are situated at this precise level that Hashemi claims need to be rethought.

The foundation of the European Enlightenment and political liberalism in general was a limited state whose powers are checked, based on a mutually agreed social contract. On the philosophical underpinnings of the liberal nation-state, Stephen Eric Bronner writes:

> The constitution was the jewel in the crown of the new world. The individual would no longer be an object of domination, but rather a subject vested with rights; a citizen. Reciprocity, rather than artificially imposed forms of hierarchy would define the formal relations between individuals. Each would be a part of an undertaking intent on constraining the arbitrary exercise of power under the liberal idea of 'the rule of law.' (1999: 26)

Despite the triumph of liberalism as the dominant political paradigm and general social discourse in the West, fundamental questions about the nature of the social contract—one of the core postulates of liberalism—remain unanswered.

John Locke was one of most important early Enlightenment figures who articulated his own version of the social contract. At the core of Lockean social contract theory is the premise that individuals leave the state of nature and form societies based on their own rational consent and free will primarily in order to provide greater protection to their person and their property. According to Locke;

> Men being, as has been said, by nature, all free, equal, and independent, no one can be put out of his estate, and subjected to the political power of another, without his own *consent*. The only way whereby anyone divests himself of his natural liberty, and *puts on the bonds of civil society* is by agreeing with other men to join and unite into a community, for their comfortable, safe, and peaceable living one amongst another, in a secure enjoyment of their properties, and a greater security against any that are not of it. (Locke [§95], quoted in Cox (Ed.) 1982: 58)

The basis of Locke's social contract derived from the introduction of private property into the previously unclaimed state of nature. "Whatsoever then he removes out of the state that nature hath provided, and left it in, he hath mixed his labor with and joined to it something that is his own, and thereby makes it his property" (Locke [§27], quoted in Cox (Ed.) 1982: 18). When man first mixed his labor with the natural resources of the land, thus claiming a parcel of it as his own, the need for the social contract arose out of the necessity for man to protect his land and his body from outside invaders and robbers. The social contract for Locke derives purely from material means; within Locke's worldview, man was under no moral obligation to ever even leave the state of nature.

The state of nature for Locke was pre-political, but it was *not* pre-moral. Locke believed that within the state of nature, there already existed the *Law of Nature* that was the basis of all morality. The Law of Nature for Locke—a deeply Christian man whose often forgotten *First Treatise* of Civil Government was almost exclusively aimed at refuting Robert Filmer's *Patriarcha from within a Christian ontological framework*—ultimately derived from God and could be understood via reason. The Law of Nature posits that we are all equal and commands that we do not harm others.[1] "And reason, which is that law, teaches all mankind, who will but consult it, that being all equal and independent, no one ought to harm another in his life, health, liberty, or possessions" (Locke [§6], quoted in Cox (Ed.) 1982: 4). This implies that man did not actually need "a state" to live a moral life, though its apparent that Locke did not believe man could actually live a meaningful life without some type of state at some point.

The standard *Sunni* and *Shī'ah* positions on man's nature hold that he is fallible, prone to violence (*'unf*), and often lost in ignorance (*jahl*). Ibn Taymiyyah (1981) argued that man was not born as a *tabula rasa* as people like David Hume or John Locke did; rather, man was born in a state of *fiṭrah*, or innate goodness (i.e., born as a Muslim), and that nature ultimately corrupted him. According to Livnat Holtzman, for Ibn Taymiyyah; "…to be born tabula rasa is neither praiseworthy nor condemnable, while Islam of course is worthy of every praise. Ibn Taymiyya then strives to establish his view that faith and unbelief are not predetermined but are rather a matter for human choice" (2010: 175).[2] Ayatollah Khomeini also believed that man was born in a state of *fiṭrah*. He believed that man was endowed with the innate ability to recognize one God, but he also recognized that man was an animal like and prone to violence (Islami 2002). We can see here that for Locke, man is born as a *tabula rasa*, and through reason can come understand the law of nature, whereas for traditional Muslim thinkers like Ibn Taymiyyah, man is born in a better position (a state of *fiṭrah*), however, though his interactions with the world, his state of *fiṭrah* soon turns into a state of *fitnah*.

Overall, I would argue that the standard Islamic view of man in the state of nature is less optimistic than Locke's—man is not capable of understanding moral law (at least in the proper Islamic way) based on his own rational faculties alone; otherwise, a revealed book like the *Qur'ān* would not be needed at all. On the other hand, the Islamic position is less pessimistic than Hobbes'—man is not inherently rotten (See *Leviathan* (1994), xiii. 3–9); rather, he is often misguided and makes poor decisions as a result. The contemporary Malaysian Islamic scholar and philosopher Syed Mohammed Naquib al-Attas succinctly commented that "Forgetfulness is the cause of man's disobedience, and this blameworthy nature inclines him toward injustice (*zulm*) and ignorance (*jahl*) ([Qur'an] 33: 72)" (1993: 140). It was through divine intervention, often through the various messages conveyed by certain chosen Prophets, that man was able to be guided back on the right path.

Based on the fact that man is forgetful and generally is unable to fully understand moral laws purely from his own rational capacities, coupled with the fact that man throughout history has often needed guidance from Prophets and/or revelation, this leads me to the conclusion that the state of nature within an Islamic epistemic framework *is* pre-moral to a certain extent. Being endowed with innate goodness as Ibn Taymiyyah or Khomeini suggested does not imply one is also endowed with a deep-rooted sense of morality and an understanding of moral laws. Since morality is essential within the Islamic worldview, and since man alone without proper guidance will struggle to live morally, man therefore *does* appear to have a moral obligation to leave the state of nature. According to Izetbegović on this matter; "Generally speaking, a Muslim does not exist as a sole individual. If he wishes to live and survive as a Muslim, he must create an environment, a community, a system. He must change the world or himself submit to change" (1990: 68).

In its ideal form, an Islamic community operates more as what Ferdinand Tönnies would call *Gemeinschaft*, whereas liberal societies today tend to operate more like *Gesellschaft*. On the basic difference between *Gemeinschaft* and *Gesellschaft*, Tönnies summarizes that; "In *Gemeinschaft* they [individuals] stay together in spite of everything that separates them; in *Gesellschaft* they [individuals] remain separate in spite of everything that unites them" (Tönnies, cited in Harris (Ed.) 2001: 52). The identity of the individual is largely reinforced by the rituals practiced within the broader Islamic community; the same can be said for communities that are *Gemeinschaft*. *Zakāt* for certain, and even *Hajj* to a lesser extent, cannot be adequately performed *without* some type of Islamic community. This helps account for why so many scholars have argued as to the importance of migration to *Dar-al-Islam*, or lands in which Islam is freely and widely practiced. The *Qur'ān* itself explicitly warns the believer to not live in lands of *fitnah*. "Lo! as for those whom the angels take (in death) while they wrong themselves, (the angels) will ask: In what were ye engaged? They will say: We were oppressed in the land. (The angels) will say: Was not Allah's earth spacious that ye could have migrated therein? As for such, their habitation will be hell, an evil journey's end" (*Qur'ān*, 4: 97). Tönnies claims that Aristotle's understanding of the ideal constitution of the city or town was also in terms of *Gemeinschaft*—within Aristotle's worldview, the city or town operates as a self-sufficient household or as an organism living in a communitarian way.

Whatever its empirical origins, its existence must be viewed as a totality, together with the individual associations and families that belong to it and are dependent on it. With its language, its customs, its beliefs, as well as its land, buildings and treasures, it forms a permanent entity that outlives the changes of many generations. (Tönnies, cited in Harris (Ed.) 2001: 48–49)

Community, optimally a close-knit community (*Gemeinschaft*), has a far more essential function within the ontological discursive framework of Islam than it has within Western liberalism. I do not think this point can be refuted.

Locke's general understanding of freedom deeply resonated with the standard liberal understanding of freedom as being primarily framed in terms of *freedom from*. "The liberal definition of freedom is normally couched in the former, in terms of "freedom from" rather than "freedom to." Negative freedom is the condition in which one is not compelled, not restricted, not interfered with, and not pressurized" (Tamimi 2001: 74). Locke's view of the social contract and society in general posited man as being primarily independent and individualistic. "The great and chief end therefore, of men's uniting into commonwealths, and putting themselves under government, is the preservation of their property. To which in the state of nature there are many things wanting" (Locke [§124], quoted in Cox (Ed.) 1982: 75). His understanding of man prefigures a liberal social and political order in which the individual takes precedent over the community. This has all the hallmarks of *Gesellschaft*. "Nothing happens in *Gesellschaft* that is more important for the individual's wider group than it is for himself. On the contrary, everyone is out for himself alone and living in a state of tension against everyone else" (Tönnies, cited in Harris (Ed.) 2001: 52). Locke's approach takes this inherent tendency toward *a state of tension* between individuals as almost unavoidable, exacerbated via the introduction of private property which necessitates man to enter into the social contract in which he exchanges his liberty for protection.

Within Islam there does exist a type of social contract. One can go back to the very beginnings of Islam and look to the Medina Charter as an example. The Medina Charter was the governing document drafted by the Prophet Muhammad (ﷺ) following the *Hijrah* in 622 CE shortly after his arrival in Medina (then known as *Yathrib*) that governed those living there. It is also believed to be the first written constitution in the history of the world (al-A'zami 2003). The Medina Constitution was the first effort at crafting a political framework for Islamic governance based on the idea of a social contract. "The most organic feature of the Medina Constitution is that it establishes an Islamic Free State on the basis of a social contract" (Khan 2006a: 206). It offered the normative establishment of a pluralistic community. There were certain rights and guarantees in the Constitution for both Muslims and non-Muslims living in Medina. On the Medina Constitution, L. Ali Khan argues;

> Conceptually, the Constitution establishes the concept of the community of believers (ummat–al mumunin). The community of believers treats all Muslims with equal respect and dignity. It dissolves the distinction between natives and immigrants, offering principles of equality and justice to all Muslims, regardless of their origin of birth, nationality, tribe, or any other ethnic or racial background. It does not allow natives to have superiority over immigrants or vice versa. (2006: 206)

At one level, the basis of an Islamic Republic, like in the West, is also an agreement, whereby people surrender some of their personal freedom in exchange for security and give the state the authority to enforce laws upon them. "Islamic law rests on the consent of the Muslim people in the same way the American Constitution rests on the consent of the American people" (al-Hibri 1992: 26). However, unlike Locke's notion of the social contract, the social contract in Islam is that the latter prioritizes the rights of the community, whereas former prioritizes individual rights. This is a major categorical distinction between the two approaches to the social contract that is irreconcilable. Ali Allawi argues that;

> The sharp dichotomy between the sacred and the profane— 'render unto Caesar the things which are Caesar's, and unto God the things that are God's'—does not hold in Islam, if it despiritualizes the foundations of both individual and collective action. Rather than separate, Islam requires the two to be reconciled. Otherwise, the teachings of Islam affirm, mankind would be denying the source of its vitality, and would be in a state of perpetual warfare with what ultimately sustains mankind's existence. (2009: 10)

The recognition of the inseparable nature of the sacred and the profane in Islam was not just limited to thinking within the more conservative *Ashā'irah* and *Atharī* traditions. Even the more "open" *Muʿtazilah* discourse, "could never entertain the idea of breaking the God-Man relationship and the validity of revelation, in spite of their espousal of a rationalist philosophy" (Allawi 2009: 11). Regardless of how one interprets the *Qur'ān*; progressive or conservative—Western liberal notions of culture, the individual, and human rights at a deep philosophical level—beyond just the content of these particular values, but rather at the existential and ontological foundations of where these values derive, in general, stand in contradistinction with an Islamic discourse that at its core is about "re-enchanting the world" and the perpetual remembrance of Allah.

Islam also does not posit that all people are equal and anyone is entitled to rule—God ordained the Prophet Mohammed's (ﷺ) rule over his community, and repeatedly in the *Qur'ān*, it is mentioned that those with religious knowledge ought to rule. The *Qur'ān* explicitly states; "O ye who believe! Obey Allah, and obey the messenger and those of you who are in authority; and if ye have a dispute concerning any matter, refer it to Allah and the messenger if ye are (in truth) believers in Allah and the Last Day. That is better and more seemly in the end" (*Qur'ān*, 4:59). Shahrough Akhavi gives a more detailed explanation of how to appropriately understand the social contract within Islam;

> As a merchant, the Prophet knew the importance of contracts, and as an arbiter of disputes and initiator of tribal alliances he gained important legal and political experience. But these compacts were not social contracts, which are formed when "each man, by right of nature, that is, by right of his human character... possessed the quality of freedom." This sort of individualism was precluded by tribal society's collective ethos. Ash'arism holds that God ordained the Prophet's rule, promising benefits to the people who accepted. This differs from people independently and freely creating a community to protect their interests. Muslims may accept or reject the revelation, but they may not negotiate or renegotiate the covenant. (2003: 24)

The social contract in Islam is more attuned to protect and promote the interests of the community, even if this comes at the expense of individual liberties they are understood in the Western discourse. Islamic conceptions of freedom fit more within the positive understanding of freedom: or the *freedom to* rather than the *freedom from*. For example, Ghannouchi understands the notion liberty within Islam primarily in its positive conception. His understanding of freedom can be paralleled to the way the enlightenment philosopher Immanuel Kant understood freedom. "Kantian freedom is the ability to realize oneself in autonomous choices, choices that will always contain an act of rational obedience toward the moral law" (Tamimi 2001: 75). Religious-based ethical systems are almost always deontological in character. Utilitarian ethical calculations, such as Bentham's crude "greatest happiness" principal, or Mill's more refined version of *rule utilitarianism*, play little role in an Islamic ethical system or a Kantian ethical system—both of which are based on a foundationalist moral source. The foundationalist source of morality in the case of Islam is revelation, while for Kant, the foundationalist source of morality was the categorical imperative which of course was deeply entrenched in a Christian existential worldview.[3]

Michael Sandel (1998) and Charles Taylor (1992) have convincingly argued that contemporary liberalism and libertarianism are grounded in an incoherent notion of the individual as existing outside of and apart from society. For Sandel and Taylor, individuals are so deeply embedded within their societies today that individual identities cannot appropriately conceptualized outside society as an abstract philosophical concept. Thus, there are no generic individuals as John Rawls (1999) leads us to believe in *A Theory of Justice*; rather, there are only "Americans" or "Germans." If this is true even for societies like those in the West that are based primarily on individual rights, then it must be even truer for Islamic societies that are deeply based in the idea of the collective as taking precedence over the individual. Once again, turning to the ideas of Wael Hallaq;

> Islamic governance (that which stands parallel to what we call "state" today) rests on moral, legal, political, and metaphysical foundations that are dramatically different from those sustaining the modern [liberal] state. In Islam, it is the Community (umma) that displaces the nation of the modern nation state. The Community is both abstract and concrete, but either case it is governed by the same moral rules. (2013: 49)

The "nation," in the West is made up of individuals who are themselves separate and distinct metaphysically from the state itself. Within the Islamic communitarian-based social structure, this separation does not exist or, at the least, is not as clearly differentiated. In Arabic, the word for the "the individual" is *al-fard*. It does not carry the same existential weight as does the notion of "the individual" in the Western context in which one thinks of a being endowed with free will, purpose, and rational faculties. According to Allawi, the word for "the individual" in Arabic "carries the connotation of singularity, aloofness, or solitariness" (2009: 11). To further illustrate Allawi's point about the meaning of *al-fard*, one needs only to look to the heavens; the brightest star in the constellation Hydra is actually called *Alphard* (derived from the Arabic word *al-fard*) or "the solitary one" because there literally are no other bright stars anywhere near it (Olcott 2004). It was originally designated *Soheil al Fard*, which translates into Latin as *Soheil Solitarius*, which literally means *the bright solitary one* (Knobel 1895). The consensus position within Islam today is that one acquires many of the qualities commonly ascribed to the individual in the West directly from God at the moment when a specific decision or action is taken; God is the creator (*khāliq*) of man's actions, and man is the acquisitor (*muktasib*). God allows or disallows an action to transpire. More simply put, within contemporary mainstream Islam's understanding of causality, your choices do *not* determine your fate—it is God who does.

The debate about the source of human action and causality within Islam was one that was largely settled centuries ago when the metaphysical positions of Al-Ghazālī and Ibn Taymiyyah won out over the *Muʿtazilah* positions that were primarily grounded in an Aristotelian understanding of causality. The Arabic understanding of "the individual" alone makes it is inappropriate to look toward Western liberalism which prioritizes an individual endowed with total free will, purpose, and independent rational faculties innate to their own physical being, over the collective good, as a *weltanschauung* to discuss Islamic governance within. In the modern world, all humans are members of some other particularistic community; the question is more a matter of degree than anything else. The degree of being members of a particularistic community is relatively high for those living in Islamic societies in comparison with other more individualistic societies.

Many early liberals saw private property as intimately connected to the life of the individual. "The defense of property rights was central in the early *lassiez* faire formulations of liberal institutionalism. The role of the state was to be constrained to enforcing a limited set of laws, adjudicating disputes, and defending property and individual rights" (Jönnson 2014: 112). Locke placed individual property rights on the same level as individual liberties. For Locke, property was an extension of one's own personal being. While Islam recognizes the importance of property rights, it does not prioritize property rights as an end in of itself in the same way that early liberals did.

Jean-Jacques Rousseau's later view of the social contract is actually closer to the Islamic conceptualization of it than was Locke's. For Rousseau, the most important aspect of the social contract was that it placed obligations and restrictions upon man. These restrictions were necessary in order for society to function.

> What a man loses as a result of the Social Contract is his natural liberty and his unqualified right to lay hands on all that tempts him, provided only that he can compass its possession. What he gains is civil liberty and the ownership of what belongs to him. (Rousseau, referenced in Barker (Ed.) 1960: 185)

Rousseau's emphasis on the necessity of certain restrictions and limitations on private property was more in line with the Islamic view of the social contract. However, Rousseau's understanding of the social contract was still secular. He placed the locus of authority in the general will, which can be understood roughly as the collectively held will that aims at the common good. For Rousseau, the ideal state expressed the general will of the people; it had no interest in anything other-worldly. Similar to Locke, the social contract for Rousseau derived primarily out of material interests that placed ultimate authority in the hands of man, not God. Rousseau praised Denis Diderot's *Encyclopédie* article titled "*Droit Naturel*" that previously had elaborated on the idea of the general will. Rousseau claimed that his version of the general will was just a development of Diderot's earlier conception. Diderot and Rousseau's writings on the general will were actually innovations on an even earlier idea of the general will that was expressed in Nicolas Malebranche's *Traité de la nature et de la grâce* that was first published in 1680. (Riley 1986). Unlike Malebranche who utilized the notion of the general will in a theological manner, Diderot and Rousseau utilized it in an entirely secular way.

Locke's claim that men freely choose to leave the state of nature to form government on their own accord based on their own mutually agreed upon principles, which really is the basis of the modern social contract, is also a highly questionable proposition to begin with. Charles Tilly (1985) offered a serious critique regarding the validity of Locke's social contract and the idea of any mutually agreed upon social arrangement in general. For Tilly, the idea of the social contract as understood in the Western context was ludicrous; nobody actually consents to it out of free will. Individuals in the modern world are born into the existing social and political order and are ultimately coerced into accepting its dominion. Individuals "tacitly consent" to be governed because they have no realistic alternative choice. This is no different from the situation one faces if they were born into a dictatorship, monarchy, or oligarchy for that matter.

There is another, even deeper fundamental problem in applying Enlightenment ideals to an Islamic political discourse that has already been hinted at in the previous sections. Locke, Rousseau and Hobbes' models of governance are all based on the secular notion of popular sovereignty. Medieval Christian thinkers like St. Thomas Aquinas argued for the primacy of natural law over man-made law, stating that where man-made law "is at variance with natural law it will not be a law, but spoilt law" (Aquinas, quoted in Grant 2003: 200). During the Enlightenment, Aquinas' idea was turned on its head—man-made law took primacy over natural law or eternal law. Popular sovereignty was a fundamental concept in framing the French Revolution and later political developments that transpired in the USA. On popular sovereignty, Donald Lutz commented;

> To speak of popular sovereignty is to place ultimate authority in the people. There are a variety of ways in which sovereignty may be expressed. It may be immediate in the sense that the people make the law themselves, or mediated through representatives who are subject to election and recall; it may be ultimate in the sense that the people have a negative or veto over legislation, or it may be something much less dramatic. (1980: 39)

Locke and Rousseau's models of a mutually agreed upon social contract are based on the idea of popular sovereignty in which ultimate legislative authority is placed in the people. A governing framework in which laws are created "by the people, for the people," is not compatible within the Islamic understanding of where the primary source of laws derives.

> A root principle in the world view of Islam is that no individual or social group, if it seeks harmony and justice, can assume the absolute power to determine its own ethical standards of conduct. [...] An ethical system of dynamic stability and justice must derive its coordinates from outside itself.

Life must derive from the 'life-giver' (*al-Hayy*); power, from the 'power-giver' (*al-Qadir*); and knowledge from the 'knowledge-giver' (*al-'Alim*). Only then can individuals and groups be guided and constrained by the only permanently legitimate form of authority. (Allawi 2009: 13)

The social contract in the Muslim world does not place ultimate authority on "the people." The social contract and political authority, in general, ultimately derive from God as understood via revelation. Even the Medina Constitution was always subservient to any new revelations of the *Qur'ān*, which was still in the process of revealed during its time (Khan 2006). For thinkers such as Abul Ala Maududi, while well-trained Muslim legal scholars may discern and apply God's law, God alone is the supreme lawgiver, and God alone is the source of all legal authority (Esposito 1987). Maududi believed that the state can create laws that are not specifically mentioned in the *Sharī'ah*, so long as these laws are not in violation of the *Sharī'ah* since the state in practice acts as God's agent or vicegerent on earth. This view actually shares much more in common with Aquinas'. Many laws are not subject to the same type of deliberative processes that laws within secular liberal legal frameworks are. Certain laws derive directly from a higher authority; in the case of Islam, many directly from Allah.

Manus Midlarsky argued that based on Islam's theological and ontological foundations, any state steeped in Islamic values will, by default, place a greater emphasis on authority than Western secular approaches to governance. "Most any government that allows revealed truth to be its guiding ideation tends to be more autocratic" (Midlarsky 1998: 493). I believe Midlarsky is correct on this point; the liturgical rulings of the Prophet Mohammed (ﷺ) were based on the *Qur'ān* and were not deliberated upon by the citizens of Mecca and Medina—they were unquestionably accepted deriving from divine revelation. However, this does not eliminate the possibility of an Islamic administered state also being democratic at some levels. "Ideas of just rule, religious or otherwise, are not fixed, even if some radicals claim they are. Such notions are debated, argued, often fought about, and re-formed in practice" (Eickelman 1997: 38). Looking toward the European Enlightenment, in which the social contract and the idea of *laws exclusively made by man, for man* is so essential, really seems to be a flawed starting point for theorizing a model of governance in the Muslim world.

Dale Eickelman argued that following the Cold War, the old, universal paradigms about politics needed to be abandoned; "The first step is to learn to elicit the cultural notions of legitimate authority and justice and to recognize the multiple voices of the Arab and Muslim world attuned to these issues" (1997: 37). This hearkens back to Aristotle who understood this point over 2000 years ago. Aristotle understood that happiness was the goal of any functional state—however, what material and ethical ends resulted in happiness differed greatly between societies.

> Now, whereas happiness is the highest good, being a realization and perfect practice of virtue, which some can attain, while others have little or none of it, the various qualities of men are clearly the reason why there are various kinds of states and many forms of government; for different men seek after happiness in different ways and by different means, and so make for themselves different modes of life and forms of government. (*Politics*, Book VII, Chap. 8, 1328a & b)

An Islamic governed state's own social contract needs to derive from its local cultural traditions (*'urf*) and be based within the generally accepted Islamic discursive framework as outlined in the *Qur'ān* and *Sharī'ah*.

While the idea of *Sharī'ah* seems unimaginable for most Americans, the majority of Muslims living in predominately Muslim countries desire to see some form of *Sharī'ah* guiding their legal framework. Almost 30 years ago in, *Islam and Politics* (1987), John Esposito argued that only "a minority elite class accepted and implemented a Western secular worldview along with its ideologies and values" and that in reality, "the majority of the Muslim population has not truly accepted and internalized a secular outlook" (1987: 212). Esposito in 2010 reaffirmed his earlier position; "…while some reformers dismiss the relationship of religion to the state, arguing for a secular state, majorities of Muslims expressed a desire for Shariah, the basis for religious values, as "a" source of law" (2010: 146).

The recent work of Sabri Ciftci empirically demonstrates that Arab people living in the Middle East are generally more likely to support some type of mix of both democracy and *Sharī'ah*. After tallying the survey results for the cases, he looked at in his overall study—Jordan, Palestine, Algeria, Morocco, Kuwait, Lebanon, and Yemen—he found that 41% of the respondents supported democracy and *Sharī'ah*, but only

14% supported democracy and without *Sharīʿah*. A significant number of people stated that they even supported *Sharīʿah* without democracy. He concluded that "democratic models incorporating Islamic values may be more feasible than strict secular democratic arrangements in Arab polities" (2013: 790). If over half of a population desires either *Sharīʿah* alone or some type of system that incorporates *Sharīʿah* and democracy, then how can one possibly believe that a state that ignores *Sharīʿah* altogether will ever be seen as legitimate in the eyes of the people?

Esposito and Ciftci's points are further bolstered by April 30, 2013, Pew Research Center Forum on Religious & Public Life, report titled "The World's Muslims: Religion, Politics and Society." This enormous project covered many topics related to the Muslim world today and involved many of the world's leading scholars. It spanned 39 different countries with sizable Muslim populations and consisted of 38,000 face-to-face interviews conducted in over 80 languages. The report notes that the desire to see *Sharīʿah* law varies from place to place throughout the Muslim world, but overall, it is generally strong. It is especially strong in the Middle East and North African countries;

> The percentage of Muslims who say they want sharia to be "the official law of the land" varies widely around the world, from fewer than one-in-ten in Azerbaijan (8%) to near unanimity in Afghanistan (99%). But solid majorities in most of the countries surveyed across the Middle East and North Africa, sub-Saharan Africa, South Asia and Southeast Asia favor the establishment of sharia, including 71% of Muslims in Nigeria, 72% in Indonesia, 74% in Egypt and 89% in the Palestinian territories. (2013: 9)

It is important to also mention that the same study notes that even in places where Muslims desire *Sharīʿah* as "the official law of the land," most Muslims still believe in religious freedom for people of different faiths. The data also showed that Muslims in general supported democracy over authoritarian leadership, "In 31 of the 37 countries where the question was asked at least half of Muslims believe a democratic government, rather than a leader with a strong hand, is best able to address their country's problems" (2013: 60). The evidence gathered from this survey and the work of Ciftci suggests that Muslims want both *Sharīʿah* and democracy and that the two are not seen as mutually exclusive (Fig. 3.1).

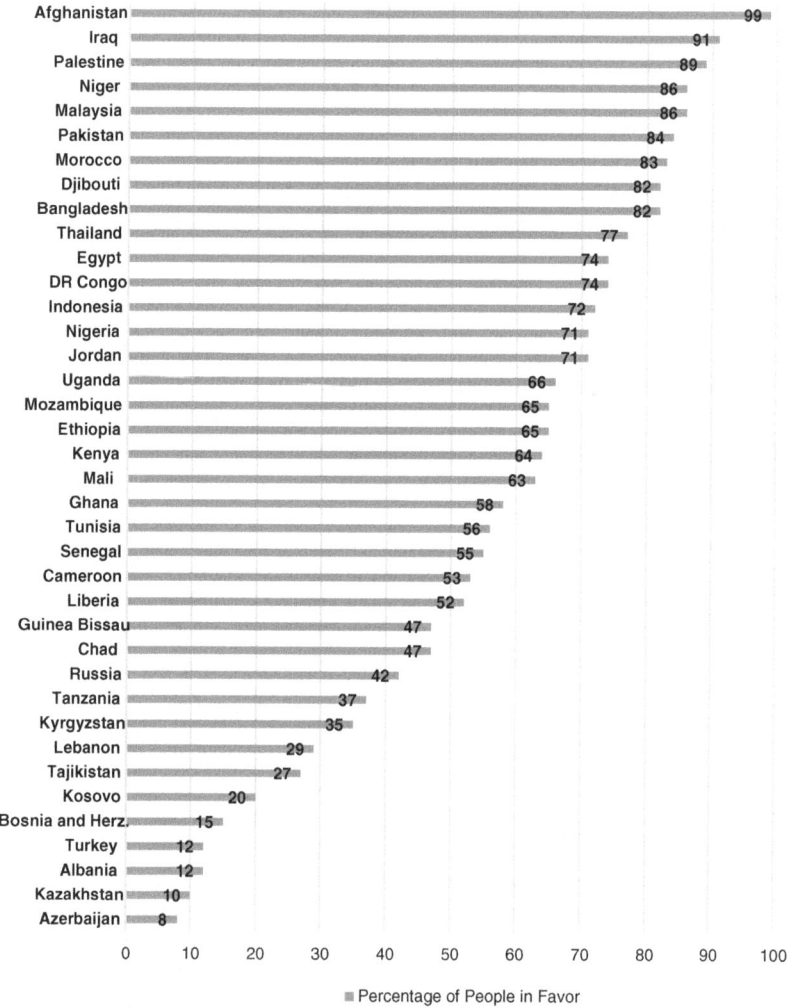

Fig. 3.1 "Do you favor or oppose making sharia law, or Islamic law, the official law of the land in our country?"[5]

A Closer Look at the Applicability of Aristotle in this Model

Aristotle was referenced in the introduction chapter on the ideal manifestation of the state. While his metaphysics might not be compatible with Islam, his understanding of the state most certainly is. The city-state for Aristotle was comprised of different classes of inhabitants who all had unique functions. Al-Fārābī, who also borrowed many ideas from Aristotle as mentioned in the previous chapter, saw the virtuous city as being organized in a similar manner as the sound body. Al-Fārābī saw that similar to the body "whose organs differ in rank or function, the parts of the city differ in rank and function, too" (Fakhry 2002: 102). The only difference between the body and the state in this regard was that the body naturally operated in this manner, whereas the state operated in this manner by social convention.

The various elements constitutive of the state for Aristotle could be understood as separate causes within his general understanding of causality. Fred Miller Jr. argues that "the city-state, like any artifact, is the product of four causes: an efficient cause (the statesman or legislator) who imposes a formal cause (the constitution) on a material cause (the inhabitants) for the sake of a final cause (the aim)." (Miller Jr., quoted in Goodman (ed.) 2007: 15) To remind the reader, Aristotle's theory of causality consisted of four distinct causes: *material causes*—"that out of which a thing comes to be and which persists..."; *formal causes*—"the form or archetype, i.e. the statement of the essence, and its genera..."; *efficient causes*— "the primary source of the change or coming to rest..."; and *final causes*—"in the sense of end or 'that for the sake of which' a thing is done..." (*Physics*, Book II, Chap. 2, 194b).

First, the city-state consisted of various classes of inhabitants whom occupied a specific given geographic territory; the people could be understood as the *material cause* of the city-state. The most important class of inhabitants in the state was citizens, who had certain unique rights and responsibilities, as opposed to non-citizen classes such as slaves and foreign visitors. These various classes of people lived under the governance of a constitution which could be understood as the *formal cause*. The constitution itself was an archetype of the ideal model of the city that was crafted by the initial lawgiver. It went beyond just being a written document; it was an internalized existential discourse. Aristotle argued that "the constitution is in a figure the life of the city"

(*Politics*, Book IV, Chap. 11, 1295a). The lawgiver's role was crucial; he served as the primary efficient cause of the city-state or *the primary source of the change or coming to rest* of the constitution of the state. "A social instinct is implanted in all men by nature, and yet he who first founded the state was the greatest of benefactors. For man, when perfected, is the best of animals, but, when separated from law and justice, he is the worst of all...." (*Politics*, Book I, Chap. 2, 1253a). A corrupt or incompetent lawgiver who crafted a poor constitution sets the precedent for a dysfunctional state with inhabitants who ultimately would come to reflect the character flaws of the original constitution. This point will be important in the next chapter that offers a model of political leadership in an Islamic governed state.

Following the creation of the constitution by the initial lawgiver, its enforcement and subsequent revisions and/or amendments were ultimately governed by politicians. Aristotle compared politicians to craftsmen, who act as the next-level efficient cause. Their tinkering with the constitution via the passing of legislation and the enactment civil codes acts as a continuation of *the source of change* initiated by the primary lawgiver. Aristotle identified the nature of a thing with its final cause. He believed that our ultimate goal in life was to realize our full potential as rational human beings. He held a teleological view of causality for both living and non-living things. On Aristotle's understanding of teleologies and final causes, Ali Çaksu comments;

> The meaning and nature of everything in the world is sought, in the end of its being. In the case of an artifact, this is an end desired by its user, and the form of the artifact is in accordance with this end imposed on its matter from outside. In the case of a living creature or of a community the end is immanent to the thing itself. (2007: 51)

Aristotle believed it was a part of human nature to ultimately adapt to life in the city-state. The constitution defines the aim of the city-state; this aim can be understood as the *final cause*. For human beings, ultimate good or happiness (*eudemonia*) consists in perfection—this is the final end for any human. Aristotle realized that the city-state could never reach this standard, but realized the closer it got to this end, the better.

Aristotle's inquiry about the ideal form of the state is a useful starting point for conceptualizing an Islamic governed state. In Book VII of, the *Politics*, Aristotle asserted that;

He who would duly inquire about the best form of a state ought first to determine which the most eligible life; while this remains uncertain the best form of the state must also be uncertain; for, in the natural order of things, those that may be expected to lead the best life are those who are governed in the best manner of which their circumstances admit. (*Politics*, Book VII, Chap. 1, 1323a; 14–19)

A careful reading of this passage about the *most eligible life* implies the necessity of some type of already existent ethical standard that exists prior to the state itself. Without addressing the question of what constitutes *the most eligible life*, one cannot really begin to tackle the question of the best form of state, because the best form of state is dependent upon some generally accepted protocol of morality or living *the most eligible life*. As one would expect, states that govern well produce citizens who are able *to lead the best life* and vice versa.

Islam, which came into being almost one thousand years after Aristotle's writings, addressed the question of *the most eligible life*. The most eligible life from an Islamic perspective is one that follows the guidance of the *Qur'ān*. "This is the Scripture where of there is no doubt, a guidance unto those who ward off (evil)" (*Qur'ān*, 2: 2). For Muslims, this literally means, the *Qur'ān* is *the* truth and it also is *the* guidance on how to live the most eligible life. "And he whom Allah guideth, for him there can be no misleader. Is not Allah Mighty, Able to Requite (the wrong)?" (*Qur'ān*, 39: 37). With Aristotle's primary question about *the most eligible life* now addressed, the next step is to craft a state based on this particular conceptualization *of the most eligible life*.

While it is obvious, the Muslim world, especially of late, has not had the most virtuous leaders, and secular liberal democracies have not been all that successful either in this regard. Alexis de Tocqueville nearly 200 years ago warned about the dangers of democratic led governments falling into the hands of incompetents. He was also concerned with the exercise of power by "the majority" over government. Tocqueville's discussion on the tyranny of the majority emphasizes this idea: "The maxim that in matters of government the majority of a nation has the right to do everything, I regard as unholy and detestable, yet, I place the origin of all powers in the will of the majority. Am I contradicting myself?" (2003: 292). Tocqueville was concerned with *the majority* dominating the political affairs and forcing imprudent action on the part of legislators, often at the expense of those in the minority. At the same time, however, Tocqueville recognized that the power legislators have derived from the will of the majority of the people. A twenty-first-century rephrasing of Tocqueville's conundrum would ask: "*How does one reconcile a politically under educated, self-interested mass public that wants both low taxes, but expensive government services at the same time?*" Something has to give. Tocqueville does not give a clear answer to this problem. At some point, a decision has to be made; does one lower the taxes or cut government services? Does one appeal to the short-term desires of their constituents or do they do what they think is in the best longer-term interests of the nation as a whole?

Within an ancient Greek political framework, the ideal political leader is one who will do what is right and not be forced into a decision by the whims of public opinion often tainted by materialism and blind self-interest. Aristotle's undeniably negative assessment of the "the mass of mankind" can be found in his *Nicomachean Ethics*. In regards to man's passions, Aristotle argued, "Now the mass of mankind are evidently quite slavish in their tastes, preferring a life suitable to beasts, but they get some ground from their view from the fact that many of those in high places share the tastes of Sardanapalus"[4] (*Nicomachean Ethics*, Book I, Chap. 5, 1095b). Aristotle's claim is that the *mass of mankind*—most specifically the poor and disenfranchised—often seeks crass worldly pleasures and that they get these ideas from those elites they so desire to be like. This general attitude toward "the mass of mankind" resonates well within an Islamic understanding of the same topic. As mentioned earlier, the general Islamic view holds that man is forgetful and needs moral guidance. The *khilāfa* was seen as being the embodiment of this moral guidance. It was viewed as the institution that brought the *ummah* stability. It remains the idealized vision of politics among millions of Muslims worldwide, and it is widely believed within the general Islamic eschatology that sometime before the Day of Judgment (*Yawm al-Qiyāmah*), it will once again be restored.

It has been well established within Islam's ethical and moral framework that worldly pleasure ought not to be the ultimate goal of Muslims. Asad Zaman further elaborates;

> In particular, pursuit of luxurious lifestyles and the pleasures of this world is not the true object of wealth: the Qur'an condemns both the pursuit of idle desires (Qur'an 45: 23) and emulation of luxurious lifestyles (Qur'an 3: 196). The modes of behaviour encouraged by the Qur'anic injunctions

are not primarily for the economic welfare of society; that is only a fringe benefit. Rather, behaving in these ways bring people closer to God, lead to spiritual growth, and develop the potential within them to achieve the "best of forms". (Qur'an 95: 4) (2013: 44–45)

Plotinus' *Enneads* argued that true human happiness lies within the contemplative capacities of the soul. "It has been shown elsewhere that man, when he commands not merely the life of sensation but also reason and authentic intellection, has realized the perfect life" (*Enneads*: I.4.4). Authentic happiness lies in the contemplation of Plato's forms and ultimately in recognizing the majesty of the all-powerful Creator and the creative process. Aristotle offers a similar commentary on the locus of true happiness. "If happiness is activity in accordance with virtue, it is reasonable that it should be in accordance with the highest virtue; and this will be that of the best thing in us" (*Nicomachean Ethics*, Book X, Chap. 7, 1177a). What Aristotle is referring to is finding happiness in the contemplative live—"That this activity is contemplative we have already said" (*Nicomachean Ethics*, Book X, Chap. 7, 1177a)—the opposite of this is finding happiness solely in what Plotinus called "the life of sensation."

In Aristotelian parlance, a mass public primarily finding happiness in the life of sensation occurs in societies that are *quite slavish in their tastes*. Money are welath are means to an end and not the end itself; "The life of money-making is one undertaken under compulsion, and wealth is evidently not the good we are seeking; for it is merely useful and for the sake of something else" (Aristotle, *Nicomachean Ethics*, Book I, Chap. 5, 1096b: 5–7). The more materialistic implications of the commonly promoted "American Dream" ought not to be the "Islamic Dream."

An effective Islamic governed state must inspire (not coerce) its citizens to seek out the version of happiness offered by Plotinus. Al-Fārābī compared the chief ruler of the city to the heart or master organ of the human body. The ruler of the city was supreme manager of the affairs of the city who should be able "to identify every action conducive to happiness and guide others to true happiness and the actions leading to it" (Fakhry 2002: 103). The governing body of state must be able to make difficult decisions, even if in the short term they may be unpopular. They ought to be cognizant of the general public will, but at the same time, have the foresight to understand that public opinion shifts like the leaves of a tree in a thunderstorm.

More recently, Bo Rothstein also wrestled with the question about how to understand the long-term interests of the public in his monumental work, *The Quality of Government: Corruption, Social Trust, and Inequality in International Perspective* (2011). One of the major questions posed by Rothstein was; "How can we distinguish between sudden changes of popular opinion and the long-term interest of the people?" (2011: 81). People often think in terms of immediate interests, rather than for the long-term good. They often become so accustomed to habit that they would rather continue doing what they are used to do, even if it is not in their best interests, rather than embrace even the simplest change. Rothstein gives the example of a 1955 Swedish referendum on determining whether or not driving should be on the left- or right-hand side of the road to illustrate his point.

In the 1955 referendum, over 80% of the population voted in favor of keeping left-hand driving out of blind habit despite the fact that many major car producers of automobiles popular in Sweden such as Volvo and Saab had already changed to make cars for right-handed driving. Recognizing the problems, this outdated policy was causing, in 1963, the Swedish parliament decided on its own to change over to right-handed driving despite the 1955 referendum results. Soon after this decision was made, it became enormously popular and has never been an issue since. He also gives the example of universal day care in Sweden as something initially that did not receive popular support when it was first launched back in the 1970s that now is a source of national pride throughout Sweden (Rothstein 2011). Rothstein's work is a modern classic that should be read by any policy maker or student of political science/public administration. An effective ruler or governing body needs to know when to compromise and when to hold firm. Leaders and governing bodies that compromise too often are seen as weak, and leaders who rarely or never compromise are seen as tyrants.

The idea of an *Islamic state* in the contemporary context of the modern nation-state did not emerge until the twentieth century and is credited to the thinking of Maududi (Nasr 1996). Anticolonial aspirations and independent autonomy for Muslims were the inspirations behind Maududi's vision of a modern-era Islamic state (Minault 1982). Maududi sought to have the leadership of Islamic states held by Muslims who were free from the corrupting influence of the colonial powers. According to Maududi;

> ...through a cruel conspiracy of circumstances, the reins of power in many a country have passed from the hands of the erstwhile imperialist powers to

this very class of west-oriented Muslims the need for a precise presentation of the Islamic case has increased manifold. (1960: 3)

Maududi's concern still resonates with millions of Muslims worldwide today. Recently deposed leaders like Egypt's Hosni Mubarak, Tunisia's Zine El Abidine Ben Ali, and even Libya's Muammar Qaddafi were viewed by their own citizens as being representative of the class of corrupt leaders under the influence of the former colonizing Western powers that Maududi warned. Maududi's vision of Islamic societies being led by morally strong leaders who are not bought and sold by monetary interests and are not under the control of foreign powers is a key point this chapter hinges upon. Arab countries have been announcing major reform and modernization policies since the 1950s (Jreisat 1992). Despite these proposed policies, administrative modernization has been largely unsuccessful. At the core of the failures have been corrupt and incompetent leaders.

The *Qur'ān* does not offer a formalized method that dictates the parameters for procedural governance in the same way the US Constitution and the Bill of Rights does.

> The Qur'an does not attempt to articulate, except in certain specific cases, detailed rules to be followed in every country or epoch. Rather, the philosophy of the Qur'an is to establish certain basic principles which could then be used by Muslims to develop specific laws suitable for their epoch, customs and needs. (al-Hibri 1992: 26)

It is the role of scholars and philosophers to use their understanding of the fundamental elements of Islam to create a state that emanates those values that are best in line with the *Qur'ān* for their time. Simply acting under the banner of Islam is not enough to guarantee success without legitimate justice.

Justice was seen by Ibn Taymiyyah as transcending any particular religion. "Verily Allah helps a just country even if it is a disbelieving one and He does not help a wrong-doing country even if it is a Muslim one. It is through justice that men are made noble and wealth is made abundant" (Ibn Taymiyyah, quoted by Sallaabee 2007: 626). The *Qur'ān* does call for leadership to be held by those with religious competence as illustrated in *sūrah* 4:59 that was referenced above. This *sūrah* does not stipulate that those in authority must be the highest-ranking Imam(s) or the individual(s) who can best recite the *Qur'ān* from memory, perfectly following the rules governing pronunciation during *Qur'ān* recitations (*tajwīd*). Rather, those who have firm faith, a reasonable level of religious knowledge, and have established themselves as respectable and trustworthy authority figures within the society are the ones to be obeyed.

Alija Izetbegović believed that many twentieth-century politicians in Muslim-majority countries discouraged Islamic thinking and practices among their citizens. Often many of these leaders openly tried to restrict such Islamic thinking and practices, while themselves indulging in Western and secular lifestyles. This was one of the reasons in his view for the overall weakness of Muslim nations. On what he called "modernizing" or secularist leaders in Muslim nations;

> They flatter and threaten, plead and goad, organize and reorganize, change names and personalities, but run up against the stubborn indifference of ordinary people, who make up the majority of the nation. Habib Bourgiba—mentioned here simply as being representative of a widespread tendency—wears European clothes, speaks French at home, isolates Tunisia not only from the Islamic but also from the Arab world, restricts religious training, calls for the abolition of the Ramadan fast "as fasting reduces productivity," while he himself drinks orange juice in public in order to set a suitable example. After all this, he wonders at the passivity and lack of support on the part of the Tunisian masses for his 'learned' reforms. (1990: 22)

In the end, such a lack of moral conviction and leadership results in passive and disinterested masses that lack direction and motivation to achieve a greater good. As mentioned in the introductory chapter, virtue and personal development are central axes on which the entire Islamic discourse is situated on. Immoral leaders are far more detrimental to the success of an Islamic nation than they are in Western liberal states whose citizenry today has almost come to expect such behaviors from their leaders. The general public disinterest following serious recent ethical lapses by major world leaders such as Silvio Berlusconi and his "*bunga bunga*" parties with underage North African prostitutes and Francois Hollande's highly publicized extra marital affair give further credence to this point. In the West, behaviors in private life are overlooked in lieu of public or political success. In the Muslim world, these kinds of transgressions are a direct assault to the core of the Islamic value system, ultimately leading to the situation described in the above quote by Izetbegović.

Conclusion

For Aristotle, a state should be formed with consideration to the nature of its inhabitants. "We should consider not only what form of government is best, but also what is possible, not only from what government is best, but also what is possible and what is easily attainable by all" (*Politics*, Book IV, Chap.1, 1288b; 37–39). The constitution of a state ought to resonate with the long-held mores and values of its inhabitants. One cannot exclude such a foundational element in the cultural identity of an Islamic majority state—the religion itself—when crafting a model of governance in this type of state. Forcing models upon states that are not in agreement with the state's general character can only lead to dysfunctionality and crisis.

Aristotle believed that even modifying an existing constitution was a difficult and dangerous enterprise in itself.

> Any change of government which has to be introduced should be one which men, starting from their existing constitutions, will be both willing and able to adopt, since there is quite as much trouble in the reformation of an old constitution as in the establishment of a new one, just as to unlearn is hard to learn. (*Politics*, Book IV, Chap. 1, 1289a; 1–5)

Being that liberal institutions and values are largely absent from the political and social framework of many Islamic countries, it seems to be unwise to utilize liberalism as a framework for governance within a state dominated by Islamic values.

Notes

1. Some have questioned how seriously Locke took natural law and have argued that his version derived from the instinct of self-preservation and natural liberty rather than from duty like most classic natural law theories. However, Jeremy Waldron points out that Locke's political thought, most specifically his understanding of equality, was in fact based on "a particular set of Protestant Christian assumptions" (2002: 13).

2. More specifically, Holtzman believes that Ibn Taymiyyah operationalizes the notion of *al-hudā wa-al-ḍalāl* (the right guidance and going astray) in a way that is meant preserve man's ability to choose or reject Islam on his own accord: "By using the fiṭra tradition Ibn Taymiyya promotes the non-deterministic concept of al-hudā wa-al-ḍalāl. He emphasizes the ability of man to transform himself from an unbeliever to a believer and vice versa" (2010: 177).
3. Kant was opposed to a Christian theocracy or the implementation of Christian law. However, he was undeniably drawn to Christianity's more abstract values. According to Nicholas Tampio, Kant and Spinoza, "historicize the Bible, and render its cognitive claims null, in order to subvert the historical rule of revealed religion;" however, Kant still "like Leibniz, cherishes Christian ethics and wishes to see a flourishing religious culture replete with churches and ministers" (2014: 181).
4. Data Source: Pew Research Center's Forum on Religion & Public life. "The World's Muslims: Religion, Politics and Society—Survey Topline Results", Question 79a, p. 201. Graph created by author in MS Excel 2016. http://www.pewforum.org/files/2013/04/worlds-muslims-religion-politics-society-topline1.pdf.
5. If one looks back into antiquity, according to the accounts of the Greek historian Diodorus, Sardanapalus was an infamous seventh century B.C.E. Assyrian emperor-king most often identified with sloth, decadence, and excess (Buckley 1996). Karl Olav Sandnes noted that "According to Cicero it was written [on Sardanapalus' tomb]: 'This I have, what I have eaten and on what my sexual desires satiated itself. These many things remain but all other riches are left behind'" (2004: 66).

REFERENCES

Akhavi, Shahrough. 2003. Sunni modernist theories of social contract in contemporary Egypt. *International Journal of Middle East Studies* 35 (1): 23–49.
Allawi, Ali A. 2009. *The crisis of Islamic civilization*. New Haven, CT: Yale Press.
Aristotle. 2001. *The basic works of Aristotle*, ed. J. McKeon. New York: The Modern Library.
al-Attas, and Syed Muhammad Naquib. 1993. *Islām and secularism*, 2nd ed. Kuala Lumpur: Art Printing Works Sdn. Bhd.
al-A'zami, and M. Muhammad. 2003. *The history of the Qur'anic text: From revelation to compilation: A comparative study with the old and new testaments*. London: UK Islamic Academy.
al-Hibri, Azizah. 1992. Islamic constitutionalism and the concept of democracy. *Case Western Reserve Journal of International Law* 24 (1): 1–27.

Barker, Ernest (ed.). 1960. *Social contract: Essays by Locke, Hume, and Rousseau*, 1st ed. New York: Oxford Press.
Brooks, Geraldine. 1995. *Nine parts of desire: Unveiling the world of Islamic women*. New York: Doubleday Publishers.
Bronner, Stephen E. 1999. *Ideas in action: Political tradition in the 20th century*. New York: Rowman & Littlefield Publishers.
Buckley, Terry. (1996). Aspects of Greek history 750-323 BC: a source-based approach. London: Routledge Press
Çaksu, Ali. 2007. Ibn Khaldun and Hegel on causality in history: Aristotelian legacy reconsidered. *Asian Journal of Social Science* 35: 46–83.
Ciftci, Sabri. 2013. Secular-Islamist cleavage, values, and support for democracy and Shari'a in the Arab world. *Political Research Quarterly* 66 (4): 781–793.
Eickelman, Dale. 1997. Muslim politics: The prospects for democracy in North Africa and the Middle East. In *Islam, democracy, and the state in North Africa*, ed. John Entilis, 17–42. Bloomington, IN: IU Press.
Esposito, John. 1987. *Islam and politics*, 2nd ed. Syracuse, NY: Syracuse University Press.
Esposito, John. 2010. *The future of Islam*. New York: Oxford Press.
Fakhry, Majid. 2002. *Al-Farabi: Founder of Islamic neoplatonism: His life and works*. New York: Oxford Press.
Gallagher, Tom. 2003. *The Balkans after the Cold War: From tyranny to tragedy*. New York: Routledge.
Ghannouchi, Rachid. 2007. The participation of Islamists in a non-Islamic government. In *Islam in transition: Muslim perspectives*, eds. J. Donohue and J. Esposito, 271–278. New York: Oxford Press.
Grant, Moyra. 2003. *Key ideas in politics*. Cheltenham: Nelson Thornes.
Hallaq, Wael. 2013. *The impossible state: Islam, modernity, and modernity's moral predicament*. New York: Columbia University Press.
Hashemi, Nader. 2009. *Islam, secularism, and liberal democracy: Toward a democratic theory for Islamic societies*. New York: Oxford Press.
Hobbes, Thomas. 1994. *Leviathan*, ed. Edwin Curley. Indianapolis: Hackett.
Holtzman, Livnat. 2010. Human choice, divine guidance and the fitra tradition-the use of hadith in theological treatises by Ibn Taymiyya and Ibn Qayyim al-Jawziyya. In *Ibn Taymiyya and his times*, ed. Y. Rapoport, and S. Ahmed, 163–188. Karachi: Oxford Press.
Ibn Taymiyyah. 1981. *Dar'u ta'arud al 'aql wa al naql*, ed. Muhammad Rashad Sa'im, vol. 8. Riyadh: Jami'at al-Imam Muhammad ibn Sa'ud al-Islamiyyah.
Islami, Hasan. 2002. *Imam khomeini: Ethics and politics*. Mansoor Limba (Trans.). Tehran: The Institute for Compilation and Publication of Imam Khomeini's Works.
Izetbegović, Alija. 1990. *The Islamic declaration: A programme for the Islamization of Muslims and Muslim peoples*. Sarajevo.

Jönnson, Christer. 2014. Classical liberal internationalism. In *International organization and global governance*, ed. Thomas G. Weiss, and Rorden Wilkinson, 105–118. New York: Routledge.

Jreisat, Jamil E. 1992. Managing national development in the Arab states. *Arab Studies Quarterly* 14 (2): 1–17.

Khan, L. Ali. 2006. Commentary on the constitution of Medina. In *Understanding Islamic law: From classical to contemporary*, ed. Hisham Ramadan. New York: AltaMira Press.

Knobel, E.B. 1895. Al Achsasi Al Mouakket, on a catalogue of stars in the calendarium of Mohammad Al Achsasi Al Mouakket. *Monthly Notices of the Royal Astronomical Society* 55 (8): 429–438.

Locke, John. 1982. *The second treatise of civil government*, ed. Richard Cox. Wheeling, IL: Harlan Davidson.

Lutz, Donald S. 1980. *Popular consent and popular control: Whig political theory in the early state constitutions*. Baton Rouge, LA: LSU Press.

Maududi, Abul Ala. 1960. *Islamic law and constitution*, ed. Khurshid Ahmad. Lahore, Pakistan: Islamic Publications.

Midlarsky, Manus. 1998. Democracy and Islam: Implications for civilizational conflict and the democratic peace. *International Studies Quarterly* 42 (3): 485–511.

Miller, Fred Jr. 2007. Aristotelian statecraft and modern politics. In *Aristotle's politics today*, ed. Len Goodman, and Robert Talisse, 13–32. Albany, NY: SUNY Press.

Minault, G. 1982. *The khilafat movement: Religious symbolism and political mobilization in India*. New York: Columbia Press.

Nasr, Vali. 1996. *Mawdudi and the making of Islamic revivalism*. New York: Oxford Press.

Olcott, William. 2004. *Star lore: myths, legends, and facts*. Mineola, New York: Courier Dover Publications.

Pew Research Center: Forum on Religious & Public Life. (2013). The world's Muslims: religion, politics and society. Project directed by James Bell. 30 April 2013. http://www.pewforum.org/files/2013/04/worlds-muslims-religion-politics-society-full-report.pdf. Accessed 1 Feb 2014.

Plotinus. 1930. *The enneads*. Stephen MacKenna (Trans.). London, UK: Medici Society.

Qutb, Seyyid. 2007. *Milestones*. Damascus: Kazi Publishers.

Qur'ān. 2001. *The meaning of the glorious Qur'an*. Mohammed Pickthall (Trans.). New York: Alavi Foundation.

Rawls, John. 1999. *A theory of justice*, 2nd ed. Cambridge MA: Belknap Press.

Riley, Patrick. 1986. *The general will before Rousseau: The transformation of the divine into the civic*. Princeton, NJ: Princeton University Press.

Rothstein, Bo. 2011. *The quality of government: Corruption, social trust, and inequality in international perspective*. Chicago, IL: University of Chicago Press.

Sallaabee, Mohammed. 2007. *The biography of Abu Bakr as-Siddique*, Trans. Faisal Shafeeq, Riyadh, Saudi Arabia: Dar-us-Salaam Publishers.

Sandel, Michael. 1998. *Liberalism and the limits of justice*. Cambridge: Cambridge Press.

Tamimi, Azzam. 2001. *Rachid Ghannouchi: A democrat within Islamism*. New York: Oxford Press.

Tampio, Nicholas. 2014. Pluralism in the Ethical Commonwealth. In *Kant's Religion within the Boundaries of Mere Reason: A Critical Guide*, ed. Gordon E. Michalson, 175–192. New York: Cambridge University Press.

Taylor, Charles. 1992. *Sources of the self*. Cambridge, MA: Harvard Press.

Tilly, Charles. 1985. War making and state making as organized crime. In *Bringing the state back in*, ed. P. Evans, D. Rueschemeyer, and T. Skocpol, 169–191. Cambridge: Cambridge Press.

Tocqueville, Alexis. 2003. *Democracy in America*. Isaac Kramnick (Trans.). New York: Penguin Classics.

Tönnies, Ferdinand. 2010. *Community and civil society*. J. Harris (Ed.) and M. Hollis (Trans.). Cambridge: Cambridge Press.

Waldron, Jeremy. 2002. *God, Locke, and equality: Christian foundations in Locke's political thought*. Cambridge: Cambridge Press.

Zaman, Asad. 2013. *Islamic economics: A survey of the literature*. Islamabad: IRI Press.

CHAPTER 4

Considering Leadership and Laws in a Contemporary Islamic Governed State

> *To know wisdom and instruction; to perceive the words of understanding; To receive the instruction of wisdom, justice, and judgment, and equity; To give subtlety to the simple, to the young man knowledge and discretion. A wise man will hear, and will increase learning; and a man of understanding shall attain unto wise counsels: To understand a proverb, and the interpretation; the words of the wise, and their dark sayings. The fear of the LORD is the beginning of knowledge: but fools despise wisdom and instruction.*
> –Proverbs 1:2–7

Introduction: A Look at Some Specific Leadership Qualities

Raphael's iconic renaissance fresco, "The School of Athens," depicts Plato holding what is believed to be the *Timaeus* in one hand, pointing toward the heavens with the other, while Aristotle is seen to his right holding a copy of his *Ethics* with his palm facing downward toward the earth. This painting perhaps best summarizes the key difference between Plato and Aristotle; Plato was the idealist looking toward the heavens for answers, while Aristotle was the pragmatic realist looking toward the material world for answers to his most perplexing questions. Aristotle believed that; "…the best is often unattainable, and therefore the true legislator and statesman ought to be acquainted, not only with (1) that which is best in the abstract, but also with (2) that which is best relatively to circumstances" (*Politics*, Book IV, Chap. 1, 1288b; 25–28). Aristotle and Plato will both be referenced in this chapter; however, Aristotle's pragmatic model of political leadership will be more requisite to the general arguments presented in this section.

The recent work of Rick D. Hackett and Gordon Wang offered an Aristotelian approach to leadership. They specifically look at leadership qualities desirable in the business world. They outline seven different types of leadership: ethical, moral, spiritual, servant, charismatic, transformational, and visionary. Each type of leadership has its own corresponding set of virtues. The virtues they discuss, however, can also be applied to political leadership. I chose to incorporate their work into my overall conception of leadership in an Islamic governed state because it is concise, clearly written, and easily fits within the parameters of an Islamic discourse. As has been mentioned earlier, any scholarship that has kernels of wisdom contained within should be incorporated in any project that seeks to build a modern Islamic governed state.

The four Aristotelian cardinal virtues are courage, temperance, justice, and prudence. In regard to leadership, the first thing that they argue is that a leader must have the disposition or character traits of a leader (i.e., be recognized as a leader by the larger community); second, that virtue is acquired through learning and continuous practice; third, the leader's virtue is expressed voluntarily; and forth, leader virtue is defined through specific situations and interactions (Hackett and Wang 2012). These four traits are found in the Prophet Mohammad (ﷺ) who was revered for his courage in battle and domestic issues, his temperance and clemency toward his people, his focus on justice and fairness, and his prudence and willingness to make difficult decisions[1] (Mubarakpuri 2002; Ramadan 2009; Armstrong 2007).

Any political leader must be flexible and capable of grappling with difficult situations. Hackett and Wang argue that "all Aristotelian virtues are described in accordance with specific situations. For example, courage is discussed with respect to situations that provoke fear; justice is discussed with respect to situations calling for distributing resources" (2012: 870). The table on the next page offered by Hackett and Wang shows individual virtues linked to seven specific leadership concepts. The leader of any Islamic governed state should look toward the Prophet of Islam (ﷺ) as an exemplary of both domestic and international leadership. Models of business leadership are useful for articulating virtues of a political leader; however, one must remember the two enterprises (political leadership and business leadership) have some very serious differences as well. The way success and "profits" are measured differ in many distinct ways between political leadership and business leadership. The ideal leader should embody the various virtues outlined by Hackett and Wang. Many of the aforementioned virtues in the left-hand column overlap with the seven different leadership categories outlined by Hackett and Wang. As one can see, there is quite a long laundry list of traits that are desirable of a leader under this particular Aristotelian model of leadership (Table 4.1).

The terms "king" and "monarch" are used rather interchangeably in the European context. In Arabic, however, there are multiple terms for understanding the European equivalent of "a king." Both *khalīfah* and *malik* refer to a political leader, but carry very different meanings. "The Arabic term used as the translation of 'king' in modern Arab political discourse is *malik*, a term which has historic negative connotations" (Voll 1997: 10). Voll argued that the controversial founder of the Umayyad Caliphate, *Mu'āwiyah I*, was branded with the title *malik* as a disparaging term by some of the people living in his time. On the other hand, the term *khalīfah* refers to what is conceived as the nature of a proper successor to the Prophet Mohammad (ﷺ) based on that individual's personal qualities such as piety, justice, and righteousness.

A governing structure led by those who are wise and capable that make serious efforts to *genuinely* follow the divine prescripts of Islam (i.e., act more like a *khalīfah* rather than a *malik*) should never fall into tyranny, since by definition they are accountable to Allah and they take this accountability seriously. Plato uses the famous "ship of state" metaphor to describe effective political leadership—"the true pilot must give his attention to the time of year, the seasons, the sky, the winds, the stars, and all that pertains to his art if he is to be a true ruler of a ship...." (*Republic*, Book VI, 488d). Likewise, the leader in a modern Islamic governed state must be intimately connected to all aspects of their society and understand both the art and the science of leadership.

In the *Republic*, Plato argued that the ideal ruler should be one who does not actively seek political office for their own gains. They should be appointed by the people due to their inherent qualities. They must be civically minded (*Republic*, 338b–342a). One particularly salient *hadīth* from the highly regarded *Riyadh-us-Saliheen* collection of Imam Nawawi echoes very closely to Plato's own sentiment.

> Abdur Rahman din Samurah reported: The messenger of Allâh [s.a.w] said to me, "Do not ask for position of authority. If you are granted this

108   J.J. KAMINSKI

Table 4.1 Leadership styles and corresponding attributes

Virtues	Moral leadership	Ethical leadership	Spiritual leadership	Servant leadership	Charismatic leadership	Transformational leadership	Visionary leadership
Ability				x			
Acceptance				x			
Ambition							x
Autonomy							
Benevolence				x		x	
Caring	x	x	x	x	x		x
Compassion	x	x	x	x	x		x
Competence	x						x
Concern for authors		x	x	x	x		
Conscientiousness		x					
Consideration						x	
Consistency					x		
Cooperativeness							
Courage/fortitude	x	x	x	x	x	x	x
Creativity					x	x	x
Dedication						x	x
Dependability		x	x				x
Determination		x				x	x
Discipline				x	x		x
Empathy		x		x	x	x	x
Enthusiasm		x					x
Equity				x			
Faithfulness\faith\loyalty	x	x	x				
Fidelity		x					x
Forgiveness			x	x			
Friendliness						x	

(continued)

Table 4.1 (continued)

Virtues	Moral leadership	Ethical leadership	Spiritual leadership	Servant leadership	Charismatic leadership	Transformational leadership	Visionary leadership
Generosity				x			
Honesty	x	x	x	x	x	x	x
Honour				x			x
Hope			x				
Human-heartedness						x	
Humility	x	x	x	x		x	x
Independence							x
Integrity	x	x	x	x	x	x	x
Justice\fairness	x	x	x	x	x	x	x
Kindness				x			
love	x	x	x	x	x	x	x
loyalty		x	x	x			x
Magnanimity							
Modesty			x				
openness							x
Passion	x					x	x
Patience		x	x	x	x		
Perseverance\persistense		x	x	x		x	x
Pride		x					
Prudeness	x	x	x	x	x	x	x
Reliability		x					
Respect for others	x	x	x	x			
Responsibility\Accountability\duty	x	x	x	x	x	x	x
Righteousness					x	x	
Self-sacrifice		x		x	x	x	

(continued)

Table 4.1 (continued)

Virtues	Moral leadership	Ethical leadership	Spiritual leadership	Servant leadership	Charismatic leadership	Transformational leadership	Visionary leadership
Senstivity		x	x				
Service to common good				x			
Temperance\moderation\Self control	x	x	x	x	x	x	x
Tolerance		x	x				
Toughness				x			
Trustworthiness	x	x	x	x	x	x	x
Truthfulness	x				x		
Wisdom		x	x	x		x	x

Reprinted with permission from Emerald Group Publishing Limited, originally published in *Management Decision*, Vol. 50, No. 5, © Emerald Group Publishing Limited 2012 position without asking for it, you will be helped (by Allâh) in discharging its responsibilities; but if you are given it as a result of your request, you will be left alone as its captive. If you take an oath to do something and then find a better alternative, you should adopt the latter and expiate for your oath. (*Riyadh-us-Saliheen*, #674)

Islam immediately recognized the corrupting nature of power. One who seeks power will often become enslaved to their passions and act in self-aggrandizing, rather than civic-minded ways. Noah Feldman (2008) noted that often Muslim immigrants to the USA were surprised by the overly flamboyant and self-aggrandizing nature of political campaigns. The ideal ruler, in essence, should loathe having political power, rather than crave it. For Plato, philosophers must become kings or those who are kings "must take to the pursuit of philosophy seriously and adequately..." (*Republic*, Book V, 473d). Plato understood that true philosophers were the only ones truly qualified to rule because they were most familiar with *the good* and understood it better than anyone else. Al Fārābī's model of the chief leader in *The Virtuous City* was not only heavily based on Plato's model of the chief leader offered in the *Republic* but also "invested him [the chief leader] with prophetic qualities in addition to Plato's philosophic traits" (Fakhry 2002: 104). Understanding Plato's forms in an Islamic context can roughly be paralleled to understanding the essence of the *Qur'ān* and the *Sunnah* of the Prophet (ﷺ).

The late dissident Iranian cleric, Ayatollah Hussein-Ali Montazeri, was clear that those who possess religious knowledge do not necessarily possess all those qualities needed to run a government. While an individual may excel in one area, they most likely will be weaker in others. On this matter, Montazeri states that; "...a person might be the most knowledgeable in terms of issues related to worship, but less so when it comes to political and penal issues of Islam" (2000: 7). An individual may be strong in the philosophical and religious sciences, but lack the ability to be effective statesmen without help from others. Montazeri's point echoes an argument made by Alexis de Tocqueville in the mid-nineteenth century on the difference between the art of political rule and the science of politics.

For Tocqueville, the art of political rule and the science of politics were two very different things. In an unpublished address given to the *Séances et Travaux de l'Académie de Sciences Morales et Politiques* in 1852, Tocqueville sapiently comments that; "The art of writing, indeed, brings about in those who have long practiced its habits of mind ill adapted to the conduct of public affairs" (1852: 28). This implies that great thinkers and philosophers often are not capable of moving beyond their own ideas, thus failing to adequately account for the will of the public. Such a disjunction between theory and practice mitigates the possibility for effective rule. The great thinker's quest for philosophical fidelity "forces them to abide by the logic of ideas, whereas the crowd only obeys the logic of its passions" (Tocqueville 1852: 28). With this being said, the role of advisors trained in the art of rule and other disciplines is essential to the political leader; the two must complement each other. Those who advise the leader must also be of superior intellectual quality; leadership based on greed, material possessions, and other such avarice ultimately leads to failure. This means that Islamic regimes need rulers and advisors who put justice ahead of profits in their vision of governance. In Platonic terms, an Islamic leader must have some familiarity with *the good* as it is understood within the Islamic discursive framework—there can be no shirking on this.

Socrates compares the difference between knowledge and *the good* to the difference between vision and light, and the sun. He reminds the Glaucon that while vision and light are "sun like" they are not actually the sun. The sun exists independently from both vision and light.

> But as for knowledge and truth, even as in our illustration, it is right to deem light and vision sunlike, but never to think they are the sun, so here it is right to consider these two their counterparts, as being like the good or boniform, but to think that either of them is the good is not right. Still higher honor belongs to the possession and habit of the good. (*Republic*, Book VI, 509a)

Plato goes on to further explain to Glaucon that—"you are to say the objects of knowledge not only receive from the presence of the good their being known, but their very existence and essence is derived from it, though the good itself is not essence, but still transcends essence in dignity and surpassing power" (*Republic*, Book VI, 509b). If one offers an interpretation of truth from an Islamic perspective, truth is something that has always and will always exist, but was previously beyond the grasp of man. In Plato's, *Theatetus*, Socrates ultimately fails to come up with a conclusive definition of epistemological certainty, or knowledge, in his dialogue with the young Theatetus. The reader of the *Theatetus* is left in the undesirable position of accepting the final position on this matter of the later influential Greek skeptic, Sextus Empiricus.

Sextus Empiricus who wrote a few hundred years after Plato advocated for the suspension of judgment in regard to questions relating to epistemological certainty. According to Sextus Empiricus;

> Now whether one should say that all appearances are true, or that these are true and those false, or that all are false is impossible to say; for we have no agreed standard through which to judge which we are to prefer, nor are we equipped with a proof which is both true and judged because we are still investigating the standard of truth through which true proofs should properly be decided. (*Outlines of Skepticism:* Book II: 53)

For the Pyrrhonian skeptics, there was no "standard of truth through which true proofs should properly be decided" in which to base judgments of reality upon. This did not just apply to the physical world, but the ethical world as well.

In the eyes of its followers, Islam and its Prophet (ﷺ) were sent as a mercy to mankind to allow for man to understand ethical truths in a way previously not possible. Within the Islamic discourse, the *Qur'ān* always has been the "agreed standard through which to judge" as articulated by Sextus Empiricus in his *Outlines of Skepticism*. For the true believer, it meets the qualification being Plato's *the good*, in corporeal form, within Islam. According to al-Attas; "The Holy Qur'an is the complete and final Revelation, so that it suffices for man's guidance and salvation; and there is no other knowledge—except based upon it and pointing to it—that can guide and save man" (1993: 144). Operationalizing Plato's analogy of vision and light, and the sun in an Islamic context— the *Qur'ān* is Plato's sun, or *the good*, and the wisdom that emanates from it is the light. When our cognition, which can be roughly understood as vision in Plato's analogy, fixates on the *Qur'ān*, we gain wisdom; however, if our cognition turns away from the *Qur'ān*, it is as if our eyes turned away from the sun and as a result, we are left in darkness—"when the eyes are no longer turned upon objects whose colors light the day fall but that of the dim luminaries of night, their edge is blunted and they appear almost blind, as if pure vision did not dwell in them" (*Republic*, Book VI, 508c). Muslims believe that it is through the teachings of the Prophet (ﷺ) and the words of the *Qur'ān* that truth can be deciphered.

While the sacred text of Islam is *the truth* or *the good* within Islam, this does not guarantee that the reader of the *Qur'ān* will properly understand and implement its lessons, just as simply possessing a car does not guarantee one will arrive safely at their final destination. The driver of the car must possess the skills requisite to properly operate the vehicle otherwise it will not go anywhere, or worse, it will end up crashed into a tree. This is why it is so essential for an Islamic governed state to have a leader who possesses a sufficient level of religious knowledge and personal virtue, yet remains willing to heed advice from his advisors and other legislative bodies. It is important for political actors to be receptive to non-Islamic sources in regard to political institutions and governance, yet still recognize when an institution is operating outside the acceptable bounds of Islam.

BALANCING POWER WITH RESTRAINT

The rule of the leader should by no means be unlimited or uncontested. While the executive should be capable of effectively ruling without excessively stifling oversight, they must be held to an extremely high moral standard. This was made explicit in Ayatollah Khomeini's model of governance. In his own words; "The ruler must also possess excellence in morals and belief; he must be just and untainted by major sins" (1970: 32). These moral standards extend beyond their actions while in office, but into their personal lives as well. This was one of the essential points in the model of Islamic governance outlined by Ayatollah Khomeini.

While in Najaf, the exiled Khomeini gave a series of 19 lectures to a group of his students between 21 January 1970 and 8 February 1970. Eventually, these lectures became a book published under three different titles. The most widely known title is *Hukumat-e islamī: velāyat-e faqīh* (*Islamic Government: Rule of the Jurist*). One of the main points in Khomeini's theory was that monarchy and despotism were unIslamic. According to Ervand Abrahamian;

> Muslims, Khomeini insisted, have the sacred duty to oppose all monarchies. They must not collaborate with them, have recourse to their institutions, pay for their bureaucracies, or practice dissimulation to protect themselves. On the contrary, they have the duty to rise up (qiyam) against them. (1993: 24)

Although Khomeini's writings are situated within the *Shī'ah* theo-political discourse, some of the basic principles he outlines can be applied to states predominantly situated within the *Sunni* tradition as well.

Khomeini argued that religious judges had a divine right to rule. While this model of Islamic governance is not going as far as to making that claim, this model does see merit in having those intimately familiar with Islamic jurisprudence hold political positions and advisory roles at high levels within the state. Having such figures in positions of authority gives the state more legitimacy and ought to serve as a check and balance on those at the highest levels of political leadership. In reality, there are currently no *Sunni* majority states where political leadership is truly dominated by those whose knowledge of Islamic law and justice surpass all others in knowledge; no *Sunni* majority state today even tries to make such a claim. While actually having a leader who truly meets this qualification in the literal sense may be impossible, modern Islamic governed states should seek leaders who are well versed in various disciplines, including the Islamic sciences. This is to not-so-subtly suggest that a large bank account and connections to people or families in high places are in no way a qualification for being a political leader in this model of political leadership in an Islamic governed state.

Khomeini's position on the centrality of moral excellence as a foundational quality of a legitimate ruler parallels Aristotle's position on this particular matter. Aristotle believed that immoral leadership ultimately filtered down into the ethos of the people being governed. An earlier quote on this matter referenced how the masses are slavish in their tastes; however, they get their inspiration for such attitudes from the elites who they seek to be like. On the importance of creating an office or body that oversees those in power and makes sure the leader is conducting his personal affairs in an appropriate manner, Aristotle commented that "since innovations creep in through the private life of individuals also, there ought to be a magistracy which will have an eye on those whose life is not in harmony with the government, whether oligarchy or democracy or any other" (*Politics*, Book V, Chap. 8, 1308b: 20–25). An Islamic governed state ought to be organized in a way in which the leaders of the regime are subject to regulation and scrutiny from some type of independent authority in which they do not control.

Following Khomeini's passing in 1989, Grand Ayatollah Montazeri was slated to be Iran's next Supreme Leader, but due to personal disagreements between Khomeini and Montazeri, prior to Khomeini's death, the position was given to the lower ranking and much more conservative, Ayatollah Ali Khamenei. Montazeri would live another 20 years as an outcast. During this time, his religious school was shut down, his was office looted, and he would actually spend 6 years under house arrest. Following his death, Iran's official state news agency (IRNA) "did not use the *ayatollah* title in its early reports of Grand Ayatollah Montazeri's death and referred to him as the "clerical figure of rioters"" (BBC News 2009: *online*). Montazeri was widely seen as more of a moderate and a reformer, despite still holding some controversial opinions, such as accepting the permissibility of executing apostates.[2] If he would have succeeded Khomeini, Iran's political discourse would likely be much different than it is today. In an interview on the topic of Iranian participation in the larger global community, Montazeri stated;

> Of course in Iran we cannot accept those laws that are against our religion. But the necessity of not becoming globally isolated requires that we should collaborate with international organizations. But on certain occasions that these laws contradict the very clear text of the Qur'an, we cannot cooperate. (Montazeri, interviewed in Bashi 2003: 19)

Montazeri showed a willingness to engage with non-Islamic organizations and ideas, so long as they are not in direct violation of the *Qur'ān* and *Sharī'ah* as understood within the Iranian context.[3] Montazeri references a statement made in 1979 by Khomeini that explicitly mentioned that *faqīh* must be just and not oppress the people.

> The *faqih* does not seek to oppress the people. If a *faqih* [expert in Islamic law] sought to oppress the people, he would not be fit for *veylat* (religious jurisprudent) anymore. It is Islam; in Islam the law will rule. Even the Holy Prophet obeyed the law, obeyed the divine law and could not violate it. There is no dictatorship. (Khomeini referenced in Montazeri 2000: 9)

An immensely unpopular or immoral leader cannot remain in power. In a properly functioning Islamic administered state, there would be no dictatorship, since by definition; a dictator is the one who has all the vested power. In Islam, only Allah has the authority to create universal rules as he pleases. Many Western writers have made similar assertions in regard to the danger of unchecked power. In particular, Tocqueville articulates this point in a way that really resonates well with the broader

Islamic understanding of where power and authority ultimately lie. In *Democracy in America* (2003), on omnipotence in terms of worldly power, Tocqueville commented that it "seems self-evidently a bad and dangerous thing. Its exercise appears to be beyond man's powers, whoever he might be, and I see that only God can be omnipotent without danger because his wisdom and justice are always equal to his power" (2003: 294). When wisdom and justice are unequal to power, problems immediately arise. Tocqueville did not believe any one man could properly balance the three on his own.

In today's age of hyper-communication and social networking, absolute rule with unchecked power is even more impossible than ever. The groundbreaking work of Douglass North (1990), eloquently articulated how economics and institutions are often impacted not only by formal legal constraints, but also by vast networks of informal constraints;

> Even the most casual introspection suggests the pervasiveness of informal constraints. Arising to coordinate repeated human interaction, they are (i) extensions, elaborations, and modifications of formal rules, (ii) socially sanctioned norms of behavior, and (iii) internally enforced standards of conduct. (1990: 40)

Some of the informal constraints on institutions today include things such as social media, traditional mainstream media, "whistle-blowers" and *hacktivism*, and public opinion. North argued that the public ultimately plays a role in how formal rules are construed and modified in both the institutional and the economic arenas. Mass publics often directly influence not only the formal rules of institutions, but also even the behavior of actors within the institutions themselves. Recent examples in the Middle East have shown that even within the most authoritarian regimes, public discontent and social mobilization can force the hand of even the most obstructive bureaucrats and political actors.

Unlike the 1979 Iranian Revolution, the protest movements in Egypt, Libya, and Tunisia were not shaped by any type of unwavering devotion to all-encompassing ideology or particular charismatic leader. Oliver Roy claimed that these movements were driven by "the ideals of democracy, pluralism, and good governance" (2012: 14). He notes that none of the 2011 Arab Revolutions relied on calls to *jihād* or efforts to mobilize a transnational Islamic community. National organizations and national agendas were at the core of the various Islamist groups that have risen to prominence in the places that they have. National-based Islamist movements of recent vintage have taken on the mantle of pragmatic reform as opposed to radical revolutions and calls to violence (Gerges 2013). Many movements that constituted the broader phenomenon that was the Arab Revolutions focused on what are considered legal rights-based related issues by Western scholars and observers. However, this is not to suggest that Western articulated "natural legal rights" are somehow universal axioms or that the values of the West were what the people of the Arab Revolutions sought. These standards of legal rights, much like norms, are culturally specific (North 1990). Therefore, legal rights must be understood within culturally specific settings, rather than as universal axioms. In an Islamic governed state, legal rights derive from the *Qur'ān-* and *Sharī'ah*-based laws, not from Enlightenment era philosophical developments and discourses.

Prominent leaders even in the most conservative countries have recognized the need for state leadership to allow for dissent. Ayatollah Montazeri argued that stifling peaceful dissent and "depriving people of their legal freedoms is not only a sin and encroachment on the natural rights of people, but will also discourage them and lead to estrangement between the nation, government, and officials" (2000: 6). Montazeri astutely understood that doing this was unacceptable for not only moral reasons, but for more practical reasons as well. As mentioned in this book's introduction, the means of social and political organizing have taken on new forms that even a dictator cannot completely control.

Online political mobilization began in Egypt right around 2000. It also played a key role in galvanizing opposition to the authoritarian rule of Bashar al-Assad in Syria a decade later. Eltantawy and Wiest (2011) argued that as early as 2008, cyber activism in Egypt began to directly challenge the authority of the state. Social media literally mobilized millions of Egyptians against Hosni Mubarak and ultimately prevailed in removing him from power. There are disproportionately large youth populations in the Middle East in comparison to Europe and North America. The Middle East now accounts for 5% of total world population; this has doubled from 2.5% in 1950. In 1950, there were approximately 60 million people living in the Middle East. As of 2005, that number is at 271 million (*United Nations Population Division* 2008). The youth in Egypt were largely responsible for the overthrow of the Mubarak regime. "The use of social media to organize the youth was paramount in bringing about regime change in Egypt, and in protests

across the Middle East writ large" (LaGraffe 2012: 73). People between the ages of 15–24 who were disproportionately clustered in urban centers like Cairo were equipped to challenge the unpopular political leadership in a way previous generations could not. At this point in history, the leader of any state should be fully aware of the power of disenfranchised youth populations and social media. Muslim leaders need to appeal to their younger populations if they are to be successful. Now that the internet and social media are rudimentary elements that have been incorporated into new social movements, at this point, there is no turning back.

One of the primary factors that ignited the 2011 Arab Revolutions was despotic rulers, underperforming bureaucracies, and stagnant economies. Milan Svolik's empirical research has shown that "the probability of successful power sharing declines in the dictator's power. In other words, the moral hazard associated with authoritarian power sharing intensifies as the dictator gains more power" (2009: 487). This is to suggest that there exists a quantifiable correlation between power sharing and levels of authoritarianism. The more power a dictator has, the less likely there will be much power sharing, even among the other political elites inside the dictator's own coalition. When authoritarian regimes lack power sharing, even among those actors sympathetic to the regime, the regime moves from being authoritarian to totalitarian.[4]

An ideal state operating within the framework of Islam would never allow for the emergence of a Stalin or a Mao. The Ancients recognized that *the good* of the nation must come prior to the good of the individual, especially if the good of the individual interferes with the good of the nation. Aristotle states in his *Nicomachean Ethics*, "The attainment of the good for one man alone is, to be sure, a source of satisfaction; yet to secure it for a nation and states is nobler and divine" (Book I: Chap. 3, 1094b). Leaders must not use the state as a means of expanding their own personal wealth. Aristotle was aware of this reality when he wrote his *Politics*—"But above all every state should be so administered and so regulated by law that its magistrates cannot possibly make money" (Book V: Chap. 8, 1308b). Aristotle argued that this must be the case for all regimes; people get especially angry when they know their rulers and politicians are stealing public monies for private uses. The Athenian city-state was a regime of laws. This is a common theme that runs throughout ancient Greek thought. Plato's *Laws* are several hundred pages in length consisting of a total of 12 books, all dealing with the importance of just laws.

The same meticulous concern with just laws should also be present for any functioning twenty-firstcentury Islamic governed state. A concern for the rule of law and justice can be found within the history of Islam dating all the way back to the inaugural address of Islam's first Caliph, Abu Bakr as-Saddiq. In this address, he implored to his audience;

> You must be Godfearing, for piety is the most intelligent practice and immorality is the most foolish. Indeed I am a follower, not an innovator: if I perform well, then help me, and if I should deviate, correct me.... O gathering of the Ansar [sc. Madinan Muslims], if the caliphate [lit. "this matter"] is deserved on account of inherited merit and attained on account of kinship, then the Quraysh is more noble than you on account of inherited merit and more closely related to you [to the Prophet]. However, since it is deserved on account of moral excellent in religion, then those who are foremost in precedence from among the Muhajirun [sc. the Makkan emigrants to Madina] are placed ahead of you in the entire Qur'an as being more worthy of it compared to you. (Abu Bakr as-Saddiq, quoted in Afsaruddin 2006: 55)

States that claim to be acting in accord with the rules of Islam, yet in reality have become bastions of corruption and nepotism, led by figures that view themselves as more than human, by their very nature, are not Islamic governed states. Such governments should be toppled by the people. This model of an Islamic governed state in no way endorses ideologies popular among certain Middle Eastern "court scholars"—to borrow a term from Giles Kepel (2004)—who oppose political activism by arguing that challenging a ruler, even if the ruler is unjust, leads to *fitnah*, and that one ought not cause *fitnah* even if the ruler is unjust.[5] Such reasoning mitigates any realistic possibility for justice and transparency since such logic makes a leader almost completely unaccountable.

Even earlier scholars who are widely celebrated by many more conservative Muslims today such as the iconic fourteenth century *Ḥanbalī/Atharī* theologian Ibn Qayyim al Jawziyyah recognized the inherent limitations on worldly rulers. Ibn Qayyim recognized that no ruler was above the law or the dictates of the scholars who Ibn Qayyim sees as having a closer connection to the Prophet (ﷺ) due to their knowledge than any worldly ruler. According to Ibn Qayyim on the matter;

Properly speaking, the rulers (*al-umarā'*) are obeyed [only to the extent] that their commands are consistent with the [articulations] of the religious sciences (*al-'ilm*). Hence, the duty to obey them [the rulers] derives from the duty to obey the jurists (*fa-ṭā'atuhum taba' li-ṭā°at al-'ulamā'*). [This is because] obedience is due only in what is good (*ma'rūf*), and what is required by the religious sciences (*wa mā awjabahu al-'ilm*). Since the duty to obey the jurists is derived from the duty to obey the Prophet, then the duty to obey the rulers is derived from the duty to obey the jurists [who are the experts on the religious sciences]. Furthermore, since Islam is protected and upheld by the rulers and the jurists alike, this means that the laity must follow [and obey] these two [i.e., the rulers and jurists].[6] (Ibn Qayyim, referenced in Abou El Fadl 2012: 49)

The people also are only obliged to obey that "in what is good". This implies that if a ruler is not promoting that which is good within the Islamic context, then people have no obligation to obey these specific commands. It is ironic that many nations that unequivocally identify the likes of Ibn Qayyim and the tradition of Abu Bakr as-Sadiq and *ahl as-sunnah wa l-jamā'ah* have completely jettisoned the aforementioned foundational premise of leadership passing through moral excellence rather than inherited merit, and instead have political systems in which leadership passes through blood relations.

A Closer Look at Some of the Ideas of Ayatollah Khomeini

The twentieth century Italian philosopher Gaetano Mosca claimed that "societies in which religious beliefs are strong and ministers of faith form a special class, a priestly aristocracy almost always arises and gains possession of a more or less important share of wealth or political power" (1939: 59). Mosca's key point was that in societies dominated by religious values, one is more likely to see a small group of religious elites emerge as leaders. Iran in 1979 is perhaps the clearest example of Mosca's observation originally made in the 1920s. If Mosca is correct in his assertion that there is a natural propensity for societies with strong religious beliefs to gravitate toward institutions that have leaders who reflect those values, then the question should not be how to keep these types of people out, rather it should be how to have people in power with such religious propensities do their jobs in justly and successfully.

While it is obvious that post-1979 Iran has engaged in numerous human rights violations and has been rather dismal in regard to women's issues, one cannot deny that it is one of the few successful attempts to establish an Islamic state that is not ruled by an absolute monarch and has some levels of democratic participation. Khomeini believed that in "a true Islamic state those holding government posts should have knowledge of *Sharī'ah*, and the country's ruler should be a *Faqīh* who 'surpasses all others in knowledge' of Islamic law and justice" (Khomeini 1981: 59). Not surprisingly, Khomeini was heavily influenced by Plato. Khomeini believed that Plato deeply understood the essential Islamic notions of oneness or *tawḥīd* and divine knowledge based on his own readings of Plato's *Timaeus*. Khomeini was also deeply influenced by Plotinus' *Enneads* (Martin 2007). He sought to encourage *Sunni-Shī'ah* unity against oppression and imperialism. According to Reza Aslan;

> Under Khomeini's guidance, the constitution was a combination of third-world anti-imperialism mixed with the socioeconomic theories of legendary Iranian ideologues like Jalal Ali Ahmad and Ali Shariati, the religio-political philosophies of Hasan al-Banna and Sayyid Qutb, and traditional Shi'ite populism. (2005: 251)

This present discussion is not arguing that the current manifestation of what some scholars have called "Khomeinism" is model that should be blindly imitated. The current Iranian regime in many ways has regularly violated basic human rights within an Islamic worldview (Moghadam 1991; Sedghi 2007; Afary 2009). Ayatollah Montazeri was well known for his view that an Islamic state was important, but that Iran was not acting as one. My argument is that the broader themes encompassed within the notion of *velāyat-e faqīh* are worth further considering when crafting a model of governance in the contemporary Muslim world.

The term *faqīh* or jurist of Islamic law derives from the word *fiqh* which means Islamic jurisprudence. Tariq Ramadan argues *fiqh* can be understood as "The state of juridical reflection reached by Muslim scholars at a certain time in a certain context in light of their study of the *Sharī'ah*" (2006: 3). One of the central arguments in Khomeini's writings is that Islam already has a general framework outlined for governance. The problem has been finding a government willing to actually implement it. Khomeini believed that guardianship should be vested in one jurist, while other Iranian religious figures, such as Mohammed al-Husayini al-Shirazi, favored a modified iteration of *velāyat-e faqīh* in which not a single cleric, but a council of scholars should govern an Islamic State. A central element of al-Shirazi's theory was a consultative system of leadership composed of senior clerics.

Khomeini, similar to Maududi, argued that imperialism had forced non-Islamic governance and institutions on Islamic societies resulting in previously unimaginable levels of corruption—the aftermath of 1952 CIA led coup of the democratically elected Mohamed Mossadeq is just one of many examples of this. Following *Operation Ajax*, Mossadeq was replaced by the authoritarian Shah Mohammed Reza-Pahlavi (Kinzer 2003; Capehart and Milanovich 2007). The Shah was widely loathed by the population who viewed him as an excessive decadent product of Western imperialism. On Shah Pahlavi's 47th birthday, he crowned himself king. As a part of the celebration festivities, 17,532 roses were dropped from planes over Tehran, each rose representing a day that the Shah had been alive (January 2008). The festivities were capped off with a 101-gun salute and a million-dollar firework show dedicated to Pahlavi. The failings of the Shah along with other more contemporary Middle Eastern dictators have resulted in an intellectual backlash against Western modes of government and values.

> Nationalistic answers that once seemed heady and progressive, buttressed by a purported superiority of cultural and intellectual values originally imported from the west, now fall flat before the whispered—or shouted suspicion that they are actually symptoms of the malignancy of cultural imperialism. (Bulliet 1994: 4)

Khomeini believed that imperial dominance over any Islamic state was unacceptable. The laws of any Muslim nation cannot be forced onto it by foreign powers. The laws must develop organically based on local norms and culture and reflect the *Sharī'ah*. This means that simply having laws that reflect *Sharī'ah* is not sufficient—especially if the government pays lip service to these laws, and engages in rampant corruption. According to Khomeini;

> A body of laws alone is not sufficient for a society to be reformed. In order for law to ensure the reform and happiness of man, there must be an executive power and an executor. For this reason, God Almighty, in addition to revealing a body of law (i.e., the ordinances of the shari'ah),

has laid down a particular form of government together with executive and administrative institution. (1970: 18)

Khomeini's view was that the government must be organized in a way in which there is an executive who makes certain these laws are followed. However, even within the framework of Khomeini's very hierarchical system of governance, other senior Iranian clerics argued that there still must be room in all societies for dissent and opposition.

Ayatollah Montazeri was quite critical of the overly intrusive nature of the Iranian regime. The *Qur'ān* is a guide for human behavior; it is not meant to be a science book or understood as a book of procedural administration over menial matters. While both the *Qur'ān*, and more specifically the various collections of *'aḥādīth*, address some of the more seemingly personal issues, such as eating behaviors and rules regarding how to properly fast, this does not mean that all of these matters are subject to any codified legal proceedings or formal sets of worldly sanctions if these edicts are violated. For example, there is no *ḥudūd* punishment if one eats with their left hand instead of their right. While Islam may have many rulings and decrees pertaining to various aspects of one's life, many of these rulings and decrees have no formal punishments ascribed to them. While one is supposed to raise their child in an Islamic way, if the child turns out to be a criminal, there is no "legal punishment" for the parent. The same goes for something like performing prayers or *ṣalāt*. Even though *ṣalāt* is considered absolutely essential to true faith, there is no formal worldly punishment for missing a prayer.

Throughout the various collections of *aḥādīth*, it is made clear that the individual is not subject to draconian arbitrary punishments. First, it is important to remember the severity of inappropriately labeling someone a disbeliever, or doing *takfīr* on someone. One *ḥadīth* on this matter reports that;

> Ibn 'Umar said; The Messenger of Allah [s.a.w] said, When a person calls his brother (in Islam) a disbeliever, one of the will certainly deserve the title. If the addressee is so as he asserted, the disbelief of the man is confirmed, but if it is untrue, then it will revert to him. (*Riyadh us-Saliheen*, #1732)

Another famous *ḥadīth* contends that when one commits a minor sin that nobody witnesses, they are to keep it to themselves. They are to consider the matter between themselves and Allah only. The quote from the *'aḥādīth* collection of Imam Bukhārī on this matter states;

> It was narrated that Abu Hurayrah said: I heard the Messenger of Allah (peace and blessings of Allah be upon him) say: "All of my ummah may be forgiven except those who commit sin openly. It is a kind of committing sin openly if a man does something at night, then morning comes and Allah has concealed his sin, but he says, 'O So and so, I did such and such last night,' when his Lord has concealed him (his action) all night but in the morning he reveals that which Allah had concealed for him. (*Ṣaḥīḥ al-Bukhārī*, #5721)

This means that behavior inside one's house or in private locations is generally not subject to legal scrutiny. The purpose of the laws is to maintain a stable society: not to place one's entire life in some type of totalitarian prison.

Even those penalties that have been traditionally interpreted by scholars and jurists as warranting corporal punishment within Islam are often difficult to prove and are unfairly enforced on those at the bottom of their respective societies. Omid Safi argues that;

> The majority of the *ulamā'*, historically and today, are of the opinion that these penalties are on the whole Islamic but that the conditions under which they should be implemented are nearly impossible to reestablish. Conditions for the application of these punishments are not met. (2010: 88)

This unfair distribution of justice most certainly goes against the very essence of the faith itself which posits that no individual is above the laws. Tariq Ramadan emphasizes that *ḥudūd* punishments are disproportionately administered to the marginalized of society: women, poor, prison inmates, in today's context.

> A still more grave injustice is that these penalties are applied almost exclusively to women and the poor, the doubly victimized, never to the wealthy, the powerful, or the oppressors. Furthermore, hundreds of prisoners have no access to anything that could even remotely be called defense counsel. (Ramadan, quoted in Safi 2010: 89)

Ramadan is quite careful to affirm that the *ḥudūd* has always been and will continue to be a part of the *Sharī'ah*. Ramadan's argument "is based on the fact that the conditions that the hudud call for are difficult to realize justly in today's society, and as a result the enforcement of the hudud must be suspended" (Safi 2010: 88). Contemporary Islamic governed states must be absolutely certain to properly administer penalties and punishments in a fair manner, otherwise the fundamental legitimacy of the state is at risk.

SHARĪʿAH VERSUS *FIQH*—TWO DIFFERENT TERMS WITH TWO DIFFERENT MEANINGS

Now that the terms *Sharīʿah* and *Fiqh* have been introduced, and it is necessary to go into greater detail explaining what these two concepts mean and their role in postulating a theory of an Islamic governed state. The word "*Sharīʿah*" actually derives from the Arabic word "*Sharʾee*" which literally translates into *street*. Irshad Abdal-Haqq defines *Sharīʿah* as meaning the "pathway, path to be followed or clear way to be followed" and in its original context, it literally meant the "road to the watering place or path leading to water, i.e., the way to the source of life" (2006: 4). This literally means that *Sharīʿah* is the path which one follows that leads them to success. According to Bernard Weiss (1998), the idea of "the pathway to water" is significant because water represented the lifeblood of Arab society in the harsh and unforgiving desert. *Sharīʿah* is inextricable form Islam itself.

Following the emergence of the four main schools of jurisprudence within the *Sunni* tradition (*Mālikī, Ḥanafī, Shāfiʿī,* and *Ḥanbalī*), it was recognized that more formalized procedures were needed to articulate *Sharīʿah*.

> The most important of these instruments was the *ijma* (consensus), which was to become in its own right a pillar upon which the shari'a rests (holding a position of priority next to the Qur'an and hadith, in this order). *Qiyas* (analogy with a rule derived from any of the other three) was then added as the fourth foundation for the shari'a (and its lowest in hierarchy). (Nawas 1996: 706)

In order to ensure legitimacy, early jurists recognized how important it was to have laws derived from *'aḥādīth* collections that were deemed authentic via some formal procedure. During the first two centuries of Islam, accounts and stories of the actions of the Prophet (ﷺ) were compiled into various collections gathered all throughout the Muslim world. Many of the *'aḥādīth* originally collected were "concoctions" that often were reflective of local customs, laws, tastes, and desires, written down by fallible human beings (Juynboll 1983; Nawas 1996). It was up to scholars and jurists to determine what was authentic and what was fabricated. By the later part of the eighth century CE, intense studies of the *'aḥādīth* and their validity were already underway. It was within the four main *Sunni* schools of jurisprudence that much of the classification and collation of *'aḥādīth* were done. "This corpus served as a mainspring on which definitive canonical compilations, such as those of al-Bukhari, Muslim, and others drew" (Nawas 1996: 706). The original principles of the *Sharīʿah* evolved during the early period of Islam based on a new, uniquely Islamic science dedicated toward validating the authenticity of the sources used to create the Islamic legal framework.

Despite the lack of a coherent, final document defining *the Sharīʿah*, there still are elements of *Sharīʿah* that are broadly more accepted than others. According to Jan Michel Otto, "When people refer to *the* Shari'a, they are in fact referring to *their* Shari'a, in the name of the eternal will of the Almighty God" (2008: 7). According to Hallaq, the *Sharīʿah* is not a stagnant remnant from centuries ago, rather it is constantly evolving in its efforts to understand God's will.

> The Shari'a consists of the hermeneutical, conceptual, theoretical, practical, educational, and institutional system that we have come to call Islamic Law. It is a colossal project of building a moral-legal empire whose foundational and structural impulse is summed up in the ever continuing attempt to discover God's moral will. (2013: 51)

Hallaq in many ways echoes Maududi, who on the nature of *Sharīʿah* similarly stated that "This scheme of *Sharīʿah* is, however, divided into many parts. Aspects of it do not need any external force for their enforcement they are and can be enforced only by the ever-awake conscience by his faith" (Maududi, quoted in Euben and Zaman 2009: 97). The *Sharīʿah* can be enforced at multiple levels, including within the individual's own soul and in the courts of public opinion. "Other parts are enforced by Islam's program of education, training of man's character, and the purification of his heart and morals" (Maududi, quoted in Euben and Zaman 2009: 97). Maududi also was clear that the external legalistic form of *Sharīʿah* can only be adequately practiced within an actual practicing Islamic governed state. This means that rag-tag bands of rebel armies or militia groups do not have the authority to enforce *Sharīʿah* law as happened in Mali, where Al Qaeda of the Islamic Maghreb (*Tanẓīm al-Qāʿidah fī Bilād al-Maghrib al-Islāmī*), have infiltrated Tuareg society and imposed their own brutal form of *Sharīʿah*. Most recently this has been happening in Iraq and Syria, where ISIS has engaged in horrific misapplications of *Sharīʿah*. For Maududi and most contemporary scholars of Islamic jurisprudence, this informal application of *Sharīʿah* would be wholly unacceptable.

While there are certain elements of *Sharīʿah* more specific than others, the twentieth century Oxford University historian Albert Hourani argued that it is most commonly "expressed in terms of general principles." He goes on to argue that *Sharīʿah* "contains some specific commands, for example, in regard to marriage and the division of a Muslim's property after death, but these are limited, and for the most part God's will is expressed in terms of general principles" (1991: 65). These specific commands were absolutely essential during the seventh and eighth centuries CE to ensure that widowers were properly compensated and that the wealth rightfully due to orphans was not stolen by unscrupulous characters. While some of the idiosyncrasies of Islamic property law may seem arcane today, the original purpose of these laws was to protect those weakest members of society from exploitation.

The terms "*Sharīʿah*" and "*fiqh*" are regularly misused in the media and in public discussions—often when people refer to *Sharīʿah*, they in fact mean *fiqh* and vice versa. "*Sharīʿah*" refers to immutable moral codes as expressed in the *Qurʾān* and *Sunnah*. "*Fiqh*" refers to interpretative law which is based on *Sharīʿah* principals that continuously evolves (Khan 2003). Khaled Abou El Fadl argued that *fiqh* "quite literally means 'understanding' or 'comprehension,'-not *the* understanding or *the* comprehension, but *an* understanding or a comprehension" (2012: 809). Oussama Arabi argues that modern Islamic law should be seen as being based on *Sharīʿah* rather than being seen as a set of some type of a priori set of assumptions.

> Modern Islamic law is better viewed as what present day Muslim jurists, legislators, judges, and theologians take to be Islamic provisions and rulings in the altered, complex world of today rather than an a priori

constrained corpus that is conserved, albeit in an astoundingly rich variety, in classical legal manuals. (Arabi 2001: 18)

Arabi is clear that while in Islam, laws are generally based on previous rulings, there still remains room for modern interpretations.

For Abou El Fadl, Arabi, and Hallaq, *Sharī'ah* should be understood as a living breathing discourse rather than as an outdated and rigid set of laws that it often caricaturized as by Islam's contemporary detractors. The issue of balancing tradition with modernity permeates all aspects of the entire debate surrounding Islam and its application. Since there are so many uniquely modern issues that are not really addressed within *Sharī'ah*, the only logical way to approach *Sharī'ah* is to look at it as one source among many for crafting law and policy. This has also been the approach of recent moderate Islamist movements such as Tunisia's *Ennahda* Movement and the Egyptian Muslim Brotherhood.

Regardless of whether one understands *Sharī'ah* as being a set of immutable principles, as a set of standards meant to be continually re-evaluated, or somewhere in between, there still are important things to consider when articulating the *Sharī'ah*. Malevolently claiming something is *Sharī'ah* when it is not is a grave matter within Islam. Issuing legally binding *fatāwā* or rearticulating *Sharī'ah* principles are things that only the best-trained jurists who have spent their entire lives studying Islamic law have the authority to do. Trying to articulate the complex issue of *Sharī'ah* and its proper interpretation goes well beyond the scope of this project. Since I am not a trained expert or qualified jurist on *Sharī'ah*, I will not offer any normative claim as to the "proper way" to interpret specific instances falling within the rubric of *Sharī'ah*. However, adhering to the widely held jurisprudential standard of consensus (*ijmā'*) seems to be an appropriate starting place for articulating a more specific vision of *Sharī'ah*.

Since there is no universal final, codified version of "the" *Sharī'ah*, each individual state's iteration of *Sharī'ah* should be interpreted by the local qualified authorities within that particular state. It would make no sense to have a set of Ḥanbalī Gulf State scholars articulate their interpretation of *Sharī'ah* in a state dominated by Shāfi'ī or Mālikī jurisprudence. Positive law must develop based on local culture/customs ('*urf*) and each local culture's own understanding of Islam. On the importance of '*urf* as a source of law, the renowned fourteenth century Andalusian Makilite scholar, Abū Isḥāq al-Shāṭibī (1970), in his *al-Muwāfaqāt fī Uṣūl al-Aḥkām*, argued that interpretations of *Sharī'ah* should always consider the overall public interest, and that it is in the public interest that *'urf* and *'ādah* (usage) are relied upon as supporting legal sources so long as they are not in contradiction to the *Sharī'ah*.[7]

Qānūn/siyāsa, or laws promulgated by Islamic rulers that were outside the direct purview of *Sharī'ah*, were common throughout Islamic history. Such laws were meant to supplement *'urf*, but in a more formalized manner. Said Amir Arjomand argues that the "word *Qānūn* had entered into Arabic in the early Middle Ages. It retained its original Greek fiscal connotations as regulation of land taxes, but also acquired the more general sense of state law" (1993: 77). *Qānūn* is believed to have originated as early as during the rule of *'Umar* and continued to develop throughout the centuries. As mentioned by Arjomand, *qānūn* often addressed issues related to taxation and administrative practices, however, it also addressed penal issues as well. It was especially common during the era of the Ottoman Empire. Each particular Islamic governed state should have their own set of scholars and jurisprudential standards that ought to be consulted when crafting their respective localized and national level jurisprudential frameworks, for both *Sharī'ah* and *qānūn*.

Transitioning states also ought to not immediately enforce laws that they lack the capacity to properly enforce. Ramadan's point about the importance of properly and justly applying *ḥudūd* punishments should be taken very seriously. One ought to remember that it was reported by Abu Hurairah that the Prophet (ﷺ) said; "Ward off the legal punishments as much as you can" (*Sunan Ibn Majah*, # 2545). The great *Shāfi'ī* legal expert, al-Suyuti, in his *al-Ashbāh wal-Naẓā'ir* (see 2/122) also argued that legal punishmenets should be suspended if their exists any doubts. A transitioning state would be well advised in taking a guarded approach if it chooses to implement some of the more controversial *ḥudūd* punishments. Even the prohibition of alcohol occurred in three gradual stages during the time of the Prophet (ﷺ) (Qaradawi 2001). Finally, there also ought to be special courts related to family matters for those minorities living within a state. Such courts have existed throughout the Muslim world for centuries, perhaps best embodied through the Ottoman *Millet* system in which separate courts existed pertaining to personal/family law under which a confessional community was allowed to rule itself under its own jurisprudential system. Similar systems exist in many parts of the Muslim world today.

Conclusion

Ibn Khaldun commented that Islamic "religious law does not censure royal authority as such and does not forbid its exercise. It merely censures the evils resulting from it, such as tyranny, injustice and pleasure seeking" (2005: 157). While Ibn Khaldun is specifically talking about the *khilāfa*, royal authority should not simply be conceived of as an undemocratically chosen monarch who comes to power through brute force and conquest, rather it should be understood in terms of justified rational political leadership. In his words on the function religious law in Islam, "The [Islamic] religious law practices justice, fairness, the fulfillment of religious duties, and the defense of religion" (Ibn Khaldun 2005: 157). It is *royal* in the sense that it adheres to the foundational elements of Islam in accordance with the divine rules prescribed by God.

This chapter did not try to suggest that Sunnism and Shi'ism are the same despite the repeated references to the Iranian model—the doctrinal differences are obvious. The clerical organizational structure between the two is also significantly different. Shi'ism has recently been compared to the Roman Catholic Church, whereas Sunnism claimed to be similar to Protestantism in structure (Bill 2001). While it may be true that the *Shī'ah* hierarchical clerical structure might facilitate the modeling of an Islamic government, by no means is this particular religious organizational structure a pre-condition to forming an Islamic governed state—such states can take on many forms. The point here is that the general model of governance offered in the project is meant to be applicable to *any* Islamic governed state.

This chapter explored the essential role of leadership and law in conceptualizing an Islamic governed state. Since Islam is so heavily entrenched in authority derived from a *foundational* source, it is essential for any Islamic governed state to have a strong *foundation*. This begins by considering the role of the leader, as goes the leadership, so does the state, especially in the very beginning when the state is at its most fragile. Along with strong leadership, understanding *Sharī'ah*, what it actually is and how it can be used, is the second fundamental element of an Islamic governed state that must be evaluated. As important as political leadership may be, it is only one element in reconceptualizing governance in a twenty-first century Islamic governed state. The next chapter will go into greater detail examining other critical features in this discussion on crafting a modern Islamic governed state. It will look at bureaucratic development and the role of democracy and civic engagement in the next chapter.

Notes

1. The Prophet Mohammed (ﷺ) was described as *al-Insān al-Kāmil* or the perfect person in Ibn 'Arabi's, *Fuṣūṣ al-Ḥikam*, among other places. *Al-Insān al-Kāmil* can be further extrapolated upon to also refer to "a wise person who has acquired qualities of high virtue. [...] The bearers of the Prophet's spiritual heritage today possess both the physical warrior qualities [Max] Weber alludes to [in his *Sociology of Religion*] and the rational qualities to which he does not allude" (Kaminski 2016: 47).
2. Such cases are actually quite rare in Iran, and there is no evidence that Montazeri actually was responsible for anyone's execution for apostasy.
3. One can see Montazeri's sentiment on the importance of Iran avoiding global isolation finally beginning to be realized with the United Nations Security Council's (UNSC) unanimous endorsement of the long awaited the nuclear arms agreement between Iran and the P5+1 powers on 14 July 2015.
4. It should be clear that "authoritarian" and "totalitarian" are two different concepts. An authoritarian state does not necessarily have to be totalitarian. According to Paul Sondrol, "Totalitarian self-conceptions [unlike authoritarian] are typically teleological. The tyrant is less a person than an indispensible 'function' to guide and reshape the universe" (Sondrol 2009, 600). This is to say, the "Messianic function" of the dictator was not present in cases of authoritarian leaders like Hosni Mubarak or Zine El Abidine Ben Ali, while it was in the cases of totalitarian leaders like Stalin, Hitler, and Mao. The extent to which a state is "totalitarian" is that to which it can effectively cut off the intermediary bonds of civil society through a repressive coercive state apparatus that is literally involved in almost all aspects of daily life; public and private. As the individual becomes more alienated from, and even fearful of friends and family who *could* be potential agents of the secret police, the individual ultimately is forced to identify with the only source that seems "safe," the tyrant himself.
5. See Gilles Kepel (2004), *The War for Muslim Minds: Islam and the West*. Pascale Ghazaleh (Trans.). Cambridge: Belknap Press, p. 253, for more discussion of pro-regime, court scholars in the Middle East.
6. Andrew March comments that this statement by Ibn Qayyim "suggests that the scholars themselves, as the custodians of the law, are the true sources of sovereignty and the ones entitled to transform a usurping warlord's possession of coercive capacity into legitimate authority. But it also points to a third major concept, namely the division of authority into a sphere for secular rulers and one for the scholars" (March 2013: 298). This statement reaffirms the often-misunderstood notion within Islam that the laws are divine, *not* the rulers themselves.

7. Abū Isḥāq al-Shāṭibī was one of the major figures of the *maqāṣid* literature which sought to contextualize *fiqh* within the notion of "the greater purpose" of the *Sharī'ah*, which is based on *al maṣlaḥa*. According to Mavani, "The major objectives and principles set out under the *maqasid* literature (i.e., the preservation of life, religion, intellect, property, and lineage) are of a universal and overarching nature that allows the public to negotiate with is most suitable for a particular time, place, context, circumstance, and custom of convention (*'urf*)" (Mavani 2013: 218).

References

Abou El Fadl, Khaled. 2012. The centrality of Shari'ah to government and constitutionalism. In *Constitutionalism in Islamic countries: Between Upheaval and continuity*, ed. Rainer Grote and Tilmann J. Roder, 35–61. New York: Oxford Press.
al-Attas, Syed Muhammad Naquib. 1993. *Islām and secularism*, 2nd ed. Kuala Lumpur: Art Printing Works Sdn. Bhd.
al-Shatibi, Abu Ishaq Ibrahim. 1970. al-Muwāfaqāt fi uṣūl al-aḥkām, ed. M.Muyhi al-Din 'Abd al-Hamid. Cairo: Matab'at Muhammad Ali Subayh.
Abdal-Haqq, Irshad. 2006. Islamic law—An overview of its origin and elements. In *Understanding Islamic law—From classical to contemporary*, ed. H. Ramadan, 1–42. New York: Altamira Press.
Abrahamian, Ervand. 1993. *Khomeinism: Essays on the Islamic republic*. Berkeley: University of California.
Afary, Janet. 2009. *Sexual politics in modern Iran*. Cambridge: Cambridge University Press.
Afsaruddin, Asma. 2006. Obedience to political authority: An evolutionary concept. In *Islamic democratic discourse*, ed. M.A. Muqtedar Khan, 37–60. Lanham: Lexington Books.
Arabi, Oussama. 2001. *Studies in modern Islamic law and jurisprudence*. New York: Kluwer Law International.
Aristotle. 2001. In *The basic works of Aristotle*, ed. J. McKeon, New York: The Modern Library.
Armstrong, Karen. 2007. *Mohammed: A prophet for our time*, Reprint ed. New York: Harper One Publishers.
Arjomand, Said Amir. 1993. Religion and constitutionalism in Western history and in modern Iran and Pakistan. In *The Political Dimensions of Religion*, ed. S.A. Arjomand, 69–99. Albany: SUNY Press.
Aslan, Reza. 2005. *No God but God: The origins, evolution, and future of Islam*. New York: Random House Publishers.
Bashi, Goldbarg. 2003. Eyewitness history: Ayatollah Montazeri. [Interview]. www.parstimes.com/women/bashi-montazeri.pdf. Accessed 1 Mar 2015.

BBC News. 2009. Crowds gather to mourn reformist Iran cleric Montazeri. 20 December 2009. http://news.bbc.co.uk/2/hi/middle_east/8423319.stm. Accessed 2 June 2013.
Bill, James. 2001. *Roman Catholics and Shi'i Muslims: Prayer, passion, and politics*. Chapel Hill: University of North Carolina Press.
Bulliet, Richard. 1994. *Islam: The view from the edge*. New York: Columbia University Press.
Capeheart, Loretta, and Dragan Milovanovic. 2007. *Social justice: Theories, issues, and movements*. Piscataway: Rutgers Press.
Empiricus, Sextus. 2000. In *Outlines of scepticism*, ed. Julia Annas and John Barnes. Cambridge: Cambridge University Press.
Eltantawy, Nahed, and Julie Wiest. 2011. Social media in the Egyptian revolution: Reconsidering resource mobilization theory. *International Journal of Communication* 5: 1207–1224.
El Fadl, Abou, and Khaled. 2012. Conceptualizing Shari'a in the modern State. *Villanova Law Review* 56 (5): 803–818.
Fakhry, Majid. 2002. *Al-Farabi: Founder of Islamic neoplatonism: His life and works*. New York: Oxford Press.
Feldman, Noah. 2008. *The fall and rise of the Islamic state*. Princeton: Princeton Press.
Gerges, Fawaz A. 2013. The Islamist moment: from Islamic State to Civil Islam? *Political Science Quarterly* 128 (3): 389–426.
Hackett, Rick, and Gordon Wang. 2012. Virtues and leadership: An integrating conceptual framework founded in Aristotelian and Confucian perspectives on virtues. *Management Decision* 50 (5): 868–899.
Hallaq, Wael. 2013. *The impossible state: Islam, modernity, and modernity's moral predicament*. New York: Columbia University Press.
Hourani, Albert. 1991. *A history of the Arab peoples*. New York: Warner Books.
Khaldun, Ibn. 2005. *The muqaddimah: An introduction to history*, trans. ed. N.J. Dawood. Franz Rosenthal. Princeton, NJ: Princeton University Press.
Juynboll, G.H.A. 1983. *Muslim tradition: Studies in chronology, provenance and authorship of early hadith*. Cambridge: Cambridge Press.
LaGraffe, David. 2012. The youth bulge in Egypt: An intersection of demographics, security, and the Arab Spring. *Journal of Strategic Security* 5 (2): 65–80.
January, Brendan. 2008. *Pivotal moments in history: The Iranian Revolution*. Minneapolis, MN: 21st Century Books.
Kaminski, Joseph. 2016. Beyond capitalism: Exploring the limitations and weaknesses in Max Weber's general understanding of the Islamic discourse. *Intellectual Discourse* 24 (1): 35–58.
Kepel, Giles. 2004. *The war for Muslim minds: Islam and the West*. Pascale Ghazaleh, trans. Cambridge: Belknap Press.

Khan, L.Ali. 2003. The reopening of the Islamic code: The second era of ijtihād. *University of St. Thomas Law Journal* 1 (1): 341–385.
Khomeini, Ayatollah Ruhollah. 1970. In *Islamic government: Governance of the jurist*, ed. Hamid Algar, Tehran, Iran: Institute for the Publication of Imam Khomeini's Works.
Khomeini, Ayatollah Ruhollah. 1981. In *Islam and revolution: Writings and declarations of Imam Khomeini 1941–1980*, ed. Hamid Algar. Tripoli, Lebanon: Mizran Publications.
King James Version Reference Bible. 2005. New York: Oxford University Press.
Kinzer, Stephen. 2003. *All the shah's men: An American coup and the roots of Middle East terror.* New York: Wiley.
March, Andrew. 2013. Genealogies of sovereignty in Islamic political theology. *Social Research: An International Quarterly* 80 (1): 293–320.
Martin, Vanessa. 2007. *Creating an Islamic state: Khomeini and the making of a new Iran.* New York: St Martin's Press.
Maududi, Abul Ala. 2009. The Islamic law. In *Princeton readings in Islamist thought*, ed. R. Euben, and M. Zaman. Princeton: Princeton University Press.
Mavani, Hamid. 2013. *Religious authority and political thought in twelver Shi'ism: From Ali to post-Khomeini.* New York: Routledge.
Mubarakpuri, Safi-ur-Rahman. 2002. *The sealed nectar: Biography of the noble Prophet.* Brooklyn: Dar-us-Salaam Publishers.
Moghadam, Valentine. 1991. The reproduction of gender inequality in Muslim societies: a case study of Iran in the 1980's. *World Development* 19 (10): 1335–1349.
Montazeri, Ayatollah Hussein-Ali. 2000. *Democracy and constitution*. (pp. 141). http://www.amontazeri.com/farsi/fl.asp. Accessed on May 1, 2015.
Nawas, John A. 1996. The *Mihna* of 218 A. H./833 A. D. revisited: An empirical study. *Journal of the American Oriental Society* 116 (4): 698–708.
North, Douglass. 1990. *Institutions, institutional change, and economic performance.* Cambridge: Cambridge University Press.
Otto, Jan M. 2008. *Sharia and national law in Muslim countries: Tensions and opportunities for Dutch and EU foreign policy.* Amsterdam: Amsterdam University Press.
Plato. 1961. *The collected dialogues of Plato including the letters*, ed. Edith Hamilton and Huntington Cairns. New York: Pantheon Books.
Qaradawi, Yusuf. 2001. *The lawful and the prohibited in Islam*, 2nd ed. K. al-Hilbawi, M. Siddiqi, and S. Shukri, trans. Cairo: Al Falah Foundation for Translation.
Ramadan, Tariq. 2009. *In the footsteps of the Prophet: Lessons from the life of Mohammed.* New York: Oxford Press.
Ramadan, T. 2006. *Ijtihad* and *Maslaha*: Foundations of Governance. In *Islamic Democratic Discourse*, ed. Muqtedar Khan, 3–20. Lanham: Lexington Books.

Roy, Oliver. 2012. The transformation of the Arab world. *Journal of Democracy* 23 (3): 5–18.

Riyadh-us-Saliheen. 1999. Compiled by Abu Zakariya Nawawi. Muhammad Amin and Abu Usamah Al-Arabi bin Razduq, 2 Vols. trans. New York: Dar-us-Salam Publications.

Safi, Omid. 2010. Between 'ijtihad of the presupposition' and gender equality: Cross-pollination between progressive Islam and Iranian reform. In *Rethinking Islamic studies: From orientalism to cosmopolitanism*, ed. Carl Ernst, 72–96. Columbia, SC: University of South Carolina Press.

Ṣaḥīḥ al-Bukhārī. 2002. Compiled by Muhammed bin Ismail Bukhari, ed. M. Matraji and F. A. Z. Matraji, vols. 9. New Delhi: Islamic Book Services.

Sedghi, Hamideh. 2007. *Women and politics in Iran: Veiling, unveiling, and reveling*. Cambridge: Cambridge University Press.

Sondrol, Paul. 2009. Totalitarian and authoritarian dictators: A comparison of Fidel Castro and Alfredo Stroessner. *Journal of Latin American Studies* 23: 599–620.

Sunan Ibn Mājah. 2007. Compiled by Ibn Majah al Qazwini. Hafiz Abu Tahir Zubair 'Ali Za'i (Ed.) and Nasiruddin al-Khattab, 5 Vols. trans. Houston, TX: Darussalaam Publishers.

Svolik, Milan. 2009. Power sharing and leadership dynamics in authoritarian regimes. *American Journal of Political Science* 53: 477–494.

Tocqueville, Alexis. 1852. The art & science of politics. Unpublished address given to the *Séances et Travaux de l'Académie de Sciences Morales et Politiques*.

Tocqueville, Alexis. 2003. *Democracy in America*. Isaac Kramnick, trans. New York: Penguin Classics.

United Nations Population Division. 2008. World Population Prospects: 2008 Revision Population Database. http://www.un.org/esa/population/. Accessed 4 Apr 2013.

Voll, John. 1997. Sultans, saints, and presidents: The Islamic community and the state in North Africa. In *Islam, democracy, and the state in North Africa*, ed. J. Entilis, et al., 1–17. Bloomington: Indiana University Press.

Weiss, Bernard. 1998. *The spirit of Islamic law*. Athens: University of Georgia Press.

CHAPTER 5

Considering Bureaucracy and Democracy in a Contemporary Islamic Governed State

INTRODUCTION

Islamic societies require their own interpretations of what is constitutive of an appropriate mode of political discourse and action for their respective societies. Nasr aptly notes that;

> What is certain is that the Islamic response to western liberalism is turning more and more to Islamic solutions rather than simple imitation of western ideas and institutions; these simply cannot be imported from the West without important modifications. (2010: 37)

While the West can provide ideas for the Muslim world, Western political systems cannot simply be grafted onto it. The USA and others learned this lesson following the most recent wars in Iraq and Afghanistan. Economists and political scientists have developed some benchmarks for understanding development and how states in transition get from point A to point B. They have also established some more general principles about public administration and democracy that can also be engaged with when modeling an Islamic governed state. This chapter will explore some of these benchmarks and further explore how they can be applied in an Islamic governed state.

Economic Development → Institutional Development → Electoral/Civil Rights

Manus Midlarsky's research in the late 1990s suggested that for a liberal democracy to take root in the Muslim world, free and fair elections ought to be prioritized. On the ideal trajectory of political development for a Muslim state transitioning toward liberal democracy and ultimately political legitimacy, he argued; "First, political rights in the form of basic electoral freedoms would be achieved, followed by the establishment of strong institutions and then the granting of civil liberties associated with liberal democracy" (1998: 505). A little over a decade after Midlarsky's claims, in 2011 Bo Rothstein came to an opposite conclusion—he argued that electoral democracy is not necessarily the key to establishing political legitimacy. Instead he argued that political legitimacy ultimately derives from functioning institutions; "political legitimacy depends more on the quality of government and less on the quality of elections or political representation" (2011: 80). Rothstein actually suggested that in developing nations experiencing economic and social upheaval, elections often further destabilize the state. In some cases, this unrest results in civil war.

Noah Feldman also discussed the importance of institutions. He argued that an Islamic society's ability to actually adhere to the rule of law "depends ultimately upon the Islamists' ability to develop new institutions that would find their own original and distinctive way of giving real life to the ideals of Islamic law" (2008: 147). Feldman is clear that effective institutions must be representative of the general will of the people—the biggest hindrance to a just Islamic state is when the executive branch usurps power from the judicial and legislative elements of the state, and ultimately circumvents its own self-imposed restraints and legal obligations. Rothstein and Feldman would agree with Midlarsky on the importance of representative institutions as an ultimate goal of any modern Islamic governed state.

This work argues against Midlarsky's conclusion that one ought to prioritize democratic elections over institutions when crafting a new democratic state in the Muslim world. First, as the previous chapter argued, the ultimate goal of an Islamic governed state should not be liberal democracy in the American or European sense. There are too many essential features that undergird liberalism are incompatible with the Islamic understanding of the world.

Second, it is important to mention that Midlarsky looked at the USA as an example of how the evolution from electoral rights to functioning institutions slowly took root, ultimately resulting in a functioning liberal democratic state. Muslim states did not come into being in the same way as did the USA. One can look at the writings of Tocqueville for a detailed discussion of the unique conditions in which the USA found itself. For Tocqueville, Protestantism, the lack of a landed aristocracy, and a blueprint of rule derived from European nations—most specifically English Common Law (i.e., no historical traditional of *Sharī'ah* or any other revealed legal system)—played a critical role in how "democracy in America," so to speak, took root (Tocqueville 2003). These variables were largely lacking in much of the Muslim world's process of development.

Midlarsky even recognized that the historical precedent of British colonial rule and the rather unique operation of representative institutions in the USA *may* have impacted why political freedoms came prior to institutions. "Their prior experience with colonial representative institutions may have imbued the founders of the American polity with the necessity for this sequential ordering [of political rights prior to institutions]" (Midlarsky 1998: 505). Muslim states that have an entirely different process of historical development cannot be expected to follow such a model.

His taxonomy does, however, reference one important variable that seems to facilitate in the realization of basic political rights that ultimately facilitates democratic development: economic development. His regressions showed that in the Muslim case, economic development had a greater impact of the development of basic political rights than on liberal democracy in the Western sense. "The net effect of economic development on basic political rights appears to be much greater than that on liberal democracy" (Midlarsky 1998, 503). He goes on to argue that "[t]his finding has implications for the influence of economic development on the generation of a basic democracy in Muslim societies, albeit not liberal democracy" (1998, 504). The dominant view of political development during the first years of the twenty-first century held that institutions ultimately shape economics (North 2005; Acemoğlu et al. 2005). However, others have more recently argued that economic performance is the ultimate determinate of institutions. Ha-Joon Chang (2011) makes the point that even when institutions are functional, their upkeep and maintenance can result in serious opportunity-costs, and that "even for an institution that we are certain will bring a lot of benefit, we have to consider the costs needed for its establishment and future running, before we recommend it" (2011: 488). Not having enough financial resources at hand often means the implementation of one well-intentioned program entails the slashing of other social welfare and educational programs that already are in place.

This model firmly supports Chang's general assessment of the relationship between economic performance and institutions. Paldam and Gundlach (2008) also found in their econometric research that democratic development was in many ways dependent upon increasing levels of income. One would be hard-pressed to find many examples today of nations with well-functioning bureaucracies and high levels of electoral freedoms that are very poor. Mahathir prioritized economic development over electoral and civil rights when modernizing Malaysia in the 1980s. A similar approach was taken by Indonesia's longtime strongman, Suharto, as well. Despite the many well-founded critiques that can be levied against the authoritarian tendencies of both aforementioned South Asian political leaders, one cannot deny Malaysia and Indonesia's relative success, especially in comparison with other Muslim countries that have been far less successful in modernizing over the past half century.

Grand Transition Theories (GT-Theories) posit that when a nation embarks on a journey whereby that nation moves from being a poor and less-developed country to a wealthy developed country, a total transformation in almost all aspects of that society occurs. Economic growth opens previously unforeseen doors each time a state passes through a stage of economic development. This is to suggest that one cannot even fully conceive of all the possibilities at *Time* (T + 1) while situated at *Time* (T) because so much happens during the transition itself from (T) to (T + 1).

> The key idea of the GT-theory is that development is a path where the whole society changes in much the same way. Thus the GT consists of a set of transitions in all proportions and institutions in society. The GT is not a unique path, but rather a zone around such a path. (Paldam, in Svendsen and Svendsen (Eds.), 2009: 357)

This holds true for not just economic opportunities, but institutions and institutional development as well. Even though all countries are different and follow unique paths, once the full transition has been made, Paldam notes that one finds countries that begin at very different starting point, often arrive at a similar post-transition destination.

Paldam and Gundlach (2008) also found that there was a very significant correlation between countries perceived as corrupt and poverty, and countries conceived of as honest and wealth. They found that the scores on Transparency International's honest/corruption measure index differed by almost seven full points (based on 10-point scale) between the poorest 10% of nations and the wealthiest 10% of nations. Based on this metric, the best way to tackle corruption and perceptions of corruption (which can be equally bad, if not worse than unnoticed corruption itself) is to raise incomes.

I would argue that ideally, the trajectory of political development in a transitioning Islamic governed state would roughly follow in this order:

1. Foreign and Domestic policies that promote economic growth and development, that foster;
2. Functioning institutions, which then promote, uphold, and ultimately advance;
3. Electoral rights and civil rights.[1]

States that lack reasonable economic resources and prosperity ought to make tacking the issue of economic development their first priority. Voting rights do not put food on the table, and sadly, the lack of enough food on the table in many households throughout the Muslim world today remains a problem of critical import.

The main point here is that one can have all the voting rights they want, but if the state lacks the financial or institutional resources to pay workers to pick up the trash, to distribute welfare benefits in a timely and efficient manner, or maintain minimal standards for schools and hospitals, then political participation does not really mean much. Lebanon serves as a testament to this reality. Despite having extensive voting rights, Lebanon's notoriously faulty political institutions, coupled with poor city planning, directly facilitated in uncollected festering piles of trash lining the streets of Beirut bringing life to a near halt in the midst of a typical hot Levantine Summer in 2015. Lebanon's "You Stink!" campaign was not just talking about the cities pungent odor. On 21 September 2015, "[t]housands marched through the streets of Beirut earlier in the day to press their demands for holding government officials accountable and new parliamentary elections. They also called for a sustainable solution to the trash piling in the streets of Beirut" (*Al Arabiya English* 2015: *online*). One would be hard-pressed to find any Lebanese citizens these days pleased with their government, despite universal suffrage for all Lebanese citizens of age.

The importance of functioning institutions for a new government to succeed cannot be underestimated. Sherri Berman believes that it is all too obvious that "what Egypt and many other Arab countries need most at this point is not stronger civil societies, but rather more effective and responsive political institutions" (2003: 266). Berman's claim is further backed by the research of Öberg and Melander (2010) who used bureaucratic data gathered from 41 countries from 1984 to 2004 to conclude that bureaucratic quality was a very significant variable for explaining the outbreak of civil war. Weak political institutions in unstable nations ultimately foster a more radicalized form of civil society that can lead to violence.

Eva Bellin has also argued that crafting effective institutions is at the foundation of any functioning state; "In the absence of effective state institutions, removing an oppressive coercive apparatus will lead, not to democracy, but rather to authoritarianism of a different stripe or, worse, chaos" (2004: 153). Judging by the way many Muslim-majority states have been organized and have operated over the last century; it is apparent that the people will deal with limited political freedoms, but when the institutions deteriorate to a certain point, uprising will occur. Perhaps Egypt and Tunisia are the best examples of this. Both of these generally ethnically homogenous nations did not have the same sectarian issues to contend as did Iraq and Syria. These revolutions did not occur because a specific sect or ethnicity felt they were being slighted or oppressed; these revolutions can be directly attributed to institutional failures.

The previous chapter focused specifically upon political leadership and the role of law in conceptualizing a twenty-first century Islamic society. Based on the structure and content of the *Qur'ān* and *Sunnah*, leadership and law must be at the center of an Islamic governed state. Without these two elements, there simply is *no* Islamic governed state. The rest of this chapter will explore the next set of essential ideas to consider when creating a general model of an Islamic governed state—bureaucracy and democratic participation. States in transition ought to prioritize economic and institutional development if they hope to eventually have meaningful electoral rights.

The Importance of a Modern and Efficient Bureaucracy

The importance of administrative policy within Islam is nothing new. Almost 1000 years ago, the prominent *Ḥanbalī* scholar from Baghdad, Ibn 'Aqil (1040–1119 CE), discussed how the primary goal of Islamic administrative policy should be to promote good and discourage evil and corruption. Rachid al-Ghannouchi also notes that *aṣ-ṣaḥābah* even took it upon themselves to issue decrees regarding administration even if the were not directly referenced in the *Qur'ān*:

> Ibn 'Aqil defined *As-Siyasah Ash-Shar'iyah* (Islamic administrative policy) as the actions which bring the people closer to good and distance them from evil, even if such actions were not advocated by the Prophet or revealed from the Heavens. [...] After all they [*aṣ-ṣaḥābah*] initiated many new policies and took numerous measures in order to fulfill the needs of the society in response to new developments or changing circumstances. (2007: 275–276)

A couple hundred years later, in 1412 CE, Ahmad al-Qalqashandi completed his 14-volume *magnum opus* that was titled *Subh al-a 'sha* (The Dawn of the Blind) which covered numerous topics directly related to administration. Qalqashandi's work shed light on the inner workings and history of Egyptian administration and showed the similarities between Egyptian administration and administration elsewhere.

Political institutions are critical in all regime types. Even in the most authoritarian regimes, they serve as a check on the governing elite's power. "Political institutions in dictatorships, such as governing councils, legislatures, or parties, may therefore function to allow members of the governing authoritarian elite to reassure each other that none of them is trying to acquire more power at others' expense" (Svolik 2009: 493). If political institutions can serve as a check on an authoritarian regimes power, then it logically follows that such institutions also mitigate some of the potential hazards that come with regime change in general. When looking to seriously transform the daily affairs of Islamic political society after looking at the role of political leadership and the rule of law, the place to begin is with formal political institutions, specifically, with the bureaucracy.

Bureaucracy is absolutely rudimentary for the success and growth of any modern nation-state. In the words of the iconic American scholar of bureaucracy, Anthony Downs; "It is ironic that bureaucracy is still a term of scorn, even though bureaus are among the most important institutions in every nation in the world" (1965: 439). In a previous work on the importance of bureaucracy in the Muslim world, I argued that "Islamic states must seriously consider the importance of a well-developed and functioning bureaucracy. Scholars who study public administration in Arab States recognize the need for administrative reform in these regions" (2013: 3–4). Almost 100 years ago, Max Weber articulated three different sources of legitimate authority—traditional, charismatic, and rational-legal. As a state becomes more advanced, rational-legal authority becomes more salient, while authority based primarily on traditional and charismatic sources tends to wane.

For Weber, an effective bureaucracy was the embodiment of rational-legal authority. Modern bureaucracies ought to operate within the framework of codified written laws that can be referred to for guidance. If one has a grievance, there is a formal procedure and body that exists for adjudicating their grievance.

> The principle of office hierarchy and of the successive stages of appeal requires a clearly ordered system of authority and subordination involving supervision of the lower offices by the higher ones; a system which simultaneously accords the governed the possibility of appealing, in a regulated fashion, the finding of a lower agency to the corresponding superior agency. (Weber 1964: 60)

This also means that individuals cannot act on their own accord when deciding procedures. A well-organized bureaucracy can help with the flow of government and can cut down on violence and uprisings due to popular resentment resulting from arbitrary enforcement of the laws. The notion of fairness is emphasized and embodied within the confines of a well-functioning bureaucracy.

Khomeini was very critical of bureaucracy when he crafted his model of an Islamic state. "In addition, superfluous bureaucracies and the system of file-keeping and paper-shuffling that is enforced in them, all of which are totally alien to Islam, impose further expenditures on our national budget not less in quantity than the illicit expenditures of the first category" (Khomeini 1970: 31). He goes on to say, "These superfluous formalities, which cause our people nothing but expense trouble, and delay, have no place in Islam" (1970: 31).

The first critique of Khomeini's condemnation of bureaucratic procedures can be challenged at the level of the *Qur'ān* itself. The *Qur'ān* directly makes reference to the importance of record keeping. It also emphasizes the importance of using the tool of writing to keep records for things such as private debts;

> Oh ye who believe! When ye contract a debt for a fixed term, record it in writing. Let a scribe record it in writing between you in (terms of) equity. No scribe should refuse to write as Allah hath taught him, so let him write.... (*Qur'ān*, 2:282)

If the records of debts and contracts between individuals are to be recorded in writing, then there is no reason why debts, contracts, and other formal agreements between the state and other entities, public and private, should also not be formally recorded. In regard to making oaths or promises, the *Qur'ān* unequivocally states; "Make not your oaths a deceit between you, lest a foot should slip after being firmly planted and ye should taste evil forasmuch as ye debarred (men) from the way of Allah, and yours should be an awful doom" (*Qur'ān*, 16:94). Not recording such agreements and transactions in a transparent way only further exacerbates the possibility of corruption on the parts of individuals and the state itself.

A second critique of Khomeini's position on bureaucracy can be better understood through the lens of history. Ibn 'Aqil and Qalqashandi were mentioned at the beginning of this section as important figures who wrote about administration, however, perhaps the greatest Islamic polymath of the Middle Ages, Ibn Khaldun, also make detailed references to what today would be understood as public administration. In regard to *positions of the pen,* Ibn Khaldun commented that;

> Each of the instruments through which help may be given has many different subdivisions. 'The pen' has such subdivisions, for instance, as 'the pen of letters and correspondence', 'the pen of diplomas and fiefs', and 'the pen of bookkeeping,' which means the offices of chief of tax collections and allowance and of minister of the army. (2005: 189)

The need for written records has always been important in the Muslim world. In the view of Muslims, the *Qur'ān* itself is a written account of God's decrees and commands. Ibn Khaldun argued throughout

The Muqaddimah that when an empire begins to enter into a stage of decline, often the first notable crack in empire is seen in the arena of public administration. Individuals working within these agencies become less accountable and their actions become less transparent. Ultimately the bureaucratic apparatus of the state becomes irreparably corrupt. As public administrators become increasingly corrupt, the ruling class soon follows suit. The repeated dereliction of administrative duties generally signaled the beginning of the end for any dynasty.

One of the best examples of an extensive bureaucratic apparatus that actually existed in the Muslim World was that of the Ottoman state. Albert Hourani argued that during the Ottoman era, bureaucracy was integral to the functioning of the empire. He notes that it "was a bureaucratic state, holding different regions within a single administrative and fiscal system" (1991: 207). The Ottoman state also had a specific administrative vernacular, known as *fasih Türkçe*, which translates to "eloquent Turkish." This was the language spoken in poetry and politics; it is "Ottoman Turkish" in its strictest sense. This administrative language differed from *orta Türkçe*, (Middle Turkish) which was more commonly spoken by the upper and middle classes, and *kaba Türkçe*, (Rough Turkish) which was spoken by the lower classes. Many of the administrators were converts from all over the empire.

The various Ottoman sultans recognized the importance of effective and competent public administration for the success of their Empire. "Periodically, the Sultan was required to tour local governments in disguise to ensure that magistrates and justices were operating justly. If the Sultan believed that an injustice was being committed against the people, he would interfere directly and overturn the decision" (Kapucu and Palabiyik 2008: 75). Recognizing the need for modernization, at the beginning of the nineteenth century, Sultan Mahmud II initiated what came to be known as the *Tanzimât* reforms. Following his death in 1839, the new Sultan, Abdülmecid I, issued an imperial edict known as the Edict of Gülhane or the Tanzimât *Fermânı* (Imperial Edict of Reorganization).

The Edict of Gülhane called for the introduction of new institutions to improve administration throughout the Empire. It ushered in a period of major administrative reforms that included the creation of new administrative bodies to meet the needs of a changing world (Liebesny 1975). It also reorganized the ossified Ottoman financial and legal systems. Similar reforms continued over the next few decades. The year

1840 saw the first Ottoman paper bank notes and the first Empire post office. Other notable reforms during this period were the first Ottoman census of 1844 and the abolition of the slave trade and slavery in 1847. These reforms also further demonstrate the willingness of the Caliph to use (and modify) *qānūn* laws in the name of the public good.

The sources of *Sharī'ah* are also hierarchically organized, much like an effective bureaucracy. In Islam, the *Qur'ān* and *Sunnah* are primary sources of legislation, followed by secondary sources such as *ijmā'*, *qiyās*, and *'urf*. "A well-organized modern bureaucracy in practice should also have a well-defined vertical hierarchy of organization, in which each position has a specific, well-defined task that they are responsible for executing" (Kaminski 2013: 4). Such organization makes accountability easier and allows for easier transitions within the bureaucracy itself. On contemporary issues surrounding bureaucracy and bureaucratic development in the OIC states, I previously argued;

> The recent Middle Eastern uprisings have not happened because of trivial bureaucratic quagmires, such as long lines at the Bureau of Motor Vehicles or extensive paperwork to receive tax benefits. Rather, these uprisings and government overthrows have occurred due to the arbitrary enforcement of the rules, especially on those who are in power or are closely connected to it. (2013: 7)

In Muslim-majority states, particularly in the Gulf States, bureaucracy and public administration during the last century have been ineffective to say the least. Written formal procedures have not taken shape in the Gulf States the way they have in the West. Information has often not been properly recording surrounding policy decisions. Often times the information transmitted has been inaccurate, reflecting the personal preferences of senior leaders and other elites (Common 2008; Jreisat 1999).

The pathologies behind the of the lack of transparency and properly recorded information can be traced back to two fundamental scourges that have hampered Arab—and Islamic governance in general for that matter—since its very earliest days, nepotism and cronyism. In the words of the renowned scholar of public administration in the Arab world, Jamil Jreisat, on public administration in the Arab world;

> Political regimes are deliberate in limiting the scope and directions of change. Political leaders often endorse personnel training or simplification

of procedures; they also sprinkle their public statements with calls for more efficient and effective management. At the same time, these political leaders continue to promote to senior government positions unqualified relatives, cronies, and loyalists and to protect various corrupt practices in conducting the public's business'. (1999: 22)

Highly centralized, authoritarian states breed corruption and unaccountability. "Authoritarian states are less transparent and critical of procedural protocol" (Kaminski 2013: 7). Jreisat goes on to argue that imperialism has been a major obstacle for the development of functioning public administrative institution in the Arab world. Colonialism has kept the Arab states fragmented for centuries. "The British during their control of the Middle East regularly did numerous things to weaken any efforts at legitimate local bureaucratic legislation, via payoffs and other underhanded deals" (Kaminski 2013: 7). The centralized control of things such as public utilities, banks, railways, gas, electricity, and other major aspects of public life, along with the disproportionate number of people under thirty years of age has placed new burdens on bureaucratic performance.

Overstaffing and low productivity have also negatively impacted bureaucratic performance over the past few decades. Arab states still need to modernize and utilize the new models of information systems available. Many of these states have not been quick enough in acquiring and incorporating new information technologies into their bureaucratic frameworks. "It is via modernization that bureaucracies are better equipped to address and confront issues related to performance" (Kaminski 2013: 8). Despite the costs associated with acquiring and incorporating these new technologies in the civil service, at this point, such essential acquisitions can no longer be avoided.

It has also been suggested that properly organized bureaucracies can help bridge the increasingly salient digital divide by facilitating the transmission of technological advances to both the public and private sectors in developing nations (Jreisat 1999). Howard and Mazaheri claim that "some public supervision of the telecommunications sector—perhaps by a professional bureaucracy rather than elected politicians—may be a positive step toward narrowing the digital divide" (2009: 1166). The research of Hanifizadeh et al. (2009) has shown that there are empirically statistically significant correlations between Gross National Income, per capita and information, communication, and technology (ICT) infrastructure and access. As one would intuitively expect, higher GNI per capita generally correlates to higher ICT infrastructure and access scores.

Bureaucratic development and competency have repeatedly been shown to also play a major role in the diffusion and implementation of modern technology (Howard and Mazaheri 2009; Corrales and Westhoff 2006; Milner 2006). Hanifizadeh et al. argues that a lack of competition in places like Saudi Arabia where the government monopolizes telecommunications services has had an adverse impact on quality,

> A probable explanation is that the government has monopoly on providing telecommunications services such as the Internet and mobile cellular in these countries and the market is not competitive. Therefore, the costs of access to telecommunication services are high and their quality is low. (2009: 396)

Other states that monopolize telecommunications have seen similar results in service quality as the KSA. Hanifizadeh et al. do note one very positive example of rapid ICT growth, access, and access quality in one particular GCC state, the United Arab Emirates, "[b]y offering facilities, stimulating the private sector, and fulfilling the essential requirements for attracting foreign investment, this country has been able to develop ICT and moved up remarkably in the world rankings in this field in recent years" (2009: 397). Qatar has also made efforts to modernize its ICT as well.

In the case of telecommunications technology, foreign investment and market-based solutions have been more effective at ushering in modernization than have centralized state control of telecommunication technologies. Agency independence, transparency, and discretion helped explain the growth of internet users and internet hosts in many developing countries at the beginning of the twenty-first century (Wallsten 2005). Fink and Kenny's (2006) research also suggested that liberalizing telecommunications industries has resulted in an increase in per capita means of communication in developing countries. Cheaper, higher quality service has resulted in such places that look toward the telecommunications organizational models offered by Hanifizadeh et al., Wallsten, and Fink and Kenny. Government monopolies on telecommunications technology seem to retard technological development in developing nations. Reasonable bureaucratic oversight as opposed to direct state control of these industries seems to be the best solution in this particular case. As the world becomes more technologically advanced, Arab and non-Arab Islamic, states are going to have to be even more focused on developing their ICT infrastructure and bureaucratic administrations.

A Brief Overview of Contemporary Theoretical Approaches to Bureaucracy

Over the last 35 years, there have been two main theoretical approaches to public administration. The first approach to management theory gained prominence in the 1980s at the height of Reagan era privatization and deregulation policies. *New public management* (NPM) sought to emphasize improvements in service quality and employee empowerment (Kaboolian 1998; Jreisat 1999). Deregulation and agency autonomy were core strategies of NPM. NPM also sought to increase competition among bureaucratic agencies by breaking various agencies down into smaller competing parts. The iconic American public choice scholar, William Niskanen (1975), convincingly argued that competition between agencies improves overall productivity. His approach argues that consolidating agencies actually results in "greater monopoly power of the remaining bureaus" (1975: 640). When agencies lack competition, instead of competing based on efficiency and overall results, they seek total monopoly demands for their services, ultimately resulting in greater inefficiency and greater budgetary demands.

The peak of *New Public Management* occurred during the 1980s and 1990s when deregulation was popular among reformers of government agencies and neoliberal economic think tanks in the USA and the United Kingdom. The twenty-first century has seen a move away from the older NPM paradigm. According to Patrick Dunleavy et al.;

> The intellectually and practically dominant set of managerial and governance ideas of the last two decades, new public management (NPM), has essentially died in the water. This cognitive and reform schema is still afloat, and a minority of its elements are still actively developing. But key parts of the NPM reform message have been reversed because they lead to policy disasters, and other large parts are stalled. (2005: 468)

Catastrophic security failures such as the 9/11 attacks on the USA and regulatory failures involving high-profile financial scandals involving widely respected firms like Enron and Lehman Brothers during the first decade of the twenty-first century accelerated the retreat from the old model (Kaminski 2013; Dunleavy et al. 2006). NPM theories have been replaced by a newer approach called *Digital Era Governance*.

Digital Era Governance (DEG) approaches to public administration argue that NPM's insistence on fragmented, competing agencies ultimately resulted in avoidable communications breakdowns among agencies that have should be cooperating rather than competing in the first place. Under the NPM model, corruption was easier to get away with and accountability was more difficult that it needed to be.

> Risks of greater corruption, malversation and the encouragement of 'club' effects figure large in egalitarian critiques of NPM. Egalitarians claim that such abuses are easier in the decentralized accountability framework of NPM and in the extension of areas covered by doctrines of commercial confidentiality and contract privity. (Dunleavy and Hood 1994: 12)

DEG approaches toward management focus on agency reintegration and maximizing digitization. Newer approaches to public administration have moved away from the old axiom that championed multiple competing agencies within a bureaucracy. Agency reintegration is seen as essential in the digital age and in the age of transnational security threats that more than ever require collaboration as opposed to competition. DEG fits in-line with Rothstein's (2011) general claim that contrary to earlier public choice models; high quality of governance (QoG) cannot simply be understood as smaller government.

Modern information technologies are critical to DEG approaches to government agency reform and improvement. More recently, Dunleavy and Margetts (2013) argued that DEG has entered a second phase.

> Since 2010, social Web developments have contributed to a further bending of the modernization main course away from NPM patterns, and a stronger differentiation of the three DEG themes (reintegration, holism and digital changes) from the previous quasi-paradigm. The DEG approach remains 'insurgent', an 'ideal type', and its implementation is patchy in even the most 'advanced' industrial states. (2013: 3)

New web-based services have been effective at reducing redundancy in service delivery chains. These services have also been invaluable in this age of fiscal austerity.

> In austerity conditions, reintegration saves governments money by pulling functions back from executive agencies into central ministries; cutting out the extra management costs of multiple agencies; and recentralizing controls over spending and over areas such as the online Web estates of public sector agencies. (Dunleavy and Margetts 2013: 7)

The ultimate goal of DEG 2.0 is to merge delivery chains when possible and maximizing efficiency for citizens. "The key implication is the joining up (eventually merging) of previously separate delivery chains, adding to the DEG1 pressures for one-stop shops and windows" (Dunleavy and Margetts 2013: 9). Islamic administered states should consider these theoretical developments in public administration theory when improving their own bureaucracies.

States in the Muslim world today need to immediately transform their largely patronage-based bureaucracies into ones that are competitive and meritocratic. Empirical research on bureaucratic performance has suggested that meritocratic systems perform significantly better than patronage-based systems (Rauch and Evans 2000; Mueller 2009; Schnose 2015). The quantitative work of James Rauch and Peter Evans shows "that several relatively simple, easily identifiable structural features constitute the key ingredients of effective state bureaucracies: competitive salaries, internal promotion and career stability, and meritocratic recruitment (2000: 65). They found in 35 less-developed countries the vast majority were patronage-based bureaucracies. Hannes Mueller's work suggests that the "lack of competition under patronage can imply increased rent extraction and loss of welfare" (2009: 2). Under patronage models, bureaucrats are chosen due to their political affiliations or family/tribal connections rather than because of their overall administrative abilities. Under such models, when regimes do shift, often the bureaucrats from the previous regime are also changed. This leads to bureaucratic instability and hinders overall agency effectiveness.

Meritocratic bureaucracies can serve as an effective "check and balance" on state power. Islam is explicit in articulating that no individual is above the law. The laws must apply equally to all citizens within Islamic society, which most certainly does not happen throughout much of the Muslim world today. Political elites must be held accountable, and one way of holding such actors accountable is via bureaucratic institutions that have tenured employees who perform their duties diligently without fear of being made redundant when a new regime assumes power.

There are strong correlations between meritocratic institutions and democracy. "Meritocratic institutions have been introduced in most developed countries throughout the last two centuries. Often, meritocratic reform coincided with a trend towards more open and democratic elections" (Mueller 2009: 2). In meritocratic systems, bureaucrats often are free from the interference of political actors. Bureaucrats in meritocratic systems generally hold long tenures, often holding their positions through multiple leadership changes. "Meritocracy shields bureaucrats from the volatility of political competition and, thus, provides relatively high levels of competence" (Mueller 2009: 3). As one would expect, such a system also tends promote policy stability. Bureaucratic professionalism has been empirically shown to correlate at a statistically significant level to policy stability throughout the world.

Developed countries with the highest levels of bureaucratic professionalization almost always show higher levels of policy stability than do undeveloped countries that generally have lower levels of bureaucratic professionalization. According to Viktoriya Schnose, "[p]olitical systems, especially in developed countries, often rely on principles of "neutral competence" and efficiency of outcomes to rationalize merit-based selection of bureaucrats (2015: 2). She goes on to give the example of the civil service in the UK where bureaucrats are "recruited primarily on the basis of merit, ascertained through a combination of competitive examinations, interviews, and observed groups exercises that involve role playing hypothetical policy scenarios" (2015: 2–3). Germany also requires civil servants to possess certain educational certificates and training. Such rigorous recruitment techniques ought to be emulated in Islamic governed states that seek to raise their own administrative standards.

Bureaucracies, as mentioned above, should also have well-defined hierarchies, in which individual roles are clearly defined. This allows for greater fairness and helps minimize excess and waste (Moe 1984). Well-defined bureaucracies can also allow for a standard of evaluation that the people can use when evaluating the efficiency of a particular bureaucracy's leadership structure. Are the leaders adhering to the codified legal codes, or are they arbitrarily exercising power? Questions like this can only be addressed within a well-codified set of procedures and laws.

The concept of *al-shūrā* (the council) is one of the core principles of organizing an Islamic governed state. The concept of a consultative council that assists in the process of decision-making dates all the way back to the very beginnings of Islam. According to Abou El Fadl;

> There are many historical reports suggesting that the Prophet consulted regularly with his companions regarding affairs of the state. In addition, shortly after the death of the Prophet (ﷺ), the concept of *shura* (consultative deliberations) had become a symbol signifying participatory politics and legitimacy. (2004: 16)

There are some key elements of *al-shūrā* that most scholars today agree upon. Hai and Nawi (2007) posit that the *condiciones sine quibus non* of *al-shūrā* includes the following:

- Meeting or consultation that follows the teachings of Islam
- Consultation following the guidelines of the *Qur'ān* and *Sunnah*
- There is a leader elected among them to head the meeting
- The discussion should be based on *mushawarah* (consensus) and *mudhakarah* (remembrance of the *sunnah* and *ḥādīth*)
- All the members are given fair opportunity to voice out their opinions
- The issue should be of *maṣlaḥa 'ammāh* (public interest)
- The voices of the majority are accepted, provided that it does not violate with the teachings of the *Qur'ān* or *Sunnah*

Al-shura's basic framework can be applied to the way all bureaucracies operate in an Islamic governed state. According to Azizah al-Hibri;

> ...the Shura Principle could readily become applicable to all the different branches of democratic government and thus take different, more complex forms than it did in the early days of Islam. It also could become applicable to each branch of government at its various levels. This complexity, of course, is to be expected in the era of the technetronic society. (1992: 22)

The rules, if properly observed, could easily transform the way decision-making and public administration is handled throughout the OIC states.

Indeed, bureaucracy is not only compatible to Islamic political institutions—it is foundational. This problem of arbitrary enforcement of laws is at the core of the corruption that plagues the Islamic world. Many states in the Islamic world do not have well-defined bureaucracies that treat individuals equally. The adjudication of disputes must be handled in a fair and even manner. This is also something that is inherent within the original framework outlined by the Prophet Mohammed (ﷺ). At the core of the recent uprisings in the Middle East is anger at the perceived incompetence and corruption of governments led by dictators. The leaders of Tunisia and Egypt were uprooted as a result of their corruption and failing policies, not simply because they were undemocratic. Well-defined bureaucratic procedures can mitigate civilian anger at perceived unfairness.

The Role of Democracy and Civic Participation

Robert Dahl's classic work, *Polyarchy: Participation and Opposition* (1971), offered a functional definition of democracy that has been widely accepted by many scholars over the past 45 years. This definition can serve as a benchmark for democracy in an Islamic governed state. What makes Dahl's model useful for considering democracy in the Islamic case is the fact that his model of democracy is not inextricably liberal. Dahl's notion of polyarchy can be seen as being an intermediary between liberal democracy and electoral democracy (Veenendaal 2015). A couple of decades later, Dahl (1989) admitted that no state fully meets the standards of true "democracy," and that his vision of democracy can be seen as an ideal-type rather than representative of any particular state that exists in the world today. His basic point by 1989 was that politically advanced countries should be thought of as polyarchies to varying degrees. For a political system to be completely polyarchic, eight conditions must be met. Dahl's conditions include the following:

1. Freedom to form and join organizations
2. Freedom of expression
3. Right to vote
4. Eligibility for public office
5. Right of political leaders to compete for support and votes
6. Alternative sources of information
7. Free and fair elections
8. Institutions for making government policies depend on voters and other expressions of preference (1971: 3).

Dahl's characterization of polyarchy can be placed into two general categories, *contestation* and *inclusiveness*. According to Wouter Veenendaal;

> On the one hand, the dimension of contestation (or competition) refers to the extent to which public offices are open to public and political competition, and therefore also to the opportunities for the existence of a political opposition. On the other hand, the dimension of *inclusiveness* stands for the proportion of citizens who are allowed to participate in the political process. In this regard, active and passive suffrage rights have generally been regarded as the most important indicator. (2015: 46)

Veenendaal's characterization of contestation and inclusiveness is quite similar to Kenneth Bollen's earlier distinction between *political rights* which parallel *contestation*, and *political liberties* which parallel *inclusiveness*. According to Bollen;

> Political rights exist to the extent that the national government is accountable to the general population and each individual is entitled to participate in the government either directly or through representatives. Political liberties exist to the extent that the people of a country have the freedom to express any political opinions in any media and the freedom to form or to participate in any political group. (1990: 10)

Dahl's notion of democracy was much more robust than earlier, less ambitious efforts to articulate a vision of democracy, such as the one offered by Joseph Schumpeter, which held that "the democratic method is that institutional arrangement for arriving at political decisions in which realizes the common good by making the people itself decide issues through the election of individuals who are to assemble in order to carry out its will" (1942: 250). Dahl's eight basic conditions can be met within an Islamic framework under certain conditions.

In the previous chapter, Rachid al-Ghannouchi's definition of Islamic governance was used as the benchmark for defining the overall framework of the model of Islamic governance being proposed in this work. His two main points were that supreme legislative authority is derived from the *Sharīʿah*, which transcends all other man-made laws, and that political power ultimately is vested in the community which adopts a form of *shūrā* or system of mandatory consultation in which there is some type of oversight over political actors. The entire Islamic governance model presented here hinges upon both of these premises—if one is absent then the whole model collapses. If the latter is present, but that former is not, one does not have an Islamic governed state at all; if the former is present, but the latter is not, one has tyranny.

This is to suggest that for a state to legitimately operate within the model offered in this work, it must (1) derive its supreme legislative authority from the *Sharī'ah* and (2) the people must ultimately consent to this without coercion and take an active participatory role in the oversight of the state. So long as these two fundamental premises take lexical priority over man-made laws and political processes, none of Dahl's conditions appear to be at odds with the model of an Islamic governed state offered here.

Civil Society is also essential for any functioning modern nation-state (Almond and Verba 1963; Barber 1984; Putnam 2001). Benjamin Barber argued that "it is vital to establish the educational and civic conditions necessary to cultivating engaged citizenship before constructing an elaborate top-down constitution that in fact can function properly only when nurtured by a competent citizenry" (1984: xvii). Strong civil societies possess the ability to challenge and even overthrow unpopular autocratic regimes. This was the case in Egypt and Tunisia most recently.

Sherri Berman almost a decade before the Egyptian Revolution of 2011 noted this possibility when examining the strength of Islamist movements in Egypt, "What the Egyptian case seems to indicate, then, is that in some ways the capture of civil society can be as powerful an agent of revolutionary change as the capture of the state itself" (2003: 266). Indeed, less than a decade later, the state itself was overthrown. The basic idea of political accountability goes back to the earliest days of Islam. The Mu'tazilite scholar Abu Bakr al-Asam who lived during the ninth century argued that there must be a general consensus over the ruler; the ruler could not act as an unaccountable autocrat and that each person under the ruler's authority must give their consent to be ruled.

In regard to the individual's right of self-expression in an Islamic society, Maududi commented that in an Islamic society, "every sane adult Muslim, male or female, is entitled to express his or her opinion, for each one of them is the repository in the Caliphate" (Maududi 1960: 151–152). Thus far, throughout much of the Muslim world, Maududi's standards have not been met. Esposito claims that; "Unfortunately, Mawdudi [sic: read Maududi] did not indicate how Muslims can safeguard against rulers who falsely use the banner of Islam to legitimate their rule, impose their will, and stifle dissent" (1987: 147). Any modern Islamic governed state needs to address civil society and its importance. At the same time, Muslim societies must be aware that often corrupt individuals use their right to speech often coupled with their wealth to put themselves or their special interests in positions of power to the detriment of society as a whole. This issue is perhaps as important as any in regard to free speech and political participation.

The situation surrounding democratic participation, like bureaucratic efficiency and quality in the twentieth century in Middle Eastern and OIC Member states in general has been bleak to say the least. First, the previous section explored how formal functioning and transparent institutions in OIC states have been limited. The transition to democracy or more transparent forms of government are dependent upon functioning institutions. In an earlier section, it was argued that at the very least, minimally functioning institutions must come prior to political freedoms or civic participation. High levels of civic participation coupled with failing or nonexistent institutions often result in fundamentalist backlash (Berman 2003).

Since institutions in many Islamic countries tend to be weak, it is not surprising that the situation surrounding political and social freedoms as weak as well. According to the Freedom House's 2011 ratings, the situation in most Muslim countries regarding freedom has changed little over the past 40 years. According to the Freedom House's 2011 report;

> Despite a few noteworthy gains, primarily Indonesia's embrace of democracy and civil rights, Muslim-majority countries have failed to make significant progress over the past decade. Only two are ranked as Free, with 19 Partly Free and 26 Not Free. While practically no improvements were registered in the Middle East and North Africa, some gains were recorded in Muslim-majority countries outside the region. (Puddington 2011: 3)

The Freedom House ratings are not the only research projects that place Arab states at the bottom in regard to political and social freedoms. The immensely important work of Alfred Stepan and Graeme Robertson also argue that, *specifically*, the Arab states have been the least free in comparison with their other Muslim counterparts. More political freedoms, especially in terms of elections, are in enjoyed in the non-Arab Muslim states. Stepan and Robertson emphatically comment;

How many Muslims live in Arab League member states with electorally competitive regimes? None. Moreover, Arab League members have the world's highest percentage of "electorally underachieving" countries. Thus as things stand now, half of all Muslims outside the Arab League, despite their greater poverty, live under electorally competitive regimes. (2004: 143)

Stepan and Robertson showed two major things over a decade ago. First, they showed that one must not look at Islam simply as a monolithic entity, local cultures cannot be simply ignored. Second, they show that regimes that have democratic elections are not, *ipso facto*, wealthier nations. The poorer, non-Arab states have more democratic freedom than the richer Arab states. The coercive capacity and will of a state also impact democratic transition. "Democratic transition can be carried out successfully only when the state's coercive apparatus lacks the will or capacity to crush it" (Bellin 2004: 143). In recent rebellions in Libya and Syria, the world witnessed firsthand that some Arab states were willing to do whatever it took to crush opposition, even if it meant using chemical weapons on its own civilian population as is evident now in Syria.

Twentieth century public intellectual and influential scholar, Eqbal Ahmad, in regard to the state of affairs in the Arab world states;

> The pro-Western Gulf States have pretense neither to military power nor radicalism. Led by Saudi Arabia, they plead with Washington to save Arab face and the dynastic future. But they are prisoners of dependency and uneven development. They have acquired wealth without working and made enormous profits without producing. Their countries are littered with expensive machines, but they have no technology. Their economies are run by foreigners. Their investments are linked symbiotically with America. They own billions of dollars but control no capital. They lack the will and capacity to translate their wealth into power. (2006: 358)

This excerpt from his essay, "On Arab Bankruptcy," was written in 1982. How much has really changed in the last three decades? It is clear that there has been some shift in the patterns of dependency that Arab states face, but the overall analysis offered by Ahmad over 30 years ago remains the same; "Without radical democratization, the Middle East cannot escape recurrent defeats and recolonization" (2006: 358). Despite vast oil reserves and other natural resources, for quite some time Arab states have been perceived as among the world's most corrupt and unequal nations.

While there remain undeniably high levels of corruption throughout much of the Muslim world, this does not mean that change is impossible. Recently, the conservative economist Frederic Pryor commented that; "The fact that some predominantly Muslim nations have relatively respectable degrees of political freedom suggests that this deficit may not be a permanent condition" (2007: 57). Political freedoms and rights are necessary to break up authoritarian dictatorships and pockets of corruptly held wealth. What *democracy* actually consists of remains the great philosophical question. Richard Bulliet believes that democracy should be understood within "dialogue of discourses," rather than one discourse dominated by Western liberal principles. Timothy Sisk quoted Bulliet, who on democracy and Islamic political evolution stated;

> And the degree to which democracy is a part of all this [Islamic state evolution] will depend not upon the correspondence between the features of that new synthesis and our current views of democracy (our own views are, of course, always evolving as well), but it will depend upon the reshaping of the concept of democracy within world terms in which there is a dialogue of discourses, and not simply a western hegemonic discourse. (Bulliet, quoted in Sisk 1994: 59)

Bulliet's point ought to be taken seriously. The entire concept of democracy must be freed from the oppressive grips of the West that feel they have the only *authentic* (i.e., liberal) understanding of a very complex philosophical approach to governance. Allawi echoes the earlier point made by Hallaq as to the universalizing tendency of Western liberalism; "In many ways, the prized tolerance of these [Western] societies has an obverse side in the form of an intolerance or disregard for other civilizations, which may not subscribe to the 'universal' nature of western values" (2009: 172). *Democracy* is a multifaceted concept with numerous caveats and intricacies that are dependent upon local culture and customs, not to mention each nation's own unique historical path of development.

An Islamic society that seeks to follow teachings of the Prophet Mohammed (ﷺ) and the other Prophets of the past, at its core, simply is not compatible with the type of "Democratic" governing models that are present in Europe and North America. As mentioned in the previous section, Western liberal governments do not take seriously certain laws derived from any higher authority. Divine law and laws made by the collective interests of fallible individuals are in conflict. An ideal Islamic-oriented political system must be led by individuals who are intimately familiar with the sources of Islamic laws; these sources include the *Sunnah, Sharī'ah*, and to a lesser extent *'aḥādīth*. These individuals must also be just and possess superior moral qualities. Returning to Montazeri; "No government could continue to rule through force, coercion, or inculcating mandatory behavior and only a democratic government could survive" (2000: 5). The consensus of contemporary scholars would agree that there is room for scholarly interpretation (*ijtihād*) of the intent and meaning of these laws, but from within the Islamic framework. There are no clearly defined Qur'anic rulings on things such as the Internet, automobiles (or those who can drive them), and nuclear weapons. Generally, scholarly rulings on such matters are based on the spirit of the *Qur'ān* and *Sunnah*, but are not as fixed or Islamically binding as are other rules formally specified in the *Qur'ān* or the *Sunnah*. The people of the particular Islamic governed state should make their opinions and voices heard, especially in regard to uniquely modern issues that many religious jurists may be out of touch or unfamiliar with. It is the natural right of any Muslim or individual living in a Muslim nation to freely assemble and protest government acts they feel are oppressive or in violation of the *Sharī'ah*.

Conclusion

Aristotle discussed some of the necessary qualifications for governors and bureaucrats in his *Politics*.

> There are three qualifications required in those who have to fill the highest offices—(1) first of all, loyalty to the established constitution; (2) the greatest administrative capacity; (3) virtue and justice of the kind proper to each form of government; for, if what is just is not the same in all governments, the quality of justice must also differ. (*Politics*, Book V, Chap. 9, 1309a; 33–39)

Aristotle's understanding of the qualifications necessary for working in public service seems to fit well within the model discussed in this chapter. It is actually hard to envision any model of public administration in which Aristotle's aforementioned qualities are *not* desirable. In any state—secular, religious, or otherwise—bureaucrats need to support the constitution of the state they work for, possess a certain level of competence pertaining to the task of administration, and have a sense of ethics and personal responsibility that compliments the general ethical values of the particular society in which they reside. One must remember, however, that Aristotle argues that unlike the case of a military general—when it comes to any office of trust or stewardship, if one must choose, it is better to have a public servant who possesses virtue rather than skill since "more virtue than ordinary is required in the holder of such an office, but the necessary knowledge is of a sort which all men possess" (*Politics,* Book V, Chap. 9, 1309b). This is to suggest the bureaucrat must be loyal and just in their actions—two qualities have been lacking in the Muslim world as this chapter showed. Rachid al-Ghannouchi at the end of the twentieth century emphatically claimed that; "Our main task now is to combat despotism in favor of a genuine and true transition to democracy" (2007: 278). Sadly, even today, this transition from despotism to democracy still has not been realized in most of the Muslim world.

Ideally, an Islamic governed state should be a mix of democratic rule and rule by the wise. This is similar to the vision of American government promoted by Thomas Jefferson. Interestingly enough, despite not recognizing the authority of the Prophet Mohammed (ﷺ), Jefferson was far more receptive to Islam than other religious value systems that were more commonly practiced in the colonial USA.[2] Jefferson explicitly argued that there was only one God.

> The doctrines of Jesus are simple, and tend all to the happiness of man. 1) That there is one only God, and he is all perfect. 2) That there is a future state of rewards and punishments. 3) That to love God with all thy heart and thy neighbor as thyself is the sum of religion. (Jefferson—cited in Aspland 1843: 632)

Jefferson felt it was essential to have a group of intelligent leaders who are capable of making sure the society doesn't run amok. The power of greed and corruption can easily turn a moral society into a corrupt one. The state must, as Aristotle discussed, be active in promoting civic virtue. This is far different from Enlightenment era philosophies that argued that governments should not to be interested in "crafting the soul." At the core of Islamic society are the teachings of the Prophet Mohammed (ﷺ). According to Izetbegović, "There can be neither peace nor coexistence between the Islamic religion and non-Islamic social and political institutions" (Izetbegovic 1990: 30). Governments representing these values need to make efforts to keep individuals on the rightly guided path. M.A. Muqtedar Khan argued that;

> In the twentieth century we have witnessed the emergence of two distinct approaches to Islamic political theory. The Islamists who advocate the establishment of an Islamic State, an authoritarian and ideological entity whose central concepts are *al-Hakimiyyah* (the sovereignty of God) and *Sharia* (the law of God), and the liberal Muslim political theorists who advocate an Islamic democracy whose central themes are *Shura* (consultation) and *Sahifat al Madinah* (Constitutionalism *a la* the Compact of Medina). (2006b: 160)

While Khan's characterization of what transpired in the past may be true, one cannot simply deduce that those who support of God's sovereignty (*al-Hakimiyyah*) and the law of God (*Sharī'ah*), by default are opposed to consultation (*shūrā*) and constitutionalism (*sahifat*). The previous two chapters have argued for a nuanced blending of all four elements outlined in Khan's taxonomy of Islamic guiding principles as commonly articulated in contemporary Islamic political theory. If one wants to argue for a non-Islamic governed state in the Muslim world—then ignoring the principles of the sovereignty of God and the *Sharī'ah* is perfectly fine. However, this work is not doing that; it is arguing for an Islamic polity. An Islamic polity that does not recognize the central role of God's ultimate sovereignty and the *Sharī'ah* is not an Islamic polity at all.

Notes

1. When presenting a section of this chapter at the 2016 International Political Science Association Biennial World Congress in Poznań, Poland, Professor Zillur R. Khan noted that this model of development constituted what he called a "virtuous cycle." He agreed with the lexical ordering offered in my model and also added that each element actually also reinforces and strengthens each previous element. For example, when this order of development is followed, not only do functioning institutions lead

to electoral rights, but electoral rights also help strengthen the functioning institutions. I thank him for this very insightful observation.
2. In a letter addressed to John Adams, Jefferson stated, "I can never join Calvin in addressing his god. He was indeed an Atheist, which I can never be; or rather his religion was Daemonism. If ever man worshipped a false god, he did" (Jefferson, 11, April 1823).

References

Al Arabiya English. 2015. Lebanon's 'you stink' protests return to Beirut, Sept 21 http://english.alarabiya.net/en/News/middle-east/2015/09/21/Lebanese-protesters-face-off-with-security-forces-in-Beirut.html. Accessed 22 Feb 2016.
al-Hibri, Azizah. 1992. Islamic constitutionalism and the concept of democracy. *Case Western Reserve Journal of International Law* 24 (1): 1–27.
Acemoğlu, D., S. Johnson, and J.A. Robinson. 2005. Institutions as the fundamental cause of long-run growth. In *Handbook of economic growth*, ed. P. Aghion, and S. Darlauf, 385–472. Amsterdam: North-Holland Publishing Co.
Ahmad, E. 2006. The selected writings of Eqbal Ahmad. C. Bengelsdorf, M. Cerullo & Y. Chandri (eds.). New York, NY: Columbia University Press.
Allawi, Ali A. 2009. *The crisis of Islamic civilization*. New Haven, CT: Yale UniversityPress.
Almond, Gabriel, and Sidney Verba. 1963. *The civic culture: Political attitudes and democracy in five nations*. Princeton, NJ: Princeton University Press.
Aristotle. 2001. *The basic works of Aristotle*. ed. J. Mckeon. New York: The Modern Library.
Barber, Benjamin. 1984. *Strong democracy: Participatory politics for a new age*. Los Angeles, CA: UCLA Press.
Bellin, Eva. 2004. The robustness of authoritarianism in the Middle East: Exceptionalism in comparative perspective. *Comparative Politics* 36 (2): 139–157.
Berman, Sheri. 2003. Islamism, revolution, and civil society. *Perspectives on Politics* 1 (2): 257–272.
Bollen, Kenneth A. 1990. Political democracy: Conceptual and measurement traps. *Studies in Comparative International Development* 25: 7–24.
Chang, Ha-Joon. 2011. Institutions and economic development: Theory, policy and history. *Journal of Institutional Economics* 7 (4): 473–498.
Common, Richard. 2008. Administrative change in the gulf: Modernization in Bahrain and Oman. *International Review of Administrative Sciences* 74: 177–193.
Corrales, Javier, and Frank Westhoff. 2006. Information technology adoption and political regimes. *International Studies Quarterly* 50 (4): 911–933.
Dahl, Robert. 1971. *Polyarchy: Participation and opposition*. New Haven, CT: Yale University Press.

Dahl, Robert. 1989. *Democracy and its critics.* New Haven, CT: Yale Press.
Downs, Anthony. 1965. A theory of bureaucracy. *The American Economic Review* 55 (1): 439–446.
Dunleavy, Patrick, and Christopher Hood. 1994. From old public administration to new public management. *Public Money & Management* 14 (3): 9–16.
Dunleavy, Patrick, and Helen Margetts. 2013. The second wave of digital-era governance: Aquasi-paradigm for government on the Web. *Philosophical Transactions of the Royal Society* 371 (1987): 1–17.
Dunleavy, Patrick, Helen Margetts, Simon Bastow, and Jane Tinker. 2006. *Digital era governance: IT corporations, the state and e-government.* New York: Oxford University Press.
Patrick, Dunleavy, Helen Margetts, Simon Bastow, and Jane Tinker. 2005. New public management is dead. Long live digital-era governance. *Journal of Public Administration Research and Theory* 16 (3): 467–494.
Esposito, John. 1987. *Islam and politics*, 2nd ed. Syracuse, NY: Syracuse University Press.
Feldman, Noah. 2008. *The fall and rise of the Islamic state.* Princeton, NJ: Princeton Press.
Fink, Carsten, and Charles Kenny. 2006. W(h)ither the digital divide? *Info* 5 (6): 15–24.
Ghannouchi, Rachid. 2007. The participation of Islamists in a non-Islamic government. In *Islam in transition: Muslim perspectives*, eds. J. Donohue, and J. Esposito, 271–278. New York: Oxford Press.
Hai, Jeong Chung, and Nor Fadzlina Nawi. 2007. *Principles of public administration: An introduction.* Kuala Lumpur: Karisma Publications.
Hanifizadeh, Mohammed Reza, Abbas Saghaei, and Payam Hanifizadeh. 2009. An index for cross-country analysis of ICT infrastructure and access. *Telecommunications Policy* 33 (7): 385–405.
Hourani, Albert. 1991. *A history of the Arab peoples.* New York: Warner Books.
Howard, Philip N., and Nimah Mazaheri. 2009. Telecommunications reform, internet use, and mobile phone adaptation in the developing world. *World Development* 37 (7): 1159–1169.
Ibn Khaldun. 2005. *The muqaddimah: An introduction to history.* ed. N.J. Dawood. Franz Rosenthal (trans.). Princeton, NJ: Princeton University Press.
Izetbegović, Alija. 1990. *The Islamic declaration: A programme for the Islamization of Muslims and Muslim peoples.* Sarajevo.
Jefferson, Thomas. 1843. Thomas Jefferson, letter to Benjamin Waterhouse, June 26, 1822. In *The Christian reformer; or, Unitarian magazine and review,(Vol 10)*, ed. Robert Aspland. London: UK.
Jefferson, Thomas. 1823. Thomas Jefferson to John Adams, April 11, 1823, *The Thomas Jefferson papers series 1. General correspondence. 1651–1827.* http://hdl.loc.gov/loc.mss/mtj.mtjbib024623. Accessed 25 Aug 2015.

Jreisat, Jamil E. 1999. Administrative reform and the Arab world economic growth. *Policy Studies Review* 16 (2): 19–40.
Kaboolian, Linda. 1998. The new public management. *Public Administration Review* 58 (3): 189–193.
Kaminski, Joseph J. 2013. Bureaucracy and modernity: A comparative qualitative analysis of bureaucratic development in the US and OIC states. *Politics, Bureaucracy, and Justice* 3 (2): 1–10.
Kapucu, Naim, and Hami Palabıyık. 2008. *Public administration: From tradition to the modern age*. Ankara, Turkey: International Strategic Research Organization.
Khaled, Abou El Fadl. 2004. Islam and the challenge of democracy. In *Islam and the challenge of democracy*, ed. K. Abou El Fadl, J. Cohen, and D. Chasman, 3–48. Princeton, NJ: Princeton University Press.
Khan, M.A. Muqtedar. 2006b. "The politics, theory, and philosophy of Islamic democracy". In *Islamic Democratic Discourse*, ed. M.A. Muqtedar Khan, pp. 149–171. Lanham, MD: Lexington Books.
Khomeini, Ayatollah Ruhollah. 1970. *Islamic government: Governance of the jurist*. Hamid Algar (ed.). Tehran, Iran: Institute for the Publication of Imam Khomeini's Works.
Liebesny, Herbert. 1975. *The law of the near and Middle East readings, cases, and materials*. Albany, NY: State University of New York Press.
Maududi, Abul Ala. 1960. *Islamic law and constitution*.ed. Khurshid Ahmad. Lahore, Pakistan: Islamic Publications.
Midlarsky, Manus. 1998. Democracy and Islam: Implications for civilizational conflict and the democratic Peace. *International Studies Quarterly* 42 (3): 485–511.
Milner, H. 2006. The digital divide: The role of political institutions in technology diffusion. *Comparative Political Studies* 39 (2): 176–199.
Moe, Terry. 1984. The new economics of organization. *American Journal of Political Science* 28 (4): 739–777.
Montazeri, Ayatollah Hussein-Ali. 2000. *Democracy and* constitution, 1–41. Ayatollah Montazeri Official Website. http://www.amontazeri.com/farsi/fl.asp. Accessed 1 May 2015.
Mueller, Hannes. 2009. Patronage or meritocracy: Political institutions and bureaucratic efficiency. Spanish National Research Council. Unpublished.
Nasr, Sayeed Hossein. 2010. *Islam in the modern world*. New York: Harper One.
Niskanen, William. 1975. Bureaucrats and politicians. *Journal of Law and Economics* 18: 617–643.
North, Douglass. 2005. *Understanding the process of economic change*. Princeton, NJ: Princeton University Press.
Öberg, Magnus and Erik Melander. 2010. On the effect of quality of governance as compared to, e.g., democracy, on civil war Ooutbreak. Paper presented at

the annual meeting of the American Political Science Association, Washington DC, Aug 31–Sep 3.

Paldam, Martin. 2009. The macro perspective on generalized trust. In *Handbook of social capital: The troika of sociology, political science and economics*, ed. G. Svendsen, and G. Svendsen, 354–375. Cheltenham, UK: Edward Elgar.

Paldam, Martin, and Erich Gundlach. 2008. Two views on institutions and development: The grand transition vs the primacy of institutions. *Kyklos* 61 (1): 65–100.

Pryor, Fredric. 2007. Are Muslim countries less democratic? *Middle East Quarterly* XIV: 53–58.

Puddington, Arch. 2011. Freedom in the World 2011: The authoritarian challenge to democracy. Published by Freedom House. http://www.freedomhouse.org/images/File/fiw/FIW_2011_Booklet.pdf. Accessed 8 July 2014.

Putnam, Robert. 2001. *Bowling alone: The collapse and revival of American community*. New York: Simon & Schuster.

Qur'ān. 2001. *The meaning of the glorious Qur'an*. Mohammed Pickthall (trans.). New York: Alavi Foundation.

Rauch, James, and Peter Evans. 2000. Bureaucratic structure and bureaucratic performance in less developed countries. *Journal of Public Economics* 75: 49–71.

Rothstein, Bo. 2011. *The quality of government: Corruption, social trust, and inequality in international perspective*. Chicago, IL: University of Chicago Press.

Schnose, Viktoryia. 2015. Who is in charge here? Legislators, bureaucrats, and the policy making process. *Party Politics* 1–22. doi:10.177/1354068815597896.

Schumpeter, Joseph. 1942. *Capitalism, socialism and democracy*. New York: Harper.

Sisk, Timothy. 1994. *Islam and democracy: Religion, politics, and power in the Middle East*. Washington, D.C.: United States Institute of Peace.

Stepan, Alfred, and Graeme Robertson. 2004. Arab, not Muslim exceptionalism. *Journal of Democracy* 15 (4): 140–146.

Svolik, Milan. 2009. Power sharing and leadership dynamics in authoritarian regimes. *American Journal of Political Science* 53: 477–494.

Tocqueville, Alexis. 2003. *Democracy in America*. Isaac Kramnick (trans.). New York: Penguin Classics.

Veenendaal, Wouter. 2015. *Politics and democracy in microstates*. New York: Routledge Press.

Wallsten, S. 2005. Regulation and internet use in developing countries. *Economic Development and Cultural Change* 53: 501–523.

Weber, Max. 1964. *The theory of social and economic organization*. New York: The Free Press.

CHAPTER 6

The Importance of Involving Women in the Political Apparatus of a Contemporary Islamic Governed State

Introduction—Tracing the Pathology of Reactionary Attitudes Toward Women Today in the Muslim World

One of the most revolutionary aspects of the *Qur'ān* was the rights it gave to women. According to Riffat Hassan;

> Within the Islamic tradition both negative and positive attitudes are found toward women and women's issues. However, the Qur'an, which *is* the primary source on which Islam is founded, consistently affirms women's equality with men and their fundamental right to actualize the human potential that they possess equally with men. (1999: 275)

Hassan's claim is supported by the *Qur'ān*, which states;

> Lo! men who surrender unto Allah, and women who surrender, and men who believe and women who believe, and men who obey and women who obey, and men who speak the truth and women who speak the truth, and men who persevere (in righteousness) and women who persevere, and men who are humble and women who are humble, and men who give alms and women who give alms, and men who fast and women who fast, and men who guard their modesty and women who guard (their modesty), and men who remember Allah much and women who remember—Allah hath prepared for them forgiveness and a vast reward. (*Qur'ān*, 33:25)

Women are explicitly given the same status as men in the eyes of Allah for their actions and deeds. Women in Islam have explicit social, economic, and political/legal rights as well. Some examples of these rights include the right to work and earn money, the right to keep their earnings, the right to negotiate the terms of marriage, the right to divorce, the right to custody of her children following a divorce, the right to property, and the right to education.

The rights the *Qur'ān* granted to women were something quite revolutionary for its time. Once again, returning to Islam's historical moral resources, numerous *'aḥādīth* exist that reference the prominent role the Prophet's (ﷺ) wives played during Islam's formative years. According to Reza Aslan;

> ...women like Aisha and Umm Salamah [both wives of the Prophet (ﷺ)] acted not only as religious but also as political—and on at least one occasion military—leaders; and in which the call to gather for prayer, bellowed from the rooftop of Muhammad's house, brought men and women together to kneel side by side and be blessed as a single undivided community (2005, 136).

Women's empowerment and rights also were not necessarily alien to later Islamic juridical rulings either. One particularly famous *fatwā* issued by the great fifteenth-century Ottoman *faqīh*, Ebu Su'ud Efendi, noted that women have an obligation to fight back against men who try to sexually assault them and even use deadly force if necessary to do so. Colin Imber reports one particular legal scenario referenced in a ruling by Ebu Su'ud Efendi related to this matter;

> Zeyd enters Hind's house and tries to have intercourse forcibly. Since Hind can repel him by no other means, she strikes and wounds him with an axe. If Zeyd dies of the wound, is Hind liable for anything?
>
> *Answer:* She has performed an act of Holy War. (Ebu Su'ud Effendi—referenced in Imber 1997: 230)

Imber goes on to argue that "by wounding and ultimately killing her assailant, the woman has prevented an act of fornication, which is an offense against God, and hence Ebu-su'ud's enthusiasm for her action" (1997: 230). He also notes that Ibn Bazzaz made a similar ruling on the matter of rape.¹ Even though these rulings had more to do with a perceived violation to the rights of Allah, rather than to the rights of women; nonetheless, at least in practice, they offered women some level of legal protection from would-be predators.

Despite all of this, there most certainly has been discord between the rights of women as expressed in the *Qur'ān* and the actual situation in the world today as mentioned by Hassan. An effective modern Islamic governed state must come to terms with the rights given to women in the *Qur'ān* and make active efforts to include women in the political processes of the state. The pathology of the reactionary attitudes held toward women today in the Muslim world can be traced back to how earlier scholars interpreted the meanings of the *Qur'ān* which resulted in some of the more specific rulings and eventual laws that discriminated against women. Exegetes from the classical period in Islamic history often read the *Qur'ān* one *āyah* at a time, without making any real efforts to connect *āyāt or suwar* into a larger coherent theme (Mir 1986). Asma Barlas paraphrases Mustansir Mir who argued that past scholars "relied on a "linear-atomistic" method that takes a "verse-by-verse" approach to the Quran" (Mir, quoted in Barlas 2001: 8). Mir believed that even when scholars did make efforts to connect two or more *āyāt*, there never was any general hermeneutic principal for connecting syntactical structures or overarching motifs.

The lack of a generally agreed to hermeneutic principle has resulted in scholars reading texts primarily from the locus of their own subjective experiences. Adis Duderija argues that "the semi-contextualist nature of traditional Qur'ān–Sunna hermeneutics is unable to break the shackles of the Qur'ān's revelatory historicity in order to free it from the spatio-temporal constraints within which it initially operated" (2016, 594). This is to suggest that if one was a misogynist living in a highly patriarchal or repressive society, they were likely to interpret and offer commentaries (*tafsīr*) on the *Qur'ān* that reflected these values, since there was never any established widely held hermeneutic principal for guidance. Considering the highly patriarchal nature of almost all societies (Muslim or not) during the Middle Ages, it is hardly surprising that such commentaries would often offer misogynistic interpretations of woman and their respective roles in society.

Duderija goes on to argue; "…we can conclude that traditional Muslim thought subscribes to a number of assumptions regarding appropriate gender roles and norms, which were based on certain customary beliefs and practices that were absorbed by Islamic law" (2016, 592). Duderija's broader project here suggests the following: Since many norms regarding women are based primarily on old customs (*'urf*) that were later incorporated into Islamic law, there is a possibility to reconceptualize these norms and values in a more contemporary sociopolitical context and to then change the old laws, *i.e.*, there is nothing "divine" about many of the gender norms that dominate many parts of the Muslim world today. This seems to be a worthwhile enterprise so long as this can be done organically without uncritically accepting whatever norms and values are *en vogue* in non-Muslim, Western secular societies—values that often stand in stark contrast to even the most basic Islamic values. As one can see, this is a massive long-term project that most certainly will take quite some time, enormous patience, and immense scholarly efforts. While it is obligatory for any Muslim to believe in the perfection of the *Qur'ān*, it would not only be foolish, but even un-Islamic to believe in the perfection of commentaries on the *Qur'ān*, even from the most iconic commentators of the past and present.

Recent scholars such as Jean-Jacques Waardenburg have argued for the necessity of developing a consistent methodology underlying *tafsīr*. Waardenburg suggests that scholars should separate their emotional response to certain verses of the *Qur'ān* from their study of the meaning of the text.

> A scholar studying the exegesis of Qur'anic texts may feel attraction or repulsion for certain texts on an emotional level. But inasmuch as scholarship is an attempt to arrive at knowledge that is generally valid, include knowledge about Scriptures and the ways in which they have been read, we should avoid taking an attitude either for or against the contents of the text. Our concern should be the text itself and its meaning, including the meaning people have found in the text and the way they have interpreted it. (2002: 112)

The obvious question here is whether this is even possible. On the surface, this seems like an almost impossible task, since all human beings are situated subjective beings with unavoidable biases, "pre-judgements," and unique understandings of the meanings of words and the world in general (Gadamer 2004; Shanks 1992). Even if scholars were to craft some type of standard hermeneutic protocols for interpreting Qur'anic texts, is it even realistic to believe that such protocols would ever actually be agreed upon? If scholars cannot even agree on the proper translation of certain words from Arabic to English in the various translations of the *Qur'ān* that have been published over the past couple hundred years, one can imagine how difficult it would be to come up with an entire system of hermeneutics that is universally assented to by all of the various scholars, schools of thought, and competing sects within Islam today.

Tafsīr and *'aḥādīth*, in general, tend to be much more conservative in their interpretation of the role of women in Islam than the actual writings on women contained in the *Qur'ān* (Rahman 1982; Spellberg 1994; Stowasser 1994). In recent times, some scholars such as Fazlur Rahman have suggested that *tafsīr* and *'aḥādīth* have "come to eclipse the Qur'an's influence in most Muslim societies today" (Barlas 2001: 9). While I believe that this point is highly debatable, the fact remains that *tafsīr* and *'aḥādīth* do often serve as substitutes for those who lack the ability or time to actually read the *Qur'ān* for themselves—it is much easier and less time-consuming to listen to a YouTube lecture by someone deemed reputable than it is to read the original text.

The late Moroccan feminist scholar, Fatima Mernissi, argued that a questionable *ḥadīth* compiled by Imam Bukhari sets the table for keeping women out of politics many centuries ago.

> According to al-Bukhari, it is supposed to have been Abu Bakra who heard the Prophet say: "Those who entrust their affairs to a woman will never know prosperity." Since this Hadith is included in the *Sahih* - those thousands of authentic Hadith accepted by the meticulous al-Bukhari - it is a priori considered true and therefore unassailable without proof to the contrary, since we are here in scientific terrain. (1991: 49)

Mernissi goes on to argue why this particular *ḥadīth* may very well be problematic or even wrong.

> Even though it was collected as *sahih* (authentic) by al-Bukhari and others, that Hadith was hotly contested and debated by many. The *fuqaha* did not agree on the weight to give that Hadith on women and politics. Assuredly there were some who used it as an argument for excluding

women from decision making. But there were others who found that argument unfounded and unconvincing. (1991: 61)

The famous ninth-century Persian *mufassir*, al-Ṭabarī, was one of those religious authorities who questioned this *ḥadīth*, justifying the exclusion of women from politics. Mernissi argues that even *ṣaḥīḥ*-rated *ḥadīth* must be constantly reinvestigated for authenticity.

> So nothing bans me, as a Muslim woman, from making a double investigation – historical and methodological- of this Hadith and its author, and especially of the conditions in which it was first put to use. Who uttered this Hadith, where, when, why, and to whom? (1991: 49)

The most damning evidence against the reliability of this particular *ḥadīth* was based on the fact that the narrator of this *ḥadīth*, Abu Bakra, was known to have lied to the Caliph 'Umar and was flogged as punishment for giving false testimony about a woman engaging in illegal sexual behavior. This fact alone is enough for some scholars to discredit this *ḥadīth*. "If one follows the principles of Malik for *fiqh*, Abu Bakra must be rejected as a source of Hadith by every good, well-informed Malikite Muslim" (Mernissi 1991: 61). Mernissi goes on to argue that by the second-century A.H., there were known to already exist over 500,000 fabricated *'aḥādīth*. A similar criticism was levied by a nineteenth-century Indian scholar as well, questioning the overall veracity of *'aḥādīth*. According to Moulvi Cheragh Ali;

> The vast flood of tradition soon formed a chaotic sea. Truth, error, fact and fable mingled together in an undistinguishable confusion. Every religious, social, and political system was defended when necessary, to please a Khalif or an Ameer to serve his purpose to support all manner of lies and absurdities or to satisfy the passion, caprice, or arbitrary will of the despots, leaving out of consideration the creation of any standards of test. (Ali, quoted in Guillaume 1966: 97)

Mernissi and Ali's statements do not mean that *'aḥādīth* should be ignored or abandoned as a guiding source. However, it does mean that one must recognize that even *ṣaḥīḥ* rated *ḥadīth* are fallible and that scholars must continue to investigate the validity of even these *'aḥādīth*, especially if they sound like something that one would not expect the Prophet Mohammed (ﷺ) to actually say or do.

WOMEN IN PUBLIC ADMINISTRATION AND POLITICS—THE KEY MISSING VARIABLE TO COMBAT THE AUTHORITARIANISM THAT DOMINATES MANY PARTS OF THE MUSLIM WORLD TODAY?

The women role of women in positions of political power and public administration must be taken seriously if a modern Islamic governed state is to succeed. One of the central planks of the contemporary Islamist discourse on women is that God has intended different functions for men and women and that denying this reality is unjust to women. The prominent Iranian clerical figure and ideologue of the Iranian Islamic Republic, Murtaza Mutahhari, commented that; "The western world is now attempting to create uniformity and identicalness in laws, regulations, rights, and functions, between women and men, while ignoring the innate and natural differences" (Mutahhari in Euben et al. (eds.) 2009: 260). According to one anonymous activist involved in the 2011 protests in Egypt—"If you ask someone if they want gender equality, that's a loaded term here. Do you mean all women should be like men? Most would say no. If you mean women have choice and equal protection under the law, most would say yes" (Finn 2011: *online*).

While some have argued that those who try and make women "identical" in all aspects to men are in actuality oppressing women by fundamentally altering their own natural tendencies, nonetheless, regardless of the biological differences between the sexes, women have historically played an important role in Islamic society. Earlier an example was given of two of the Prophet Mohammed's (ﷺ) later wives that attests to this reality; however, the most well-known example of a Muslim woman possessing great power and independence can be found in his first wife, Khadija, who was a highly respected and wealthy business woman. The renowned ninth-century Arab biographer Ibn Sa'd reported in his *Kitāb al-Ṭabaqāt al-Kubrā* that that Khadija's caravan equaled the caravans of all other traders of the Quraysh tribe put together (Ibn Sa'd 1995). Over time she has come to be known as *Khadija al-Kūbra*, or "Khadija the Great" for her piety, charity, and personal strength.

One can also look back to the 1979 Iranian Revolution as a more recent example of female empowerment in Islam. Women were an essential part of the Iranian Revolution even though many of the Revolution's more conservative figures were initially concerned about their participation. Iranian women played an undeniable role in the overthrow of Shah Pahlavi, and the legitimacy of female participation in the Revolution was never again questioned by Iran religious authorities. It is also evident that women played an important role in the recent Arab uprisings as well. In Egypt, Yemen, and Syria, women did not just participate in the protests against their oppressive regimes, but they also provided material support for all involved via medical, food, and other essential resources needed in any revolutionary social movement.

> The Arab Spring was not about gender equality. Women involved in all countries say that. But many are alarmed that their efforts risk going unrewarded, and that men who were keen to have them on the streets crying freedom may not be so happy to have them in parliament, government and business boardrooms. (Finn 2011: *online*)

There is no real reason within an Islamic governed state why women cannot only be involved in politics, but can also play a fundamental role in helping shape the discourse.

The social and political roles of women throughout the Muslim world vary greatly by location. Women have had more access to politics in South Asian Muslim countries than in the Gulf States and north Africa (Kaminski 2013). In some places, such as Pakistan and Bangladesh, women have made inroads to positions of leadership and other well-respected positions in the civil services. In the early 1970s, the Pakistani system of public administration banned castes and made efforts to limit wanton corruption that marked administration in Pakistan during the colonial era. Women in Pakistan were also given more access to positions within the government.

While females have greater influence in the realm of public administration in Pakistan and Bangladesh than in the Gulf States, they still are underrepresented and not treated equally by Western standards. Women rarely reach the highest echelons of the pay scale in public administration in any country, let alone Muslim ones. During the first decade of the twenty-first century, it was noted that in Pakistan, compared "to some 800 men in the BPS scales 20 and above, there are only 19 women holding posts in these grades" (Islam 2005: 167). The cultural norms in Pakistan and Bangladesh, like the Gulf States, undeniably have severely mitigated a woman's upward social mobility; this is especially true within the realms of public administration. In many of these societies, women are strongly encouraged to take on domestic roles, get married early, and soon after, start having children (Islam 2005). Males still have a great deal of influence on the type of work their wives do and often husbands actively discourage their wives from working outside the house, regardless of household income. While economic realities in the West have caused most men to be accepting of their wives working outside the house, many Muslim men, especially in the Muslim world, would rather choose poverty than allowing their wives to work outside the house.

Afghanistan and Pakistan are regularly cited as examples of places where women's rights lag behind the rest of the world. It should not be surprising then that both of these countries have very low female literacy rates as well. As of 2008, in Pakistan the literacy rate of women between the ages of 15 and 24 was a meager 59% and the literacy rate of women between the ages of 15 and 24 in Afghanistan was an unfathomable 18% (UNICEF 2010). While there seems to be a correlation between the rights of women and literacy levels, this should not be misunderstood as a universal trend. In Saudi Arabia, 96% of women are literate, yet still lack many basic rights enjoyed by women in the West.

As mentioned in the introduction of this chapter, many positions on women that are described as "Islamic" are actually tribal and local customs and mores that are grafted onto an Islamic framework. Al-Hibri argues that "If we want to go back to a pristine understanding of what it is really that Islam said about basic issues [we will find] a very gender equitable view" (al-Hibri, quoted in Sikimic 2011: *online*). Different parts of the Islamic world have vastly different cultural traditions which result in different standards of treatment of women. Often, these cultural traditions cannot be readily found in the *Qur'ān*. One such example is the often-misunderstood reality of women and face veiling (*niqāb*) that many in the West mistakenly believe is universally considered mandatory within Islam for all Muslim women.

> Ultraconservative Muslims have gone even further, requiring that a woman also cover her face. Certainly there are no Qur'anic statements which justify the rigid restrictions regarding segregation and

veiling which have been imposed on Muslim women in the name of Islam. (Hassan 1999: 275)

Regarding face veiling, Hassan is talking specifically about the general *Ḥanbalī* legal standard that holds that women should not show their hands or faces in public. However, others have argued that this is not obligatory. The *Qur'ān* states; "And tell the believing women to lower their gaze and be modest, and to display of their adornment only that which is apparent, and to draw their veils over their bosoms, and not to reveal their adornment save to their own husbands ... (24.33)." According to Ibn Ṭabari in his *Tafsīr al- Ṭabarī*, the *ṣaḥābī* and cousin to the Prophet (ﷺ), 'Abdullah bin 'Abbās was asked about this *āyah*, and he commented that "only that which is apparent" was referring to the face and hands, which means that a woman's face and hands may be uncovered (Khan 2016). There also exists multiple 'aḥādīth that seem to suggest that *niqāb* is not *farḍ*. Even the prominent Salafi scholar Nasiruddin al-Albani, despite not technically being *Ḥanbalī* (who nonetheless is often seen as having many positions that fit within the *Ḥanbalī* tradition), argued that this was not mandatory. He based his argument on evidence gathered from critically exploring the *'aḥādīth*.[2] The point here is not denounce the *niqāb* or societies/individuals that choose to promote it, rather it is to promote further discussion on this and other social topics that are inclusive and take into consideration the possibilities for change if a particular society feels the need for such. In order to break the cultural barriers that limit the rights and participation of women, improving education and communication must be paramount.

From a more practical perspective, positive attitudes toward women and gender equality in general have been shown by Norris and Inglehart to play an essential role in facilitating democracy and good governance. Less restrictive attitudes on gender equality also facilitate in promoting tolerance and equality. "A society's commitment to gender equality and sexual liberalization proves time and again to be the most reliable indicator of how strongly that society supports principles of tolerance and egalitarianism" (Inglehart and Norris 2003: 65). They found that states with more progressive attitudes toward women tended to be more democratic. However, they also recognized that modernization and economic stability also played a major factor in shaping more progressive attitudes toward women in general.

In particular, modernization compels systematic, predictable changes in gender roles: Industrialization brings women into the paid work force and dramatically reduces fertility rates. Women become literate and begin to participate in representative government but still have far less power than men. Then, the postindustrial phase brings a shift toward greater gender equality as women move into higher-status economic roles in management and gain political influence within elected and appointed bodies. Thus, relatively industrialized Muslim societies such as Turkey share the same views on gender equality and sexual liberalization as other new democracies. (Inglehart and Norris 2003: 68)

Without focusing on industrialization and economic modernization as a requisite for changing attitudes toward gender equality, the hope for promoting viable democratic structures in post-authoritarian states is in an even more perilous position.

In places where there is a great deal of inequality between men and women, the state tends to be more authoritarian. According to Steven Fish, "Muslim societies are not more prone to violence, nor are they less 'secular' than non-Muslim countries; and interpersonal trust is not necessarily lower in Muslim countries. But one factor does help explain the democratic deficit: the subordination of women" (2002: 5). Fish's research showed that *Freedom House* (*FH*) aggregates freedom ratings rise in correlation with the percentage of women occupying positions in government.

> Each additional 1 percent of officialdom that is occupied by women is associated with an improvement of .08 in the FH score. Thus, the difference between a government that is 5 percent women and one that is 25 per cent women is associated with a difference of 1.6 points—nearly one quarter of the empirical range—in the dependent variable. (2002: 28)

FH scores range from 1 (most free) to 7 (least free). To make the point more clearly, what this means is that a nation that has a FH score of 5.6 that has 5% of women in the government could expect its score to drop to 4.0 if 25% of its government was composed of females.

Fish's overall conclusion was that the status of women is the *most* important factor in understanding levels of authoritarianism in a state, more important than religiosity or any other economic factors. In places where women earn significantly less than men, where women are significantly less literate than men, and have significantly less representation in government than men, level of authoritarianism is highest. Fish's (2002) findings are backed by Stefanczak and Connolly (2015) who more recently showed that women still have less representation in Arab and Post-Soviet states—which generally are considered more authoritarian— than women living in other parts of the world. "The level of women's representation [in Post-Soviet states] has remained comparatively low at 18.6% in 2015, only slightly above the regional average for Arab states at 18.1%, and below the regional average for sub-Saharan Africa at 22.7%, Europe at 25.3% and the Americas at 26.5%" (Stefanczak and Connolly 2015: 2). Like many Arab states, many Caucasus states have strong central leaders, weak and fragmented party systems, and cultural mores that discourage women from working in government.

Education and Change

The importance of formal education that was mentioned earlier in regard to creating a skilled and professional bureaucratic class is no less important in getting women involved in the political process as well. In Chimamanda Ngozi Adiche's critically acclaimed novel, *Half of a Yellow Sun* (2007), Odenigbo, a radical revolutionary professor comments to his mistress Olanna on the legacy of European colonialism, "The real tragedy of our postcolonial world is not that the majority of people had no say in whether or not they wanted this new world; rather, it is that the majority have not been given the tools to negotiate this new world" (Adiche 2007: 101). Education is the most essential tool for women trying to successfully express themselves politically and economically in post-colonial societies. When one lacks a sufficient vocabulary, they actually lack their ability to even adequately articulate the nature of their own oppression. Billions of women in the colonized world today *know* that they are oppressed, but often lack the power, and even more importantly, the words to make their oppression *known*.

The role of education in the Islamic sense goes beyond the traditional secular notion of education that is practiced in the West. Nasr argues that the role of Islamic education "was not only the training of the mind, but that of the whole being of the person" (2010: 131). The education of women in the Muslim world is at the forefront of the current transformation of the status quo that is taking place. According to Hassan;

> Male-centered and male-dominated Muslim societies have continued to assert, glibly and tirelessly, that Islam has given women more rights than any other religion, while keeping women in physical, mental, and emotional confinement and depriving them of the opportunity to actualize their human potential. (1999, 250)

For Hassan, education is the key to liberation and political rights. Patriarchal stereotypes about women must be broken for real change to happen in any of the currently authoritarian Muslim countries. Emphasis on the improvement of education, including making sure that women are aware of their inherent rights given to them by the *Qur'ān*, is essential.

It is also essential to teach young males about the rights that women have in Islam. The battle of ideas literally begins in the kindergarten classroom. Boys and girls need to be taught from the very beginning of their individual educational endeavor that the *Qur'ān* and traditions of the Prophet (ﷺ) provide certain standards and expectations of behavior that apply to all people. Stereotypes and discriminatory attitudes will only be broken when children grow up in a world where they can see incremental progress in this arena. Teaching children about the rights women have in the *Qur'ān* at the age of 16 is too late; these lessons need to be taught at the age of 6.

Improving literacy is also essential in improving the opportunities women have to engage in political processes. The best place to formally improve literacy is in the classroom where students can learn under the aegis of a teacher. However, another way to improve literacy outside the traditional classroom is via technological modernization, specifically through computers and Internet access. Scholars of primary and secondary education have noted that the Internet can be as valuable, if not more so, than traditional print literature for improving literacy and critical thinking skills.

> ...internet readers have taken the strategies used for reading print text and applied them to the reading of Internet text. Along with knowing how to navigate the internet, they also know how to read it through the use of prior knowledge about the topic and structure of the text. (Schmar-Dobler 2003: 85)

Even while Web browsing, listening to music, or *Facebook* chatting, simply through the process of repetition and typing, literacy can be expected to improve as well. As Schmar-Dobler notes, knowing how to navigate the Internet is a valuable skill in and of itself. Perhaps in some of the least developed places, getting every household up-to-date computer hardware and Internet access may be a stretch, but getting local libraries technologically modernized seems to be a reasonable place to start.

It is a fact that women in the Middle East lag behind their male counterparts in regard to formal educational achievement and literacy. UNESCO data on literacy development show that overall global literacy is steadily on the rise; however, a disproportionate number of people who are remained illiterate are female. "The global adult literacy rate, for the population 15 years and older, was 80% for women and 89% for men in 2012" (UNESCO 2014: *online*). According to UNESCO's international literacy data for 2014 (based on 2012 data);

> Despite these gains, 781 million adults still could not read or write – two-thirds of them (496 million) were women. In more than a dozen countries, mostly in sub-Saharan Africa, fewer than half of all adults had basic literacy skills. Among youths, 126 million were illiterate, of which 77 million were female. Even though the size of the global illiterate population is shrinking, the female proportion has remained virtually steady at 63% to 64%. (UNESCO 2014: *online*)

Cultural norms play a major role on how women are treated as a whole by the particular society they live in Tonso (1996). Access to formal education in the West for Muslim women has increased steadily over the past 20 years (Marcotte 2010). Contemporary female Islamic scholars come from numerous academic disciplines. Such academic diversity is critical for combating backwardness, and it is also essential for combatting misconceptions of Muslim women by those in the West with negative sentiments toward Islam.

Effective communication is at the heart of transforming the reactionary and patriarchic aspects of the contemporary Islamic discourse. Communicative and associational rights for educated and informed political participants are essential for democracy to work. Looking briefly at Jürgen Habermas' theory of communicative action can help further elucidate this point. For Habermas, rationality lies directly within the dynamics of interpersonal communication, rather than within the isolated individual subject in the sphere of Plato's forms. Through communication, the individual subject understands, comprehends, and ultimately shapes the world. According to Habermas;

> Communicative action serves to transmit and renew cultural knowledge, in a process of achieving mutual understandings. It then coordinates action towards social integration and solidarity. Finally, communicative action is the process through which people form their identities. (1985: 140)

Effective communication fosters new ideas and increasing social camaraderie. It is not meant to be an exercise in rhetoric. At the root of Habermas' theory is the importance of action. "Action refers not only to the system of explicit norms and rule of a form of life, but also always to a background which can generate new norms" (Taylor 1991: 26). The communicative process facilitates in the generation of new modes of understanding, and potentially new norms. For Habermas, the communicative process must be inclusive and allow for diverse opinions. However, just because an opinion is introduced, does mean that it has to be accepted. In many ways, an ideally functioning *Shūra* council work engages with many of Habermas' ideas. Communicative action theory is meant to be critical—at its core is a scathing critic of the current global capitalist order and the status quo (Habermas 1985; Taylor 1991). In short, communicative action theory is meant to have a revolutionary dynamic; it is meant to allow for a non-repressed critical discourse on existing institutions and ideologies. This can also easily include shaping the discourse in the Muslim world on the role of women, going back to the fundamental subconscious ways women are conceived. Communicative action theory is meant to break through the wall of seemingly unshakable stereotypes and distorted perceptions of reality that are perpetuated by governments and mass media.

While the often-complicated and painful process of globalization has its obvious drawbacks, one positive aspect of it is that it offers new possibilities of communicative discourse. The key to effective communicative action lies in free expression of ideas in the public sphere. The public sphere in the twenty-first century has gone global.

> Multiple translocalities and the luminal hybrid spaces they open up provide Muslim women with a variety of opportunities to reflect critically on their own experiences and to question both religious interpretations and traditional hegemonic discourses which the former rely. (Marcotte 2010: 155)

Global education and spaces for authentic discourse are essential to redefine the role of women in Islamic societies. In a *ḥadīth* contained in Imam Nawawi's collection, it states, "Abu Hurairah reported: Messenger of Allâh (s.a.w) said, "The believers who show the most perfect Faith are those who have the best behavior, and the best of you are those who are best to their wives"" (*Riyadh us-Saliheen*, #278). Being good to one's wife or women in general must extend beyond the domestic sphere and into the realm of political and public social discourse. If contemporary OIC member states are to be competitive in an increasingly global economy, they need to tap all the resources they have; these resources include females who can offer balance and new approaches to politics and governance.

Conclusion

Nawaal El Sadaawi informs her readers in *The Hidden Face of Eve: Women in the Arab World* (2007) that understanding the plight of women in the Arab world requires an intersectional approach. On the basic premise behind intersectionality, Oprisko and Caplan argue, "that experiences are buried by a rush to study primary constructions without looking at the intersections between other axes" (2014: 39). They then go on to reference the work of Purdie-Vaughns and Eibach (2008) who "refer to this phenomenon as intersectional invisibility where individuals who are outside of the predetermined norm are ignored or marginalized"[3] (2014: 39). On the way intersectional research should be conducted, Oprisko and Caplan go on to argue that multiple axes must be explored in tandem in order to determine which axes and levels of analysis are the most relevant and have the most explanatory power. Contemporary scholars "should engage as many axes as possible in as many combinations as is allowable in order to determine the salience of the intersectional group(s) for the research being conducted" (Oprisko and Caplan 2014: 38). Intersectional research can highlight distinctions within and between oppressed groups.

El Sadaawi's writings concur with Oprisko and Caplan, claiming that women's struggles in other parts of the world cannot simply be conceived of in the same manner as struggles for women's rights in the West. She also points out that non-Western women are generally *the least advantaged of the least advantaged*;

> It is necessary at all times to see the close links between women's struggles for emancipation and the battles for national and social liberation waged by people in all parts of the 'Third World' against foreign domination and the exploitation exercised by international capitalism over human and natural resources. If this link is forgotten, feminist movements in the West may be used not to further the cause of women's liberation but instead to participate in holding back the forces of freedom and progress in the countries of Asia, Africa, and Latin America. (2007: xxiv)

Much like the earlier example given about democracy and bureaucracy, Western models of feminism cannot simply be grafted on women living in the Muslim world. An imposition of Western feminist values onto the Muslim world could easily result in Muslim women themselves retreating into even more conservative positions in defense of their own indigenous cultures against secular Western values. If one identifies as a "Muslim" prior to any specific gender, then this possibility becomes the likely result due to misguided Western feminists who fail to take seriously the roles of Islam and local culture.

An intersectional approach to women's rights in the Muslim world allows for one to consider all the variables that have contributed to the of Muslim women. Without fully exploring the role of colonialism, transnational capitalism, *along* with patriarchal attitudes among Muslim males based on sometimes questionable *'aḥādīth* sources and non-Islamic cultural norms and mores, one does not understand the complete picture. Khaled Abou El Fadl reminds us that;

> The thorough and fair-minded researcher would observe that behind every single Qur'anic revelation regarding women was an effort to protect the women from exploitative situations and from situations in which they are treated inequitably. In studying the Qur'an, it becomes clear that the Qur'an is educating Muslims how to make incremental but lasting improvements in the condition of women that can only be described as progressive for their time and place. (2005: 262)

The role of women and rights of women in the Muslim world must continue to be explored by scholars such as Duderija, Abou El Fadl, Hassan, and El Sadaawi that make efforts to understand women from within an Islamic discursive framework and to understand women in the Muslim world in relation to larger geopolitical historical realities and trends.

It is important to remember that even in the West, women only recently gained the rights they have, and even in these cases, in no serious way could one rightfully claim women enjoy equal rights as men. Simply arguing that reactionary Muslim male attitudes toward their female counterparts is why women are in the position that they are is not enough. While such attitudes may be a part of the pathology of the problem, this reality cannot simply be essentialized as being its root cause.

NOTES

1. According to Imber, Ibn Bazzaz ruled that "If a man coerces a woman, she may kill him" (1997: 230).
2. Nasiruddin Al-Albani famously justified his position that the *niqab* was recommended, but not mandatory by referencing the following hadith: "It was narrated from Aishah that Asma bint Abi Bakr entered upon the Messenger of Allah (peace be upon him) wearing a thin garment. The Messenger of Allah (peace be upon him) turned away from her and said: 'Oh Asma, when a woman reaches the age of menstruation, it is not proper for anything to be seen of her except this and this,' and he pointed to his face and hands" (*Sunan Abī Dāwūd*, #4104). Despite Abu Dawud noting that this hadith was *mursal* (hurried), i.e., could only be traced back to the *taabi'i* (Muslim's who saw or met *Sahaab'i*) and not the *sahaba* themselves, Al-Albani argued this hadith was strengthened due to the fact that a similar incident was referenced in the writings Al-Bayhaqi, Al-Mundhiri, and adh-Dhahabi.
3. Oprisko and Caplan's reference to "Purdie-Vaughns and Eibach (2008)" refers to, Purdie-Vaughns, Valerie, and Richard Eibach. "Intersectional Invisibility: The Distinctive Advantages and Disadvantages of Multiple Subordinate-Group Identities." *Sex Roles*, 59:1 (2008): 377–391.

REFERENCES

Abou El Fadl, Khaled. 2005. *The great theft: Wrestling Islam from the extremists*. New York: Harper Collins.
Adichie, Chimamanda N. 2007. *Half of a yellow sun*. Toronto: Knopf Canada.
Aslan, Reza. 2005. *No God but God: The origins, evolution, and future of Islam*. New York: Random House.
Barlas, Asma. 2001. *"Believing women" in Islam: Unreading patriarchal interpretations of the Qu'ran*. Austin: University of Texas Press.
Duderija, Adis. 2016. The custom (urf) based assumptions regarding gender roles and norms in the Islamic tradition: A critical examination. *Studies in Religion* 45 (4): 581–599.

El Sadaawi, Nawal. 2007. *The hidden face of Eve: Women in the Arab world*, 2nd ed. London: Zed Publishing.
Finn, Tom. 2011. Women have Emerged as Key Players in the Arab Spring. 22 April, 2011. *The Guardian*. http://www.theguardian.com/world/2011/apr/22/women-arab-spring. Accessed 21 July 2015.
Fish, Steven M. 2002. Islam and authoritarianism. *World Politics* 55 (1): 4–37.
Gadamer, Hans-Georg. 2004. *Philosophical hermeneutics*, ed. David Linge Berkeley, CA: University of California Press.
Guillaume, Alfred. 1966. *The traditions of Islam—An introduction to the study of the hadith literature*. Beirut: Khayats.
Habermas, Jürgen. 1985. *The Theory of Communicative Action*, ed. Thomas McCarthy, vol. 2. Boston, MA: Beacon Press.
Hassan, Riffat. 1999. Feminism in Islam. In *Feminism and world religions*, ed. A. Sharma, and K. Young, 248–278. Albany: SUNY Press.
Ibn Saʿd, Muhammad. 1995. *Tabaqat* Vol. 8. 'The Women of Madina,' Aisha Bewley, trans. London, UK: Ta-Ha Publishers.
Imber, Colin. 1997. *Ebu's Suʿud: The Islamic legal tradition*. Palo, Alto: CA: Stanford Press.
Inglehart, Ronald, and Pippa Norris. 2003. The true clash of civilizations. *Foreign Policy* 135: 62–70.
Islam, Nasir. 2005. National culture, corruption, and governance in Pakistan, In *Administrative culture in a global context*, eds. J. Jabbra and Dwivedi. Whitby, Ontario: De Sitter Publications.
Kaminski, Joseph J. 2013. Bureaucracy and modernity: A comparative qualitative analysis of bureaucratic development in the US and OIC states. *Politics, Bureaucracy, and Justice* 3 (2): 1–10.
Khan, Mateen. 2016. Niqab: An approach based on the proofs. The Institute for the Revival of the Traditional Islamic Sciences. https://bukhari2013.files.wordpress.com/2016/12/niqab-an-approach-based-on-the-proofs.pdf. Accessed on 30 Dec 2016.
Marcotte, Roxanne D. 2010. Muslim women's scholarship and the new gender jihad. In *Women in Islam*, ed. Z. Kassam, 131–162. Denver: Praeger Publishers.
Mernissi, Fatima. 1991. *The veil and the male elite: A feminist interpretation of women's rights in Islam*, trans. and ed. Mary Jo Lakeland. New York: Perseus Publishing.
Mutahhari, Mortaza. 2009. The human status of women in the Qur'an. In *Princeton readings in Islamist thought*, ed. R. Euben, and M. Zaman, 254–274. Princeton: Princeton University Press.
Nasr, Sayeed Hossein. 2010. *Islam in the modern world*. New York: Harper One Publishers.

Oprisko, Robert and Caplan, Josh. 2014. Beyond the cake model: critical intersectionality and the relative advantage of disadvantage. *Epiphany: Journal of Transdisciplinary Studies,* 7 (2): 35–54.

Purdie-Vaughns, Valerie, and Richard Eibach. 2008. Intersectional invisibility: The distinctive advantages and disadvantages of multiple subordinate-group identities. *Sex Roles* 59 (1): 377–391.

Qur'ān. 2001. *The meaning of the glorious Qur'an,* trans. and ed. Mohammed Pickthall. New York: Alavi Foundation.

Rahman, Fazlur. 1982. *Islam and modernity: Transformation of an intellectual tradition.* Chicago: University of Chicago Press.

Riyadh-us-Saliheen, (2 Vols.). 1999. Compiled by Abu Zakariya Nawawi, trans. and ed. Muhammad Amin and Abu Usamah Al-Arabi bin Razduq. New York: Dar-us-Salam Publications.

Schmar-Dobler, Elizabeth. 2003. Reading on the internet: The link between literacy and technology. *Journal of Adolescent & Adult Literacy* 47 (1): 80–85.

Shanks, Michael. 1992. *Experiencing the past: On the character of archaeology.* London: Routledge Press.

Sikimic, Simona. 2011. Activist Highlights Women's Rights in Islam. 16 June, 2011. *The Daily Star.* http://www.dailystar.com.lb/News/Local-News/2011/Jun-16/Activist-highlights-womens-rights-in-Islam.ashx#ixzz1PSKdmW4L. Accessed 14 June 2014.

Spellberg, Denise A. 1994. *Politics, gender, and the Islamic past: The legacy of Aisha bint Abi Bakr.* New York: Columbia University Press.

Stefanczak, Karolina, and Eileen Connolly. 2015. Gender and political representation in the de facto states of the Caucasus: Women and parliamentary elections in Abkhazia. *Caucasus Survey* 3 (3): 1–11.

Stowasser, Barbara. 1994. *Women in the Qur'an: Traditions and interpretations.* New York: Oxford University Press.

Sunan Abī Dāwūd , (5 Vols.). 2008. Compiled by Abu Dawud. Hafiz Abu Tahir Zubair 'Ali Za'I ed. and trans. Nasiruddin al-Khattab. Houston, TX: Darussalaam Publishers.

Taylor, Charles. 1991. Language and society. In *Axel Honneth and Hans Joas,* ed. Communicative Action, 23–35. Cambridge: MIT Press.

Tonso, Karen L. 1996. The impact of cultural norms on women. *Journal of Engineering Education* 85 (3): 217–225.

UNICEF, 2010.Report on World Countries: Education Statistics.http://www.unicef.org/search/search.php?q=Education%20statistics&type=Main. Accessed 23 June 2011.

Waardenburg, Jean Jacques. 2002. *Islam: Historical, social, and political perspectives.* Berlin: Walter de Gruyter.

CHAPTER 7

The Importance of Economic Justice in a Contemporary Islamic Governed State

Economic Justice—A Two-Way Street

The final foundational element to be discussed in Part I of this work that reconceptualizes a modern Islamic governed state is the issue of economic justice. The 2011 revolutions in the Middle East can largely be attributed to the fact that unemployment was high and opportunities to succeed financially and professionally were low for most people living in these nations. People with high levels of education were not getting opportunities, and small classes of powerful elites remained firmly in control of the economic resources. Powerful corporatist coalitions have been receiving large financial benefits in exchange for political obedience throughout North Africa for decades (Waterbury 1997). While the Western media focused on the abstract notion of "democracy," in actuality, the primary material factors that led to the Arab uprisings were economic stagnation and staggering levels of inequality.

The 2014 findings of Alverado and Piketty suggest that in recent times, the Middle East has been among the most unequal regions in the world; "According to our benchmark estimates, the share of total Middle East income accruing to the top 10% income recipients is currently 55% (vs. 48% in the USA, 36% in Western Europe, and 54% in South Africa)" (2014: 6). In their high-inequality estimates, they found that the top 10% in the Middle East control 61% of the total income, and the top 1% account for over 25% of the total income. They also go on to note that there was a relatively constant level of high inequality in the Middle East

© The Author(s) 2017
J.J. Kaminski, *The Contemporary Islamic Governed State*,
Palgrave Series in Islamic Theology, Law, and History,
DOI 10.1007/978-3-319-57012-9_7

from the period 1990 to 2012. However, they add the caveat that based on population growth primarily from poor foreign workers living and working in Middle East countries that their model did not account for, future estimation models that include different variables could actually show growing inequality during the period 1990–2012 (Alverado and Piketty 2014). If one looks back at the one particular event that sparked the Arab Revolutions that began in 2011, it was immediate economic desperation coupled with a broader sense of economic hopelessness that caused an unknown Tunisian street vendor named Mohammed Bouazizi to set himself on fire.

Within democratic state formation itself, economic development is essential (Przeworski and Limongi 1997; Inglehart and Norris 2003, and Chang 2011). Economic development is a key factor in shifting attitudes. A previous chapter already referenced Ha-Joon Chang, who argued that there exists a great deal of historical evidence suggesting that economic development improves institutions, rather than the inverse.

> Today's rich countries acquired most of the institutions that today's dominant view considers to be prerequisites of economic development *after, not before, their economic development* –democracy, modern bureaucracy, IPRs, limited liability, bankruptcy law, banking, the central bank, securities regulation, and so on. (2011: 476)

This is to suggest that one cannot simply build effective and efficient institutions without some economic prosperity and development already in place.

Even if a "democratic" state replaces an authoritarian one, its survival is dependent on many different factors. Any developing state must seek exogenous sources of income in the form of foreign direct investment. A state in transition needs economic success, not only macro-level success, such as high GDP and large levels of foreign capital investment, but also micro-level success, such as individuals having a reasonable per capita income. Income inequality must be tackled. The landmark research of Adam Przeworski and Fernando Limongi found a strong correlation between individual economic achievement and democratic survival in regimes that were already democratic.

In their research, they found that "[t]hirty-two democracies spent 736 years with [personal] income above $6055, and not one collapsed, while thirty-nine out of sixty-nine democracies did fall in countries that were poorer" (Przeworski and Limongi 1997: 164). Their measure was based on the 1985 PPP in US dollars. If one adjusts the 1985 GDP per capita PPP amounts for inflation today, the corresponding dollar amount today would be around 13,400.87 USD. An Islamic governed state must promote economic justice, especially at the individual and local levels. For the sake of my argument, I am defining "economic justice" simply as meaning that adult male and female individuals, regardless of their ethnic or religious background, have fair access to the necessary financial resources to live a comfortable life.

Modern Islamist thinkers have also discussed the importance of economic justice. Rachid al-Ghannouchi makes clear the need for economic justice throughout his line of argumentation. Ghannouchi argues that since the beginnings of Islam, one of the state's primary functions was to protect those members of society who were socially and economically weakest, such as women and non-Muslims living within the state. He believes that *'adl* or justice is not an impossible dream; rather it is something that must be realized in a universal manner, transcending any particular religion or ethnicity within an Islamic governed state (Abdullah 1999). For Ghannouchi, it is incumbent upon an Islamic governed state to promote economic justice among its Muslims and non-Muslims citizens.

Ibn Khaldun on Basic Economic Principals

Earlier Islamic scholars did not have large datasets containing thousands of pieces of economic data at their disposal, nor did they have the advanced statistical computer program packages that would allow them engage in the same mathematical models and empirical statistical studies of economic systems the way contemporary scholars do today. However, these earlier scholars did understand many of the same basic economic principles that have still dominant debates among economists and political scientists today. One such example is that of Ibn Khaldun.

The basic ideas of Ibn Khaldun on economics are worth reconsidering when articulating some of the basic principles of a modern Islamic economic system. He represents a major figure within the Islamic tradition that most certainly meets Hallaq's criterion of being a "historical moral resource" for guidance that was discussed in Chap. 3. Today, Ibn Khaldun is primarily remembered as a great historian. However, he was also a great economist in his own right who was centuries ahead of his time in terms of originality. Jean David Boulakia argued that Ibn Khaldun "discovered the virtues and the necessity of a division of labor before Smith and the principle of labor value before Ricardo," and that he "elaborated a theory of population before Malthus and insisted on the role of the state on the economy before Keynes" (1971: 1117). Boulakia goes on to argue that "Without tools, without preexisting concepts, he elaborated a genial economic explanation of the world. His name should figure among the fathers of economic science" (1971: 1118).

Ibn Khaldun shared many similarities with the late Douglass North. Both argued that increasing specialization coupled with a clearly demarcated division of labor would result in institutional growth which would culminate in more complex political structures and cultural innovation (Khalid 2015). Like modern economists, Ibn Khaldun acknowledged that the transfer of wealth and power between individuals and governing bodies was essential to understanding the economic well-being of a state. "The finances of the dynasty, in turn, correspond to the wealth and number of the subjects. The origin of it all is civilization and its extensiveness" (Ibn Khaldun 1958: 291). Ibn Khaldun recognized the essential function of markets and the role governments play in commerce.

> If government business slumps and the volume of trade is small, the dependent markets will naturally show the same symptoms, and to a greater degree. Furthermore, money circulates between subjects and ruler, moving back and forth. Now if the ruler keeps it to himself, it is lost to the subjects. (1958: 103)

For Ibn Khaldun, irrational government spending and decadence ultimately led to the breakdown of the state. An ever widening "inner circle" of individuals, businesses, and special interests facilitates in the delegitimization of economic policy and government authority in general. As public funds continue to be squandered and misappropriated, the state quickly transitions into a kleptocracy, and the group that holds power becomes more firmly entrenched with the help of their cronies who they provided benefits to in the first place. The state begins to resemble a corrupt dynasty and begins to take on an increasingly despotic character. Ultimately, this means more money for friends and less money for the average citizen. According to Ibn Khaldun, when the ruler and his entourage stop spending, "business slumps and commercial profits decline because of the shortage of capital" (1958: 92).

Almost 600 years before, James Carville's internal memorandum that reminded the 1992 Clinton presidential campaign—"It's the economy, stupid"—became a part of American political vernacular; Ibn Khaldun understood the dangers of long-term economic stagnation and decline for regime survival. He believed that the state was responsible for raising the expectations of prospective entrepreneurs by implementing essential public works projects periodically to generate employment and build confidence. Such public works projects also would provide a means of employment for many lower skilled laborers. In order to promote stability, the state should build roads, bridges, trade centers, and other engage in other infrastructure-building-related activities that encourage production and trade. It is important to remember that Ibn Khaldun believed that an overly involved state in the market would result in negative economic growth and ultimately economic stagnation.

Ibn Khaldun also recognized the cyclical nature of economics. On his general theory of social systems, Dieter Weiss commented that; "In modern terms, he deals with processes that recur *cyclically* during relatively normal phases, but from time to time undergo sharp ruptures leading to fundamental changes of the system" (1995: 27). Ibn Khaldun divided income into three categories: salary, profit, and taxes, and offered an optimum level for each one of these categories. He was also realistic and realized that these optimum levels could not be permanently sustained. As a result, he realized that "cycles of the economic activity must occur" (Boulakia 1971: 1113). "Cycles of economic activity" can be understood today as a flexible monetary policy. Here, one can see a type of proto-Keynesianism in Ibn Khaldun's thought; the government should promote a mixed economy that is predominantly driven by the private sector, however there ought to be government intervention during recessions and in times of economic instability. This chapter will go on to argue that middle path between unbridled capitalism and a centralized economy should be the goal of a contemporary Islamic governed states' economic system. Such a middle path resonates well with Islam's general existential view that seeks to find a middle path between extremes.

Islam as the Middle Path

Islam is supposed to represent the moderate way of life. This point is repeated numerous times in the Qur'ān. Al–wasaṭiyyah implies moderation and balance; it lies between excessiveness (*ifrāṭ*) and laxity (*tafrīṭ*) and derives from the word '*wasaṭ*' which means middle, fair, or moderate. Perhaps the most well-known invocation of the notion of *wasaṭiyyah* occurs at the very beginning of the *Qur'ān*: "Thus We have appointed you a middle nation [*ummatan wasaṭan*], that ye may be witnesses against mankind [*shuhadā' 'alā al-nās*] and the messenger may be a witness against you…" (*Qur'ān*: 2: 143). The concept of *al-wasaṭiyyah* has been popularized by the likes of Muhammad Rashid Rida, Hasan al-Banna, and more recently, Yusuf al-Qaradawi and Mohammed Hashim Kamali. According to Ibn Kathir, *wasaṭ* "means the best and the most honored" (2003: 422). Kamali argues that *wasaṭiyyah* "is primarily a rational concept with little or no dogmatic connotations, but [it is] also religiously virtuous since the Qur'an has recommended it" (2015: 10). As Kamali notes, despite being primarily a rational concept, its meaning goes beyond merely referring to something physical; *wasaṭiyyah* has a normative dimension as well. *Wasaṭ, wuṣṭā*, and other similar words are referenced in numerous verses in the *Qur'ān* (See, *Qur'ān* 2:238, 5:89, 68:28, and 100:5).

The idea of *al-wasaṭiyyah* has also been utilized by more recent Islamic scholars in regard to Islamic economics; the notion of fairness and a concern for the common good—*al maṣlaha*—is a key feature of Islamic economics. Hasan al-Banna emphatically argued that "Any good economic system is welcomed by Islam, which urges the nation to promote it and puts no obstacles in its path" (2009: 67). The cold war years saw the emergence of two radically different economic dogmas that at numerous times nearly resulted in nuclear war. Iranian scholar, Sayyed Mujtaba Musavi Lari, in the 1970s wrote: "The rivalry for absolute power between these two ideologies hangs over the modern world with a menace like the sword of Damocles" (2011: 63). An Islamic economic system should not be shackled by ideological dogma. According to the Iraqi cleric, Ayatollah Mohammed Baqir al Sadr;

> Thus it [Islamic economics] lays down the principle of multifaceted ownership—that is ownership in a variety of forms—instead of the principle of only one kind of ownership, which capitalism and socialism have adopted. It believes in private ownership, public ownership, and state ownership.
> (al Sadr referenced in Euben and Zaman (Eds.), 2009: 187)

Islam economics recognize the necessity of different modes of ownership at different levels. Chang noted that certain industries operate more effectively and efficiently under communal, rather than private ownership. Many wealthy nations today such as France, Finland, Norway, and Taiwan have numerous, wealthy state-owned enterprises (SOEs) "that were not just efficient in the narrow allocative sense but also led to their country's economic growth process through technological dynamism and export successes" (Chang 2011: 480). It is the job of the state to appropriately determine which mode of ownership is appropriate for each level. Such ownership is "defined by clearly defined intellectual bases and rule, and which is put forward within a special framework of values and concepts" (al Sadr referenced in Euben and Zaman (Eds.), 2009: 187). Turkish scholar Murat Çizakça argues that;

> Providing the wealth is earned through halal means and spent on one's family's needs and for the good of the society, the Shari'ah approves of capital accumulation. Al-Ghazali even considers the acquisition of goods for the fulfillment of needs as a form of worship. Wealth, for instance, is needed for the fulfillment of the pilgrimage. [...] In short, Islamic capitalism allows accumulation of capital subject to ethical and voluntary self-controls and redistribution of wealth. (2007: 111)

Justice and fairness are at the core of the framework of values and concepts discussed by al-Sadr and Çizakça.

There is no reason to believe that Islam is opposed to private property or economic liberties. "Islam as a political ideology accepts the basic tenets of capitalism, such as the sanctity of private property, validity of debt contracts, and the legitimacy of commercial profits" (Üşenmez 2007: 216). Üşenmez goes on to argue, however, that Islamic political movements, especially in the case of Turkey, have actually become co-opted by neoliberal models of economic organization which have ultimately undermined autonomy and workers' rights. I agree with Üşenmez's broader position that unchecked neoliberal economic systems ultimately harm lower income workers and sustainable development. The working class and underclass must be protected in any viable Islamic political system. There is no reason to assume protecting workers and supporting labor unions is in some way fundamentally at odd with Islam's basic values.

Despite the general openness to different economic approaches, certain principles such as moderation and economic fairness have been present throughout Islam's history. Under the rule of 'Umar ibn Al-Khattāb, governors and other individuals in positions of authority were expected to live moderately and were held accountable for ill-gotten gains. ʿUmar even established a type of social welfare system which led to a reasonable minimal standard of living for everyone. Under his rule, the state even provided an annual stipend to the elderly and those who fought in previous battles (Hamid 2013). *Al-Khulafā'u ar-Rāshidūn* was one of the world's first welfare states (Crone 2005). The reforms introduced by ʿUmar ibn Al-Khattāb and his successor, ʿUthmān ibn ʿAffān, helped lead to economic prosperity for the nascent Islamic Empire. Al-Shāṭibī and Ibn Taymiyyah later engaged with similar topics (Choudhury and Malik 1992). Ibn Taymiyyah wrote about the need to regulate markets in his *Al-Ḥisba fī al-Islām*, and Al-Shāṭibī wrote about the need to prioritize the production and consumption of necessary goods over comfort goods in an effort to avoid waste and ostentatious displays of wealth in his *Al-Muwāfaqāt*.

Asad Zaman argues that "Islamic economics is neither positive, nor normative, but it is transformative" (2015: 6). Unlike secular economic models, Islamic models seek "to change society, and all individuals within society, towards an ideal" (Zaman 2013: 48). The transformative ideal Zaman alludes to is one in which compassion and justice take priority over profits; "Compassion and concern for all human beings and passionate engagement in improving their lot is a central teaching of Islam" (2013: 49). Neo-classical economics, much like liberal politics, prioritize the individual over the community. Islamic economics stresses cooperation and harmony and has a deep concern with internal satisfaction beyond just observable empirical outputs, such as cash or property.

Two major obstacles that have historically hindered all economic systems are widespread poverty and high levels of inequality. The overall accountability of political leadership in most Arab states has been minimal for a very long time now. Over the past century, "direct political accountability were eschewed with the result that dissatisfaction could be expressed and accountability exerted only by indirect means" (Waterbury 1997: 142). The "indirect means" of expression often utilized by those living in Arab states included sabotaging machines and essential equipment within the workplace and the shirking of responsibilities, which only further exacerbated patterns of low productivity and economic stagnation. It is a well-known fact that many Middle Eastern autocrats for generations have lived lavish and decadent lifestyles much to the chagrin of their citizenry and the rest of the world at large. Such inequality fosters hopelessness, and as we can see with the Arab uprisings of 2011, ultimately revolution.

Islam very early developed a notion of economics based on Aristotelian thought. "At its heart was a notion of property circulated and purified, in part, through charity. Thus did donors imitate God, who made a gift of his surplus *(faḍl)* and sustenance *(rizq)*, without ever expecting it to be returned" (Bonner 2005: 392). At the core of economic justice within an Islamic framework is the idea of individual spiritual growth and Enlightenment. In the words of Zaman, "Muslims struggle for justice, equitable economic outcomes, etc. because such struggles will bring about an inner spiritual transformation" (2009: 526). Islam directly addresses the question of social justice within the framework of its five pillars.[1] One of those pillars is *zakāt*.

In the *Qur'ān*, the importance of the *zakāt* or religiously mandated alms-giving (or "poor-tax") that every able citizen must pay cannot be ignored or downplayed. In Arabic, *zakāt* literally means "that which purifies" and its proper timely payment is seen as a major virtue. In regard to spending in the way of charity, the *Qur'ān* states "The likeness of those who spend their wealth in Allah's way is as the likeness of a grain which groweth seven ears, in every ear a hundred grains. Allah giveth increase manifold to whom He will. Allah is All-Embracing, All-Knowing" (*Qur'ān*, 2:261). An interesting point about *zakāt* that is often forgotten today is that during the life of the Prophet Mohammed (ﷺ), neither he nor his descendants were allowed to receive any of that money—these funds were only meant for the poor and the needy. This set an important precedent; the ruler of an Islamic governed state is not supposed to take public monies for personal use. From the very beginning of Islam, the leadership has been held to a standard of economic integrity that very few leaders today could attest to. *Sūrah* 9:60 states unequivocally;

> The alms are only for the poor and the needy, and those who collect them, and those whose hearts are to be reconciled, and to free the captives and the debtors, and for the cause of Allah, and (for) the wayfarer; a duty imposed by Allah. Allah is Knower, Wise. (*Qur'ān*, 9:60)

It is not meant to be abused or squandered on projects cloaked in the language of "urban development" that really are meant to line the pockets of a particular entrepreneur or government official.

While the *zakāt* is one of the five inviolable pillars of Islam, it is not enough to ensure a functioning society with a safety net for all citizens.

Larger scale economic reforms must support increased equality in the long term. Redistributive thought has been common throughout many parts of the Muslim world for decades now (Kaminski 2012). The Soviet Union had a great deal of influence throughout the 1970s and 1980s in numerous domestic issues in Middle Eastern and Central Asian countries. Numerous treaties and agreements between the Soviet Union and places such as Iraq and Afghanistan attest to this fact. One must remember, however, that there is a major difference between Islamic- and Marxist-influenced economic approaches in regard to what metaphysical outcomes are prioritized. All traditional Marxist-based economic systems emphasize material ends over spiritual or metaphysical ends (Marx 1977, and Bronner 1999). Unlike Marxist-influenced systems, an Islamic economic system prioritizes spiritual ends. The material gains of any economic system within an Islamic worldview are a *means* to a spiritual end and not *the end*, in of itself.

This is not to suggest material comfort is somehow *UnIslamic*; quite the opposite actually is true. Islam openly condemns the type of monasticism that many movements with Christianity have embraced over the centuries.

> Then We caused Our messengers to follow in their footsteps; and We caused Jesus, son of Mary, to follow, and gave him the Gospel, and placed compassion and mercy in the hearts of those who followed him. But monasticism they invented - We ordained it not for them - only seeking Allah's pleasure, and they observed it not with right observance. So We give those of them who believe their reward, but many of them are evil-livers. (*Qur'ān*, 57:27)

Another quote from the *Qur'ān* on this matter states;

> Say: Who hath forbidden the adornment of Allah which He hath brought forth for His bondmen, and the good things of His providing? Say: Such, on the Day of Resurrection, will be only for those who believed during the life of the world. Thus do we detail Our revelations for people who have knowledge. (*Qur'ān*, 7:33)

Muslims are commanded to enjoy those things Allah has made lawful for them and to avoid that which is explicitly unlawful. There is no reason why any Islamic system cannot embrace redistributive economic approaches, yet still promote private property ownership within a communitarian ethical framework that prioritizes social accountability.

The twentieth and twenty-first centuries have shown that totalitarian communist states are not viable, nor are they widely supported by the masses. This is true even among the most extremist Islamic figures. Many cold war era veterans of the Soviet invasion of Afghanistan, who are currently engaging in violent terrorist-related activities against the Western powers, remain steadfast in their opposition to "Godless" Communism. Anwar al-Awlaki (2006) was as critical of Soviet Communism, and he was of US capitalism and imperialism. The twenty-first-century Islamic economies must be regulated to prevent corruption, but at the same time promote entrepreneurship and growth. The Soviet Union showed the inherent limitations of a centrally planned economy; it could not out produce Western competitors, promote enough innovation, or create sustainable growth domestically (Rutland 1985, 1993, and Sakwa 1998). This example does not, however, disprove the necessity of regulations on industry and trade.

Harry Targ recently has discussed the need for developing states to adopt modified models of socialist economic systems if they are to succeed that allow for regulated marketplaces. In regard to Cuba and Vietnam, Targ comments that;

> With the collapse of state socialism as a world force and the shift virtually everywhere to neoliberal economic policies, Vietnamese and Cubans came to the realization that transitioning to 21st century socialism would require the construction of a more complicated economic model that continued to support a renovated state sector, allowed a regulated marketplace, and encouraged local socialist forms, such as workers cooperatives. (Targ, 2013: *online*)

He notes that both of these states have begun to adapt to the changing world historical landscape. The model of socialism presented by Targ does not adhere to any dogmatic interpretation of Marxism or any other economic system. It offers a nuanced understanding of need to balance the private and public sectors in a way that promotes growth and fairness in a way that prevents one from trumping the other. Such an approach to economics would be ideal for developing countries in the Muslim world. Ayatollah Khomeini's popularized slogan *"nah sharqī, nah gharbī, jumhūrī-i Islāmī"* (neither East, nor West, Islamic Republic) offers a contemporary precedent for conceptualizing a unique discursive framework that fits within the more general Islamic notion of *wasaṭiyyah*, even if in practice such rhetoric has not actually met this standard. The main point this section seeks to make is that an Islamic governed state cannot simply graft onto itself a particular Western economic model without taking into consideration a multitude of other factors unique not only to Islam, but also to that particular state.

Usury and Islam

There are certain key considerations that must be taken in modeling a genuinely *Islamic* economy. For example, in the *Qur'ān*, usury or *ribā* is categorically forbidden. It is hard to imagine living in a world without usury, but it is a categorical demand from Allah that comes directly from the *Qur'ān*.

> Those who swallow usury cannot rise up save as he ariseth whom the devil hath prostrated by (his) touch. That is because they say: Trade is just like usury; whereas Allah permitteth trading and forbiddeth usury. He unto whom an admonition from his Lord cometh, and (he) refraineth (in obedience thereto), he shall keep (the profits of) that which is past, and his affair (henceforth) is with Allah. As for him who returneth (to usury) - Such are rightful owners of the Fire. They will abide therein. (*Qur'ān*, 2:275)

Usury was considered one of the "seven great destructive sins" according to the Prophet Mohammed (ﷺ).

> Abu Huraira narrated that the Prophet said: Avoid the seven great destructive sins. They (the people) asked: O Allah's Apostle! What are they? He said: To join partners in worship with Allah; to practice sorcery; to kill the life which Allah has forbidden except for a just cause (according to Islamic law); to consume riba, to consume the property of an orphan; to give one's back to the enemy and fleeing from the battlefield at the time of fighting, and to accuse chaste women who never even think of anything which violates chastity and are good believers. (*Ṣaḥīḥ al-Bukhārī*, #4061)

According to this *ḥadīth*, *ribā* is on the same level of destructiveness as murder and adultery. If one simply looks at contemporary examples of financial corruption and their impact on global affairs, this is certainly not an issue to take lightly. There are Islamic banking systems that currently exist that make efforts to avoid this *ḥarām* practice. This is one of the key features of an Islamic banking system that differentiates it from other banking systems. Zaman describes Islamic banking as a system in which "lenders must participate in the risks of business, in order to earn a reward. Thus, collateral for business loans cannot be seized in the event of business failure? That is, Shylock cannot get his pound of flesh if the ships of Antonio sink" (Zaman 2009: 543). Zaman notes that the main end, in theory, for an Islamic banking system is spiritual growth and fulfillment rather than just profits. At the core of an Islamic system of economics is justness. "If God is *al-'Adl* (justness), as per the Qur'ān (6:115), man's theomorphism could not be divorced from that Divine attribute. In the affairs of man, this dimension essentially relates to his participation in the collective existence" (Azhar 2009: 128). Since man is modeled after God, man must do as best he can to apply the divine attributes of God.

A concern for the *al maṣlaḥa* is incumbent upon any system of Islamic governance. The common good must be defined broadly and seek to benefit society in general. It also must not be in contradiction of the *Qur'ān* and *Sunnah* (Ramadan 2006). *Economic fairness is Islam is a moral category*. The rules for economic justice are spelled out in the basic principles of Islamic jurisprudence. "Islamic jurisprudence is filled with rules for financial transactions, and it has given them in such minute detail as to obviate further elaboration" (Al-Banna 2009: 67). At the heart of these rules mentioned by al-Banna is the centrality in an Islamic economic system to promote justice and fairness. Justice and fairness is a two-way street in Islam; the state must act justly in economic decisions, but the people must also take personal responsibility for being just and fair themselves. Individual responsibility, in this regard, is actually prior to collective responsibility. "What is significant at this stage of the argument is that in Islam, the idea of collective responsibility is made subservient to the idea of individual responsibility, for it could not be otherwise in a Divinely ordained system" (Azhar 2009: 131). This helps address the free-rider problem (Olson 2002). One cannot simply latch on the system like a parasite and collect its benefits. One has a moral obligation to make a contribution to the collective, or at least to try if they are mentally and physically capable.

Conclusion

Andrew March astutely commented that "Islam does bequeath a powerful political impulse, but this prevents neither Islam itself from changing nor Muslims from assimilating a variety of novel values and desires in politics" (2015: 174). Islamic political and social structures must constantly adapt for their own contemporary circumstances.

> Every age and every generation has the task of implementing the message of Islam in new forms and by new means. There are immutable Islamic principles which order relations between people, but there is no Islamic economic, social, or political structure which cannot be changed. (Izetbegović 1990: 31)

Chapters 3–7 sought to address a few key issues. These chapters showed that an Islamic political discourse cannot be conceived in the same way as Western liberal democracies are conceived. The foundation of the Islamic governed state is based on revelation. Ancient political thought is more conducive in conceptualizing an Islamic governed state than modern thought. Islamic governed states must strive to have wise and incorruptible leadership that still has restraints. Simply having a government "organized in the name of Islam" does not in of itself guarantee justice. It is important to remember, as Feldman reminds us, "a government organized in the name of Islam can be as constitutionally corrupt as a secular autocracy, and so may find itself equally unpopular with its citizens" (2008: 147). Modernizing bureaucratic institutions, ensuring democratic participation, and actively seeking to include women and minority groups in the political apparatus are all at the forefront of adequately theorizing the modern Islamic governed state. According to Khan, "The key features of Islamic governance that I have found in Islamic sources—Quran and the Prophetic precedence (Sunnah), and contemporary Muslim discussions on the Islamic State—are Constitution, Consent, and Consultation." (2014: 96) Promoting economic justice is also essential in an authentic Islamic governed state. Achieving this "will require a public financial system that is transparent both in terms of budgetary and nonbudgetary components and that can be scrutinized in order for citizens to hold officials accountable for their actions" (Amin, et al. 2012, 48). Without such transparency and accountability, economic justice will never be reached in any Islamic governed state.

One point that cannot be forgotten is that economic growth cannot be the only goal for modern emerging Muslim states. The 2011 World Happiness Report argues that overall citizen "happiness" is based on a combination of factors.

> A household's income counts for life satisfaction, but only in a limited way. Other things matter more: community trust, mental and physical health, and the quality of governance and rule of law. Raising incomes can raise happiness, especially in poor societies, but fostering cooperation and community can do even more, especially in rich societies that have a low marginal utility of income. It is no accident that the happiest countries in the world tend to be high-income countries that also have a high degree of social equality, trust, and quality of governance. (Helliwell et al. 2011: 8)

This report nicely sums up the key factors in establishing a functioning state with a content population. Muslim countries should not only strive to raise incomes, but also have high levels of community trust, mental and physical health, and quality governance. In the words of Joseph Stiglitz; "Development is about transforming the lives of people, not just transforming economies. Policies for education or employment need to be looked at through this double lens: how they promote growth and how they affect individuals directly" (2006: 50). The report concludes that sustainable development goals for all nations should be based on four central pillars: ending extreme poverty, environmental sustainability, social inclusion, and good governance. All of the aforementioned concepts discussed in this particular report and this chapter can be done while remaining firmly within the framework of the *Qur'ān* and the *Sunnah* of the Prophet (ﷺ).

The remaining chapters in this book will be contemporary case studies. It is important to look at real world examples when articulating a model of an Islamic governed state. Albeit in a context much different than a practical theory of Islamic governance, Antonio Gramsci famously made the point in the early twentieth century that philosophy completely detached from history and politics is nothing more than metaphysics. This project is meant to be practical. The cases explored in these upcoming chapters will give concreteness to the theoretical model offered thus far in this project.

None of the cases chosen are necessarily "Islamic governed states," but nonetheless, they all do have Islamic political parties and movements that do directly engage in local and national politics. They all offer something to the more general discourse surrounding Islamic governance that was offered in the first half of this work. These next few chapters will look at contemporary states in the Muslim world and explore what can be drawn from these states that would useful to consider when reconceptualizing a contemporary Islamic governed state based on the model offered thus far in this work. Despite the fact that each state has its own unique particularities, I still remain confident that some general principles can be derived from each case explored.

NOTE

1. *The five pillars of Islam* are considered the foundation of the faith; they are *Shahadah*, which means to assert with sincere intent that there is "No God but God, and Mohammed is the Prophet of God"; *ṣalāt*, which is the obligatory prayers each Muslim is expected to offer; *zakāt*, which is the poor tax all capable Muslims are expected to pay; *Ḥajj*, which is the once in a lifetime pilgrimage to Mecca that all able-bodied and financially capable Muslims are expected to make; and the observation of the obligatory month long fast between sunrise and sunset during the month of *Ramaḍān* which all capable Muslims are to observe.

REFERENCES

Abdullah, Saeed. 1999. Rethinking citizenship rights of non-Muslims in an Islamic state: Rashid al-Ghannushi's contribution to the evolving debate. *Islam and Christian-Muslim Relations* 10 (3): 307–323.
al-Awlaki, Anwar. 2006. Allah is Preparing us for Victory, Parts I and II. [Audio podcast]. http://www.sendspace.com/file/ls3oa9 and http://www.sendspace.com/file/ov2c7b. Accessed on May 8, 2013.
al-Banna, Hassan. 2009. Toward the light. In *Princeton readings in Islamist thought*, ed. R. Euben, and M. Zaman, 56–78. Princeton, NJ: Princeton University Press.
al-Sadr, Mohammed Baqir. 2009. The general framework of the Islamic economy. In *Princeton readings in Islamist thought*, ed. R. Euben, and M. Zaman, 186–206. Princeton, NJ: Princeton University Press.
Alverado, Facundo and Thomas Piketty. 2014. Measuring top incomes and inequality in the Middle East: Data limitations and illustration with the case of Egypt. Economic Research Forum Working Paper Series, Working Paper No. 832. 1–45.

Amin, Magdi, et al. 2012. *After the spring: Economic transitions in the Arab world*. New York: Oxford University Press.
Azhar, Rauf A. 2009. *Economics of an Islamic economy*. Leiden: Brill E-Books.
Bonner, Michael. 2005. Poverty and economics in the Qur'an. *Journal of Interdisciplinary History* 35 (3): 391–406.
Boulakia, Jean David. 1971. Ibn Khaldûn: A fourteenth-century economist. *Journal of Political Economy* 79 (5): 1105–1118.
Bronner, Stephen E. 1999. *Ideas in action: Political tradition in the 20th century*. New York: Rowman & Littlefield Publishers.
Chang, Ha-Joon. 2011. Institutions and economic development: Theory, policy and history. *Journal of Institutional Economics* 7 (4): 473–498.
Choudhury, Masudul A., and Uzir Malik. 1992. *The foundations of Islamic political economy*. New York: Palgrave.
Çizakça, Murat. 2007. Democracy, economic development, and *maqāsid al-Sharī'ah*. *Review of Islamic Economics* 11 (1): 101–118.
Crone, Patricia. 2005. *Medieval Islamic political thought*. Edinburgh, UK: Edinburgh University Press.
Feldman, Noah. 2008. *The fall and rise of the Islamic state*. Princeton, NJ: Princeton Press.
Hamid, Shadi. 2013. An Islamic alternative? equality, redistributive justice, and the welfare state in the caliphate of Umar. *Renaissance: Monthly Islamic Journal, 13*. http://www.monthly-renaissance.com/issue/PrintVersion.aspx?id=355. Accessed on October 30, 2016.
Helliwell, John, Richard Layard, and Jeffrey Sachs. 2011. *World happiness report*. New York: The Earth Institute Columbia University.http://www.earth.columbia.edu/sitefiles/file/Sachs%20Writing/2012/World%20Happiness%20Report.pdf. Accessed on October 30, 2016.
Ibn Kathir. 2003. *Tafsir ibn Kathir* (Abridged Vol. 1). Saifur-Rahman al-Mubarakpuri (Trans.). Houston, TX: Dar-us-salaam.
Ibn Khaldun. 1958. Muqaddimah of Ibn Khaldun, (An Introduction to History). Franz Rosenthal (Trans.). Princeton, NJ: Princeton University Press.
Inglehart, Ronald, and Pippa Norris. 2003. The true clash of civilizations. *Foreign Policy* 135: 62–70.
Izetbegović, Alija. 1990. The Islamic declaration: A programme for the Islamization of Muslims and Muslim peoples. Sarajevo.
Kamali, Mohammad H. 2015. *The middle path of moderation in Islam: The Qur'ānic principle of wasaṭiyyah*. New York: Oxford Press.
Kaminski, Joseph J. 2012. The importance of historical understanding: Evaluating the strengths and weaknesses of the current counter-narcotics strategy in Afghanistan. *Review of International Law and Politics* 8 (29): 109–141.

Khalid, Haniza. 2015. The role of institutions in driving economic change: Comparing the thoughts of Ibn Khaldūn and Douglass C. North. *Intellectual Discourse* 23 (2): 177–199.

Khan, M.A. Muqtedar. 2014. "What is Islamic Democracy? The 3 Cs of Islamic Governance," in T., Poirson and R. Oprisko (eds.), *Caliphates and Global Islamic Politics.* 94–99. E-International Relations Publications.

Lari, Sayyed Mujtaba Musavi. 2011. *Western civilization through Muslim eyes.* F.J. Goulding (Trans.). Qom, Iran: Al-Hadi Press.

March, Andrew. 2015. Political Islam: Theory. *Annual Review of Political Science* 18: 103–123.

Marx, Karl. 1977. *A contribution to the critique of political economy.* Moscow: Progress Publishers.

Olson, Mancur. 2002. *The logic of collective action.* Cambridge, MA: Harvard Press.

Przeworski, Adam, and Fernando Limongi. 1997. Modernization: Theories and facts. *World Politics* 49 (2): 155–183.

Qur'ān. 2001. *The meaning of the glorious Qur'an.* Mohammed Pickthall (Trans.). New York: Alavi Foundation.

Ramadan, Tariq. 2006. Ijtihad and maslaha: Foundations of governance. In *Islamic democratic discourse*, ed. Muqtedar Khan, 3–20. Lanham, MD: Lexington Books.

Rutland, Peter. 1993. *The politics of economic stagnation in the Soviet Union: The role of local party organs in economic management.* Cambridge, UK: Cambridge University Press.

Rutland, Peter. 1985. *The myth of the plan: Lessons from the Soviet planning experience.* London, UK: Hutchinson and Co. Ltd.

Ṣaḥīḥ al-Bukhārī. 2002. Compiled by Muhammed bin Ismail Bukhari M., Matraji, and F. A. Z. Matraji (Eds.). vol. 9. New Delhi, India: Islamic Book Services.

Sakwa, Richard. 1998. *Soviet politics: In perspective*, 2nd ed. New York: Routledge.

Stiglitz, Joseph E. 2006. *Making globalization work.* New York: W.W. Norton & Company.

Targ, Harry. 2013. *Transitional Steps to a Socialist Future: Part 1, the Vietnam Case.* The Labor and Working—Class Studies Project, Working Class Studies Association. Madison College. Madison, Wisconsin. 12–15 June, 2013.

Üşenmez, Özgür. 2007. Backlash: A neo-Gramscian approach to the rise of political Islam in Turkey. Ph.D. Dissertation. City University of New York- Graduate Center.

Waterbury, John. 1997. From social contracts to extraction contracts. In *Islam, democracy, and the state in North Africa*, ed. J. Entilis, et al., 141–176. Bloomington, IN: Indiana University Press.

Weiss, Dieter. 1995. Ibn Khaldun on economic transformation. *International Journal of Middle East Studies* 27 (1): 29–37.

Zaman, Asad. 2009. Islamic economics: a survey of the literature: II. Islamic Studies 48 (4): 525–566.

Zaman, Asad. 2015. Crisis in Islamic economics: Diagnosis and prescriptions. In *Islamic economic: Theory, policy and social justice*, ed. H.A. El-Karanshawy, et al., 1–11. Doha, Qatar: Bloomsbury Qatar Foundation.

Zaman, Asad. 2013. *Islamic economics: A survey of the literature*. Islamabad, Pakistan: IRI Press.

PART II

Case Studies in the Contemporary Muslim World

CHAPTER 8

The Case of Turkey: Soft Power and Economic Growth

INTRODUCTION

The case of Turkey and its current government under the leadership of President Recep Tayyip Erdoğan is a very interesting and relevant case to discuss when considering this model of a contemporary Islamic governed state for many reasons. Turkey is a regional and global power and its economic growth over the past decade is undeniable. "Turkey relies on its role in regional and international security, its impressive economic growth and regional political clout to spread its message and its positive image" (Ennis and Momani 2013: 1128). While many economies have been unable to recover from the 2008 global financial recession, the Turkish economy expanded by 9.2% in 2010 and 8.5% in 2011, even though things have gotten noticeably worse over the past couple years. Until very recently, Turkey was one of the fastest growing economies in Europe, and one of the fastest growing economies in the world. In 2012, Turkey's credit rating went up because of its established economic strength. "Fitch upgraded Turkey's long-term foreign currency Issuer Default Rating (IDR) to 'BBB−' from 'BB+' and the Long-term local currency IDR to 'BBB' from 'BB+'. The outlooks on the long-term ratings are stable" (Butler 2012: *online*). In 2013, Moody's also raised their rating of Turkey government bond ratings to the lowest investment grade Baa3, which is a major improvement from its previous non-investment grade/junk bond long-term investment rating.

The Justice and Development Party (AKP) and Soft Power

Erdoğan's election in 2003 as the 36th Prime Minister of the Republic of Turkey ushered in a major shift from the previous Turkish mode of international politics that could be best characterized as submissive engagement with Western powers, often at the expense of historical regional allies. Turkey's new strategy emphasized soft power and diplomacy.

> What continues to set Turkey somewhat apart from these other ascending geopolitical players is that it has staked its claims to regional and global influence partly through its foreign minister's articulation of a clear vision of world order that includes an explicit emphasis on soft power instruments of diplomacy combined with an enunciated resolve to minimize hard power tactics of threat of and recourse to force to resolve international conflicts. (Falk 2013: 355–356)

While the charismatic Erdoğan and AKP (*Adalet ve Kalkınma Partisi*) have altered Turkey's political discourse in a more Islamic-oriented manner over the past decade, the real intellectual inspiration behind the Turkey's geopolitical strategy at the turn of the century was its previous Prime Minister, Ahmet Davutoğlu.

Before entering into politics, Davutoğlu was a Professor of Political Science at Marmara University. His most prominent work is titled *Stratejik derinlik: Türkiye'nin uluslararsi Konumu* (2001), and it undeniably plays a major role in contemporary Turkish foreign policy.[1] It offers a vision of a Turkish state that reasserts itself in global affairs as an autonomous actor, without the same dependency on the West that it had for decades. The renowned international relations expert, Richard Falk, on the merits of Davutoğlu's *magnum opus* comments;

> The book sets forth lucidly the conceptual framework for rethinking the Turkish approach to foreign policy in a manner sensitive to the pulls and opportunities of economic globalization as well as to the pitfalls and opportunities associated with traditional state-centric diplomacy. (2013: 361–362)

He goes on to argue that, "Davutoğlu has provided coherent public explanations for Turkey's policy positions that have been consistently informed by a deep historical, cultural, and strategic understanding" (Falk 2013: 362). Davutoğlu's affinities for Turkey's historical and cultural tradition should not be understood as a subtle signal that his foreign policy agenda was inherently anti-American or anti-West. He openly declared support for Turkey's entry into the EU. In an official statement on Turkey's Ministry of Foreign Affairs Web site as recently as 2015, he commented that;

> We are of the opinion that Turkey deserves EU membership and [the] international system needs, more than ever, Turkey as an EU member. An EU including Turkey will have a strong voice in the world affairs and will be more effective. (T.C. Dişişeri Baklanliği website 2015a: *online*)

Secularists and Kemalists have tried to label his approach as *Neo-Ottomanism*, a term which he fervently denies. "There is no common identity that drives both the JDP's [AKP] domestic agenda and its foreign policy; rather, a unique "strategic identity" blends both ideology and Realpolitik" (Kardaş 2010: 123). Turkey's twenty-first-century foreign policy has thus far been much more complicated than reductionist explanations that simply claim that Turkey is now run by Neo-Ottoman revivalists with a romantic desire for a return to the days of Sultan's and *Paşa's*.

> Turkey's assertive new foreign policy is the product of a unique combination of factors: the reconfiguration of power power relations in the international and regional systems, transformations in Turkish domestic politics, the agency and identity of the ruling elite, and public opinion. (Kardaş 2010: 117)

In comments that appeared in 2009 in the popular Turkish Publication, *Daily Sabah*, on the topic of Neo-Ottomanism, Davutoğlu made it clear that he saw Turkey as a nation-state that was equal with any other nation-state in the Balkans region. He also explicitly noted that Turkey does not seek hegemony or domination over anyone and that his government only seeks to contribute to the establishment of a lasting peace in the region: "We are trying to establish an order and such a thing [an attempt] is not wrong. Yet we are trying to establish it in a modern framework and around the parameters of the equality of nation-states"[2]

(Batur 2009: *online*). Turkey's regional security is dependent upon regional peace and stability.

Turkey's desire for global stability and peace should not be seen as a sign of capitulation and genuflection to the West, however. In recent times, Turkey has certainly been willing to go against the will of the Western powers regarding some of their foreign policy decisions which have included staunch support for the Palestinian cause. In an address to the UN General Assembly while Prime Minister, Davutoğlu on the topic Palestinian statehood boldly stated;

> We are all aware that the right of the Palestinians to a State has been unfortunately denied for decades. The denial of this right to the Palestinians has no justification on any grounds, be it moral, political or legal. Last year, the Palestinian President Mahmoud Abbas made the application for Palestine for U.N. membership. Unfortunately the application has been left unanswered at the Security Council. Here comes the second chance. We call on the international community, the members of this August body, to honor their already belated obligation to the Palestinians and grant them the status of a "non-member state." It is high time for all of us to uphold the universal values of justice and dignity. (Davutoğlu UN Speech 2012: *online*)

The "New Turkey" showed moral support for the Morsi led Egyptian Muslim Brotherhood government. It also long maintained its own stance of non-direct intervention in regards to getting involved in the battle against ISIS out of well-founded strategic self-defense and internal security-based reasons, until finally being forced to take action in July 2015 because multiple incursions inside of Turkey by both ISIS and PKK [*Partiya Karkerên Kurdistanê*] terrorists.[3] Turkey's previous long-standing policy of non-direct intervention was a part of its *Zero Problems with Neighbours Policy*. "The 'Zero Problems with Neighbours policy' revitalized its Ottoman legacy but also attempted to increase interdependence with Arab neighbours and minimize any negative spill-overs" (Ennis and Momani 2013: 1129). This policy sought to reengage former allies and other Arab states in a less hostile, more open and diplomatic manner. It was a major reversal from decades of tense relations with its neighbors at the hands of Kemalist political elites and the Turkish military.

Turkey has not limited its regional engagement to only Arab states and traditional allies. Turkey has also played a pivotal role in bringing order and sustainability to Somalia over the past few years. According to Mehmet Özkan, since 2011;

> Turkey provided Somalia with essential infrastructure projects. Turkey built field hospitals, giving doctors the much-needed medical infrastructure to care for approximately one 1200 patients daily. Also, a hospital with a 200-bed capacity was opened. The Turkish Cooperation and Coordination Agency (TIKA) cooperated with the State Hydraulic Works (DSI) to drill wells, providing for the water needs of one hundred and twenty six thousand people, in a country struggling with drought. And an Agricultural School was opened in Somalia to educate Somalis on how to prevent drought and foster awareness of the richness of their land. (2014: 23)

Turkey's efforts in Somalia have been generally promising despite recent setbacks. While other nations provided aid in terms of security, Turkey provided direct aid in regard to the most tangible things that all Somalis deal with on a daily basis. Turkish aid focused on promoting sustainable development, especially in the areas of health, agriculture, and education. This has strengthened Turkey's relations with Somalia and also can serve as an example for other nations in handling humanitarian crises in Africa.

Turkey's reengagement with its regional neighbors does not, however, imply uncritical acceptance of injustices committed by these same neighbors. Turkey has been highly critical of the brutal civil war led by Basher al-Assad on his own people. On Turkey's support for the Syrian refugees, Davutoğlu at an *iftār* dinner in Gaziantep (an area rife with Syrian refugees) said: "We will stand by the Syrian people until the end of this oppression, until Syrian people regardless of their religion, sect and ethnic origin live with honor and in peace in all around Syria. Our support will continue" (T.C. Dişişeri Baklanlığı website 2015c: *online*). Most recently, Turkey has been supporting the Free Syria Army rebel group with weapons and ground troop support in its efforts to defeat ISIS. In a matter of hours, Turkey was able to liberate parts of Jarablus and Dabiq from years of brutal ISIS occupation—feats neither the Russians nor the American's ever even came close to achieve throughout the course of their inept carpet bombing campaigns.

As of March 2015, Turkey had already welcomed around 1.7 million Syrian refugees since the beginning of the Syrian civil war levied by Assad on his own people. On the quality of a recently built refugee camp in

Kobani, located right on the Syrian border, a UNHCR report comments that "The tented camp, one of 24 built by the government for refugees (currently 230,000) across Turkey, is essentially a well-run and safe small town with shops, restaurants, a school under construction, water distribution network, electricity, fire station and more" (UNHCR 2015: *online*). The Kobani camp serves as a model for future camps that might sadly need to be built in Turkey because of the ongoing Syrian civil war.

Going back to the earlier model discussed in this book, Turkey has most certainly been effective in recent times at asserting its autonomy and independence from the former European colonial powers. This has been one of the main points of most all twenty-first-century scholars' writings on Islamic governance: the critical importance of autonomy and national self-determination. "Turkish motivations are to be a role model in the region for Arab states to emulate, particularly on the question of how to be a responsible Islamist, democratic and economically successful government in the global community" (Ennis and Momani 2013: 1128). It has not allowed colonial powers to dictate its foreign and domestic affairs like many other states in the Muslim world have recently done. While Turkey has not outright rejected many of the ideas proposed by the Western powerbrokers, it no longer will uncritically be told what to do by them either.

Turkey's efforts to reconnect with their former allies are an important step in building solidarity among other Muslim nations. "From involvement in the Mashreq to investment and partnership in the Arabian Peninsula, Turkey is brandishing its economic influence" (Ennis and Momani 2013: 1139). Turkey has also been investing in places outside the Arabian Peninsula and Africa as well. One such example is in the Balkans.

> Let's take a quick survey of some of the major Turkish investments in various countries of the region. Through the Turkcell telecommunications company, Turkey has managed to buy and become a major shareholder of Telekom Srbija; well-known Turkish construction companies have managed to win a tender to build a 445-kilometer-long highway in Serbia linking Belgrade with Bar in Montenegro; a Free Trade Agreement (FTA) was signed between two countries; and there was even some discussion about Turks buying Serbia's national carrier, JAT Airways. Turkey has long been in the banking industry of Bulgaria, Serbia, Bosnia, Albania and

Macedonia. For instance, Ziraat Bankası and IK Bank (a sister company of Halk Bank) are well-established banking systems in Macedonia, while TEB (Türk Ekonomi Bankası) is already among the key players of Kosovo's banking industry. (Idriz 2011: *online*)[4]

As mentioned by Idriz, Turkey has also made significant investments in the war-torn Balkan nation of Bosnia and Herzegovina. Bosnia and Herzegovina, historically the European westernmost Ottoman-administered territory, has openly welcomed Turkish investment in its struggling economy.

Turkey has invested around 80 million Euros in Bosnia and Herzegovina for many important industrial-, cultural-, and infrastructure-related projects. This money has gone toward building hydroelectric power plants, bridges, hospitals, and very urgently needed housing and road reconstruction projects. "Turkey is ranked 9th in the list of direct foreign investors of Bosnia and Herzegovina. Large private companies manufacturing, glass, paper and packaging materials, made a wide range of investments in Bosnia and Herzegovina" (T.C. Dişişeri Baklanliği website 2015b). Turkish Airlines, ranked fifth in the world and number one in all of Europe in 2014 according to the Passengers Choice Awards, has helped bridge the two nations with deep historical ties. As this manuscript is being prepared, one can get a direct flight twice daily from Sarajevo to Istanbul on Turkish Airlines for less than 100 Euros. This is another concrete example of Turkey's economic success in the past decade and the increasing investment by Turkish companies in Bosnia and Herzegovina.

The year 2015 was especially fruitful for Bosnian–Turkish cultural exchange. Turkish aid assisted in refurbishing crumbling streets in Sarajevo's historic Baščaršija district, it renovated the oldest Turkish bath in Sarajevo, Isa-beg Hamam, and it provided the support necessary to rebuild the historic *Emperor's Masjid* that was originally built in the fifteenth century by Isa-Beg Ishaković (İshakoğlu İsa Bey) that suffered extensive damage during the 1992–1995 Bosnian War. Turkey also donated five much-needed street-trams to the Sarajevo public transportation operator GRAS.

Democracy, Bureaucratic Modernity, and Turkey

Despite recent setbacks which can be largely attributed to the increasing security concerns that come with being situated in an incredibly rough neighborhood that includes ISIS, Al-Qaeda, various Kurdish militant/terrorist groups, Syria, Iraq, Iran, and the most recent problem, Russia, Turkey was more democratic during the early years of AKP rule. During the AKP's first term in power, Paul Kubicek noted that;

> They touched on issues such as expanding freedom of expression and association, minority (including Kurdish and non-Muslim) rights, strengthening gender equality, a ban on the death penalty and antitorture laws, and curtailing the prerogatives of the military. (2015: 66)

Things have not been as positive over the past few years, however, as Turkey's security has been challenged by enemies from near and abroad, with some enemies even coming from within Turkey's own military establishment.

One of the reasons why Turkey enjoyed so much domestic stability for the first 15 years of the twenty-first century was due to the fact that the military was firmly under the control of the regime and was no longer an independent variable in Turkish politics as it had been in the past. On July 15, 2016, however, a botched military coup led by supporters of the exiled cleric Fetullah Gülen challenged this control. The coup had little support within the military and was quickly put down. In the aftermath of the coup effort that left hundreds of people dead, Turkey enacted an indefinite state-of-emergency that has resulted in a crackdown on tens of thousands of academics, journalists, politicians, and judges believed to be connected to the outlawed movement that is now known in Turkey by the acronym *FETÖ* (*Fethullahçı Terör Örgütü*). However, it is widely believed that other dissidents not necessarily linked to *FETÖ*, especially Kurds and journalists critical of the regime, have also been targeted in these purges. Only time will tell how long these purges of suspected Gülenists will continue.

The importance of any Islamic governed state keeping its military out of domestic politics will be examined further when the case of Egypt is covered in the next chapter. Ümit Cizre referred to the AKP's earlier dealings with the Turkish armed forces as "a strategy of confrontation avoidance" (2004: 15). Burhanettin Duran called this the "politics of patience" and noted the success that the AKP had in maintaining control over national security issues and foreign policy while at the same time not angering the military elites (Duran, in Cizre (Ed.) 2008: 95). Even to this day, despite the coup effort, the vast majority of Turkish armed force members remain fiercely loyal to the regime.

On August 10, 2014, Turkish citizens for the first time directly voted for their president, previously parliament made this decision. This time, however, the head of state was chosen in a two round popular vote process. In the 2014 presidential election, there were examples of voters who one would not normally identify with a specific party, embracing that party nonetheless.

> Accordingly, this election campaign has witnessed some unlikely political clustering: a group of LGBTs supporting the AKP under the name AK-LGBT, some very pious and some very secularist groups supporting the same candidate against the AKP, and liberals in their 30s excited over a candidate whose traditional Kurdish constituency they had been taught were separatist traitors and against whom they were mobilised during their military service in the 1990s. (Goksel 2014: *online*)

Goksel saw this as a positive sign for Turkey: "Such symbolic examples have created awareness that society is not inevitably trapped in age-old divisions, or civilisational clashes" (2014: *online*). Turkish voters have not fallen for simple slogans that lack content. David Ghanim on Turkish Islamism states;

> Whether they are called Islamists or liberals is not very significant, if the essence of the democratic process exists. More important is that this distancing from extremism not only ensured success for them as a political party, it also proved to be in the interests of the Turkish people. The Islamists of Turkey did not subscribe to the destructive fallacy that "Islam is the solution," a slogan that not only failed to prove viable, but also exacerbated the political, economic and intellectual crises in the Middle East. Instead, they advanced the idea that Islamists can respect and engage in the democratic process. (2009: *online*)

In the June 2015 Turkish parliamentary elections, following growing discontent with the ruling AKP regime in Ankara, a newly formed pro-Kurdish Party, the HDP (*Halkların Demokratik Partisi*) was able to meet the 10% voter threshold and has representation in Parliament. This is another positive sign for Turkey's democracy; alternative political positions continue to have official representation in Turkish politics. Due to the failure of a coalition government being formed following the June 2015 elections, a snap second election was held in November 2015 that saw the AKP surprise all analysts and win enough votes to for a return to single-party rule. Despite the AKP's victory, the pro-Kurdish HDP managed to meet the 10% threshold and still has a voice in parliament. Once again it is important to note here that with the failed military coup being only a few months in the past as this is being written, it is impossible to tell exactly which direction Turkey's experiment with Islamic influenced democracy will go.

Other than through democratic elections, one of the most concrete ways Turkey has promoted democracy is via the introduction of e-governance. "In the past several years Turkish officials argued that it is necessary to develop [the] so-called Prime Ministry Management Information Center in order to provide services and information through only one website on the model of USA Firstgov Portal" (Oğurlu 2014: 18). The new e-governance system in Turkey allows citizens access to their government in ways that are not possible in many other places. Yücel Oğurlu on the goals of e-governance in the Turkish context comments that;

> One of the major aspects of e-government is how to bring customers (citizens, business, other governments and NGOs) closer to their governments aiming at simplifying procedures but keeping the privacy and security of its clients. Therefore, there are four main, very broad, categories or models which e-government encompass that represent the scope of e-government: Government-to-Citizens (G2C), Government-to-Business (G2B), Government-to-Government (G2G) and Government-to-NGO (G2N). (2014: 19)

Turkish citizens today can access a wide range of government documents, datasets, and services online. For example, a Turkish citizen living abroad can go to their local embassy and request a copy of their criminal record in less than 1 min for less than 3 or 4 Euros. Even in the USA, citizens must go through extensive procedures and wait weeks for their records sent to their overseas residence via snail mail. Such bureaucratic smoothness makes working and living abroad a much easier experience.

Turkey has also engaged in multiple major domestic infrastructure building projects in recent years. Two years ago, Turkey completed an ambitious project building a rail link beneath the Bosporus. It has been considered a major breakthrough and an engineering marvel. Eventually, it is expected to handle 1.5 million commuters daily. The most recent project is a monorail system that will link the areas outside the center of Istanbul in an efficient and environmentally friendly manner.

> ...Istanbul started the process of building the largest monorail network Europe has ever seen. Covering 47 kilometers (29 miles) and ultimately carrying 200,000 passengers a day, Turkey's largest city will one day have a total of eight monorail lines snaking across it, adding missing links to a still-developing transit system. (O'Sullivan 2015: *online*)

This new monorail system will include one key inner city link from Beyoğlu to Sisli and a much-needed connection to Istanbul's Sabiha Gökçen Airport located on the Asian side of the city. These new mass transit systems will go a long way in relieving Istanbul's notorious traffic congestion that is on par with the rush-hour traffic in Manhattan or Los Angeles.

SOME SERIOUS ISSUES FOR TURKEY TO CONSIDER

Like any government, the AKP majority government currently in power also has some important issues to address as it moves forward. H. Ertuğ Tombuş has argued that the AKP embraced democracy and reforms during its first decade of rule, but as their rule become further entrenched, they became less supportive of democratic principles and became more concerned with maintaining and extending their power. He argued that in more recent times, the AKP has become increasingly similar to the Kemalists they so denounced in their efforts to gain support in the first place; "A great deal of evidence exists and has been pointed out to show the authoritarian nature of the Kemalist establishment has been absorbed by the AKP and informs the limits of the AKP's dedication to democratic ideas and values" (2013: 314). İshan Yilmaz calls the recent AKP discourse "Kemalo-Islamism" in that it justifies its efforts to control society by acting in the name of upholding the sanctity of the state. "It seems that some of our Islamists have cognitively emulated the six arrows of Kemalism (republicanism, nationalism, populism, revolutionism, secularism and statism) and added 'Islamism' as the seventh arrow" (Yilmaz 2013: *online*).

Many secularists and ethnic minorities have argued that the state is moving in the wrong direction and that Turkey's secular and cosmopolitan identity is being threatened. These groups feel they are not only being discriminated against in cultural life, but also in terms of public employment. "Many Kurds and Alevis are increasingly frustrated since they believe that the ruling elite is discriminating against them especially in public recruitment policies" (Taşkin 2013: 298). Critiques have also been levied against the current government in regards to cronyism.

> The governments in Turkey are still enjoying disproportional state power to re-shape even the class configurations. Despite lip service to "the interests of *vatandaş*," (citizen) it is an open secret that the governments are serving mostly to their *yandaş*, (partisans) as the management of economy and state are not significantly separated—a significant precondition of democratization. (Taşkin 2013: 298)

Turkey's long tradition of state-mandated secularism dating back to the founding of the Republic in 1923 makes the integration of Islamic values directly into the governance of the state a more difficult case. However, the AKP has won generally fairly contested elections repeatedly over the past 15 years signaling a general sense of national support despite opposition efforts.

The 2013 demonstrations at Gezi Park over the building of a shopping center in a historic area was another controversial issue the Turkish government had to handle. The Gezi Park occupation began on May 28, 2013, in protest of a wildly unpopular urban management project. "When the police brutally intervened and used aggressive force, the Gezi movement gained new momentum from the massive support of the Middle Class and the expansion from Istanbul to other urban cities" (Göle 2013: 7). Citizens were quick to take to the streets following word of widespread police brutality, and things quickly spiraled out of control. The Gezi Park demonstrators were a broad cross-section of Turkish society that included not just leftists, but also many Islamists, Nationalists, Kemalists, and others dissatisfied with the government plan to change the local scenic landscape in Taksim. Many argue the government was too heavy handed in this affair. The AKP representatives claimed that protestors were driven by ulterior motives and claimed that alcohol was provided some protestors, thus facilitating in an even more volatile environment. This led to an opposition party calling for further investigation of these claims levied by the AKP.

> A group of main opposition Republican People's Party (CHP) deputies has demanded a parliamentary inquiry into the controversy over claims that alcohol was consumed in Istanbul's Dolmabahçe Mosque during the intense first week of the Gezi Park protests. (*Hurriyet Daily News* 2013: *online*)

The idea that people may have been consuming alcohol or illicit drugs should not be too shocking for anyone has participated in such a mass protest before. One of the first things one will generally notice at such demonstrations is a few severely intoxicated protesters looking for trouble. However, this is not a valid excuse for the tragic deaths that occurred at the hands over an overzealous police force. In the end, the government did make concessions to the demonstrators and agreed to put up thousands of trees instead thus keeping Istanbul's picturesque urban landscape beautiful and green. This was a wise decision on the government's part. In the end, it managed to survive this potential catastrophe without any serious long-term damage. A little over three years after Gezi Park incident, the ruling AKP appears to be as firmly in control as it has ever been.

Perhaps the most distressing long-term trend in regards to Turkish politics today has been its increasingly censored presscensored press. According to *Reporters without Borders*;

> Freedom of information has declined alarmingly in Turkey since its first Universal Periodic Review during the 8th session in May 2010. It was then ranked 138th out of 178 countries in the Reporters Without Borders press freedom index. In the past four years it has fallen 16 places and is now ranked 154th out of 180 countries in the 2014 index. (*Reporters without Borders* 2014: 1)

Following the January 2015 *Charlie Hebdo* murders by Al-Qaeda-affiliated extremists, Turkish police raided the offices of the prominent Kemalist Turkish daily newspaper, *Cumhuriyet*, without any court order on the claims that it was said to be republishing images deemed offensive to the Prophet Mohammed (ﷺ) (*Today's Zaman* 2015a: *online*).

Today's Zaman also reported that a court in Southeast Turkey had blocked access to a Web site portraying the *Charlie Hebdo* cover: "A Diyarbakır court has ruled to block web pages featuring a controversial cover of the French satire magazine Charlie Hebdo, which became the target of a fatal attack last week" (*Today's Zaman* 2015b: *online*). Other news sites critical of the AKP have also come under increasing scrutiny from government officials. The previously referenced *Today's Zaman*, with connections to the outlawed Fetullah Gülen Movement, was raided at midnight on March 4, 2016 (well before the July 15 coup attempt), and the newspaper was put under administrative control. Many other media outlets have been raided since the July 15 failed coup. According to *Reporters without Borders* in 2014;

> Although the media are still very diverse, more and more leading media are owned by businessmen who support the government or depend on being awarded state contracts. This allows the government to exercise increasing influence over editorial policies and endangers diversity. (*Reporters without Borders* 2014: 5)

Turkey ought to be aware of the importance of press freedom. Its leaders must preserve freedom of speech if it expects to continue receiving support from important EU and Western political actors in an increasingly globally interdependent world. There is nothing within Islam to suggest that the state ought to censor citizen's access to international news sources or limit the discussion on relevant current events.

The Lesson Learned from Turkey

Turkey's balance of religion and moderation, especially in the beginning years of the twenty-first century, makes it an inspirational figure for many other regional actors who seek stability and economic success. While Turkey is not an "Islamic governed state" and secularism is deeply entrenched within Turkey's current constitutional model, Islam is clearly present within the nation's contemporary political discourse. Kubicek calls the AKP "an Islamic-oriented party" (2015: 63). Mehmet Özkan makes the argument that Turkey can serve in some ways as a model for other regional states as an example of a state that was able to settle internal ethnic conflicts without bloody civil war.

If Turkey today, with the AKP's coming to power, has consolidated or partly settled its center—periphery relations without civil war, therein lies the 'Turkish model' for the Middle East and possibly even for the third world. Most of the problems in the Middle East emanate from home rather than from outside. Naturally, the starting point should be to usher in democracy, peace, and prosperity. Democratic consolidation in Turkey has much to offer the Middle East where the problems between the centre and periphery are acute. With the AKP consolidating its position in Turkey, the new Turkey can be a much better model for the region and beyond. (2013: 536–537)

It is important to remember, however, Turkey has vast economic and military resources which make it a much different case than somewhere like Somalia or Afghanistan. One also cannot forget that the coercive power of the Turkish state is quite significant. In more direct terms—Turkey's military power thus far has prevented the Kurdish issue from escalating into an all-out civil war as has been the case in other places in the region with high sectarian tensions such as Syria, Iraq, Libya, and Yemen where in each case, the state's coercive apparatus was significantly weaker.

During the early years of AKP rule, efforts were made to reach out to the Kurdish minority that predominantly lives in the eastern part of the country, but a lasting peace agreement has yet to be reached. "They are still oscillating between a softer approach based on Islamic brotherhood and a harder line that unveils their disappointment from the failure of this strategy" (Taşkin 2013: 299). In July 2015, AKP–Kurdish relationstook another hit with Turkish forces targeting Kurdish fighters in Syria along with ISIS following two separate terrorist attacks in Southeastern Turkey. YPG (*Yekîneyên Parastina Gel*) forces claimed that it "had been shelled in the Kurdish-held village of Zormikhar, west of Kobane, on Sunday [26.7.2015] evening. It added that, an hour later, one of its vehicles had come "under heavy fire from the Turkish military east of Kobane in the village of Til Findire" (BBC News 2015: *online*). Turkey claimed it was only targeting PKK terrorists. On October 9, 2015, a horrific terrorist attack attributed to ISIS ripped through a peaceful leftist protest in Ankara killing close to 100 people. The leftists and pro-Kurdish HDP Party immediately blamed the ruling AKP government for not making better efforts to provide security in Kurdish regions for Kurdish people. Time will show how this all eventually impacts long-term AKP-Kurdish relations.

Turkey's relative autonomy from the pull of the other major global actors is something to be admired by other developing regions in the Muslim world. According to Richard Falk;

> Despite the setbacks of the past two years, the combination of economic success, political stability, and diplomatic independence continue to make Turkey a generally admired and trusted presence in the region, and a continuing source of inspiration for those social and political forces seeking moderation and a more equitable pattern of development while trying to fulfill the democratizing promises of the Arab Spring. (2013: 355)

Islamic governed states ought to avoid being pulled into the hopeless vortex of US–Iranian political influence and dependence; autonomy in foreign affairs is essential to autonomy in domestic affairs. "Above all it is to Turkey's great advantage in the current atmosphere in the Middle East to not be too closely associated with either the US or the Iranian model of governance, the two other political narratives that have exerted influence throughout the region in past decades" (Falk 2013: 355). The most important lessons Turkey can provide for an Islamic governed state are the importance of autonomy, economic growth, building a modern infrastructure, international trade, and the importance of making efforts to reach out to minority groups.

Notes

1. In the West, this work is commonly referred to simply as: *Strategic Depth*.
2. I translated this from the original text which was in Turkish: "Biz düzen kurmaya çalışıyoruz, böyle bir şey yanlış da değil. Ama bunu modern çerçevede bu ulus devletlerin eşitliği parametreleri etrafında kurmaya çalışıyoruz."
3. As this manuscript is being prepared, multiple terrorist incidents have recently transpired in Ankara and Southeastern Turkey against Turkish police officers and military personnel. This has caused policy makers in Ankara to rethink their non-interventionist position. As things stand as of November 2016, Turkey has been regularly bombing PKK and YPG positions in Northern Syria. Both groups are widely believed to be committing acts of ethnic cleansing on local Arab and Turkmen populations in

previously ISIS held territory in Northern Syria and are believed to be primarily responsible for attacks on Turkish police and military forces inside Turkey.

4. In the end, the JAT acquisition effort fell through, and on August 1, 2013, JAT Airways and Etihad Airways entered into a strategic partnership agreement in which Etihad took a 49% stake in JAT Airways and would hold management rights over the airline for the next five years. The other 51% of the company was retained by the Republic of Serbia. JAT launched its inaugural flight under its new name "Air Serbia" on October 26, 2013.

References

Batur, Nur. 2009. Yeni Osmanılıar sözü iyi niyetli değil. *Daily Sabah*, Dec 4. http://www.sabah.com.tr/siyaset/2009/12/04/yeni_osmanlilar_sozu_iyi_niyetli_degil. Accessed 8 Feb 2015.

BBC News. 2015. Syrian Kurds accuse Turkey of attacking their forces. July 27. http://www.bbc.com/news/world-europe-33675760. Accessed 28 July 2015.

Butler, Daren. 2012. Turkey regains investment-grade rating after long wait. *Reuters*, Nov 5. http://www.reuters.com/article/2012/11/05/turkey-fitch-rating-idUSL5E8M56DZ20121105. Accessed 9 Feb 2015.

Cizre, Ümit. 2004. The catalysts, directions and focus of Turkey's agenda for security sector reform in the 21st century. Paper presented at the July 12–13 workshop on "Challenges of security sector governance in the Middle East," Geneva Centre for the Democratic Control of Armed Forces (DCAF), Working Paper No. 148: 1–25.

Davutoğlu, Ahmet. 2001. *Stratejik Derinlik: Türkiye'nin Uluslararası Konumu*. Istanbul: Küre Yayınları.

Davutoğlu, Ahmet. 2012. Statement by Dr. Ahmet Davutoğlu, Minister of Foreign Affairs of the Republic of Turkey Nov 29, at the U.N. General Assembly regarding Palestinian statehood. *Washington Report on Middle East Affairs*, 32(1), (Jan/Feb2013). http://www.wrmea.org/2013-january-february/three-views-the-u.n.-welcomes-the-state-of-palestine.html. Accessed 30 Oct 2016.

Duran, Burhanettin. 2008. The justice and development party's 'new politics': Steering toward conservative democracy, a revised Islamic agenda or management of new crises? In *Secular and Islamic politics in Turkey: The making of the Justice and Development Party*, ed. Ümit Cizre, 80–106. New York: Routledge.

Ennis, Crystal and Bessma Momani. 2013. Shaping the Middle East in the midst of the Arab Spring uprisings: Turkish and Saudi foreign policy strategies. *Third World Quarterly* 34 (6): 1127–1144.

Falk, Richard. 2013. Turkey's new multilateralism: A positive diplomacy for the twenty-first century. *Global Governance* 19: 353–376.

Göksel, Diba. 2014. The presidential elections that have changed Turkey. *Al Jazeera Online*, 7, August. http://www.aljazeera.com/indepth/opinion/2014/08/presidential-elections-changed-tu-2014871389569858.html. Accessed 18 Feb 2015.

Göle, Nilüfer. 2013. Gezi—Anatomy of a public square movement. *Insight Turkey* 15 (3): 7–14.

Ghanim, David. 2009. Democracy and political Islam. *Middle East Policy*, 16 (1), http://www.mepc.org/journal/middle-east-policy-archives/turkish-democracy-and-political-islam. Accessed 19 May 2015.

Hurriyet Daily News. 2013. Turkey's main opposition CHP seeks probe into 'alcohol in.mosque' Gezi protest claim, Dec 9. http://www.hurriyetdailynews.com/turkeys-main-opposition-chp-seeks-probe-into-alcohol-in-mosque-gezi-protest-claim.aspx?pageID=238&nID=59301&NewsCatID=338. Accessed 17 Feb 2015.

Idriz, Mesut. 2011. Balkans between two worlds: Turkey and Europe. *Today's Zaman*, Oct 9. http://www.todayszaman.com/op-ed_balkans-between-two-worlds-turkey-and-europeby-mesut-idriz-_259260.html. Accessed 13 April 2014.

Kardaş, Şaban. 2010. Turkey: Redrawing the Middle East map or building sandcastles? *Middle East Policy* 17 (1): 115–136.

Kubicek, Paul. 2015. *Political Islam and democracy in the Muslim world*. Boulder, CO: Lynne Rienner Publishers.

Oğurlu, Yücel. 2014. 'E-Government portal' and e-government services in Turkey. *Epiphany Journal of Transdisciplinary Studies* 7 (2): 17–26.

O'Sullivan, Feargus. 2015. Why Istanbul is building the largest monorail network in Europe? Feb 4. *CityLab*. http://www.citylab.com/commute/2015/02/istanbul-monorail/385162/. Accessed 18 Feb 2015.

Özkan, Mehmet. 2013. Turkey, Islamic politics, and the 'Turkish model'. *Strategic Analysis* 37 (5): 534–538.

Özkan, Mehmet. 2014. *Turkey's involvement in Somalia: Assessment of a statebuilding in Progress*, 1–66. Istanbul, Turkey: SETA Publications.

Reporters Without Borders. 2014. Contribution to universal periodic review United Nations Human Rights Council, second cycle—21st session—Jan-Feb 2015. Written contribution by reporters without Borders on freedom information in TURKEY June 2014. http://fr.rsf.org/IMG/pdf/turkey_upr_en-2.pdf. Accessed 9 Feb 2015.

Taşkin, Yuskel. 2013. Hegemonizing conservative democracy and the problems of democratization in Turkey: Conservatism without democrats? *Turkish Studies* 14 (2): 292–310.

Today's Zaman. 2015a. Turkish police check newspaper over Charlie Hebdo cartoons, Jan 14. http://www.todayszaman.com/national_turkish-police-check-newspaper-over-charlie-hebdo-cartoons_369741.html. Accessed online: 9 Feb 2015.

Today's Zaman. 2015b. Turkish court rules to block web pages featuring Charlie Hebdo cover, Jan 14. http://www.todayszaman.com/_turkish-court-rules-to-block-web-pages-featuring-charlie-hebdo-cover_369784.html. Accessed 9 Feb 2015.

Tombuş, H. Ertuğ. 2013. Reluctant democratization: The case of the Justice and Development Party in Turkey. *Constellations* 20 (2): 312–327.

T.C. Dişişeri Baklanliği (Turkish Ministry of Foreign Affairs) official website. 2015a. Foreign Minister Davutoğlu, EU membership has been our strategic goal for almost 50 years and will continue to be. http://www.mfa.gov.tr/foreign-minister-davutoglu-_eu-membership-has-been-our-strategic-goal-for-almost-50-years-and-will-continue-to-be.en.mfa. Accessed 8 Feb 2015.

T.C. Dişişeri Baklanliği (Turkish Ministry of Foreign Affairs) official website. 2015b. Relations between Turkey and Bosnia and Herzegovina. http://www.mfa.gov.tr/relations-between-turkey-and-bosnia-and-herzegovina.en.mfa. Accessed 9 Feb 2015.

T.C. Dişişeri Baklanliği (Turkish Ministry of Foreign Affairs) official website. 2015c. Foreign Minister Davutoğlu we will stand by the Syrian people until they live with honor in all around Syria. http://www.mfa.gov.tr/foreign-minister-davutoglu-we-will-stand-by-the-syrian-people-until-they-live-with-honor-in-all-around-syria.en.mfa. Accessed 18 Feb 2015.

UNHCR UN Refugee Agency. 2015. Kobani refugees encouraged to move into Turkey's newest and largest camp, Feb 16. http://www.unhcr.org/54e1efe39.html. Accessed 18 Feb 2015.

Yilmaz, İhsan. 2013. Kemalo-Islamism in full force. *Today's Zaman*, Oct 23. http://www.todayszaman.com/columnist/i-hsan-yilmaz/kemalo-islamism-in-full-speed_329588.html. Accessed 27 Feb 2016.

CHAPTER 9

The Case of Egypt: Revolution, Counterrevolution, and a Return to Brutal Dictatorship

INTRODUCTION—THE FALL OF HOSNI MUBARAK

Any serious effort to conceptualize a theory of Islamic governance in the twenty-first century must evaluate the case of Egypt considering the rise and fall of the Egyptian Muslim Brotherhood's formal power in politics over such a short span of time. By the final years of the twentieth century, it was evident that Egypt was run by a dictator and that democratic reforms were not coming anytime soon under the incumbent regime. According to Muhamad Olimat; "The Mubarak regime in Egypt continued its oppressive treatment of opposition, both secular and Islamist. In 2003 it claimed that Egypt enjoyed 'all kinds of democracy,' but in reality, political participation was at its lowest levels since Mubarak took over in 1981" (2014: 8). The Muslim Brotherhood was finally allowed to participate in the 2005 Egyptian political elections. In these elections, they won 90 out of 150 parliamentary seats. This caused such fear among the Mubarak regime that they postponed the 2006 National Assembly elections for 2 years. Things continued to deteriorate for the Mubarak regime during this time. Finally, by January 2011, the revolution in Egypt had started. After over 30 years of absolute power, the people finally were able to rise up and topple Mubarak's inept and corrupt regime.

In 2012, for the first time in Egypt's history, dating all the way back to the Pharaohs of antiquity, Egypt held democratic elections. In these elections, Dr. Mohammed Morsi won the presidency of Egypt with

51.7% of the total vote. According to the *New York Times*, the atmosphere immediately after Morsi victory was jubilant.

> Smiling riot police officers put down their helmets to exchange congratulations with bearded protesters. Beaming Brotherhood supporters streamed in, swelling the crowd to perhaps 100,000 by nightfall. In a carnival atmosphere, fireworks were set off and vendors hawked cotton candy or threw pieces of fruit into the laughing crowd. (Kirkpatrick 2012: *online*)

The same article goes on to report comments from one of Morsi's supporters. "'I feel like there is hope again,' said Mohamed Ahmed, 20, an activist with the secular April 6 Youth Movement, one of many demonstrating with the Brotherhood in Tahrir Square" (Kirkpatrick 2012: *online*). Despite the initial hopes of millions of young and enthusiastic supporters like Mohamed Ahmed, the Egyptian Revolution quickly turned sour for many reasons. One year later, President Morsi was overthrown in a military coup, and his democratic regime was replaced with a brutal military junta that has brutally cracked down on the Muslim Brotherhood, Muslim Brotherhood members, and those who voiced support for the Morsi regime.

THE MUSLIM BROTHERHOOD EXPERIMENT

The history of the Egyptian Muslim Brotherhood (Egyptian MB) is well documented (Mitchell 1993; Rubin (ed.) 2010; Laub 2014). It was created by the iconic Islamic scholar and schoolteacher, Hasan al-Banna, in 1928. Originally, the Egyptian MB was primarily a youth organization that sought to engage in charitable and social activities. "Though establishing an Islamic state based on sharia was at the core of the Brotherhood's agenda, the group gained prominence by effectively providing social services where the security state failed" (Laub 2014: *online*). In the 1940s, it moved toward active political life and sought to establish an Islamic state. Its leader, Hasan al-Banna, was murdered in February 12, 1949, and the movement was banned in the 1950s by Egypt's then President Gamal Abdel Nasser. Many of its prominent leaders were jailed and executed, including the iconic Syed Qutb in 1966 by Egyptian authorities. During the 1970s, Egyptian President Anwar Sadat and the Muslim Brotherhood began a brief period of *détente* that abruptly ended following his assassination in 1981 at the hands of Khalid

Islambouli, an Islamist who also held the rank of First Lieutenant in the Egyptian army—who like many Arabs in general—felt that Sadat sold out the Palestinians to the Israelis during the 1979 Camp David Peace Accords.

Immediately following Sadat's assassination, the new President, Hosni Mubarak, clamped down on the Muslim Brotherhood. The Muslim Brotherhood was regularly denied direct access to the formal political structure as an organized political party. "Throughout the 1980s, there was a tacit agreement whereby the Brothers could expand their presence in civil society in exchange for their respect [of] the regimes 'red lines'" (Soage and Franganillo 2010: 45). Despite their lack of political power, their influence over labor unions and other aspects of civil society continued to grow. "Islamist organizations became the main focus of cultural and community life in many parts of Egypt, especially in poorer areas" (Berman 2003: 260). In many cases, Islamist organizations in Egypt were more efficient providers of health care, employment, and education than the formal Egyptian government itself. Political maneuvering continued throughout the 1980s and 1990s, with Brotherhood members contesting elections under the banner of other recognized Egyptian political parties until finally, in 2005, the Muslim Brotherhood were formally allowed field candidates for the People's Assembly. Their electoral success in this election signaled the beginning of the end of the Mubarak regime.

During the next 6 years, the Egyptian economy continued to struggle and discontent with Mubarak and his regime grew stronger. Following the 2011 Revolution in Egypt that removed Mubarak, the Muslim Brotherhood was legalized. In April 2011, the newly legalized Muslim Brotherhood created a civic political party called the *Freedom and Justice Party* (FJP) to contest elections, including the 2012 presidential election where its candidate, Mohamed Morsi, became Egypt's first democratically elected president. The Freedom and Justice Party was separate from the Muslim Brotherhood. It was, at least in principle, meant to be an inclusive political organization that was not limited to Muslim Brotherhood members.

> There will be a complete separation between the political branch of the Muslim Brotherhood and the organization itself, Abdel Ghaffar said, noting that the Freedom and Justice Party) also has Christian deputy candidates and party Vice President Dr. Rafik Habib is a Christian. "The

Freedom and Justice Party will work without any interference from the movement," he said. (Yezdani 2011: *online*)

The Freedom and Justice Party sought to incorporate *Sharī'ah* into the new Egyptian legal system; however, it was meant to be a source of laws and not necessarily the only legal system. It offered a more socially conservative vision for Egypt, yet was still welcoming of tourists and engagement with the West. Dr. Ashraf Abdel Ghaffar, one of the leaders of the Egyptian Muslim Brotherhood, in an interview with the Turkish media outlet, *Hürriyet Daily News*, commented, "Egyptian people are religious people, whether Muslim or Christian; we cannot let things happen like people hanging around without clothes in a village or gambling in casinos"; however, he goes on to note that "anyone who would like to come to Egypt in order to visit the pyramids or Alexandria is more than welcome" (Ghaffar, quoted in Yezdani 2011: *online*). Once in power, Morsi made appeals to the world about the need for toleration and mutual respect. President Mohammed Morsi, in his first address to the United Nations as Egypt's leader, spoke out against both extremism from Islamic actors and international provocations against Islam;

> We must join hands in confronting these regressive ideas that hinder cooperation among us. We must act together in the face of extremism, discrimination, and incitement to hatred on the basis of religion or race. The General Assembly, as well as the Security Council, has the principal responsibility in addressing this phenomenon that is starting to have implications that clearly affect international peace and security. The obscenities recently released as part of an organized campaign against Islamic sanctities is unacceptable and requires a firm stand. We have a responsibility in this international gathering to study how we can protect the world from instability and hatred. (Morsi 2012: 14)

Morsi made it clear that Islamophobia had serious implications on international security and peace. Western forms of discrimination against Arab and Muslim populations at home ultimately impact the way policies are crafted within OIC member states. Quelling the flames of Islamophobia abroad is essential in bringing domestic stability to OIC nations, especially those in the midst of major political transitions. Discrimination against Muslims in the USA and in Western Europe ultimately only leads to policies and attitudes more hostile to Christian and Jewish minority communities in the OIC member states. This principle is understood in the international relations literature as the notion of *reciprocity*, and it plays an essential role in how domestic and international affairs play out.

Shortly after the Morsi assumed the office of the Presidency, things quickly spiraled out of control. Morsi's party sought to rush through a new constitution, riding the wave of popular support that put it into office. According to Muqtedar Khan;

> In the one year during which President Morsi governed, he rushed through a hastily written constitution, tried to assume extra-constitutional powers to preempt the judiciary, and focused more on consolidating his party's power over government institutions than providing good governance. (2014: 79)

Despite these valid points made by Khan, the fact remains that anti-MB parties and candidates sought to have more influence in the process than was warranted based on the electoral results. Khan even goes on to note that from the beginning, the previous regime made efforts to interfere with new political leadership. Islamists were also unhappy because of the power still held by the military. Nathan Brown argues that;

> Non-Islamists felt their fears of Islamist majoritarianism deepening; Islamists discovered that their parliamentary majority meant little because the military had taken care in the constitutional declaration to ensure that the new parliament would have no power to oversee the cabinet or pass legislation without the generals' approval. (2013: 47)

The military powers also were unhappy because as the situation stood, their influence was only temporary; "Once a new president was sworn in, the military would have no formal role and no clear tools with which to influence the outcome of the constitutional process" (Brown 2013: 47). All of these events eventually came to a head on June 30 as millions of Egyptian protestors along with other shadowy foreign agents with regional interests took the streets and demanded Morsi's removal. The military forcibly overthrew the democratically elected leader on July 3, 2012. Following Morsi's removal, top MB aides were arrested, including Morsi himself. Pro-MB media outlets were also shut down, and a brutal crackdown on all of its activities ensued.

From the beginning, the anti-MB forces in Egypt and abroad were never willing to work with the Morsi government.

> Major opposition actors not only tried to stave off or boycott several elections; even when they found one they could like (the mid-2012 presidential balloting, for example), they ended up seeking to overturn its results with street protests. Oppositionists complained about the make-up of the constituent assembly but did little to articulate their own constitutional vision, instead simply pressing non-Islamists to withdraw from the body. (Brown 2013: 51)

Many scholars, including Muqtedar Khan, were critical of the Morsi regime following its overthrow; however, as noted above, Khan still admitted that there were obvious efforts by elements loyal to old regime to hinder to the MB; "Clearly, there is evidence that the previous regime had worked to subvert the Morsi government, but that should have been evident to those wielding the levers of power" (2014: 79). Indeed, the Muslim Brotherhood leadership should have been more cognizant of these realities, but nonetheless, even if the Morsi government realized this, there was little that they could do in regard to the media propaganda apparatus that was also largely against the regime. The concerted efforts of anti-MB groups with connections and funding from questionable sources also facilitated in the regime's eventual collapse. "Egyptian media were fed a steady stream of outlandish information (in 2011, directed primarily against revolutionary youth; in 2012 and especially in 2013, aimed mostly at the country's newly elected leadership) that undermined trust" (Brown 2013: 52). While this book argues that the press in any Islamic governed state ought to be free, one must still consider the dangers of false information and its impact on a newly established regime. The state must have some mechanisms at its disposal to, at the least, offer a counter narrative to hostile anti-regime sources and their motivations. Perhaps this is not as important as in the case of long-established states like the USA and Turkey, where there exists an overall general sense of stability, but this point seems undeniable in the case of newly emerging regimes.

Muslims around the world hoped that the democratically elected Muslim Brotherhood and Dr. Mohammed Morsi could be an example of an Islamic government that showed wisdom and pragmatic governing skills; after decades of talk, an actual Islamist political party was given the authority by the people to rule over an entire nation. However, after one year in power, it was clear that Morsi and the Brotherhood were not getting the job done.

> The real setback began the day after they ascended to the helm of power, when they began to rule: when the movement became the regime. It was astonishing to see such an erosion of sympathy, support, and legitimacy, and so many defections in the course of just two years. If Mohamed Mosri had remained to end his presidential term in defeat, that would have had more serious implications for the future of Islamism as such than his removal by the military intervention. (Bayat, quoted in Al Arian et al. 2013: *online*)

After Morsi's first 100 days in office, an article that appeared in the *Washington Post* stated in reference to the current situation in Egypt; "Piles of garbage continue to line some streets of the capital. Strikes over wages and overdue benefits have halted some public-sector services, particularly in Egypt's woefully underfunded hospitals" (Hauslohner 2012; *online*). Following the Morsi regime's formal assumption of power, the "economy declined, the crime rate rose precipitously, social divisions became more pronounced and the quality of life fell significantly" (Khan 2014: 79). According to a 2011 African Development Bank Group Report, over 40% of the Egyptian population are still living on less than $2 a day and 21% of the population live on less than $1 a day (*Africa Bank Development Group* 2011). This number did not improve during Morsi's 1 year of leadership. However, in all fairness, one must remember the Morsi inherited a very bad situation, including an enormous national debt and major obstructionism from secular and pro-Mubarak elements within the government itself. It is unreasonable to think any newly appointed leader could fix the mess of the 30 years reign of Hosni Mubarak within their first year.

THE "NEW EGYPT" UNDER ABDUL FATTAH AL-SISI

Isaac Newton's 3rd Law of Motion famously posited that for every action, there is an equal and opposite reaction. The Sisi-led government in Egypt most certainly qualifies as Newton's aforementioned opposite reaction to the Morsi regime. The current Egyptian government under the iron-fisted rule of Abdul Fattah al-Sisi almost immediately turned Egypt back into an authoritarian police state. The situation under Sisi deteriorated so rapidly that on May 12, 2015, the Obama Administration issued an unclassified formal statement signed by Secretary of State John Kerry that goes into detail explaining the multiple failures of the military junta new regime;

> While Egypt has implemented part of its "democracy roadmap," the overall trajectory of rights and democracy has been negative. A serious of executive initiatives, new laws, and judicial actions severely restrict freedom of expression and the press, freedom of association, freedom of peaceful assembly, and due process, and they undermined the prospects for democratic governance. (*Egypt Report* 2015: 1-2)

The statement goes on to mention in some detail the more specific failings. Included in the assessment was the State Department's concern with the arrests of members of the Muslim Brotherhood for no legitimate reasons.

> According to the Egyptian security authorities' estimates in March, 16,000 persons were arrested between July 2013 and March 2015; many of those have been detainees are accused of membership in the Muslim Brotherhood (MB) and/or violating a demonstration law that does not comport with international standards for protecting freedom of assembly. (*Egypt Report* 2015: 1-2)

The restrictions on freedom of press and thought alluded to in the Congressional Report can be extended outside the realm of politics and even into the classroom. The Sisi government has even gone as far as burning books in schools that are believed to possess Muslim Brotherhood "propaganda" including many well-known Islamic books that have no connection to the MB.

Daily News Egypt reported in April 2015 that the Sisi-led Egyptian government had issued a decree to remove certain books from schools and libraries. "More than 60 books were mentioned, the majority of them discussing Islamic jurisprudence, women in Islam, the phenomenon of terrorism, and Islam in science" (Youssef 2015: *online*). At the same school in Giza that conducted the book-burning campaign picture above, the government took control of the school's administration and has begun its own "re-education" process.

Fadl is one of the many private schools of which the government took over administration, accusing them of being "managed by the Muslim Brotherhood". Hundreds of schools and NGOs were either confiscated or closed by the Egyptian government, which feared they are controlled by the now outlawed Muslim Brotherhood. (Youssef 2015: *online*)

The term *re-education* is not meant to be taken simply as a colorful figure of speech in this case—the newly appointed headmaster of the Giza school commented that "burning the books is a "first step" toward the Minister of Education's demand for a "guarantee that our children are raised the right way" (Youssef 2015: *online*). On June 23, 2015, the situation surrounding books in Egypt got even worse after a decree was issued by the Egyptian government banning books that are often found in *masjid* libraries based on the claim that they "contradict the leniency of Islam." According to one of the officials in the Ministry of Religious Endowments, Ahmed Fahmy, the Ministry's desire is "to purge them [*masjids*] of books that call for fundamentalism and extremism and call for the opposite of moderates Islam" (Fahmy, quoted in İnanç 2015: online). Fahmy goes on to declare that; "A committee will examine the books in every city to evaluate and remove them. Any book, irrespective of its author or publishing house, that contradicts the teachings of Islam, will be confiscated" (Fahmy, quoted in İnanç 2015: online). Included thus far in this purge are all works written by Muslim Brotherhood members including Sayyed Qutb, Yusuf al-Qaradawi, Hassan al-Banna, and other very commonly read works that predate contemporary fundamentalism by hundreds of years such as Mohammad ibn 'Abd al-Wahhāb and Ibn Taymiyyah. Such rhetoric from various ministers on books in schools and mosques hardly sounds like something one would expect from a new government that seeks to be recognized by other nations as democratic and civilized; rather, such cryptic utterances sound like something taken from the pages of Ray Bradbury or George Orwell. Such efforts to suppress opposing views go far beyond anything ever attempted during the year of rule under Mohammed Morsi.

The actions of the Sisi-led military junta have caught the attention of human rights scholars and activists already. Mohammed Lofty commented that via Sisi's heavy-handed and undemocratic actions, he is actually "creating a new generation of terrorists, and exporting them to Syria and Iraq…" (Lofty, quoted in Kirkpatrick 2015: *online*). The continued oppression of Islamists ultimately will only lead to further radicalization and instability not just in Egypt, but throughout the Middle East. Each continued act of oppression against Islamists only gives further credence to their claims of oppression and discrimination by a regime already considered illegitimate by millions of Egyptians.

Women in Egypt have also faced new forms of discrimination under the Sisi regime. According to a May 2015 FIDH report on recent sexual harassment in Egypt;

> Since the military takeover in July 2013 and resumed control by the army and the police, there has been a surge in sexual violence perpetrated by the security forces in Egypt. While sexual violence has long been a characteristic of state violence, today it indiscriminately targets those apprehended by the security forces: in addition to opponents of General el-Sisi's regime, victims include NGO representatives, protesters, individuals perceived as going against the moral order, as well as common-law detainees. (FIDH Report 2015: 4)

The same report goes on to note that such sexual violence has been aimed at stifling protest and maximizing state coercive power, and that "the Egyptian authorities have failed to take action to prevent torture and other forms of sexual violence" (FIDH Report 2015: 28). Along with sexual violence, many tourist hot spots such as the wealthy Sharm-el-Sheik area have harassed, and even gone as far as banning women from wearing *hijāb* in restaurants, businesses, and other places of leisure. In her poignant analysis of the ideological dimensions of gender-based oppression and violence in Egypt today, Diana Alghoul writes;

> It's important to take this issue to its ideological roots, as well as focus on gender-based violence, in which Al-Sisi is currently pushing a form of nationalization of Islamic thought. In a bid to defeat the Muslim Brotherhood, he understands that he needs to depart from what the majority of scholars throughout Islamic history have recognized to be legitimate opinions and compete with them ideologically as well as militarily and politically. (2015: *online*)

Sisi's war against women who choose to cover is a part of the larger *re-education* of Egyptian society. These policies have nothing to do with the red herring claim that such clothing promotes extremism; rather, the real reason is that Sisi seeks to recreate his own authoritarian version of Islam that crushes all dissent and criticism. It should be no surprise that Arab dictatorships today fawn over their authoritarian brother-in-arms who has sought to destroy any vestiges of democratic political Islam in his country.

WHAT IS TO BE LEARNED FROM THE CASE OF EGYPT?

According to Fareed Zakaria;

> Egypt under Morsi was a textbook illiberal democracy. But the Egyptian military is not a force for liberty or the rule of law. This is the regime that ran Egypt for six decades, abusing human rights, crushing economic freedom, banning free media and jailing political opponents. The choice in Egypt is not between bad democrats and a Singapore-style efficient and open autocracy. It is between illiberal generals and illiberal politicians. (Zakaria 2013: 36)

The Egyptian case showed many things. Perhaps most importantly, the military must stay out of domestic politics in any newly emerging Islamic governed state. The military cannot act as an unchecked independent actor in domestic affairs. "Responsible and accountable security forces reduce the risk of conflict, provide security for citizens and create the right environment for sustainable development" (DFID 2003: 30). The elected political leader of an Islamic governed state must hold authority over military actors within the state. In many OIC states, the military historically has often been in direct competition with the political leadership for power, often acting as a shadow government.

This was the story in Algeria for decades. This was perhaps best exemplified in 1992 when the military stopped free elections in fear of the Islamist FIS party (*Islamic Salvation Front*) coming to power. This usurpation of power from the voters of Algeria resulted in a long and bloody civil war. Algeria's first contested, democratically elected president, Abdelaziz Bouteflika, made security reform a priority when he came to office in 2004. According to a Bonn International Center for Conversion report on security reform in Algeria;

> President Bouteflika has reshuffled some of the higher ranks of the military in order to reduce their influence in political affairs. He has publicly emphasized the importance of restoring the authority of the state, reforming the judiciary, and strengthening human rights. (Bonn Report 2013: 1)

Turkey also had a highly politicized military that for many decades made regular incursions in domestic politics, most notably the 1960 and 1980 military coup d'état's. Transitioning states in the Muslim world should consider the model the USA adopted in which the political head of state is, by default, also the commander-in-chief of the military. This power was given to the President of the USA by constitutional decree when the constitution was first drafted. Article II, Sect. 2 of the US Constitution, also known as the *Commander-in-Chief Clause*, categorically declares that; "The President shall be Commander in Chief of the Army and Navy of the United States, and of the Militia of the several States, when called into the actual Service of the United States [...]" (*U.S. Constitution*, art. II, § 2). A military-led coup against a sitting US president within the context of the US Constitution would be almost unthinkable and tantamount to treason in almost any case.

In the Middle of the Korean War on April 11, 1951, President Truman dismissed General George MacArthur—an overzealous yet enormously popular WWII hero—once he felt the General had overstepped his authority when he violated a presidential directive order to not make public statements on policy matters surrounding the Korean War. Truman went ahead with ordering MacArthur's removal even though he did not technically violate a Joint Chiefs of Staff order (Clayton 1985). Such executive authority is necessary to ensure the stability of a newly emerging Islamic governed regime. The breakdown of the hierarchical chain of command within the state between the presidency and the military ultimately leads to the breakdown of the state's legitimacy and ability to act decisively.

The second thing to be learned from the Egypt case is the importance of timing, foresight, and patience of Islamic governed regimes when they actually hold power. The timing of the Egyptian elections was questionable. "Had parliamentary elections been successfully scheduled for the second quarter of 2013, it is likely that significant opposition energies would have gone into campaigning rather than street protests, thereby forestalling any mass uprising" (Brown 2013: 50). The Morsi government also failed to appropriately integrate all various groups into the political process. According to Brown;

> Egypt had no rules of accepted democratic behavior. For instance, when forming the constituent assembly, the Brotherhood's parliamentary

deputies agreed that half the drafters would be nonpartisan representatives of various institutions and organizations in Egyptian society—but then chose numerous formally "nonpartisan" people with Islamist inclinations. (2013: 50)

While it is impossible to guarantee perfect balance and impartiality, better efforts could have been made to include a more diverse cross section in choosing the drafters of the constitution. Morsi was already in power. He could have waited longer before rushing elections and maintained his legitimacy even in the eyes of some of his detractors.

Finally, the Egyptian Muslim Brotherhood experiment should serve as a reminder to other nations seeking to establish an Islamic governed state that counterrevolutionary forces and remnants from the previous regime will remain issues to contend with, even after the successful transfer of power occurs. There exists ample evidence that the US government was active in propping up anti-Morsi activists via large-scale covert financial assistance programs in which millions of dollars were filtered through a complex network of agencies within the US State Department who then re-routed much of this money to anti-Morsi political parties and movements who doubled as NGO activists. Emad Mekay from the Investigative Reporting Program at UC-Berkeley reported that their investigation found;

> Activists bankrolled by the [US State Department 'democracy assistance'] programme include an existed Egyptian police officer who plotted the violent overthrow of the Morsi government, an anti-Islamist politician who advocated closing mosques and dragging preachers out by force, as well as a coterie of opposition politicians who pushed for the outset of the country's first democratically elected leader, government documents show. (2013: *online*)

One also should not expect help from other Muslim "allies"—Saudi Arabia's utter intransigence toward Egypt's nascent effort at democratic Islamic governance attests to this reality. Authoritarian Islamic states very well may be even worse enemies to democratic Islamic governed states than the secular West. A successful Islamic governed Egypt would have been a nightmare for the Saudi regime who most certainly would have felt increased pressure from its own citizens to follow Egypt's model. Even the support provided by Turkey was primarily only moral.

The failed experiment and overthrow of the Morsi regime do not mean "the end" of political movements based on Islam in the rest of the Muslim world, or even in Egypt. I find myself partial to the balanced and reasonable view of the future of Islamism in Egypt offered by John Voll who claims;

> What this means for the future of the Muslim Brotherhood and Islamism in Egypt seems to me to be the following: the parliamentary elections confirmed the support for Sharia-based political morality by three-quarters of the Egyptian population (as reported in a recent Pew survey). However, the broadly-based opposition to the Morsi presidency indicates that this religiously political mood does not necessarily translate into support for the Muslim Brotherhood. Egypt is in a time when it is possible to speak of both post-Islamism and post-secularism. I suggest that what is emerging in Egypt (and elsewhere) is a religious secularism and a secularist religionism that will probably produce new styles of movements and organizations that may keep old labels (like "Muslim Brotherhood" and "Nasserite") but will be significantly different from their twentieth-century ancestors. (Voll, quoted in Al Arian et al. 2013: *online*)

Voll believes that Egyptian Islamism will ultimately learn from its past mistakes; it will continue to reconfigure itself, and it will likely make greater efforts to find a balance between secularism and religion.

While it seems improbable that any genuine "Islamist movement" would denounce *Sharī'ah* or Islamic laws as a primary guiding source for legislation and social morality, it does seem likely that future Islamist movements in Egypt will make better efforts to be more inclusive in their decision-making processes and more cautious to placing people in positions of administrative power solely because of revolutionary credentials or charismatic authority as understood by Max Weber. Some seem to believe that this is already happening in the post-Morsi Egypt.

> In Egypt itself, there are other manifestations of Islam — salafi and sufi, for example — both of which have entered the public sphere. The Al-Nour party has a strong salafi orientation, and the leadership of Al-Azhar University has once again begun to revert to its sufi heritage. Both Islamic alternatives to the Brotherhood have in the past two years demonstrated a willingness to work within a democratic context and be less politically rigid than the Brotherhood. (Khan 2014: 80)

If one applies the Morsi government as a case study juxtaposed against my work, it gives even greater empirical credence to my claims about what is necessary for an Islamic government to succeed: strong, yet pragmatic Aristotelian leadership, bureaucratic modernity and competence, women having access to political institutions, toleration and genuine representation for minority groups, and most importantly, economic balance that promotes sustainable growth and provides social welfare benefits to those most in need. This can all be accomplished within an Islamic framework, and after one year, the Morsi government had yet to effectively meet any of these aforementioned standards during the short period that it was in power.

References

al Arian, Abdullah, et al. 2013. Roundtable on the future of Islamism: A starting point. *Jadaliyya*. http://www.jadaliyya.com/pages/index/15112/roundtable-on-the-future-of-islamism_a-starting-po. Accessed 12 July 2015.

Africa Bank Development Group. 2011. The African development bank group in North Africa—2011. http://www.afdb.org/fileadmin/uploads/afdb/Documents/Publications/RAPAfriquenordAnglais.pdf. Accessed 26 May 2015.

Alghoul, Diana. 2015. The hijab ban is part of a wider war against women. *Middle East Monitor*. https://www.middleeastmonitor.com/articles/africa/20315-the-hijab-ban-is-part-of-a-wider-war-against-women. Accessed 10 Aug 2015.

Berman, Sheri. 2003. Islamism, revolution, and civil society. *Perspectives on Politics* 1 (2): 257–272.

Bonn International Centre for Conversion (Bonn Report). 2013. Security sector reform in Algeria. 1–10. https://www.bicc.de/ssr_gtz/pdf/algeria.pdf. Accessed 19 Sep 2016.

Brown, Nathan. 2013. Tracking the Arab Spring: Egypt's failed transition. *Journal of Democracy* 24 (4): 45–58.

Clayton, James D. 1985. *Triumph and disaster 1945–1964: The years of MacArthur*, vol. 3. Boston, MA: Houghton Mifflin.

Department for International Development (DFID). 2003. The global conflict prevention pool: a joint UK government approach to reducing conflict. 1–41. London, UK. http://webarchive.nationalarchives.gov.uk/+/http:/www.dfid.gov.uk/pubs/files/global-conflict-prevention-pool.pdf. Accessed 30 Oct 2016.

Egypt Report. 2015. Memorandum of justification for certification under section 7041(a)(6)(c) of the Department of State, Foreign Operations, and Related Programs Appropriations Act, 2015 (Div. J, P.L. 113–235). Signed by Secretary of State John Kerry, 12 May 2015. http://graphics8.nytimes.com/packages/pdf/international/2015/egyptwaiver.pdf. Accessed 1 Jan 2016.

FIDH (International Federation of Human Rights) Report. 2015. "Exposing state hypocrisy: Sexual violence by security forces in Egypt," Report No. 661a, May 2015. https://www.fidh.org/IMG/pdf/egypt_report.pdf. Accessed 3 May 2016.

Hauslohner, Abigail. 2012. Mixed reviews as Egypt's new President hits 100-day mark in office. 6 Oct 2012. *The Washington Post.* http://articles.washingtonpost.com/2012-10-06/world/35502539_1_morsi-meter-islamist-public-opinion. Accessed 9 Aug 2013.

İnanç, Yusuf Selman. 2015. Egypt to confiscate and remove Muslim Brotherhood books from libraries. 24 June 2015. *The Daily Sabah.* http://www.dailysabah.com/mideast/2015/06/24/egypt-to-confiscate-and-remove-muslim-brotherhood-books-from-libraries. Accessed 28 June 2015.

Khan, M.A. Muqtedar. 2014. Islam, democracy and Islamism after the counter-revolution in Egypt. *Middle East Policy* 21 (1): 75–86.

Kirkpatrick, D. 2015. Obama administration criticizes Egypt in report to Congress. 7 June 2015. *New York Times.*http://www.nytimes.com/2015/06/08/world/middleeast/obama-administation-criticizes-egypt-in-report-to-congress.html. *Accessed 9 June 2015.*

Kirkpatrick, D. (2012). Named Egypt's winner, Islamist makes history. 24 June 2012. *New York Times.* http://www.nytimes.com/2012/06/25/world/middleeast/mohamed-morsi-of-muslim-brotherhood-declared-as-egypts-president.html?_r=2&pagewanted=all. Accessed 15 April 2015.

Laub, Zachary. 2014. Egypt's Muslim Brotherhood. 15 January 2014. *Council of Foreign Relations Backgrounders.* http://www.cfr.org/egypt/egypts-muslim-brotherhood/p23991?cid=ppc-google-grantegypt_,uslim_brotherhood_backgrounder&gclid=CPKCtN-qm8UCFXDLtAodMgsAWg. Accessed 29 Apr 2015.

Mekay, Emad. 2013. Exclusive: US bankrolled anti-Morsi activists. 10 July 2013. *Al Jazeera.* http://www.aljazeera.com/indepth/features/2013/07/201371011352 2489801. html. Accessed 13 Sep 2015.

Mitchell, R. 1993. *The society of the Muslim brothers.* New York: Oxford Press.

Morsi, Mohammed. 2012. Statement of H.E. Dr. Mohammed Morsi President of the Arab Republic of Egypt before the 67th General Assembly of the United Nations. 26 Sep 2012. http://gadebate.un.org/sites/default/files/gastatements/67/EG_en.pdf. Accessed 19 Dec 2014.

Olimat, Mohammed. 2014. Introduction: democratization, Arab Spring and Arab women. In *Arab Spring and Arab women: Challenges and opportunities,* ed. Mohammed Olimat, 1–16. New York: Routledge International Handbooks.

Rubin, B. (ed.). 2010. *The Muslim Brotherhood: The organizational policies of a global Islamist movement.* New York: Palgrave.

Soage, Ana and J.F. Franganillo. 2010. The Muslim brothers in Egypt. In *The Muslim Brotherhood: The Organization and Policies of a Global Islamist Movement*, ed. B. Rubin, 39–56. New York: Palgrave. *U.S. Constitution*, art. II, § 2.
Yezdani, İpek. 2011. Shari'a in Egypt is enough for us, Muslim Brotherhood leader says. 23 May 2011. *Hürriyet Daily News*. http://www.hurriyetdailynews.com/default.aspx?pageid=438&n=8220shari8217a-law-in-egypt-is-enough-for-us8221-tells-a-muslim-brotherhood-leader-2011-05-23. Accessed 12 July 2015.
Youssef, Adham. 2015. Giza schools burns alleged Islamist books, 14 April 2015. *Daily News Egypt*. http://www.dailynewsegypt.com/2015/04/14/giza-schoolburns-alleged-islamist-books/#dnePhoto/0/. Accessed 15 Apr 2015.
Zakaria, Fareed. 2013. Egypt must reach out to the Islamists it is now jailing. *Time* 182 (4). http://content.time.com/time/magazine/article/0,9171,2147277,00.html. Accessed 7 Nov 2016.

CHAPTER 10

The Case of Tunisia: Pragmatism and Cooperation

INTRODUCTION—THE ONE REMAINING HOPEFUL CASE

The Arab uprisings began in Tunisia in 2011 when a young man set himself on fire in an act of protest and desperation against a decrepit authoritarian political system that had run its course. Soon after the highly public act and ensuing viral online video of Mohamed Bouazizi's tragic self-immolation, Tunisians took to the streets and eventually forced Zine El Abidine Ben Ali to flee for his life. Ben Ali had ruled Tunisia since 1987 following the overthrow of Habib Bourguiba who also had to flee for his life to Saudi Arabia.[1] Four years following the uprisings in the Arab world, Tunisia remains the one bright spot. In the words of Bruce Maddy-Weitzman, "But Tunisia was, and remains, the only Arab country whose post-authoritarian experience retains a reasonable chance of success" (Maddy-Weitzman 2014: 2507). This can widely be attributed to Tunisian political actors choosing peaceful means rather than violence in pushing their agendas. This included Tunisia's moderate Islamist *Ennahda* Party (*Ḥizbu n-Nahḍah*) that remained an Islamist party for nearly three decades until it decided to abandon its Islamist agenda in May 2016.

This chapter will look in greater detail at contemporary Tunisian politics with a focus on the moderate *Ennahda* Movement that has drawn wide praise for its pragmatism, commitment to peace, and promotion of a sensible, and most importantly, realistic, form of Islamic politics. In March 2015, Larry Diamond declared that "Tunisia remains full of promise. Alone among the Arab States, it has achieved a remarkable level of political compromise among secular parties and the principal Islamist party, Ennahda" (2015: *online*). Diamond goes on to note that *Ennahda*, along with secular parties in Tunisia, were all unequivocal and quick in their denunciation of the March 18th terrorist attacks at the Bardo National Museum in Tunis that resulted in twenty-one casualties. Why *Ennahda's* immediate denunciation of this, along with other terrorist-related attacks that have recently plagued Tunisia, has been so important will be discussed throughout this chapter.

THE *ENNAHDA MOVEMENT:* A BRIEF TIMELINE OF ITS LEADER AND GENERAL DEVELOPMENT UNTIL 2011

Ennahda is representative of a recent wave of Islamist parties that support the creation of pluralist societies that allow for dissent and opposition. According to Fawaz Gerges, in recent times, "Islamist parties are slowly moving away from their traditional agenda of establishing an authoritarian Islamic state and imposing Islamic law, to a new focus that is centered on creating a 'civil Islam' that permeates society and accepts political pluralism" (Gerges 2013: 391). Gerges goes on to argue that *Ennahda* actually prefers to align themselves with liberals and leftists rather than the ultraconservative Salafist Islamist Parties. This pragmatism comes from the ideas of *Ennahda's* co-founder, Rachid al-Ghannouchi.

Rachid al-Ghannouchi was born on June 22, 1941, in Tunisia in the midst of WWII. He grew up in a traditional village and memorized *Qur'ān* under the guidance and instruction of his father (Tamimi 2001). French imperialism had a direct impact on Ghannouchi and would play an important role in his intellectual development. According to his biographer, Azzam Tamimi;

> Ghannouchi remembers vividly that at the age of five he saw his mother weeping over the imprisonment of his uncle by the French. Although al-Bashir was imprisoned only for a few months, this was a bitter experience unprecedented in the family and causing it much distress and sorrow. Upon his release, al-Bashir emerged, in the eyes of fellow villagers, as a national hero for whom Ghannouchi had great admiration and respect. (2001: 6)

Ghannouchi studied philosophy at the University of Damascus and graduated in 1968. In his younger days, Ghannouchi was a Nasserist who supported the anti-imperialist, pan-Arabist agenda propagated by Nasser. However, soon he became disillusioned with pan-Arabism and sought an alternative path. "His Syrian experience led him to believe that in the Middle East the concept of Arabism was often opposed to Islam. He had never felt or ever thought, by virtue of his Maghreb upbringing; that Arabism meant anything other than Islam" (Tamimi 2001: 20–21). Ghannouchi never lost touch with his Islamic religious heritage, even if at times his morale was low.

Once he recognized that the secular—and even at times openly hostile—attitudes toward Islam held by pan-Arabists were at odds with his religious values, he realized he could no longer identify with or support such a movement. In June 1966, Ghannouchi experienced a deeply personal Islamic awakening and ultimately decided to leave the Arab nationalist movement altogether. According to Tamimi's highly informative biography on Rachid al-Ghannouchi, five main factors influenced the thought of Ghannouchi and his political movement.

> From the mid-1970s to the early 1980s five main factors directly influenced Ghannouchi's thought and the development of his movement's political standing. These were the liberal democratic current that emerged in Tunisia in the second half of the 1970s; the 1978 violent confrontation between the trade unions and the government; the clash and interaction on campus with the leftists; the Iranian revolution; and the socio-political thought of the Islamic movement in Sudan. (2001: 45–46)

During the 1970s, Ghannouchi realized that the *Qur'ān* provided the guidance necessary to understand the world and that denying this reality would only lead to misguidance. Ghannouchi firmly believed, based on his own readings of the *Qur'ān*, that it was acceptable and even necessary in some cases to look outside of Islam for inspiration under the condition that what was sought from the outside was not in opposition to the fundamental principles of Islam. "He came to realize that it was justice that made it possible for Ibn Rushd (Averroes) and other Muslim philosophers to interact with Greek thought, taking from it that which they believed to be compatible with Islam and rejecting that which they believed was incompatible" (Tamimi 2001, 36). He sought to move the Islamism in Tunisia away from the rigidity of the anti-democratic, deeply conservative

Salafist/Qutbist discourse and more toward the rationalist and multifaceted understandings of Islam and its relations to social and political culture held by nineteenth century reformist figures such as Rifa'ah Tahtawi, Khairuddin at-Tunisi, Mohammad 'Abduh, Abdurrahman al-Kawakibi, and Jamal al-Din al-Afghani. On the willingness of the aforementioned figures to engage with Western ideas, Tamimi commented that; "Faced with a crisis of government augmented by autocracy and corruption, they sought to legitimize the borrowing of those aspects of the Western model they believed were compatible with Islam and capable of resolving the political crisis at home" (2001: 47). This same openness to Western ideas in regard to institutions and procedural justice has been the cornerstone of Ghannouchi's political worldview.

Ghannouchi took on the mantle of supporting workers' rights alongside Marxists and Communists in the late 1970s in Tunisia noting that despite deep-seated ideological differences, both movements shared the same immediate goal of economic justice. According to Ghannouchi:

> The value of justice is the greatest value in Islam, and Just[ice] is one of the attributes of God. How could we then have embroiled ourselves in opposing those, even if they were Marxists, who struggled for securing the interests of the poor and the oppressed? Learning from the examples set by the Prophet, we decided that defending justice should be our foremost priority. (Ghannouchi, quoted in Tamimi 2001: 52)

Around the same time that conversations and protests in regard to workers' rights were being discussed in Tunisia, the Iranian Revolution took place. The 1979 Iranian Revolution was deeply inspirational for Ghannouchi and his movement (Kaminski 2015). According to Tamimi;

> For Ghannouchi, the most important intellectual contribution of the Iranian revolution was the way in which it presented the conflict between the poor and the rich. He saw in its discourse a re-presentation of the class conflict within an Islamic framework and using Islamic terminology. It was the notion of an Islamic revolution against *taghut* (a false god; or a symbol of tyranny and oppression) that drew his attention. (2001: 54)

Khomeini's movement represented a new way of understanding the relationship between social justice and Islamic values in the modern nation-state. Despite initial reservations among Tunisia's *Sunni* Muslims for supporting a *Shīʿah*-led political movement, soon after the Revolution in Iran, banners depicting images of Khomeini began appearing in Tunisian Islamist publications.

Ghannouchi also saw the Iranian Revolution as a successful organic effort aimed at uprooting Western imperialism and exploitation. At first, he saw Khomeini's model as something that could help undergird Tunisia's own nascent Islamic political movement. According to Ghannouchi; "The Iranian revolution had come at the right time to provide us with Islamic analytical tools for conflicts our traditional cultural discourse could not deal with" (Ghannouchi, quoted in Tamimi 2001: 55). Shortly after the Iranian Revolution, however, Ghannouchi became disillusioned with the Iran's new leadership who denounced his movement as not being revolutionary enough and still representing Western modes of discourse and Western values.

In the early 1980s, Tunisia's underground Islamist movement after tense deliberations among its members held an internal referendum in which 70% of the movement's members voted to make the movement public. This referendum was approved by the movement's Shura council on April 9, 1981, and two months later, Ghannouchi announced the formation of Tunisia's new Islamist movement, *Ḥarakat al-Ittijāh al-Islāmī*, or "The Movement of Islamic Tendency."

The movement from the beginning sought to be democratic. Rachid al-Ghannouchi authored the movement's manifesto that showed his movement's desire to engage in pluralistic democratic processes that included genuine power sharing, "and affirmed that the electoral process was the source of legitimacy" (Tamimi 2001: 59). Shortly after the party's formation, however, Ghannouchi, along with 500 members, was arrested, and Ghannouchi spent 1981–1984 in prison. Ghannouchi's imprisonment was a cathartic experience that gave him the time to develop his critical intellectual capacities.

During his time in prison, he spent his time reading the works of the Algerian writer and philosopher, Malek Bennabi. Bennabi argued that, for too long, Muslims have rested on their laurels, and as a result, their societies became culturally and intellectually stagnant. He addressed the question of democracy and Islam in the 1950s and 1960s—decades before the likes of Voll, Ramadan, and Esposito. Bennabi came to the conclusion that understanding the idea of democracy in Islam could not simply be reduced to formal legalistic principles—rather it had to be understood as deriving from the essence of Islam itself. The most important aspect of the democratic enterprise within an Islam context was whether or not it facilitated in strengthening one's own personal development, *imān*, and *taqwā*.

Following Ghannouchi's release from prison, he was eventually re-arrested, and this time was sentenced to death by an increasingly erratic Habib Bourguiba. However, Bourguiba was eventually removed himself from power in 1987, and Ghannouchi was freed. Islamist candidates were allowed to run as independents in the late 1980s, but due to their success, the new Ben Ali regime cracked down, and eventually Ghannouchi exiled himself to London where he continued to develop his ideas over the next two decades.

Ḥarakat al-Ittijāh al-Islāmī changed its name in 1989 to *Ḥarakat an-Nahḍah*. The movement was more radical during the 1980s. The group—or at least members of it—were widely believed to be responsible for the bombing of some popular hotels frequented by Western tourists during the 1980s. However, as time went on, the movement became more pragmatic and explicitly renounced violence and its previous affiliations with other more extremist-oriented Arab-Islamist groups. This followed a wider trend of Islamist political parties embracing a more pragmatic and moderate politics over the past few decades.

> In the last four decades, centrist Islamists skillfully positioned themselves as the credible alternative to the failed secular authoritarian order, an order that unwittingly facilitated the rise and expansion of the Islamist movement. (Gerges 2013: 390)

Ghannouchi's movement is perhaps the most successful example of what Gerges is talking about.

Ghannouchi remained abroad until his triumphant return to Tunis in the wake of the 2011 Tunisian Revolution. In the 2011 election for the Constituent Assembly of Tunisia, the *Ennahda* Movement won 89 of the 217 seats, which made it by far the strongest party in the legislature. Commenting on the 2011 elections in Tunisia, Noah Feldman commented that, "[c]ombining pragmatism and principle, mainstream political Islam has undergone an extraordinary democratic transformation" and concludes that, "[f]rom the standpoint of the global ideal of democracy, this is a victory of historic proportions" (2011: *online*).

ENNAHDA FOLLOWING 2011

Luca Ozzano (2013) offered a useful taxonomy of all religious-based parties, regardless of their particular religious orientation. His taxonomy for religious political party orientation included *conservative*, which not only has an ideology based on religious values, but also is concerned with non-religious concerns; *progressive*, which were social reform oriented, often based in a Marxist discourse; *nationalist*, which emphasized the supremacy of the group within a religious-national context; *fundamentalist*, which was labeled a "total integration" ideology that was based on a specific interpretation of a religious message; and *camp*, which were flexible and pragmatic with some core religious values.

Ozzano labeled *Ennahda* as an example of a conservative-religious party similar to Turkey's Justice and Development Party (AKP). Ghannouchi and Ennahda's leaders at one point even liked to compare their party to the Turkey's Justice and Development Party (Lewis 2011). On conservative-religious political parties such as the Turkey's AKP and Tunisia's *Ennahda*, Ozzano argues that;

> ...only part of their policies is inspired by religious values; they accept secular democratic institutions as well as social and political pluralism. Although they try to widen the role of religion in the public sphere, they do not aim at making it the only basis for state law and institutions. (2013: 7)

Following electoral setbacks, *Ennahda* dropped their insistence on Islam being the primary source of legislation recognizing Tunisia's generally more moderate political and social mores. According to Sami Brahem, "If Ennahda wants to exercise power, it must be on the same page as this modernism, or else become a radical movement" (Brahem quoted in Lambroschini 2014: *online*). Despite Tunisia's current social climate, this does not mean that in the future the people of Tunisia might not have a different opinion on the role of Islam as a source of legislation—after all only three years earlier the people voted the Islamist party into power that ran on a more religiously conservative platform.

Ozzano also noted that religious-conservative parties tended to be willing to form coalitions and often find themselves more successful at incorporating wider cross-sections of society into their movements beyond just their base. He views the impact of parties with such an orientation as promoting the overall democratization process;

Their overall impact on the quality of democracy and on democratization processes is usually quite positive because they often promote the political socialization of rural and traditional masses previously not involved in politics and attempt to create social harmony, producing public policies that balance out different economic interests. (2013: 7)

Both *Ennahda* and the AKP have been successful in their campaigns to garner support from rural religious conservatives. Tunisia's *Ennahda* Movement has been especially successful at forging coalitions with other constituencies. It has also made serious efforts to denounce radicalism and violence.

On February 6, 2013, Tunisia was rocked by the assassination of the popular left-wing politician Chokri Belaid. He was shot multiple times as he was leaving his residence in Tunis by an extremist who ISIS later claimed was working on their behalf.[2] The assassination of Belaid set off riots across Tunisia by leftists and secularists who immediately blamed *Ennahda*, and feared Tunisia turning into another failed "Arab Spring" state. Unlike the other failures, however, Tunisia was pulled from the brink largely because of Ennahda's leadership that put the stability of the country ahead of its own hold on power, even if it was not guilty of the assassination.

Shortly after February 6 assassination, Tunisia's Prime Minister Hamadi Jebali announced his resignation following a failed effort to create a technocratic unity government that could weather the political storm. Jebali stated;

> "I promised if my initiative did not succeed I would resign as head of the government, and this is what I am doing following my meeting with the president," he said at the presidential palace. "Today there is a great disappointment among the people and we must regain their trust and this resignation is a first step". (*India Today* 2013: *online*)

While Jebali's move might have in the short term weakened *Ennahda*'s position, it may have saved it from a very possible long-term fate that the Egyptian Muslim Brotherhood is currently facing. It also quelled protests and allowed for peaceful elections to take place a year and a half later. Unlike the Egyptian Muslim Brotherhood that is now banned and whose members are regularly rounded up by the totalitarian Sisi government in night pogroms on questionable charges, *Ennahda* was able to not only save face, but also win a very respectable 69 seats in the 2014 elections. It finds itself in position to reassert itself in the near future with some internal modifications and agenda re-shifting.

In Tunisia's 2014 elections, *Nidaa Tounes*, a secular Tunisian political party led by Beji Caid Essebsi—the man considered to be the spiritual father of *Nidaa Tounes*, managed to win 86 out of 217 parliamentary seats. *Ennahda* came in second, winning 69 seats as mentioned above. The other parties were much less successful in securing seats in parliament than *Nida Tounes* or *Ennahda*, the Free Patriotic Union won 16 seats, the Popular Front won 16 seats, and *Afek Tounes* won 8 seats, and no other party won more than 4. While *Nidaa Tounes* won a majority, it was not enough to rule as a single party government; they would be required to form a coalition.

Ennahda, despite the short-term setbacks in this election, recognized the importance of working within the new system. In doing so, they were able to present themselves as a party that placed public welfare over its own political success. Anouar Jamaoui argued that Tunisia's main Islamist movement "presented itself to Tunisians as a civil, democratic, party with a Muslim background, a moderate political body that favours dialogue, communication, and alliance with the political other for the sake of securing order and public welfare" (2015: *online*). The other major Tunisian secular parties, specifically *Nidaa Tounes* and the Popular Front, in the end were the ones to appear sectarian and exclusionary.

> With the coalition government, Ennahda was able to protect itself against the possible exclusionary attitude of the mainstream secular leftist current in Nidaa Tounes and the Popular Front—parties that ardently defended the exclusion of Islamists from governance. (Jamaoui 2015: *online*)

Many members in these secular parties sought to completely exclude the moderate Islamist party from any coalition because of their fundamental disagreement on the role religion should play in Tunisian politics and policies.

After facing a tough decision of whether to form a coalition with the other non-Islamist parties—a decision that would most certainly have negative reverberations throughout the ranks of Tunisia's many Islamist supporters; or join with *Ennahda*—a decision that would certainly upset secular leftist radicals within the party's ranks, *Nidaa Tounes* made the wise decision to form a coalition with *Ennahda* with the hopes of creating a large coalition of secularists and moderate Islamists. Following the disaster in Egypt after the military coup against the Muslim Brotherhood, *Nidaa Tounes* realized that if *Ennahda* was included in the new government—(1) there would less likely be mass protests outside parliament and violence, and (2) that most certainly the moderate Islamist party be more likely to "play by the rules" and minimize any extreme rhetoric or policy proposals that would most certainly anger some of the secularists in parliament.

Unexpectedly on May 20, 2016, *Ennahda* announced that they were abandoning the explicitly Islamist elements of their political platform. Ghannouchi announced to a full house at the *Ennahda* 10th party conference held at the Rades Olympic Hall that "Ennahda has changed from an ideological movement engaged in the struggle for identity to a protest movement against the authoritarian regime and now to a national democratic party. We must keep religion far from political struggles" (Ghannouchi, quoted in Souli 2016: *online*). Once again, only time will tell what this actually means and if the movement splinters between those who still seek an Islamist political agenda and those who do not. It is quite possible that this re-branding was meant to put the party in a better position for the upcoming 2017 local elections and 2019 presidential elections. Regardless of the direction the movement takes in the future, many of the elements that it sought to incorporate into its previous Islamist agenda are worth taking serious and a conceptual level.

The Lesson to be Learned from the Case of Tunisia

Tunisia showed that not all countries that were a part of the Arab uprisings were necessarily destined to failure. Pragmatism and moderation were hallmarks in getting a new constitution ratified in 2014. *Ennahda* agreed to a new constitution with the other secular parties in the Tunisian parliament in 2014. Despite its electoral defeats, *Ennahda* succeeded in having Islam declared as the official state religion in the new constitution. Title I, Article 1 of the 2014 constitution stipulates a republican political system and declares that Islam is the official state religion and that this cannot be amended. "Tunisia is a free, independent, sovereign state; its religion is Islam, its language Arabic, and its system is republican. This article might not be amended" (2014, *Title I, Art. 1*). It also agreed to strikingly cosmopolitan articles pertaining to individual rights and freedoms, including gender equality. According to Article 21 of the 2014 Tunisian constitution—"All citizens, male and female, have equal rights and duties, and are equal before the law without any discrimination. The state guarantees freedoms and individual and collective rights to all citizens, and provides all citizens the conditions for a dignified life" (2014,*Title II, Art. 21*). Tunisia's constitution allows for a great deal of flexibility. There is a lot of room for debate and discussion of more specific laws and policies within its constitutional framework.

A strong civil society seeking sustained stability was also a major factor in Tunisia's success. In 2015, Tunisia's National Dialogue Quarter, composed of various groups within Tunisian civil society including the Tunisian General Labour Union (*UGTT, Union Générale Tunisienne du Travail*), the Tunisian Confederation of Industry, Trade and Handicrafts (UTICA, *Union Tunisienne de l'Industrie, du Commerce et de l'Artisanat*), the Tunisian Human Rights League (LTDH, *La Ligue Tunisienne pour la Défense des Droits de l'Homme*), and the Tunisian Order of Lawyers (*Ordre National des Avocats de Tunisie*), society won the Nobel Peace Prize for their efforts at saving the country from ruin following the 2013 assassination of Chokri Belaid. According to the Nobel Committee's press release on the National Dialogue Quarter that was formed shortly after the assassination,

> It established an alternative, peaceful political process at a time when the country was on the brink of civil war. It was thus instrumental in enabling Tunisia, in the space of a few years, to establish a constitutional system of government guaranteeing fundamental rights for the entire population, irrespective of gender, political conviction or religious belief. (Nobelprize. org 2015: *online*)

Such cross-sector collaboration should be seen as a positive example for future Muslim states, not just in times of crisis, but in times of peace as well. Such enterprises can serve as a balance against a divided and stagnant political body. However, one must remember Tunisia was quite different from the other Arab Revolution countries. It actually had at least 7 important differences from most of the other Arab Revolution countries that need to be considered—

1. The ruling Ben Ali regime was significantly weaker than the Qaddafi, Mubarak, or Assad regime was. In the end, the Ben Ali

regime lacked the both the will, and to borrow a term often used by Charles Tilly (1985)—*the coercive capacity*—to make any serious effort at putting down an uprising. This helped account for why Ben Ali so quietly fled without much pomp and circumstance to Saudi Arabia; where many autocrats of recent vintage have been put out to pasture—Tunisia's previous dictator, Habib Bourguiba, former Yemeni despot, Ali Abdullah Saleh, ex-Pakistani premier Nawaz Sharif, and the notorious 1970s Ugandan dictator, Idi Amin Dada, immediately come to mind.

2. Tunisia's army was also a significantly weaker than the armies in other regional states like Algeria or Egypt. This helps account for why there was no military power grab following the Ben Ali regime's departure; nobody had the power to effectively make such a grab.
3. Despite Tunisia's economic weaknesses, it still had a relatively strong middle class, especially in comparison with the other Arab uprisings states. It has been long established that regimes with strong middle classes tend to be more prone to democracy, and less prone to radicalism and uncontrolled violence. In 1959, Seymour Lipset published his famous *American Political Science Review* article looking at the social requisites for democracy and noted that;

Increased wealth is not only related causally to the development of democracy by changing the social conditions of the workers, but it also affects the political role of the middle class through changing the shape of the stratification structure from an elongated pyramid, with a large lower class base, to a diamond with a growing middle class. A large middle class plays a mitigating role in moderating conflict since it is able to reward moderate and democratic parties and penalize extremist groups. (1959: 83)

In accordance with Lipset's hypothesis, Tunisia's sizeable middle class was able to mitigate tensions between the various partisan factions due to the fact they had their own economic and personal interests to consider.

4. Tunisia was not blessed (or cursed for that matter) with any particular natural resource such as oil or natural gas, which forced the government to rely primarily on tax revenues, thus making it more accountable to their citizens. *Rentier states* or states that

receive large amounts of money in the form of "rents" from global markets that do not have to rely on taxation as a source of funds generally are hostile to democratization in general. Michael Ross (2001) published a seminal work showing that oil and mineral dependence have strong negative effects on democratic development. His general findings are confirmed by Jay Ulfelder (2007) who showed a link between natural resource dependence and the survival of autocratic regimes.
5. Tunisia had little foreign funding and influence. This meant less foreign meddling in its internal political affairs like in the cases of Syria and Egypt, where multiple major international acts have a large stake in the end result.
6. As Ghannouchi himself noted, Tunisia is homogenous country had no deep underlying ethnic/sectarian tensions like Syria, Iraq, Yemen, and Bahrain. The problem with ethnic/sectarian tensions and democratic governance needs no further elaboration. One would be hard-pressed to find any state in the world with ethnic tensions to the extent that Iraq, Syria, or Yemen has, that still operates in a meaningfully democratic manner.
7. Tunisia did have a previous history of democratic and progressive reforms. In the nineteenth century, there was a constitutional order that guaranteed certain rights, and the Bourguiba presidency from 1959 to 1988, despite its autocratic tendencies, did promote public education and women's rights. The well-educated Tunisian society also fits within Lipset's rubric of factors that contribute to democracy; "The higher one's education, the more likely one is to believe in democratic values and support democratic practices" (Lipset 1959: 70). Lipset goes on to note that education was a more salient factor in support for democracy than income or occupation.

In a 2013 *Al Arabiya English* article, Senior Foreign Policy Research Institute fellow Abdullah Schleifer recalled a conversation that he had with his friend and colleague, the long-time Egyptian civil rights activist professor, Saad ad-Din Ibrahim, on the difference between the Egyptian MB's failure and Ennahda's success;

> I asked Saad-ad-Din Ibrahim (whom I seem to quote a lot) why? Saad said when he visited Tunisia after their Arab Spring moment, he asked

RachidGhannouchi, the leader of Ennahda (the Tunisian Islamist party), the same question: What was the difference? Ghannouchi replied "About 20 years," alluding to his years in exile-in England where he would sit in a café and meet Tunisian and other Arab exiles of all political persuasions, and where he could observe the actual functioning of the rule of law, unfettered freedom of speech, respectful rule and respectful opposition, and he learned much from the experience. (Schleifer 2013: *online*)

Ghannouchi's experience with Western modes of political discourse allowed for him to know how to handle his opposition in a successful and civil way. He followed Izetbegović's recommendation that the Muslim world ought to not just write of the West as immoral and corrupt. Ghannouchi learned from his time in England the importance of moderation. As a result, he was able to keep his movement on course rather than letting it implode. *Ennahda* and Tunisia's secular parties were able to find common ground despite their deep-seeded differences.

Notes

1. Ironically, Zine El Abdine Ben Ali himself fled to Saudi Arabia following his own ouster in 2011.
2. In a video released by ISIS after the shooting, Abou Mouqatel (also known as Boubakr Hakim) admitted ISIS' role in the killings of two prominent left-wing Tunisian politicians. According to the video, Abou Mouqatel said, "Yes, tyrants, we're the ones who killed ChokriBelaid and Mohamed Brahmi" (AbouMouqatel, quoted in Bacchi 2014: *online*).

References

Bacchi, Umberto. 2014. ISIS claims responsibility for murdering Tunisian politicians as election nears. Dec 19, 2014. *International Business Times.* http://www.ibtimes.co.uk/isis-claims-responsibility-murdering-tunisian-politicians-election-nears-1480280. Accessed 27 Nov 2016.

Diamond, Larry, 2015. Tunisia is still a success. *The Atlantic.* Mar 23, 2015. http://theatlantic.com/international/archive/2015/03/tunisia-is-still-a-success-terrorist-attack/388436. Accessed 30 Mar 2016.

Feldman, Noah. 2011. *Islamists' victory in Tunisia a win for democracy.* 30, October 2011. *Bloomberg View.* http://www.bloombergview.com/articles/2011-10-30/islamists-victory-in-tunisia-a-win-for-democracy-noah-feldman. Accessed 15 Dec 2015.

Gerges, Fawaz A. 2013. The Islamist moment: from Islamic state to civil Islam? *Political Science Quarterly* 128 (3): 389–426.
India Today. 2013. Tunisia PM Resigns After Cabinet Initiative Fails to Form a Technocratic Government. 20 February, 2013. http://indiatoday.intoday.in/story/tunisia-pm-resigns-after-cabinet-initiative-fails/1/250957.html. Accessed 20 May 2014.
Jamaoui, Anouar. 2015. The impact of the coalition on Ennahda and NidaaTounes. 11 March, 2015. *Open Democracy*. https://www.opendemocracy.net/arab-awakening/anouar-jamaoui/impact-of-coalition-on-ennahda-and-nidaa-tounes. Accessed 15 July 2015.
Kaminski, Joseph J. 2015. Comparing the goals and aspirations of contemporary nationalbased Islamist movements vs. contemporary transnational-based Islamist movements. In *Caliphates and global islamic politics*, eds. T. Poirson, and R. Oprisko, 46–59. Bristol, UK: E-International Publications.
Lambroschini, Antoine. 2014. Tunisia charter to uphold equality, freedom of opinion. 7 January, 2014. *Daily News Egypt*. Originally released by *Agence France-Presse* (*AFP*). http://www.dailynewsegypt.com/2014/01/07/tunisia-charter-to-uphold-equality-freedom-of-opinion/. Accessed 1 Mar 2014.
Lewis, A. 2011. Profile: Tunisia's Ennahda party. 25, October, 2011. *BBC News*. http://www.bbc.co.uk/news/world-africa-15442859. Accessed 2 May 2014.
Lipset, Seymour. 1959. Some social requisites of democracy: Economic development and political legitimacy. *The American Political Science Review* 53 (1): 69–105.
Maddy-Weitzman, Bruce. 2014. A turning point? The Arab Spring and the Amazigh movement. *Ethnic and Racial Studies* 38 (14): 2499–2515.
Nobelprize.org. 2015. The Nobel Peace Prize for 2015. https://www.nobelprize.org/nobel_prizes/peace/laureates/2015/press.html. Accessed 30 Oct 2016.
Ozzano, Luca. 2013. The many faces of the political God: A typology of religiously oriented parties. *Democratization* 20: 807–830.
Ross, Michael. 2001. Does oil hinder democracy? *World Politics* 53: 325–361.
Schleifer, Abdullah. 2013. The problems of Islamist politics in Egypt. Apr 10, 2013.*Al Arabiya English*. http://english.alarabiya.net/en/views/2013/04/10/The-problems-of-Islamist-politics-in-Egypt.html. Accessed 15 Sep 2014.
Souli, Sarah. 2016. Why Tunisia's top Islamist party rebranded itself. May 2016. *Al Monitor*. http://www.al-monitor.com/pulse/originals/2016/05/tunisia-ennahda-islamist-party-rebranding-congress.html. Accessed 19 Oct 2016.
Tamimi, Azzam. 2001. *RachidGhannouchi: A democrat within Islamism*. New York: Oxford University Press.
Tilly, Charles, and P. Evans. 1985. War making and state making as organized crime. In *Bringing the state back in Cambridge*, eds. D. Rueschemeyer, and T. Skocpol, 169–191. UK: Cambridge University Press.

Tunisian Constitution of 2014. Constituteproject.org, Translated into English by UNDP and reviewed by International IDEA. https://www.constituteproject.org/constitution/Tunisia_2014.pdf. Accessed 15 July 2015.

Ulfelder, Jay. 2007. Natural resource wealth and the survival of autocracy. *Comparative Political Studies* 40: 995–1018.

CHAPTER 11

The Case of Malaysia: Prioritizing Economic Growth and Modernization

INTRODUCTION

The final case that will be looked at in this work is that of Malaysia. Islam has a long history in Malaysia first arriving in the thirteenth century via Arab and Indian traders. Following centuries of colonial wrestling, the British assumed control of much of what today is Malaysia during the nineteenth century. After decades of struggle against British colonialism, Malaysia gained independence from the British on August 31st, 1957; however, the Federation of Malaysia, consisting of the Federation of Malaya, North Borneo, Sarawak, and Singapore, was not created until September 16th, 1963. Today, Malaysia is a federal constitutional elective monarchy whose model closely resembles the Westminster parliamentary system that it adapted from its previous British colonizers.

While not an "Islamic governed state" per se, Islam plays an undeniable role in Malaysian politics and daily life. Osman Bakar argued that Malaysia's more "moderate" general Islamic discourse "played a central role in the foundation of the nation's democratic system and in the evolution of its democratic institutions and politics" (Bakar, referenced in Khan (ed.) 2006: 76). Legislative power is divided between federal and state legislatures. Malaysia has a bicameral parliament that follows a multiparty system that consists of the lower house—the House of Representatives, and the upper house—the Senate.

WHY MALAYSIA?

When considering the case study chapters that would be included in this book, I wanted to make sure that there would be at least one case study from South Asia or Southeast Asia. Originally, I intended on including Indonesia based on my initial inclination that something could be drawn from its state ideology—*Pancasila*—that articulated a vision of pluralism and democracy that operated within the confines of an Islamic society. The Suharto regime's New Order (*Orde Baru*) program was based on *Pancasila* which literally translates from Old Javanese to "5 principles." The 5 principles constitutive of the *Pancasila* philosophy are as follows: (1) a belief in one and only one God; (2) just and civilized humanity; (3) the unity of Indonesia; (4) Democracy guided by a source of inner wisdom arising through deliberative processes among selected representatives; and (5) Social justice for all people.

To briefly elaborate, *Pancasila* is a classic example of a civil religion much like Kemalism is in Turkey. It actually can be placed in the same milieu as both Nasserism in Egypt and Kemalism, though Kemalism has been (or *was*, depending on your perspective) more durable as a foundational ideology in Turkey than Nasserism was in Egypt, or *Pancasila* was in Indonesia. Çinar and Duran defined Kemalism as: "an anti-political and state-centered paradigm that claims that Turkish society and public sphere is homogeneous and that displays distaste for political representation of differences" (2008: 26). *Pancasila* in practice displayed the same anti-political, state-centered paradigmatic characteristics that showed hostility toward the political representation of differences as does Kemalism. Unlike Kemalism, however, *Pancasila* focused more on *harmony* rather than *homogeneity* due to Indonesia's enormous cultural and linguistic diversity. Like Kemalism, *Pancasila* allowed for religious practices so long as they did not become overtly political in their mission.

While in theory, *Pancasila* seemed laudable enough, in practice, it often has been an excuse used by the ruling regimes to put down opposition movements who were conveniently labeled as *"anti-Pancasila"* similarly to how the moniker of Kemalism was selectively invoked to label religious or minority (Kurdish, Alevi, Islamist etc.) ideologies as being in opposition to the values of the modern secular Turkish state during previous decades. On the overuse of *Pancasila* as a panacea for all of Indonesian society's ills by politicians in the 1990s, Douglas Ramage commented that;

Pancasila is invoked by officials in an almost sacral, obligatory fashion. It has become part of the government mantra and citizens rarely see any connection between the invocation of Pancasila and the particular issue at hand. Several years ago the government had taken to identifying so many things as "Pancasilaist" (press, democracy, economy, etc.) that it became a joke that there was even "Pancasila football" (the national sport). (1995: 28)

Even though Indonesia modernized and its economy grew significantly under Suharto, his legacy is permanently marred by decades of brutal authoritarian repression. According to Vedi Hadiz and Khoo Boo Teik;

> Early political Islam in Indonesia had strong organization and substantial aims. Yet, overshadowed by state secularism and demobilized by brutal authoritarianism, no Islamic force emerged as a credible challenger for state power, even when a crisis of capitalism resulted in a dramatic widening of the parameters of political contestation. (2011: 481)

While researching Indonesia for this final case study chapter, I came to the conclusion that *Pancasila* was primarily a slogan aimed at keeping the peace, rather than any type of reflection upon anything specifically Islamic. It is true that Indonesia has multiple competing Islamic political parties today; however, I did not find any real clear useful lessons that could be drawn from the case of Indonesia that could be applied to this work.

I had the opportunity to discuss this conundrum with a colleague living in Malaysia and he agreed that the case of Indonesia was not the best case to engage with for this particular project. Instead of Indonesia, he recommended that I look at Malaysia where there exists a more tangible relationship between Islam and its impact on governance and the institutions that operate within it. This point corroborates with a similar point made by Kubicek in which he argued; "In contrast to Indonesia, which recognizes a number of religions under the rubric of pancasila, the state's ideology, Malaysia counts Islam as its only official religion. Islam is defined by the constitution as a core component of Malay identity" (2015: 83). Bakar argues that Islam can be seen as the foundational source of Malaysia's institutional framework based on:

(1) the special position of Islam as the sole official religion, (2) the special position of the Malays as the destined political guardians and vanguard

of Islam, thus necessitating the political dominance and special rights in various domains, and (3) the unique blending of traditional and modern western political institutions in the creation of new democratic institutions. (Bakar, referenced in Khan (Ed.) 2006: 75)

After taking my friend's invaluable advice and reading more on Malaysia, I found some really interesting things that can be drawn from this particular case. This chapter will look at how Malaysia successfully prioritized economic development over any particular dogmatic adherence to any specific ideology when modernizing in the 1980s. The chapter will conclude as did the previous chapters which aimed to show what lessons could be drawn from the case of Malaysia that can be applied to an Islamic governed state.

ENTER MAHATHIR

Mahathir bin Mohammed was born on July 10, 1925, in Alor Setar in the northwestern state of Kedah.[1] He was not born into the aristocracy or a prominent religious or political family, which is an important thing to remember when looking at his later attitudes toward Western colonial powers (Wain 2010). Like Rachid al-Ghannouchi, his early development was deeply influenced by colonialism;

> British colonial rule as well as the Japanese Occupation (1942–45) had a profound impact on Mahathir's worldview and philosophy of politics. Combined with his experience growing up in semi-rural Kedah State (unlike his three predecessors, who had aristocratic childhoods), this contributed to producing an abrasive, combative character and a tenacious will, traits that proved to be both strengths and liabilities for Mahathir. (Khalid 2011: 430)

In 1964, Mahathir was elected as the federal parliamentarian for the Alor Setar-based seat of Kota Setar Selatan. He immediately engaged with the question of the day—that of Singapore, which in 1965 was expelled from Malaysia. He continued to be a strong advocate of the ethnic Malay population over the next few years while in parliament.

On May 13th, 1969, Sino-Malay sectarian violence in Kuala Lumpur resulted in hundreds of deaths spurred on by ethnic Malays who felt as if they were second-class citizens. Despite being a nationalist Malay politician, Mahathir lost his parliamentary seat in 1969 and was subsequently expelled from the ruling United Malays National Organisation (UMNO) (*Pertubuhan Kebangsaan Melayu Bersatu*). During this time in which he found himself outside of politics, in 1970, he published *The Malay Dilemma*.[2] In this work, he argued that the ethnic Malays were the true indigenous peoples of Malaysia (*bumiputras*) and that their general tolerance and non-confrontational nature allowed for them to be subjugated by other races in their own land. He proposed a controversial program of affirmative action to mitigate the ethnic Chinese hegemony in business. While some called his program racist, others argued it was necessary to level the playing field for ethnic Malays who generally were worse off financially than the rest of the population. He was invited back into the UMNO Party in 1973 by Abdul Razak Hussein and returned to the House of Representatives in 1974. Mahathir remained active in Malaysian politics and was eventually sworn in as Malaysia Prime Minister on July 16, 1981, at the age of 56 (Wain 2010).

Mahathir's plan for Malaysia focused on economic development. The two main goals of Mahathir's modernization project were as follows: (1) to make Malaysia an economically developed country and (2) to unite Malaysia via a national integration plan that brought all of Malaysia's constituent peoples together. According to A.B. Shamsul: "The underlying philosophy of the modernization project has been homogenization through the simultaneous pursuit of entrepreneurship and social justice" (Shamsul, referenced in Hefner (Ed.) 2001: 215). Malaysia had always had a capitalist, market-based economy that moved from being generally *laissez-faire* in the late 1950s until 1969, followed by a period of more direct state intervention from 1970 until 1985, followed by a period of liberalization and deregulation during the secondhalf of the 1980s until around 1998 (Haneef 2001). Mahathir shifted Malaysia's economy from being primarily agricultural to one that focused more on manufacturing and exports.

From 1988 to 1996, Malaysia saw an 8% economic expansion per annum. Malaysia also engaged in numerous ambitious national projects during this time all aimed at continued innovation and growth.

> These included the production of Kancil, the second Malaysian car; construction of the second causeway linking Malaysia and Singapore; the Multimedia Super Corridor (msc) and Putrajaya/Cyberjaya project; the

construction of the giant Petronas Twin Towers; the launching of the maesat satellite; the completion of the country's North–South Highway; and the opening of the new Kuala Lumpur International Airport. (Shamsul, referenced in Hefner (ed.) 2001: 218)

In 1991, Mahathir announced his own economic plan known as "The Way Forward" or "Vision 2020" that outlined nine strategic challenges that Malaysia must overcome in order to be a fully developed nation by 2020. Mahathir's vision 2020 plan sought to make Malaysia both a fully economically developed and a balanced nation;

> Malaysia should not be developed only in the economic sense. It must be a nation that is fully developed along all the dimensions: economically, politically, socially, spiritually, psychologically and culturally. We must be fully developed in terms of national unity and social-cohesion, in terms of our economy, in terms of social justice, political stability, system of government, quality of life, social and spiritual values, national pride and confidence. (Mahathir 1991: 1)

He helped shift the country's economic base away from agriculture and natural resources and more toward manufacturing and exporting. Despite the fact that Malaysia's economic growth is nowhere near its early 1990s levels, its economy remains stable today.

Mahathir's Vision of Islamization for Malaysia

Mahathir's plan was to spread Islamic values in Malaysia once he became Prime Minister. In an address given very early in Mahathir's 22-year tenure as Prime Minister, he articulated his vision of Islamization;

> Islamization is the inculcation of Islamic values in government administration. Such inculcation is not the same as implementation of Islamic laws in the country. Islamic laws are for Muslims and meant for their personal laws. But laws of the nation, although not Islamic based, can be used as long as they do not come in conflict with Islamic principles. Islamic laws can be implemented if all the people agree to them. (Mahathir, quoted in Norhashimah 1996: 232)

According to Joseph Chinyong Liow, "Mahathir moved to delineate the parameters of Islamic governance and invest heavily in the Islamization of the state machinery and bureaucracy" (2009: 46). In order to do this, institutions need to be created that could foster these values. In 1983, the International International Islamic University of Malaysia (IIUM) was created. IIUM was administratively and organizationally modeled in the vein of American universities. The official IIUM web site summarizes the university's mission as: "integration, islamization, internationalization, and comprehensive excellence."[3] Milne and Mauzy argued that, "IIUM aspired to be the counterpart of the renowned Egyptian al-Azhar University where many Malay nationalists had been educated" (1999: 86). IIUM hosts multiple well-regarded peer-reviewed academic journals that generally focus on topics related to Islam and currently has an enrollment of over 20,000 students. At one time, IIUM even had Turkey's former Prime Minister, Ahmet Davutoğlu, as a lecturer in the department of political science.

Also in 1983, Mahathir took the important step of introducing Islamic banking and insurance with the establishment of the first Islamic bank in Malaysia–Bank Islam Malaysia. According to Furqani and Mulyany; "The Islamic financial system in Malaysia has evolved as a viable and competitive component on the overall financial system as a driver of economic growth and development" (2009: 60). During this time, Malaysia's financial sector began offering *Sharī'ah* compliant financial services. As mentioned in an earlier chapter, the prohibition on *ribā* or usury is taken very seriously within Islam. So serious was Malaysia about *Sharī'ah* compliant banking that it even required the Islamic banks to keep all transactions separate from conventional, interest-based banking system, so that investor funds were not in any way co-mingling.

Over the past 30 years, Malaysia has steadily expanded its Islamic banking initiative. Following a period of familiarization during the mid-1980s, in the 1990s, Malaysia's Islamic banking model encouraged increased competition. The goal was to have multiple competing banks to stimulate growth and interest in the industry. During this time, Malaysia further expanded their Islamic banking industry by allowing conventional banks to open "Islamic Windows" in which customers could get Islamic banking services at traditional banks. Since 2000, Malaysia's banking industry has been growing by an average of 18% per year in terms of assets held (Lo and Leow 2014). Quantitative research by Furqani and Mulyany demonstrated the positive future for Islamic banking in Malaysia.

> The signs and significance levels of t-statistics of ECM [Error Correction Model] for Islamic banking and investment suggests that in the long-run there is a "virtuous circle" of Islamic banking development and investment, as increase[s] in Islamic bank financing stimulates an entrepreneurial response in the productive sectors and promotes more investments, at the same time, more investment in the country facilitates Islamic banking to develop further. (2009: 69)

Islamic banks in Malaysia still only hold a fraction of the market share that non-Islamic banks in the country hold, however, as Lo and Leow argue, based on a wide range of financial services and continued success, these numbers will most certainly get bigger.

> Save for *sukuk*, most of the products concept[s] such as Mudharabah (profit-sharing), Musyarakah (joint venture), Murabahah (cost plus), Al-Ijarah (leasing), Al-Kafalah (bank guarantee) to name a few are basically functioning like the conventional banking products but structured and complied with shariah law. (2014: 528)

They go on to argue that since many of these Islamic banking products and services are already familiar to Malaysians it will be easier to gain more customers over the long term.

The Islamic Banking initiative has been wildly popular and has bolstered the United Nations Military Observer (UNMO's) Islamic credentials.

> The popularity of the Islamic Bank skyrocketed, not only among the Muslim community but also among non-Muslims who were drawn to its favorable terms, especially for personal, housing, and auto loans. So strong was the support for the Islamic Bank that it became the nation's third-largest bank within four years of its opening. (Liow 2009: 55)

Mahathir moved quickly and boldly with some Islamic initiatives during his years as Malaysia's leader; however, he was more cautious with others. Despite the broad Islamization efforts in Malaysia under Mahathir, his party (UNMO) did not try and enforce more controversial *ḥudūd* punishments. Mahathir's rationale was that Malaysia was too multi-ethnic and multireligious to effectively administer *ḥudūd* punishments (Norhashimah 1996). The more conservative PAS (*Parti Islam Se-Malaysia*) has taken on this cause with little success in recent years.

Serious Issues Malaysia Needs to Confront

Despite Malaysia's economic success during Mahathir's tenure as Prime Minister, his authoritarian tendencies cannot be ignored. Some believe that Mahathir's regime made efforts to control the ʿ*Ulamā*ʾ in order to centralize and consolidate power. Kubicek argues that in Malaysia, Islam has been "harnessed to justify both expansion of state power and [...] limit dissent. Fatwas issued by legal scholars were given force of law" (2015: 103). Often questionable *fatwās* were issued that sought to root out Western Islamic authors such as Karen Armstrong and John Esposito who were considered too provocative. The rulings of religious figures ought to factor into state legal decisions, but ought not to simply be enacted into law without sufficient oversight and legislative and judicial deliberation in an Islamic governed state.

In order to police opposition groups, Mahathir regularly invoked the notorious 1960 Internal Security Act (ISA) that allowed the government to detain individuals without trial or criminal charges under limited, legally defined circumstances. "Against the backdrop of Mahathir's Islamization agenda, the ISA became a notorious yet convenient way for the state to neutralize the political threat posed by political opposition, Civil Societygroups, and radical Islamist movements, all in the name of "national security"'" (Liow 2009: 56). This law was not changed until 2012.

Today Malaysia is mired in increasing levels of corruption that unsurprisingly have been coupled with decreases in transparency. The issue of race always looms in the background of Malaysian politics. The prominent Malaysian political scientist/political dissident Chandra Muzaffar claims that in Malaysia, the state has embraced a "selective, sectarian approach which in itself is an injustice to God's revelation" (2002: 177). Throughout Muzaffar's career, he has called for a more open Islamic discourse within Malaysia.

> The underlying theme of Chandra's philosophy is how to translate Islam's values and goals into a living reality that is relevant in the here-and-now and to extend its universalism to its utmost inclusive domain, thus bridging the gap between Muslims and non-Muslims. (Noor, in Hunter (Ed.) 2009: 218)

Making efforts to create bridges between Muslims and non-Muslims, especially those not necessarily "hostile" to Islam, should be a top priority for any newly transitioning Islamic governed state.

Tensions between ethnic Malays and those of Chinese ethnicity are not only strained, but so too are relations between Muslims and Christians. A few years ago, Malaysia was embroiled in what can be only described as a truly ridiculous national debate about whether or not Christians could also refer to God as *Allah*. After much deliberation, in 2013, the Malaysian high court reversed a ruling allowing non-Muslims to refer to God as *Allah*. Those who willfully violate this dictum can be charged with violating Malaysia's sedition laws. The aftermath of this unfortunate court decision lingers even today.

> Religion is also being politicized to almost boiling point. Relations between Muslims and Christians are at an all-tome low because of the controversy over the use of the world '*Allah*', which some Muslims claim is exclusive to them although Christians in Sabah and Sarawak have been using it long before they joined the Federation of Malaysia. (Chee 2014: 22)

Such linguistic battles ultimately have no winner; blood spilled over whether or not one group of people can refer to God with the same way as does another group of people is a sure-fire way to bolster opposition to your own movement. While such posturing may be politically expedient to bolster base support in a political election, in the long term, more harm is done than good.

Lessons to be Learned from the Case of Malaysia

Islamism in Malaysia under Mahathir was not about meaningless platitudes proclaiming "Islam is the solution," nor was it about immediately implementing and enforcing *ḥudūd* punishments—rather it was about achieving sustainable long-term economic growth in a way conducive to the values of Islam. Mahathir's efforts showed that it is possible to promote a robust agenda of economic modernization, while at the same time, moving the country away *Ribā*-based banking systems that are, as mentioned earlier, considered among the worst sins a Muslim can commit.

Entrepreneurship was also promoted and not unnecessarily stifled under Mahathir. In the words of Shamsul, in the case of Malaysia, "entrepreneurship also implies class mobility and, with it, the move from an aristocratic ascriptive society to a more meritocratic one in which any *kampung* boy or girl can succeed" (Shamsul, referenced in Hefner (Ed.) 2001: 220). Efforts at promoting social justice in Malaysia remain a work in progress; however, the important part is that both entrepreneurship and social justice were at least taken into consideration as a part of Mahathir's larger vision. Finally, Mahathir's efforts at creating a world-class Islamic University that embraces the same administrative standards and academic rigor of top Western academic institutions should about be a part of any transitioning states' long-term vision. A previous chapter on public administration emphasized the importance of a well-trained, professional meritocratic system of public administration. Such public administrators can only be adequately trained at state-of-the-art institutions of higher learning.

Discussion on Islam and Islamism in Malaysia should not be thought of as being driven solely by Malaysia's two main Islamist political parties, the UNMO and PAS. A robust public discourse along with various civil society groups and NGOs "are playing an important role either engaging, expanding, or at times even constricting the parameters of the Islamist debate in Malaysia" (Liow 2009: 15). While in many cases, Islamic political action is primarily a response to poverty and inequality, in Malaysia during the 1980's, the story was much different.

> ...the politicization of Islam was taking place in tandem with economic growth and under the watchful eye of the Mahathir administration; it was in fact mobilized to justify industrialization and development policies, which in turn were premised upon the Malay-Muslim community being benefactors of a state-driven affirmative- action program that gave them privileged political and economic access. (Liow 2009: 8)

The Malaysian example shows that the embrace of Islamization policies does not automatically correlate to a failing/failed state. Mahathir's pragmatic efforts to introduce Islamic educational and financial institutions, while avoiding getting caught up in controversial efforts to overhaul the legal system and immediately enforce *ḥudūd* punishments, should serve as an invaluable real-world example of how a state in transition should consider incrementally implementing Islamic social and political institutions in their respective societies.

One can also learn from Malaysia's weaknesses as well. Racial discrimination has no place in an authentically Islamic system. Malaysia is also another testament for the importance of third-party oversight on high-ranking political actors. The levels of oversight mentioned in earlier chapters that are necessary in an Islamic governed state were not just meant to be rhetorical—as can be been in Malaysia and Turkey, there does seem to be a tendency for leaders inspired by Islamic ideals to centralize power, often with negative consequences. Legislative, judicial, and/or other regulatory entities must have some clearly defined constitutional authority to intervene in the cases of power abuse. Iran's model has such provisions, in which the elected Assembly of Experts are vested by the Iranian Constitution with the authority to remove an erring Supreme Leader. The problem, however, is that most members of the Assembly of Experts (*Majles-e Khobregān*) in Iran today are fiercely loyal to the Ayatollah. This is clearly problematic. There ought to be some semblance of balance between ideological perspectives when coming up with such regulatory agencies.

Kubicek concludes his own analysis of democracy in Malaysia by noting that it is a "semidemocracy" and that it "has the potential to change, although whether it will turn toward more authoritarianism or greater democracy remains to be seen" (2015: 113). In order for Malaysia to continue its move toward transparency and democracy, it must root out corruption and hold firm to allowing the rule of law to reign supreme. If this can be done, Malaysia can move further up on the continuum toward democracy and ultimately prosperity.

Notes

1. Mohammed is a patronymic, not a family name. This is common with Malay names. Throughout the rest of this chapter, when mentioning 'Mahathir bin Mohammed' this article will follow the standard way of identifying such names by referring only to his given name: 'Mahathir.'
2. This work was most recently republished in 2008 in English: Mahathir bin Mohammed, *The Malay Dilemma* (Singapore: Martin Cavdendish, 2008).
3. The International Islamic Univesity of Malaysia (IIUM) Mission statement can be found on its web site is at http://www.iium.edu.my/about-iium/iium-vision.

REFERENCES

Bakar, Osman. 2006. Islam, ethnicity, pluralism and democracy: Malaysia's unique experience. In *Islamic democratic discourse* ed. M.A. Muqtedar Khan 37–62. Lanham, MD: Lexington Books.
Chee, Kee Thuan. 2014. *Can we save Malaysia please!*. Singapore: Marshall Cavendish.
Çinar, Menderes, and Burhanettin Duran. 2008. The specific evolution of political Islam in Turkey and its 'difference'. In *Secular and Islamic politics in Turkey: The making of the justice and welfare party*, ed. Ü. Cizre, 17–40. New York: Routledge.
Furqani, Hafas, and Ratna Mulyany. 2009. Islamic banking and economic growth: Empirical evidence from Malaysia. *Journal of Economic Cooperation and Development* 30 (2): 59–74.
Hadiz, Vedi R., and Khoo Boo Teik. 2011. Approaching Islam and politics from political economy: A comparative study of Indonesia and Malaysia. *The Pacific Review* 24 (4): 463–485.
Haneef, Mohamed A. 2001. Islam and economic development in Malaysia—A reappraisal. *Journal of Islamic Studies* 12 (3): 269–290.
Khalid, Khadijah. 2011. Malaysia's foreign policy under Najib: A comparison with Mahathir. *Asian Survey* 51 (3): 429–452.
Kubicek, Paul. 2015. *Political Islam and democracy in the Muslim world*. Boulder, CO: Lynne Rienner Publishers.
Liow, Joseph Chinyong. 2009. *Piety and politics: Islamism in contemporary Malaysia*. New York: Oxford Press.
Lo, Ching Wing, and Chee Seng Leow. 2014. Islamic banking in Malaysia: A sustainable growth of the consumer market. *International Journal of Trade, Economics and Finance* 5 (6): 526–529.
Mahathir. 1991. Malaysian: This way forward (Vision 2020) 1–12. http://unpan1.un.org/intradoc/groups/public/documents/apcity/unpan003223.pdf. Accessed 20 Dec 2016.
Mahathir. 2008. *The malay dilemma*. Singapore: Martin Cavdendish.
Milne, R.S., and D. Mauzy. 1999. *Malaysian politics under Mahathir*. London, UK: Routledge.
Muzaffar, Chandra. 2002. *Rights, religion and reform: Enhancing human dignity through spiritual and moral transformation*. New York: Routledge.
Noor, Farish. 2009. Reformist Muslim thinkers in Malaysia: Engaging with power to uplift the *Umma*? In *Reformist voices in Islam: Mediating Islam and modernity*, ed. S. Hunter, 208–226. New York: Routledge.
Norhashimah, Mohammed Yasin. 1996. *Islamisation/Malayinisation: A study on the role of Islamic law in the economic development of Malaysia: 1969–1993*. Kuala Lumpur, Malaysia: A.S. Noordeen.

Ramage, D. 1995. *Politics in Indonesia: Democracy, Islam, and the ideology of tolerance.* New York: Routledge.

Shamsul, A.B. 2001. The redefinition of politics and the transformation of Malaysian pluralism. In *The politics of multiculturalism: Pluralism and citizenship in Malaysia, Singapore, and Indonesia,* ed. R. Hefner, 204–226. Honolulu: University of Hawaii Press.

Wain, B. 2010. *Malaysian maverick: Mahathir Mohamad in turbulent times.* New York: Palgrave.

CHAPTER 12

Conclusion: Creating a New Discourse

Your task is not to seek for love, but merely to seek and find all the barriers within yourself that you have built against it.—Jalaludin Rumi.

INTRODUCTION—NOT MERELY A RELIGION

As mentioned in the introduction, Islam is not merely a religion; rather, it is a complete way of life. Most Muslims believe that an empirical or definitive "scientific" proof of God's existence is not possible, and that this was his ultimate will. If Allah wanted to, he clearly could have made it such that all men witnessed direct proof of his existence in an undeniable or unquestionable way. This was not the intent however. The intent was to make man utilize his cognitive faculties. The great Christian existentialist philosopher, Paul Tillich, commented that faith "is an act of the total personality. It happens in the center of the personal life and includes all its elements. Faith is the most centered act of the human mind" (1957: 4). God gave man the capacity to worship him; God also provided man with a particularly unique cognitive ability that allows for him to do so.

> And those who have no knowledge say: Why doth not Allah speak unto us, or some sign come unto us? Even thus, as they now speak, spake those (who were) before them. Their hearts are all alike. We have made clear the revelations for people who are sure. (*Qur'ān*, 2:118)

Merely, having *faith* is not enough in Islam; one must ultimately *submit* to the will of Allah. Can man, so driven by direct empirical observations and reason, transcend these cognitive boundaries and embrace the seemingly irrational? This is perhaps one of the greatest challenges God placed upon mankind in his divine project.

In order to properly understand the complete set of real numbers, one must recognize that both rational and irrational numbers comprise the set. This was understood by early medieval Islamic scholars such as the great ninth-century Persian mathematician Abu-Abdullah Muhammad ibn Īsa Māhānī. On the difference between rational and irrational numbers, Al-Māhānī commented that;

> It will be a rational (magnitude) when we, for instance, say 10, 12, 3%, 6%, etc., because its value is pronounced and expressed quantitatively. What is not rational is irrational and it is impossible to pronounce and represent its value quantitatively. For example: the roots of numbers such as 10, 15, 20 which are not squares, the sides of numbers which are not cubes etc. (Al-Māhānī, cited in Matvievskaya 1987: 259)

Just because an irrational number cannot be expressed as a simple fraction does not mean that irrational numbers do not exist. Even high school students today recognize that without the recognition of both rational and irrational numbers, one is not fully aware of all that exists within the entire set of real numbers.

The nature of some of the deepest mysteries of the physical universe can be approached in a similar manner as irrational numbers. For example, most scientists today believe in the existence of black holes due to indirect observations of gravitational interactions with other objects in the universe. Many physicists even argue that black holes do not follow the known laws of physics. Some scientists have postulated that inside the black holes, some of the most widely accepted principles of physics, such as the law of conservation of energy,[1] are regularly violated (Giddings 1995). Nonetheless, despite the fact that scientists are currently at a loss to explain what happens inside a black hole, this does not mean they simply deny their existence. These scientists look at the world around them to derive their conclusions about the existence of black holes. The *Qur'ān*, as seen in the previously quoted *āyāh*, also calls on Muslims to be cognizant of the signs of God's existence, despite not being able to directly observe Allah himself in this world.

Islam's Answer to the Great Question— "What is the Purpose of Life?"

The essence of Islam is the belief in an all-knowing (*Al-'Alīm*), all-seeing (*al-Baṣīr*) being that is unlike anything the mind can truly ever even begin grasp; man's primary purpose is to worship the all-powerful (*al-Qadīr*) one. This actually is the underpinning of all the Abrahamic religions. In the introduction to *The Chumash* [Stone Edition], Rabbi Nosson Scherman comments that God "looked into the Torah and created the world, and he designed the universe to make it possible for human beings to carry out his commandments" (1994: xxi). In the New Testament, Jesus declares; "But the hour cometh, and now is, when the true worshippers shall worship the Father in spirit and in truth: for the Father seeketh such to worship him. God is a Spirit: and they that worship him must worship him in spirit and in truth" (Holy Bible [KJV], *John* 4: 23–24). Sheikh Khalid Yasin (2006) gave a series of Islamic lectures titled: *The Purpose of Life Lectures*. Yasin argues that faithful Muslims already know the answer to this most fundamental question; the purpose of life is to worship Allah.

Contemplation and self-discipline are essential within Islam. Without each, one cannot achieve true spiritual Enlightenment. An Islamic governed state must promote these two essential values. Despite living in relative poverty and never achieving widespread fame in his lifetime, one of the finest writers on this topic was James Allen. Allen lived in England during the late nineteenth century and was dedicated for seeking spiritual Enlightenment. Allen was described as a quiet man, yet was intensely reflective and intellectual. "Allen's work embodies the influence of Protestant liberalism on the one hand and of Buddhist thought on the other" (Webb 1971: 7). Allen's ideas and works also deeply resonate with the some of the most fundamental elements of Islamic spirituality. His most widely read work titled, *As a Man Thinketh*, was inspired by the biblical proverb, "As a man thinketh, so is he" (Holy Bible [KJV], *Proverbs* 23: 7). For Allen, self-discipline was essential in reaching personal Enlightenment.

Allen describes the three stages of self-discipline as control, purification, and relinquishment. One must begin with control before moving to purification, and finally relinquishment. In Allen's words;

> A man begins to discipline himself by controlling those passions which have hitherto controlled him; he resists temptation, and guards himself

against all those tendencies to selfish gratifications which are so easy and natural, and which have formerly dominated him. (1971: 23)

Merely, restraint of the passions is not enough—one must constantly strive to purify oneself of all their worldly passions. "Without self-discipline a man drifts lower and lower, approximating more and more nearly to the beast, until at last he grovels, a lost creature, in the mire of his own befoulment" (Allen 1971: 27). In Islam, the individual is supposed to seek such Enlightenment at all times, this is especially emphasized during the month of *Ramaḍān*.

LOVE—THE ESSENCE OF THE WORSHIP AND OBEDIENCE

The realization of proper worship in Islam is obedience. Obedience itself, however, is predicated by love. Love in Islam is given a very prominent status. Along with love for Allah, Muslims are commanded to love each other. One particular *ḥadīth* in regard to loving one's brother (in Islam) for the sake of Allah notes that: "On the day of Resurrection, Allâh [s.a.w.], the Exalted, will say: 'Where are those who have mutual love for the sake of My Glory? Today I shall shelter them in My shade when there will be no Shade Except mine'" (*Riyadh us Saliheen*, #377). A second *ḥadīth* on the topic of loving one's brother in Islam states, "Mu'âdh (bin Jabal) reported: Messenger of Allâh [s.a.w] said: 'For "Allâh the Exalted has said: those who love one another for the sake of My Glory, there will be seats of light (on the Day of Resurrection), and they will be envied by the Prophets and martyrs'" (*Riyadh us-Saliheen*, #381).

Muslim's are supposed to submit to Allah, but only if they choose so out of love. As the *Qur'ān* stated in *Sūrah* 2:252, there is no compulsion in religion. Even the Prophet (ﷺ) himself did not have the authority to force one to accept something they did not in their hearts believe in. The Prophet (ﷺ) desperately hoped his uncle Abū Tālib, the man who protected him throughout his life from almost certain death at the hands of the elders of the Quraysh, would come to embrace Islam, but he never could bring himself to do so. One can only authentically submit to Allah if they love him on their own volition. On Allah's mercy and love, the *Qur'ān* states, "Say, (O Muhammad, to mankind): If ye love Allah, follow me; Allah will love you and forgive you your sins. Allah is Forgiving, Merciful" (*Qur'ān*, 3:31). It does not say the more power, or worldly possessions, or even knowledge one has will determine whether or not

12 CONCLUSION: CREATING A NEW DISCOURSE

Allah loves a person. This verse reminds believers that Allah loves and forgives his servants because they love him back.

The primacy placed on love is not unique to Islam. Martin Buber on the role of love in Judaism commented that, "a philosopher who has been overwhelmed by *faith* must speak of love" (Buber 1953: 100). True faith and love are inseparable. The more one loves, the stronger their faith will be and vice versa. Buber looked at the writings of the Kantian scholar, Hermann Cohen, who moves from looking at God as a stale psychological phenomenon to a living reality that permeates all aspects of the psyche. Buber quotes the later Cohen who commented that; "the love of God exceed all knowledge," and that "[a] man's consciousness is completely filled when he loves God. Therefore this knowledge which absorbs all others, no longer is merely knowledge, but love" (Cohen, quoted in Buber 1953: 102). Knowledge coupled with love is infinitely superior to knowledge alone. It is not knowledge that is the final step in the recognition of the object of worship, or the pinnacle of consciousness; rather, it is love. One can have all the knowledge in the world, but without the final element: a love for God—for the sake of God; one is spiritually void. It is the primary qualia that separate man from machine; a computer can contain all the knowledge in the known universe, but it cannot love knowledge and love the Creator, for the sake of love. Love is that which places humans at the apex of all Creation in the eyes of God.

Buber's recognition of the centrality of love also applies to Islam. While one can read the *Qur'ān* all they want, memorize all the prayers, and perform all the ablutions called for by Islam, one cannot be taught love. It is something that comes from within. It develops as a result of inward contemplation and divine grace. The words of *Qur'ān* may inspire love, but this can only happen if God wills it. Otherwise the words, regardless of how glorious they are, will fall upon deaf ears.

Sheikh 'Uthaymīn addressed the question of man and free will in his twentieth-century writings. There has always been confusion surrounding the question of free will and predestination within Islam. How can one be responsible for their actions if they have no free will over whether they perform them or not? As mentioned in previously, this was one of the critical metaphysical issues that differentiated the *Mu'tazilah* from the Jabbarites centuries earlier. 'Uthaymīn's position was similar to the middle road position taken by Ash'arites approximately ten centuries earlier. He argued that "man has a choice but he does not perform any action except that it is decreed by Allah because there is an authority over his authority, but Allah does not force man. Man has a choice and he acts by his choice" (2006: 54). The key point is that man has free will to decide an action on his own accord, but only if Allah decrees a certain action to be, it will be. He goes on to argue that regardless of the metaphysical reality surrounding the question of fate or free will, based on our limited perceptions—we cannot know or not know whether Allah has willed a thing for us or not. "We know that we perform actions by our own choice and decision. We do not feel anyone compelling or forcing us to do it. Rather we are the ones who want to do something, then we do it and if we want to abandon it, we abandon it" ('Uthaymīn 2006: 55). We can only do the best we can as individuals to please Allah.

The individual's relationship with Allah in Islam is complex. While God is all merciful and just, God is also the unquestioned master of the universe. Ultimately, all humans are God's servants. The great Harvard Christian Philosopher Josiah Royce in his explanation of the biblical story of *Ayyūb* (Job) states;

> Job himself pathetically insists that he never doubts for an instant, God's power to do whatever in heaven or earth he may please to do so. Nothing hinders God. No blind faith thwarts him. *Sheol* is naked before him. The abyss has no covering. The earth hangs over chaos because he orders it to do so. (Royce 2005: 834)

The biblical story of *Ayyūb* is one that resonates with Muslims all over the world. It is mentioned in the *Qur'ān* a few different times. The story reminds believers that they must remember that simply because one is pious, they are not guaranteed earthly rewards. However, in Islam Muslims, and all believers in One God, are promised that those who properly submit to Allah and his messengers will be handsomely rewarded. "And we set a just balance for the day of resurrection so that no soul is wronged in aught. Though it be of the weight of a grain of mustard seed, We will bring it. And we suffice for reckoners" (*Qur'ān*, 21:47). Life on earth is an unending test for all faithful human beings. It has been this way throughout the history. The current generations' suffering is not an anomaly.

> Or ye think that ye will enter Paradise while yet there hath not come unto you the like of (that which came to) those who passed away before you?

Affliction and adversity befell them, they were shaken as with earthquake, till the messenger (of Allah) and those who believed along with him said: When cometh Allah's help? Now surely Allah's help is nigh. (*Qur'ān*, 2:214)

One should not be discouraged by the numerous tests they receive from Allah; rather, they should be concerned if they are *not* being regularly tested. Two separate *'aḥādīth* reported in *Tafsīr al-Qur'ān al-'aẓīm*[2] address this matter. The first reports that; "The people most severely tested are the Prophets, then the righteous, then the next best and the next best [At-Tabarani 24: 245–246]" (At-Tabarani, quoted in Mubarakpuri 2003: 478). The second reports that; "A man will be tested according to his level of religious commitment; the stronger his religious commitment, the more severe will be his test [Ahmad 1: 180]" (Ahmad ibn Ḥanbal, quoted in Mubarakpuri 2003: 478). The story of *Ayyūb* reminds Muslims that life is a test; we are all here as students—our job is to pass the test.

WHAT ALL THIS MEANS FOR POLITICAL INSTITUTIONS AND GOVERNMENT

As mentioned earlier in this work, for Aristotle, the political structure and social organization of any society must reflect the values most widely held by its inhabitants. The political and social question can only be explored if one is aware of the psyche of the individuals constitutive of that society. Without Muslims, Islamic institutions are not possible. Without *honorable* Muslims, *honorable* Islamic institutions are not possible. Islam holds individual Muslims to very high standards. The same high standards ought to apply to governments and political institutions; this is why this work spends so much time emphasizing Aristotelian and Platonic thought. Unlike Enlightenment era thought, the ancients placed a much greater emphasis on the moral and ethical dimensions of leadership, and the importance of the state encouraging its citizens to behave ethically.

In any newly emerging state, especially a state in which revelation is so essential, it is even more critical to have the most capable of leaders. There are numerous standards that underpin how an Islamic governed state ultimately can be conceived. The *Qur'ān* and *Sharī'ah* must be central in conceptualizing an Islamic administered state; however, it must be remembered there are numerous interpretations and understandings of these laws and texts. It should be the goal of Islamic governed states to develop appropriate administrative procedures to handle things in a fair way. As mentioned in the previous chapters, bureaucracies and political institutions are not only acceptable within an Islamic political framework, but are ultimately essential. It is clear that within an Islamic political framework, there is a room for social change and adaptations. It is a delicate process that must be handled carefully, but as one can see in the contemporary Muslim world, it is something that desperately needs to be done.

Each Islamic governed state, within its own cultural context, must determine how it adapts to the modern world. Love is one of the essential dynamics of Islam, not only love for Allah but also for his creation, including human beings. Any serious Islamic governed state must handle issues related to minorities, women's rights, and the poor with the utmost sense of seriousness and urgency. These issues cannot be ignored when conceptualizing a modern Islamic governed state. It is also important to remember that the West also plays a role in the discourse that happens in the Muslim world (Kaminski 2014). When the West sets xenophobic and repressive precedents, one must expect similar policies in the Middle East and other parts of the Muslim world.

The worship of Allah involves far more than making daily prayers on time or paying the *zakāt*; it is an entire mind-set and way of life. It involves living life as obediently to Allah's laws as best as possible and then recognizing even this is not enough for entry into paradise, for one can only be allowed access to paradise via the grace and mercy of Allah. From this perspective, a political system that takes seriously the *Qur'ān* and *Sharī'ah* is in actuality a political system that itself is an act of worship.

Final Remarks: The Beginnings of a New Discourse

Samuel Beckett's classic twentieth-century work in absurdist theater, *Waiting for Godot*, eloquently illustrates the point that sitting around idly waiting for a savior is not acceptable. The two main characters Beckett's classic play, Vladimir and Estragon, sat by idly waiting for the mysterious *Godot* to come and save the day. At the end of the play, after Vladimir and Estragon have prattled around unproductively, they are reminded about the limited time we all have on this earth. Pozzo, an older, physically diminished, and now wiser acquaintance from the previous act reminds Vladimir: "They give birth astride of a grave, the light gleams an instant, then its night once more" (1988: 89). One clear lesson that Muslims worldwide can take from this story is that they must *act* in order to make life in this earth, or *dunyā* better. Vladimir and Estragon ultimately fail to heed Pozzo's message, and in the end resolve to commit suicide, which they could not even effectively do.

Faithful Muslims genuinely believe that Allah is going to have the final say in regard to the events that unfold on earth. In a very famous *sūrah*, commonly referred to as the *Istikhlaf* verse, it states;

> Allah has promised such of you who believe and do good works that he will surely make them succeed (the present rulers) in the earth, even as He caused those who were before them to succeed (others); and that He will surely establish for them their religion which He hath approved for them, and will give them in exchange safety after their fear. They serve Me. They ascribe nothing as partner unto Me. Those who misbelieve henceforth, they are the miscreants. (*Qur'ān*, 24:55)

Many Muslims see this verse as a divine promise that one day the *khilāfa* will be restored and that it will offer perfect worldly justice. However, this does not mean Muslims are to idly wait for this event to transpire— they must challenge injustice and offer alternative, Islamic political solutions. This is hardly a controversial or even original point—Nasiruddin al-Albani commented in his *Silsilah al-'ahādīth as- Ṣaḥīḥah:* "Muslims should not cancel their obligations and simply wait for the appearance of the Mahdi, neglecting their duty of striving hard to establish Allah's Rule on earth" (al-Albani—cited in al-Muqaddam 2013: 258). It is incumbent upon Muslims to take control of their own lives while they have the chance.

Jack Goldstone argued that the 2011 Arab Revolutions in many ways resembled both the 1848 European Revolutions against traditional monarchies and the 1989 revolutions against Communism;

> As in 1848, rising food prices and high unemployment have fueled popular protests from Morocco to Oman. As in Eastern Europe and the Soviet Union in 1989, frustration with closed, corrupt, and unresponsive political systems has led to defections among elites and the fall of once powerful regimes in Tunisia, Egypt, and perhaps Libya. (2011: 329)

However, he is quick to point out that the Arab Revolutions were unique in that they did not seek to overthrow traditional monarchies or communist dictatorships; rather, they sought replace sultanistic dictatorships. Sultanistic dictatorships rarely maintain their power for more than a generation, and these revolutions were long overdue. "Such governments arise when a national leader expands his power at the expense of formal institutions. Sultanistic dictators appeal to no ideology and have no purpose other than maintaining their personal authority" (2011: 331). Despotic leaders often pay lip service to justice—Muslims finally took heed of this in 2011 and took to the streets.

Wael Hallaq's, *The Impossible State: Islam, Politics, and Modernity's Moral Predicament* (2013), is in some ways at odds with what I am arguing *is possible* in this work. Nonetheless, I do think I share many of his views. The main thrust of his book is that Islamic values are at odds with Western or "modern" conceptions of the state. Hallaq and I agree that secular Western states do not really take seriously foundational, ethical principles that are essential to Islam. On the inherent incompatibilities between the "modern" state and an "Islamic" state, Hallaq states;

> There can be no Islam without a moral-legal system that is anchored in a metaphysic; there can be no such moral system without or outside divine sovereignty; and, at the same time, there can be no modern state without its own sovereignty and sovereign will, for no one, I think, can reasonably argue that the modern state can no more be Islamic that Islam can come to possess a modern state (unless, of course, the modern state is entirely reinvented, in which case, as we care entitled to, call it something else). (2013: 51)

The modern Western state at its core is amoral, with little or no concern about individual morality, whereas morality is a central concern with any real Islamic conception of the state or the general good. As discussed throughout this work, based on this fact, creating an Islamic governed state through an Enlightenment discourse is not reasonable within an Islamic context. However, as first mentioned in the introductory chapter, there is a difference between utilizing certain institutions or discursive methods borrowed from the West and operating within an entirely Western *weltanschauung*. The secular nature of the liberal West does not mean *all* institutions or discursive methods that are by-products of Western thought somehow, *ipso facto*, must be amoral and/or immoral.

12 CONCLUSION: CREATING A NEW DISCOURSE

Hallaq goes on to argue that the terms of history have been dictated to the Muslim world and that this is not likely to change anytime soon. He concludes his thought provoking and philosophically rigorous work by commenting that;

> Dwelling together on earth in peace is certainly a tall order, perhaps another modern Utopia, but subjecting modernity to a restructuring moral critique is the most essential requirement not only for the rise of Islamic governance but also for our material and spiritual survival. (2013: 170)

I believe that Western world, one which moves further into amorality, is not likely to resituate itself within a foundationalist ethical framework anytime soon. Nonetheless, I am not as pessimistic about the possibility of historical change in the Muslim world, or in general for that matter. History is constantly written and rewritten. Considering the unique historical circumstances, if any time was appropriate for the Muslim world to try and reshape its political systems and modes of political discourse, the time would be now. The great late Moroccan philosopher Mohammed Abed al-Jabri commented that the Muslim world must start looking forward rather than backwards; "The historical experience of the nation has to be revived, by starting a new chapter, which will enable it to adapt to the present age, the age where each and everyone of its components asserts that it is the age of posterity, not of 'ancestry'" (2009 :70). In order to transition in al-Jabri's age of posterity however, philosophers must first offer recommendations for how this can be done, even if realizing these long-term goals seem to be but a dream at this point in time. We must remember Walter Benjamin's famous quip that; "Every epoch not only dreams the next, but while dreaming impels it towards wakefulness" (1969: 172).

When walking around the various *masjids* or chatting over tea at café's, in the numerous places I have visited over the past few years in the USA, Bosnia and Herzegovina, Turkey, Lebanon, and even Iran, I have heard, and sometimes even engaged in, vibrant conversations about all the central themes covered in this book. Everyone it seems—*Sunni* or *Shī'ah*: Western or Eastern—is genuinely interested in issues of governance, institutional modernization, human rights, and economic justice and fairness. Despite the wide array of views that I have heard on each specific topic, if one general motif could be observed, it was that almost everyone agrees that all of these aforementioned topics are all essential and must be incorporated into an authentic Islamic political discourse on way or another.

Vocabularies and discourses often shift. In the words of Richard Rorty; "Interesting philosophy is rarely the examination of the pros and cons of a thesis. Usually it is, implicitly or explicitly, a contest between an entrenched vocabulary which has become a nuisance and a half-formed new vocabulary which promises great things" (1989: 9). Muslim activists and scholars must work to reshape the discourse and break free of the imperial dominated modes of communication that have marked the past few hundred years. It must also continuously struggle against the discourse being terrorized (sadly, in the most literal sense of the word lately) by extremist groups within Islam and hostile neoconservatives and dogmatic secularists outside of Islam—both of whom have been unsettlingly effective at reaching their intended audiences. Islamic political reformers need to offer a new vocabulary that blends the best elements of the Islamic tradition with new ideas and approaches to institutions and governance. Once again turning to the wisdom of al-Jabri;

> But the question which should always be asked is whether the Muslims of today are good enough for their own time, able to live in their own age, to inaugurate a new 'conduct', compatible with the old 'conduct of the forefathers', making it a living reality, suitable to be followed by future generations in building their own code of conduct. (2009: 70)

The Muslim world cannot continue to live under the yoke of oppression from foreign powers, corrupt dictators, or from rival factions that act "in the name of Islam" that ultimately only seek their own power and self-aggrandizement. Despite the surge of power that Islamist parties have experienced in recent Middle Eastern elections, they too must recognize they are ultimately accountable to the people. "Islamist parties must realize that governance is about such mundane issues as jobs, the economy, traffic and the smooth running of educational institutions, not grandiose battles between good and evil" (Khan 2014: 84). In the words of Oliver Roy;

> The islamist parties may have more power and freedom to maneuver, but they too will find themselves being pushed to adjust to the democratization process. The pushing will be done by the constraints and dynamics

characteristic of the social, religious, political, and geostrategic fields in which these parties must operate.(2012:7)

Islamist parties, even when in power, must work within a constitutional framework that keeps their power balanced.

The final step in completing the process of transformation in the Muslim world is left in the hands of the people.

> For him are angels ranged before him and behind him, who guard him by Allah's command. Lo! Allah changeth not the condition of a folk until they (first) change that which is in their hearts; and if Allah willeth misfortune for a folk there is none that can repel it, nor have they a defender beside Him. (*Qur'ān*, 13:11)

A moral public is the pillar of any successful regime. A famous *ḥadīth* narrated by Abu Dawud reports;

> It was narrated that Thawbān said: "The Messenger of Allah (ﷺ) said: 'Soon the nations will invite to partake of you, as diners call one another to a large dish.' Someone said: 'Will it be because we will be few in number on that day?' He said: 'No, rather you will be many on that day, but you will be like the refuse of the flood. Allah will take away fear of you from the hearts of your enemies, and Allah will pelt your hearts with *Wahn* (weakness).' Someone said: 'O Messenger of Allah, what is *Wahn*?' He said: 'Love of this world and dislike of death.' (*Sunan Abī Dāwūd*, #4297)

The Prophet (ﷺ) is clear that the Muslim world will be in a state of stagnation not because there will no longer be any believers. Rather, it will be in a state of stagnation because of *al-wahn*, which can be understood as a sickness that befalls nations that desire luxury and material goods at the expense of Allah and his messengers. This in many ways parallels the modern decadence and corruption that is seen in many developing Islamic nations today. This *ḥadīth* reports that the people of the future (meaning today) will be shallow and lack substance. Their decadence will cause them to love worldly pleasures in excess and forget the inevitability of death and final judgment. The rest of the world will see the increasing decadence and backwardness of the *ummah* and will not take them seriously or respect their sovereignty.

The first step for avoiding *al-wahn* is to make conscious efforts to perform acts of goodness. In Aristotle's words;

For the things we have to learn before we can do them, we learn by doing them, e.g. men become builders by building and lyre-players by playing the lyre; so too we become just by doing just acts, temperate by doing temperate acts, brave by doing brave acts. (*Nicomachean Ethics*, Book II, Chap.1, 1103a &1103b; 34(a)–2(b))

Within an Aristotelian framework, it is incumbent upon individuals within an Islamic society to work to make their society flourish. The citizens must be active participants in their regime. They must constantly perform acts of goodness and kindness. Such actions will keep public sentiment positive, the state strong, and Islam as a faith and way of life relevant. The regular God-fearing Muslim who works for a living, has a family, and struggles to pay the bills must, unlike Vladimir and Estragon, *act*. That is to say, they must make freedom and justice a reality. Otherwise, like Vladimir and Estragon, they will continue to flounder until their ultimate demise.

Notes

1. Interestingly, despite the law of conservation of energy being widely attributed to European scientists during the Enlightenment era, variations in this idea were mentioned earlier by the Ancient Greeks, The Jain thinker, Mahivira, in the sixth century B.C.E, and by the Persian scientist, Nasīr al-Dīn al-Tūsī in the thirteenth century C.E., who argued that bodies of matter never disappear; rather, they only change form or state (Alakbarli 2001).
2. Also known as *Tafsīr Ibn Kathīr*.

References

al-Jabri, Mohammed. 2009. *Democracy, human rights, and law in Islamic thought*. New York: I.B.Tauris & Co Ltd.

al-Muqaddam, M. 2013. *Al Mahdi: Truth or fiction?*. London, UK: Al Firdous.

al-'Uthaymīn, Muḥammad Ibn Ṣāliḥ. 2006. Are we forced or do we have free will? Short excerpt from, *Sharh hadeeth Jibra'eel*. Shawana Aziz, trans. Qur'an Sunnah Educational Programs Publishers. http://www.qsep.com/books/areweforced.html. Accessed 29 June 2014.

Alakbari, Farid. 2001. A 13th century Darwin?—Tusi's views of evolution. *Azerbaijan International*, 9 (2). http://www.azer.com/aiweb/categories/magazine/92_folder/92_articles/92_tusi.html. Accessed 7 Nov 2016.

Allen, James.1971. *As a man thinketh: James Allen's greatest inspirational essays.* W. Franklin, and W. Webb (eds.). Kansas City, MO: Hallmark Crown Editions.
Aristotle, and J. McKeon (eds.). 2001. *The basic works of Aristotle.* New York: The Modern Library.
Beckett, Samuel. 1954. *Waiting for godot,* 2nd ed. New York: Grove Press.
Benjamin, Walter. 1969. Paris: Capital of the nineteenth century. *Perspecta* 12: 163–172.
Buber, Martin, and Will Herberg (eds.). 1953. *The writings of Martin Buber.* New York: Meridian Books.
Giddings, Steve. 1995. The black hole information paradox. *Particles, Strings and Cosmology.* March 22–25, 1995, Johns Hopkins Workshop on Current Problems in Particle Theory 19 and the PASCOS Interdisciplinary Symposium 5.
Goldstone, Jack. 2011. *"Understanding the revolutions of 2011: Weakness and resilience in middle Eastern autocracies",* The new Arab revolts: what happened, what it means, and what comes next, 329–343. New York: Published by the Council on Foreign Relations.
Hallaq, Wael. 2013. *The impossible state: Islam, modernity, and modernity's moral predicament.* New York: Columbia University Press.
Kaminski, Joseph J. 2014. The Islamophobia industry, hate, and its impact on Muslim immigrants and OIC state development. *Islamophobia Studies Journal* 2 (2): 157–176.
Khan, M.A. Muqtedar. 2014. Islam, democracy and Islamism after the counter-revolution in Egypt. *Middle East Policy* 21 (1): 75–86.
King James Version Reference Bible [KJV]. 2005. New York: Oxford University Press.
Matvievskaya, Galina. 1987. The theory of quadratic irrationals in medieval oriental mathematics. *Annals of the New York Academy of Sciences* 500: 253–277.
Mubarakpuri, S.R. (ed.). 2003. *Tafsir ibn Kathir (Abridged),* Vol. 6 Brooklyn, New York: Dar-us-Salaam Publishers.
Qur'ān. *The meaning of the glorious Qur'an.* 2001. Mohammed Pickthall, trans. New York: Alavi Foundation.
Riyadh-us-Saliheen. 1999. 2 Vol. Compiled by Abu Zakariya Nawawi. Muhammad Amin and Abu Usamah Al-Arabi bin Razduq, trans. New York: Dar-us-Salam Publications.
Rorty, Richard. 1989. *Contingency, irony, and solidarity.* Cambridge: Cambridge University Press.
Roy, Oliver. 2012. The transformation of the Arab world. *Journal of Democracy* 23 (3): 5–18.
Royce, Josiah, and John McDermott (eds.). 2005. The basic writings of Josiah Royce (2 Vols.). New York: Fordham Press.

Scherman, Nossom (ed.). 1994. "*An overview: Torah—written and oral*", in *The Chumash: the Stone edition*. Brooklyn, New york: Mesorah Publications Ltd.

Sharh hadeeth Jibra'eel. Shawana Aziz, trans. Qur'an Sunnah Educational Programs Publishers. http://www.qsep.com/books/areweforced.html. Accessed 29 June 2014.

Sunan Abī Dāwūd 2008. 5 Vols. Compiled by Abu Dawud. Hafiz Abu Tahir Zubair 'Ali Za'i (ed.) and Nasiruddin al-Khattab (trans.). Houston, Texas: Darussalaam Publishers.

Tillich, Paul. 1957. *Dynamics of faith*. New York: Harper Row.

Webb, William. 1971. Who was James Allen? In *As a man thinketh: James Allen's greatest inspirational essays*, (ed.). W. Franklin, and W. Webb. MO. Hallmark Crown Editions: Kansas City.

Yasin, Khalid. 2006. The purpose of life lectures. Produced and recorded by 1-Islam Productions. http://www.1islam.net. Accessed 8 Aug 2015.

BIBLIOGRAPHY

Abdal-Haqq, Irshad. (2006). "Islamic law—an overview of its origin and elements," in H. Ramadan (Ed.), *Understanding Islamic law—from classical to contemporary* (pp. 1–42). New York: Altamira Press.

Abdullah, Saeed. (1999). Rethinking citizenship rights of non-Muslims in an Islamic state: Rashid al-Ghannushi's contribution to the evolving debate. *Islam and Christian-Muslim Relations, 10* (3), 307–323.

Abou El Fadl, Khaled. (2004). "Islam and the challenge of democracy," in K. Abou El Fadl, J. Cohen, and D. Chasman (Eds.), *Islam and the challenge of democracy* (pp. 3–48). Princeton, NJ: Princeton University Press.

Abou El Fadl, Khaled. (2005). *The great theft: wrestling Islam from the extremists.* New York: Harper Collins.

Abou El Fadl, Khaled. (2012a). Conceptualizing Shari'a in the modern State. *Villanova Law Review, 56* (5), 803–818.

Abou El Fadl, Khaled. (2012b). "The centrality of Shari'ah to government and constitutionalism in Islam." in Rainer Grote and Tilmann J. Roder (Eds.), *Constitutionalism in Islamic countries: between upheaval and continuity* (pp. 35–61). New York: Oxford Press.

Abou Rauf, Feisal. (2007). "What is Sunni Islam?" in V. Cornell (Ed.), *Voices of Islam: voices of tradition* (Vol. 1) (pp. 185–216). Westport, CT: Praeger.

Abrahamian, Ervand. (1993). *Khomeinism: essays on the Islamic republic.* Berkeley, CA: University of California.

Abu Rabi, Ibrahim M. (1996). *Intellectual origins of Islamic resurgence in the modern Arab world.* Albany, NY: SUNY Press.

Abusharif, Ibrahim N. (2014). "Parsing 'Arab Spring:' media coverage of the Arab Revolutions." Northwestern University in Qatar Occassional Paper Series.

Adichie, Chimamanda N. (2007). *Half of a yellow sun*. Toronto: Knopf Canada.
Acemoğlu, Daron, Simon Johnson, and James A. Robinson. (2005). "Institutions as the fundamental cause of long-run growth," in P. Aghion and S. Darlauf (eds.), *Handbook of economic growth* (pp. 385–472). Amsterdam: North-Holland Publishing Co.
Adorno, Theodor W. (2001). *Kant's critique of pure reason*. Rolf Teidemann (Ed.). Redwood City, CA: Stanford University Press.
Afary, Janet. (2009). *Sexual politics in modern Iran*. Cambridge, UK: Cambridge University Press.
Africa Bank Development Group. (2011). The African development bank group in North Africa- 2011. http://www.afdb.org/fileadmin/uploads/afdb/Documents/Publications/RAP Afr ique nord Anglais.pdf Accessed on May 26, 2015.
Afsaruddin, Asma. (2006). "Obedience to political authority: an evolutionary concept," in M.A. Muqtedar Khan (Ed.), *Islamic Democratic Discourse* (pp. 37–62). Lanham, MD: Lexington Books.
Ahmad, Eqbal. (2006). *The selected writings of Eqbal Ahmad*. C. Bengelsdorf, M. Cerullo & Y. Chandri (Eds.). New York: Columbia University Press.
Ahmad, Jamil. (1994). Ibn Rushd. *Monthly Renaissance*, 4 (9). http://www.monthly-renaissance.com/issue/content.aspx?id=744 Accessed on October 29, 2016.
Akhavi, Shahrough. (2003). Sunni modernist theories of social contract in contemporary Egypt. *International Journal of Middle East Studies*, 35 (1), 23–49.
al-Alwaki, Anwar. (2006). Allah is preparing us for victory, parts I and II. [Audio podcast]. Accessed on May 8, 2013. http://www.sendspace.com/file/ls3oa9 and http://www.sendspace.com/file/ov2c7b.
al Arabiya English. (2015). Lebanon's 'you stink' protests return to Beirut. 21 September, 2015. http://english.alarabiya.net/en/News/middle-east/2015/09/21/Lebanese-protesters-face-off-with-security-forces-in-Beirut.html Accessed on February 22, 2016.
al-Arian, Abdullah, et. al. (2013). Roundtable on the future of Islamism: a starting point. *Jadaliyya*. http://www.jadaliyya.com/pages/index/15112/roundtable-on-the-future-of-islamism_a-starting-po Accessed online: 12 July, 2015.
al-Attas, Syed Muhammad Naquib. (1993). *Islām and secularism* (2nd Edition). Kuala Lumpur, Malaysia: Art Printing Works Sdn. Bhd.
al-Atawneh, Muhammed. (2011). Wahhābi legal theory as reflected in modern official Saudi *Fatwā*s: *ijtihād*, *taqlīd*, sources, and methodology. *Islamic Law and Society*, 18, 327–355.
al-A'zami, Muhammad M. (2003). *The history of the Qur'anic text: from revelation to compilation: a comparative study with the Old and New Testaments*. London: UK Islamic Academy.

al-Banna, Hassan. (2009). "Toward the light," in R. Euben and M. Zaman (Eds.), *Princeton Readings in Islamist thought* (pp. 56–78). Princeton, NJ: Princeton University Press.
al-Fahad, Abdul-Aziz H. (2004). From exclusivism to accommodation: doctrinal and legal evolution of Wahhabism. *New York University Law Review, 79* (2), 486–519.
al-Farabi. (2011). "The political regime," in R. Lerner and M. Mahdi (Eds.). *Medieval political philosophy* (2nd Edition) (pp. 31–57). Ithaca, NY: Cornell University Press.
al-Farabi. (2001a). "Book of religion," in Charles Butterworth (Ed.). *Alfarabi, the political writings: "selected aphorisms" and other texts*. Ithaca, NY: Cornell University Press., pp. 87–113.
al-Farabi. (2001b). "Enumeration of the sciences," in Charles Butterworth (Ed.). *Alfarabi, the political writings: "selected aphorisms" and other texts*. Ithaca, NY: Cornell University Press Press., pp. 76–84.
al-Ghazali. (2002). *The Incoherence of the Philosophers* (2nd edition). Michael Mamura (Trans. and Ed.). Provo, Utah: BYU Islamic Transition Series.
al-Jabri, Mohammed. (2009). *Democracy, human rights, and law in Islamic thought*. New York: I.B.Tauris & Co Ltd.
al-Hibri, Azizah. (1992). Islamic constitutionalism and the concept of democracy. *Case Western Reserve Journal of International Law, 24* (1), 1–27.
Al Jazeera. (2015). US and Turkey to train and equip Syrian rebels. 20 February, 2015. Accessed online: 20 February, 2015. http://www.aljazeera.com/news/middleeast/2015/02/turkey-agree-train-equip-syrian-rebels-150219190258895.html.
al-Muqaddam, Muhammad. (2013). *Al Mahdi: truth or fiction?* London, UK: Al Firdous.
al-Sadr, Mohammed Baqir. (2009). "The general framework of the Islamic economy," in R. Euben and M. Zaman (Eds.), *Princeton readings in Islamist thought* (pp. 186–206). Princeton, NJ: Princeton University Press.
al-Shatibi, Abu Ishaq Ibrahim. (1970). *al-Muwāfaqāt fī uṣūl al-aḥkām*. M. Muyhi al-Din 'Abd al-Hamid (Ed.). Cairo: Matab'at Muhammad Ali Subayh.
al-'Uthaymīn, Muḥammad Ibn Ṣāliḥ. (2006a). *The great Islamic awakening*. (Faisal ibn Muhammed, Trans.). Birmingham, UK: Al Hidaayah Publishing.
al-'Uthaymīn, Muḥammad Ibn Ṣāliḥ. (2006b). "Are we forced or do we have free will?" Short excerpt from, *Sharh hadeeth Jibra'eel*. Shawana Aziz (Trans.). Qur'an Sunnah Educational Programs Publishers. http://www.qsep.com/books/areweforced.html. Accessed on June 29, 2014.
Alakbari, Farid. (2001). A 13th century Darwin? —Tusi's Views of Evolution. *Azerbaijan International, 9* (2). http://www.azer.com/aiweb/categories/magazine/92_folder/92_articles/92_tusi.html. Accessed on November 7, 2016.

Ali, Chiragh. (2002). *The Proposed Political, Legal and Social Reforms. Taken from Modernist Islam 1840–1940: A Sourcebook*. Charles Kurzman (Ed.). New York: Oxford University Press.

Alghoul, Diana. (2015). The hijab ban is part of a wider war against women. 10 August, 2015. *Middle East Monitor*. https://www.middleeastmonitor.com/articles/africa/20315-the-hijab-ban-is-part-of-a-wider-war-against-women Accessed on August 10, 2015.

Allawi, Ali A. (2009). *The crisis of Islamic civilization*. New Haven, CT: Yale University Press.

Allen, James. (1971). *As a man thinketh: James Allen's greatest inspirational essays*. W. Franklin and W. Webb (Eds.). Kansas City, MO: Hallmark Crown Editions.

Almond, Gabriel and Sidney Verba. (1963). *The civic culture: political attitudes and democracy in five nations*. Princeton, NJ: Princeton University Press.

Alverado, Facundo and Thomas Piketty. (2014). Measuring top incomes and inequality in the Middle East: data limitations and illustration with the case of Egypt. Economic Research Forum Working Paper Series, Working Paper No. 832., pp. 1–45.

Amin, Magdi, et al. (2012). *After the spring: Economic transitions in the Arab World*. New York: Oxford University Press.

Arabi, Oussama. (2001). *Studies in modern Islamic law and jurisprudence*. New York: Kluwer Law International.

Aristotle. *The basic works of Aristotle*. (2001). J. McKeon (Ed.). New York: The Modern Library.

Armstrong, Karen. (2007). *Mohammed: A Prophet for our time* (Reprint Edition). New York: Harper One Publishers.

Arjomand, Said Amir. (1993). "Religion and constitutionalism in Western history and in modern Iran and Pakistan." in S. A. Arjomand (Ed.). *The Political Dimensions of Religion* (pp. 69–99). Albany, NY: SUNY Press.

Aslan, Reza. (2005). *No God but God: the origins, evolution, and future of Islam*. New York: Random House.

Averroes. (2008). *Averroes: tahafut al tahafut: the incoherence of the incoherence* (2 Vols).Simon Van Den Bergh (Ed.). New York: Gibb Memorial Trust.

Azadpur, Mohammad. (2011). *Reason unbound: on spiritual practice in Islamic peripatetic philosophy*. Albany, NY: SUNY Press.

Azhar, Rauf A. (2009). *Economics of an Islamic economy*. Leiden: Brill E-Books.

Bacchi, Umberto. (2014). ISIS claims responsibility for murdering Tunisian politicians as election nears. 19 December, 2014. *International Business Times*. http://www.ibtimes.co.uk/isis-claims-responsibility-murdering-tunisian-politicians-election-nears-1480280. Accessed on November 27, 2016.

Bakar, Osman. (2006). "Islam, ethnicity, pluralism and democracy: Malaysia's unique experience," in M.A. Muqtedar Khan (Ed.), *Islamic democratic discourse* (pp. 37–62). Lanham, MD: Lexington Books.

Barber, Benjamin. (1984). *Strong democracy: participatory politics for a new age.* Lo Angeles, CA: UCLA Press.
Barlas, Asma. (2001). *"Believing women" in Islam: unreading patriarchal interpretations of the Qu'ran.* Austin, TX: University of Texas Press.
Barker, Ernest (Ed.). (1960). *Social contract: essays by Locke, Hume, and Rousseau* (1st Edition). New York: Oxford Press.
Bashi, Goldbarg. (2003). Eyewitness History: Ayatollah Montazeri. [Interview] www.parstimes.com/women/bashi-montazeri.pdf. Accessed on March, 1 2015.
Batur, Nur. (2009). Yeni Osmanılar sözü iyi niyetli değil. 4 December, 2009. *Daily Sabah.* http://www.sabah.com.tr/siyaset/2009/12/04/yeni_osmanlilar_sozu_iyi_niyetli_degil. Accessed on February 8, 2015.
BBC News. (2015). Syrian Kurds accuse Turkey of attacking their forces. 27 July, 2015.http://www.bbc.com/news/world-europe-33675760Accessed on July 28, 2015.
BBC News. (2009). Crowds gather to mourn reformist Iran cleric Montazeri. 20 December, 2009 http://news.bbc.co.uk/2/hi/middle_east/8423319.stm. Accessed on June 2, 2013.
Beckett, Samuel. (1954). *Waiting for Godot* (2nd Edition). New York: Grove Press.
Bellin, Eva. (2004). The robustness of authoritarianism in the Middle East: exceptionalism in comparative perspective. *Comparative Politics, 36* (2), 139–157.
Benjamin, Walter. (1969). Paris: capital of the nineteenth century. *Perspecta, 12,* 163–172.
Berlin, Isaiah. (2004). *Liberty.* New York: Oxford Publishers.
Berman, Sheri. (2003). Islamism, revolution, and civil society. *Perspectives on Politics, 1* (2), 257–272.
Bill, James. (2001). *Roman Catholics and Shi'i Muslims: prayer, passion, and politics.* Chapel Hill, NC: University of North Carolina Press.
Binder, Leonard. (1988). *Islamic liberalism: a critique of development ideologies.* Chicago, IL: University of Chicago Press.
Bollen, Kenneth A. (1990). Political democracy: conceptual and measurement traps. *Studies in Comparative International Development, 25,* 7–24.
Bonn International Centre for Conversion (Bonn Report). (2013). Security Sector Reform in Algeria (pp. 1–10). https://www.bicc.de/ssr_gtz/pdf/algeria.pdf. Accessed on September 19, 2016.
Bonner, Michael. (2005). Poverty and economics in the Qur'an. *Journal of Interdisciplinary History, 35* (3), 391–406.
Boulakia, Jean David. (1971). Ibn Khaldûn: a fourteenth-century economist. *Journal of Political Economy, 79* (5), 1105–1118.
Brooks, Geraldine. (1995). *Nine parts of desire: unveiling the world of Islamic women.* New York: Doubleday Publishers.

Bronner, Stephen E. (1999). *Ideas in action: political tradition in the 20*th *century*. New York: Rowman & Littlefield Publishers.
Bronner, Stephen E. (1995). The great divide: the Enlightenment and its critics. *New Politics*, 5 (3), 65–86.
Brown, DeNeen. (2004). Muslim refusnik incites furor with critique of faith. 19 January, 2004. *Washington Post*. https://www.washingtonpost.com/archive/politics/2004/01/19/muslim-refusenik-incites-furor-with-critique-of-faith/6e56f1aa-652b-4a9c-a59b-f454c91be366/. Accessed on October 29, 2016.
Brown, Nathan. (2013). Tracking the Arab Spring: Egypt's failed transition. *Journal of Democracy*, 24 (4), 45–58.
Buber, Martin. (1953). *The writings of Martin Buber*. Will Herberg (Ed.). New York: Meridian Books.
Buckley, Terry. (1996). *Aspects of Greek history 750–323 BC: a source-based approach*. London: Routledge Press.
Bulliet, Richard. (1994). *Islam: the view from the edge*. New York: Columbia University Press.
Burris, Greg. (2011). Lawrence of e-rabia. Facebook and the new Arab revolt. *Jadaliyya*. http://www.jadaliyya.com/pages/index/2884/lawrence-. Accessed on December 14, 2016.
Butler, Daren. (2012). Turkey regains investment-grade rating after long wait. 5 November, 2012. *Reuters*. http://www.reuters.com/article/2012/11/05/turkey-fitch-rating-idUSL5E8M56DZ20121105. Accessed on February 9, 2015.
Butterworth, Charles. (1996). Averroës, precursor of the enlightenment? *ALIF: Journal of Comparative Poetics*, 16, 6–18.
Butterworth, Charles. (1992). Political Islam: the origins. *Annals of the American Academy of Political and Social Science*, 524, 26–37.
Çaksu, Ali. (2007). Ibn Khaldun and Hegel on causality in history: Aristotelian legacy reconsidered. *Asian Journal of Social Science*, 35, 46–83.
Capeheart, Loretta and Dragan Milovanovic. (2007). *Social justice: theories, issues, and movements*. Piscataway, NJ: Rutgers Press.
Chang, Ha-Joon. (2011). Institutions and economic development: theory, policy and history. *Journal of Institutional Economics*, 7 (4), 473–498.
Chee, Kee Thuan. (2014). *Can we save Malaysia please!* Singapore: Marshall Cavendish.
Choudhury, Masudul A. and Uzir Malik. (1992). *The foundations of Islamic political economy*. New York: Palgrave.
Chronicle for Higher Education. (2011). *Adults with degree, by county*. http://chronicle.com/article/Adults-With-College-Degrees-in/125995/. Accessed on March 18, 2015.
Ciftci, Sabri. (2013). Secular-Islamist cleavage, values, and support for democracy and Shari'a in the Arab world. *Political Research Quarterly*, 66 (4), 781–793.

Cizre, Ümit. (2004). The catalysts, directions and focus of Turkey's agenda for security sector reform in the 21st century. Paper presented at the July 12-13 workshop on "Challenges of security sector governance in the Middle East," Geneva Centre for the Democratic Control of Armed Forces (DCAF), Working Paper No. 148, pp. 1–25.
Çinar, Menderes and Burhanettin Duran. (2008). "The specific evolution of political Islam in Turkey and its 'difference,'" in Ümit Cizre (ed.) *Secular and Islamic politics in Turkey: the making of the Justice and Welfare Party* (pp. 17–40). New York: Routledge.
Çizakça, Murat. (2007). Democracy, economic development, and *maqāsid al-Sharī'ah*. *Review of Islamic Economics*, 11 (1), 101–118.
Clancy-Smith, Julia Ann. (2001). *North Africa, Islam, and the Mediterranean world: from the Almoravids to the Algerian War.* London: Frank Cass & Co. Ltd.
Clayton, James D. (1985). *Triumph and Disaster 1945–1964: The Years of MacArthur* (Vol. 3). Boston: Houghton Mifflin.
Common, Richard. (2008). Administrative change in the Gulf: modernization in Bahrain and Oman. *International Review of Administrative Sciences, 74*, 177–193.
Corrales, Javier and Frank Westhoff. (2006). "Information technology adoption and political regimes," *International Studies Quarterly, 50* (4), 911–933.
Cox, Harvey. (1966). *The secular city: secularization and the urbanization in theological perspective.* New York: Macmillan.
Crone, Patricia. (2005). *Medieval Islamic political thought.* Edinburgh, UK: Edinburgh University Press.
Dahl, Robert. (1989). *Democracy and its critics.* New Haven, CT: Yale Press.
Dahl, Robert. (1971). *Polyarchy: participation and opposition.* New Haven, CT: Yale University Press.
Dallmayr, Fred. (2010). *The promise of democracy: political agency and transformation.* Albany, NY: SUNY Press.
Davis, Eric. (2005). The new Iraq: the uses of historical memory. *Journal of Democracy, 16* (3), 54–68.
Davutoğlu, Ahmet. (2012). Statement by Dr. Ahmet Davutoğlu, Minister of Foreign Affairs of the Republic of Turkey Nov. 29, 2012 at the U.N. General Assembly regarding Palestinian statehood. *Washington Report on Middle East Affairs, 32* (1), (Jan/Feb 2013). http://www.wrmea.org/2013-january-february/three-views-the-u.n.-welcomes-the-state-of-palestine.html. Accessed on October 30, 2016.
Davutoğlu, Ahmet. (2001). *Stratejik Derinlik: Türkiye'nin Uluslararası Konumu.* Istanbul: Küre Yayınları.
Delong-Bas, Natalia. (2004). *Wahhābi Islam: from revival and reform to global jihad.* New York: Oxford Press.
Department for International Development (DFID). (2003). The global conflict prevention pool: a joint UK government approach to reducing conflict (pp. 1–41). London, UK. http://webarchive.nationalarchives.gov.uk/+/http:/

www.dfid.gov.uk/pubs/files/global-conflict-prevention-pool.pdf. Accessed on October 30, 2016.

Diamond, Larry, (2015). Tunisia is still a success. *The Atlantic.* 23, March, 2015.http://theatlantic.com/international/archive/2015/03/tunisia-is-still-a-success-terrorist-attack/388436. Accessed on March 30, 2016.

Djait, Hichem. (1989). *Europe and Islam: cultures and modernity.* Berkeley, CA: University of California Press.

Downs, Anthony. (1965). A theory of bureaucracy. *The American Economic Review, 55* (1), 439–446.

Duderija, Adis. (2016). The custom (urf) based assumptions regarding gender roles and norms in the Islamic tradition: a critical examination. *Studies in Religion, 45* (4), 581–599.

Dunleavy, Patrick and Christopher Hood. (1994). From old public administration to new public management. *Public Money & Management, 14* (3), 9–16.

Dunleavy, Patrick and Helen Margetts. (2013). The second wave of digital-era governance: a quasi-paradigm for government on the Web. *Philosophical Transactions of the Royal Society, 371* (1987), 1–17.

Dunleavy, Patrick, Helen Margetts, Simon Bastow and Jane Tinker. (2006). *Digital rra governance: IT corporations, the state and e-government.* New York: Oxford Press.

Dunleavy, Patrick, Helen Margetts, Simon Bastow and Jane Tinker. (2005). New Public Management is Dead. Long live Digital-Era Governance. *Journal of Public Administration Research and Theory, 16* (3), 467–494.

Duran, Burhanettin. (2008). "The Justice and Development Party's 'new politics': steering toward conservative democracy, a revised Islamic agenda or management of new crises?" in Ümit Cizre (Ed.), *Secular and Islamic politics in Turkey: the making of the Justice and Development Party* (pp. 80–106). New York: Routledge.

Egypt Report. (2015). Memorandum of justification for certification under section 7041(a)(6)(c) of the Department of State, Foreign Operations, and Related Programs Appropriations Act, 2015 (Div. J, P.L. 113-235). Signed by Secretary of State John Kerry, 12 May, 2015. http://graphics8.nytimes.com/packages/pdf/international/2015/egyptwaiver.pdf. Accessed on January 1, 2016.

Eickelman, Dale. (1997). "Muslim politics: the prospects for democracy in North Africa and the Middle East," in John Entilis (Ed.), *Islam, democracy, and the state in North Africa* (pp. 17–42). Bloomington, IN: Indiana University Press.

El Sadaawi, Nawal. (2007). *The hidden face of Eve: women in the Arab world* (2nd Edition). London: Zed Publishing.

Eltantawy, Nahed and Julie Wiest. (2011). Social media in the Egyptian revolution: reconsidering resource mobilization theory. *International Journal of Communication, 5,* 1207–1224.
Ennis, Crystal and Momani, Bessma. (2013). Shaping the Middle East in the midst of the Arab Spring uprisings: Turkish and Saudi foreign policy strategies. *Third World Quarterly, 34* (6), 1127–1144.
Entilis, John. (Ed.). (1997). *Islam, democracy, and the state in North Africa.* Bloomington, IN:Indiana University Press.
Esposito, John. (2010). *The future of Islam.* New York: Oxford University Press.
Esposito, John. (2004). "Practice and theory," in K. Abou Fadl, J. Cohen, and D. Chasman (Eds.), *Islam and the challenge of democracy* (pp. 93–100). Princeton, NJ: Princeton University Press.
Esposito, John. (1987). *Islam and politics* (2nd Edition). Syracuse, NY: Syracuse University Press.
Fakhry, Majid. (2002). *Al-Farabi: founder of Islamic neoplatonism: his life and works.* New York: Oxford Press.
Fakhry, Majid. (2001). *Averroes (Ibn Rushd) his life, works and influence.* London, UK: Oneworld Publications.
Fakhry, Majid. (1983). *A history of Islamic philosophy.* New York: Columbia University Press.
Falk, Richard. (2013). Turkey's new multilateralism: A positive diplomacy for the twenty-first century. *Global Governance, 19,* 353–376.
Feldman, Noah. (2008). *The fall and rise of the Islamic stat e.* Princeton, NJ: Princeton University Press.
Feldman, Noah. (2011). Islamists' victory in Tunisia a win for democracy. 30, October, 2011. *Bloomberg View.* http://www.bloombergview.com/articles/2011-10-30/islamists-victory-in-tunisia-a-win-for-democracy-noah-feldman. Accessed on December 15, 2015.
FIDH (International Federation of Human Rights) Report. (2015). "Exposing state hypocrisy: Sexual violence by security forces in Egypt," Report No. 661a, May 2015. https://www.fidh.org/IMG/pdf/egypt_report.pdf. Accessed on May 3, 2016.
Fink, Carsten, and Charles Kenny. (2006). W(h)ither the digital divide? *Info, 5* (6), 15–24.
Finn, Tom. (2011). Women have Emerged as Key Players in the Arab Spring. 22 April, 2011.
The Guardian, http://www.theguardian.com/world/2011/apr/22/women-arab-spring. Accessed on July 21, 2015.
Fish, Steven, M. (2002). Islam and authoritarianism. *World Politics, 55* (1), 4–37.
Foucault, Michel. (1970). *The Order of Things.* New York: Pantheon.
Foucault, Michel. (1969). *L'Archéologie du Savoir.* Paris: Éditions Gallimard.

Furqani, Hafas and Ratna Mulyany. (2009). Islamic banking and economic growth: empirical evidence from Malaysia. *Journal of Economic Cooperation and Development, 30* (2), 59–74.

Gadamer, Hans-Georg. (2004). *Philosophical hermeneutics.* David Linge (Ed.). Berkeley, CA; University of California Press.

Gallagher, Tom. (2003). *The Balkans after the Cold War: from tyranny to tragedy.* New York: Routledge.

Gay, Peter. (1969). *The Enlightenment: An interpretation- Volume II: The Science of Freedom.* New York: Knopf Publishers.

Genequand, Charles. (1986). "Ibn Rushd's metaphysics," in Hans Daiber (Ed.), *Islamic Philosophy and Theology: Text and Studies* (Vol. 1). Leiden, Netherlands: E.J. Brill Publishers.

Gerges, Fawaz A. (2013). The Islamist moment: from Islamic state to civil Islam? *Political Science Quarterly, 128* (3), 389–426.

Ghanim, David. (2009). Democracy and political Islam. *Middle East Policy, 16*(1), http://www.mepc.org/journal/middle-east-policy-archives/turkish-democracy-and-political-islam. Accessed on May 19, 2015.

Ghannouchi, Rachid. (2007). "The participation of Islamists in a non-Islamic government," in Islam in transition: Muslimperspectives, eds. J. Donohue and J. Esposito, (pp. 271–278). New York: Oxford Press.

Giddings, Steve. (1995). "The black hole information paradox." *Particles, Strings and Cosmology.* March 22-25, 1995, Johns Hopkins Workshop on Current Problems in Particle Theory 19 and the PASCOS Interdisciplinary Symposium 5.

Glick, Thomas F. (1979). *Islamic and Christian Spain in the early middle ages.* Princeton, NJ: Princeton University Press.

Göksel, Diba. (2014). The presidential elections that have changed Turkey. 7, August 2014. *Al Jazeera Online.* http://www.aljazeera.com/indepth/opinion/2014/08/presidential-elections-changed-tu-2014871389569858.html. Accessed on February 18, 2015.

Goldstone, Jack. (2011). "Understanding the revolutions of 2011: weakness and resilience in Middle Eastern autocracies," *The new Arab revolts: what happened, what it means, and what comes next* (pp. 329–343). Published by the Council on Foreign Relations. New York.

Göle, Nilüfer. (2013). Gezi—anatomy of a public square movement. *Insight Turkey, 15* (3), 7–14.

Goodman, Len. (1999). *Jewish and Islamic philosophy: crosspollinations in the classic age.* New Brunswick, NJ: Rutgers University Press.

Grant, Moyra. (2003). *Key ideas in politics.* Cheltenham, UK: Nelson Thornes.

Griffel, Frank. (2007). "Al-Ghazālī," in Edward Zalta (Ed.), *The Stanford encyclopedia of philosophy.* http://plato.stanford.edu/archives/fall2007/entries/al-ghazali/. Accessed on July 15, 2015.

Guillaume, Alfred. (1966). *The traditions of Islam—an introduction to the study of the hadith literature*. Beirut: Khayats.
Habermas, Jürgen. (1985). *The theory of communicative action* (2 Vols.). Thomas McCarthy (Ed.). Boston: Beacon Press.
Hackett, Rick. and Gordon Wang. (2012). Virtues and leadership: an integrating conceptual framework founded in Aristotelian and Confucian perspectives on virtues. *Management Decision, 50* (5), 868–899.
Hadiz, Vedi R. and Khoo Boo Teik. (2011). Approaching Islam and politics from political economy: a comparative study of Indonesia and Malaysia. *The Pacific Review, 24* (4), 463–485.
Hai, Jeong Chung and Nor Fadzlina Nawi. (2007). *Principles of public administration: an introduction*. Kuala Lumpur: Karisma Publications.
Haj, Samira. (2002). Reordering Islamic orthodoxy: Muhammed ibn 'Abdul Wahhāb. *The Muslim World, 92* (3), 333–370.
Hallaq, Wael. (2013). *The impossible state: Islam, modernity, and modernity's moral predicament*. New York: Columbia University Press.
Hallaq, Wael. (1993). *Ibn Taymiyya against the Greek logicians*. New York: Oxford Press.
Hamid, Shadi. (2013). An Islamic alternative? equality, redistributive justice, and the welfare state in the caliphate of Umar. *Renaissance: Monthly Islamic Journal*, *13*. http://www.monthly-renaissance.com/issue/PrintVersion.aspx?id=35. Accessed on October 30, 2016.
Haneef, Mohamed A. (2001). Islam and economic development in Malaysia—a reappraisal. *Journal of Islamic Studies, 12* (3), 269–290.
Hanifizadeh, Mohammed Reza, Abbas Saghaei, and Payam Hanifizadeh. (2009). An index for cross-country analysis of ICT infrastructure and access. *Telecommunications Policy, 33* (7), 385–405.
Hansen, Allan D. and André Sonnichsen. (2014). Discourse, the political and the ontological dimension: an interview with Ernesto Laclau. *Distinktion: Scandinavian Journal of Social Theory, 15* (3), 255–262.
Hardy, Cynthia. (2001). Researching organizational discourse. *International Studies in Management and Organization, 31* (3), 25–47.
Hashemi, Nader. (2014). Rethinking religion and legitimacy across the Islam-West divide. *Philosophy and Social Criticism, 40* (4–5), 439–447.
Hashemi, Nader. (2009). *Islam, secularism, and liberal democracy: Toward a democratic theory for Islamic societies*. New York: Oxford University Press
Hassan, Mona. (2010). "Modern interpretations and misinterpretations of a medieval scholar: apprehending the political thought of Ibn Taymiyyah," in Yossef Rapoport and Shahab Ahmed (Eds.), *Ibn Taymiyyah and his times* (pp. 338–366). New York: Oxford Press.
Hassan, Riffat. (1999). "Feminism in Islam," in A. Sharma and K. Young (Eds.), *Feminism and world religions* (pp. 248–278). Albany, NY: SUNY Press.

Hauslohner, Abigail. (2012). Mixed reviews as Egypt's new president hits 100-day mark in office. 6 October, 2012. *The Washington Post*. http://articles.washingtonpost.com/2012-10-06/world/35502539_1_morsi-meter-islamist-public-opinion. Accessed on August 9, 2013.

Hay, Stephen N. and William T. De Bary, et al. (1988). *Sources of Indian tradition* (Vol 2). New York: Columbia University Press.

Helliwell, John, Richard Layard, and Jeffrey Sachs. (2011). *World happiness report*. New York: The Earth Institute Columbia University. http://www.earth.columbia.edu/sitefiles/file/Sachs%20Writing/2012/World%20Happiness%20Report.pdf. Accessed on October 30, 2016.

Himmelfarb, Gertrude. (2004). *The roads to modernity: the British, French, and American enlightenments*. New York: Knopf Publishers.

Hobbes, Thomas (1994). *Leviathan*. Edwin Curley (Ed.). Indianapolis: Hackett.

Hofstadter, Richard. (1963). *Anti-intellectualism and American life*. New York: VintagePublishers.

Holtzman, Livnat. (2010). "Human choice, divine guidance and the *fitra* tradition- the use of hadith in theological treatises by Ibn Taymiyya and Ibn Qayyim al-Jawziyya", Y. Rapoport and S. Ahmed (eds.), *Ibn Taymiyya and his times* (pp. 163–188). Karachi: Oxford Press.

Hoover, Jon. (2004). Perpetual creativity in the perfection of God: Ibn Taymiyya's hadith commentary on God's creation of this world. *Journal of Islamic Studies, 15* (3), 287–329.

Horkheimer, Max, and Theodor Adorno. (2002). *Dialectic of enlightenment*. New York: Continuum.

Hourani, Albert. (1991). *A history of the Arab peoples*. New York: Warner Books.

Howard, Philip N. and Nimah Mazaheri. (2009). Telecommunications reform, internet use, and mobile phone adaptation in the developing world. *World Development, 37* (7), 1159–1169.

Hurriyet Daily News. (2013). Turkey's main opposition CHP seeks probe into 'alcohol in mosque' Gezi protest claim. 9 December, 2013. http://www.hurriyetdailynews.com/turkeys-main-opposition-chp-seeks-probe-into-alcohol-in-mosque-gezi-protest-claim.aspx?pageID=238&nID=59301&NewsCatID=338. Accessed on February 17, 2015.

Hurvitz, Nimrod. (2000). Schools of law and historical context: re-examining the formation of the Hanbali *Madhab*. *Islamic Law and Society, 7* (1), 37–64.

Ibn Baz, Abdul Aziz bin Abdullah. (2014). "The obligation of invoking peace and blessings on the Prophet in a complete form," in *Fatwas of Ibn Baz*, compiled online by Kingdom of Saudi Arabia's Portal of the General Presidency of Scholarly Research and 'Ifta. http://www.alifta.net/Fatawa/FatawaChapters.aspx?languagename=en&View=Page&PageID=139&PageNo=1&BookID=14. Accessed on May 3, 2015.

BIBLIOGRAPHY 307

Ibn Kathir. (2003). *Tafsir ibn Kathir* (Abridged Vol. 1). Saifur-Rahman al-Mubarakpuri (Trans.). Houston, TX: Dar-us-salaam.
Ibn Khaldun. (1958). *Muqaddimah of Ibn Khaldun*, (an introduction to history). Franz Rosenthal (Trans.). Princeton, NJ: Princeton University Press.
Ibn Khaldun. (2005). *The muqaddimah: An introduction to history*. Edited by N. J. Dawood. Franz Rosenthal (Trans.). Princeton, NJ: Princeton University Press.
Ibn Qudamah. (1962). *Censure of speculative theology: an edition and translation of Ibn Qudama's Tahrim an-nazar fi kutub ahl-al-kalam wit introduction and notes*. George Makdisi (Ed.), London: Luzac and Company.
Ibn Rushd. (1954). *Al tahafut al-tahafut* (2 Vols). Simon Van Den Bergh (Trans.) Cambridge, England: EJW Gibb Memorial Trust.
Ibn Sa'd, Muhammad. (1995). *Tabaqat* (Vols. 8). 'The Women of Madina,' Aisha Bewley (Trans.). London, UK: Ta-Ha Publishers.
Ibn Sina. (1960). *Al-Ilahiyat (theology)*. M.Y. Moussa, S. Dunya and S. Zayed, (Eds.) Cairo, Egypt: Organisme General des Imprimeries Gouvernementales.
Ibn Taymiyya. (1981). *Dar'u ta'arud al 'aql wa al naql*. Volume. 8. Muhammad Rashad Sa'im (ed.). Riyadh: Jami'at al-Imam Muhammad ibn Sa'ud al-Islamiyyah.
Idriz, Mesut. (2011). Balkans between two worlds: Turkey and Europe. 9 October, 2011 *Today's Zaman*. http://www.todayszaman.com/op-ed_balkans-between-two-worlds-turkey-and-europeby-mesut-idriz-_259260.html. Accessed on April 13, 2014.
Imber, Colin. (1997). *Ebu's Su'ud: the Islamic legal tradition*. Palo, Alto: CA: Stanford Press.
İnanç, Yusuf Selman. (2015). Egypt to confiscate and remove Muslim Brotherhood books from libraries. 24 June, 2015. *The Daily Sabah*. http://www.dailysabah.com/mideast/2015/06/24/egypt-to-confiscate-and-remove-muslim-brotherhood-books-from-libraries. Accessed on June 28, 2015.
India Today. (2013). Tunisia PM resigns after cabinet initiative fails to form a technocratic government. 20 February, 2013. http://indiatoday.intoday.in/story/tunisia-pm-resigns-after-cabinet-initiative-fails/1/250957.html. Accessed on May 20, 2014.
Inglehart, Ronald and Pippa Norris. (2003). The true clash of civilizations. *Foreign Policy*, 135, 62–70.
Islahi, Abdul Aziz. (2006). Ibn Khaldun's theory of taxation and its relevance today. Paper presented to the Conference, *Organizing institutions: The Islamic Research and Training Institute*, a member of the Islamic Development Bank Group, in collaboration with Universidad Nacional de Educacion a Distance (UNED) of Spain, and Islamic Cultural Centre of Madrid. Madrid, Spain, November 3–5, 2006.

Islam, Nasir. (2005). "National culture, corruption, and governance in Pakistan," in J. Jabbra and Dwivedi (Eds.), *Administrative culture in a global context*. Whitby, Ontario: De Sitter Publications.
Islami, Hasan. (2002). *Imam Khomeini: ethics and politics*. Mansoor Limba (Trans.). Tehran: The Institute for Compilation and Publication of Imam Khomeini's Works.
Izetbegović, Alija. (1990). *The Islamic declaration: a programme for the Islamization of Muslims and Muslim peoples*. Sarajevo.
Jamaoui, Anouar. (2015). The impact of the coalition on Ennahda and Nidaa Tounes. 11 March, 2015. *Open Democracy*. https://www.opendemocracy.net/arab-awakening/anouar-jamaoui/impact-of-coalition-on-ennahda-and-nidaa-tounes. Accessed on July 15, 2015.
Jansen, Johannes. (1987). Ibn Taymiyyah and the 13th century: a formative period of modern Muslim radicalism. *Qaderni di Studi Arabi. Gli Arabi nella Sroria: Tanti Popoli una Sola Civilta*, 5 (6), 391–396.
January, Brendan. (2008). *Pivotal moments in history: the Iranian Revolution*. Minneapolis: 21[St] Century Books.
Jay, Martin. (1984). *Adorno*. Cambridge, MA: Harvard Press.
Jefferson, Thomas. (1843). Thomas Jefferson, letter to Benjamin Waterhouse, June 26, 1822, in Robert Aspland (Ed.), *The Christian reformer; or, Unitarian magazine and review* (Volume 10). London, UK
Jefferson, Thomas. (1823). Thomas Jefferson to John Adams, April 11, 1823, *The Thomas Jefferson Papers Series 1. General Correspondence. 1651–1827*. http://hdl.loc.gov/loc.mss/mtj.mtjbib024623. Accessed on August 25, 2015.
Jönnson, Christer. (2014), "Classical liberal internationalism," in Thomas G. Weiss and Rorden Wilkinson (Eds.), *International organization and global governance* (pp. 105–118). New York: Routledge.
Jreisat, Jamil E. (1992). Managing national development in the Arab states. *Arab Studies Quarterly, 14* (2), 1–17.
Jreisat, Jamil E. (1999). Administrative reform and the Arab world economic growth. *Policy Studies Review, 16* (2), 19–40.
Juynboll, G.H.A. (1983). *Muslim tradition: studies in chronology, provenance and authorship of early hadith*. Cambridge, UK: Cambridge Press.
Kaboolian, Linda. (1998). The new public management. *Public Administration Review, 58* (3), 189–193.
Kamali, Mohammad H. (2015). *The middle path of moderation in Islam: the Qur'ānic principle of wasaṭiyyah*. New York: Oxford Press.
Kaminski, Joseph J. (2012). The importance of historical understanding: evaluating the strengths and weaknesses of the current counter-narcotics strategy in Afghanistan. *Review of International Law and Politics, 8* (29), 109–141.

Kaminski, Joseph J. (2013). Bureaucracy and modernity: a comparative qualitative analysis of bureaucratic development in the US and OIC states. *Politics, Bureaucracy, and Justice, 3* (2), 1–10.

Kaminski, Joseph J. (2014). The Islamophobia industry, hate, and its impact on Muslim immigrants and OIC state development. *Islamophobia Studies Journal, 2* (2), 157–176.

Kaminski, Joseph J. (2015). Comparing the goals and aspirations of contemporary national-based Islamist movements vs. contemporary transnational-based Islamist movements, in T. Poirson and R. Oprisko (eds.), *Caliphates and Global Islamic Politics* (pp. 46–59). Bristol, UK: E-International Publications.

Kaminski, Joseph J. (2016). Beyond capitalism: exploring the limitations and weaknesses in Max Weber's general understanding of the Islamic discourse. *Intellectual Discourse, 24* (1), 35–58.

Kapucu, Naim and Hami Palabıyık. (2008). *Public administration: from tradition to the modern age*. Ankara, Turkey: International Strategic Research Organization.

Kardaş, Şaban. (2010). Turkey: redrawing the Middle East map or building sandcastles? *Middle East Policy, 17* (1), 115–136.

Kepel, Giles. (2004). *The war for Muslim minds: Islam and the West*. Pascale Ghazaleh (Trans.). Cambridge, MA: Belknap Press.

Khalid, Haniza. (2015). The role of institutions in driving economic change: comparing the thoughts of Ibn Khaldūn and Douglass C. North. *Intellectual Discourse, 23* (2), 177–199.

Khalid, Khadijah. (2011). Malaysia's foreign policy under Najib: a comparison with Mahathir. *Asian Survey, 51* (3), 429–452.

Khan, L. Ali. (2006a). "Commentary on the constitution of Medina," in Hisham Ramadan (Ed.) *Understanding Islamic law: from classical to contemporary*. New York: AltaMira Press.

Khan, L. Ali. (2003). The reopening of the Islamic code: the second era of ijtihād. *University of St. Thomas Law Journal, 1* (1), 341–385.

Khan, M.A. Muqtedar. (2006b). "The politics, theory, and philosophy of Islamic democracy," in M.A. Muqtedar Khan (Ed.), *Islamic Democratic Discourse* (pp. 149–171). Lanham, MD: Lexington Books.

Khan, M.A. Muqtedar. (2014a). "What is Islamic Democracy? The 3 Cs of Islamic Governance," in T. Poirson and R. Oprisko (Eds.), *Caliphates and Global Islamic Politics* (pp. 94–99). E-International Relations Publications.

Khan, M.A. Muqtedar. (2014b). Islam, democracy and Islamism after the counterrevolution in Egypt. *Middle East Policy, 21* (1), 75–86.

Khan, Mateen. (2016). Niqab: An approach based on the proofs. The Institute for the Revival of the Traditional Islamic Sciences. https://bukhari2013.files.wordpress.com/2016/12/niqab-an-approach-based-on-the-proofs.pdf. Accessed on December 30, 2016.

Khan, Qamaruddin. (1982). *Political Concepts in the Quran*. Lahore, Pakistan: Islamic Book Foundation.
Khomeini, Ayatollah Ruhollah. (1981). *Islam and revolution: writings and declarations of Imam Khomeini 1941–1980*. Hamid Algar (Ed.). Tripoli, Lebanon: Mizran Publications.
Khomeini, Ayatollah Ruhollah. (1970). *Islamic government: governance of the jurist*. Hamid Algar (Ed.). Tehran, Iran: Institute for the Publication of Imam Khomeini's Works.
King James Version Reference Bible [KJV]. (2005). New York: Oxford University Press.
Kinzer, Stephen. (2003). *All the shah's men: an American coup and the roots of Middle East terror*. New York: John Wiley & Sons.
Kirkpatrick, David. (2012). Named Egypt's winner, Islamist makes history. 24 June, 2012. *New York Times*. http://www.nytimes.com/2012/06/25/world/middleeast/mohamed-morsi-of-muslim-brotherhood-declared-as-egypts-president.html?_r=2&pagewanted=all. Accessed on April 15, 2015.
Kirkpatrick, David. (2015). Obama administration criticizes Egypt in report to Congress. 7 June, 2015. *New York Times*. http://www.nytimes.com/2015/06/08/world/middleeast/obama-administation-criticizes-egypt-in-report-to-congress.html. Accessed on June 9, 2015.
Knobel, Edward B. (1895). Al Achsasi Al Mouakket, on a catalogue of stars in the calendarium of Mohammad Al Achsasi Al Mouakket. *Monthly Notices of the Royal Astronomical Society*, 55 (8), 429–438.
Krishna, Sankaran. (2009). *Globalization and postcolonialism: hegemony and resistance in the twenty-first century*. New York: Rowan and Littlefield.
Kubicek, Paul. (2015). *Political Islam and democracy in the Muslim world*. Boulder, CO: Lynne Rienner Publishers.
Laclau, Ernesto. (2007). "Discourses," in R. Gooden, P. Petit, and T. Pogge (Eds.),*Contemporary Political Philosophy* (Vol. II) (pp. 541–47). Malden, MA: Blackwell Publishing.
LaGraffe, David. (2012). The youth bulge in Egypt: an intersection of demographics, security, and the Arab Spring. *Journal of Strategic Security*, 5 (2), 65–80.
Lambroschini, Antoine. (2014). Tunisia charter to uphold equality, freedom of opinion. 7 January, 2014. *Daily News Egypt*. Originally released by *Agence France-Presse* (*AFP*). http://www.dailynewsegypt.com/2014/01/07/tunisia-charter-to-uphold-equality-freedom-of-opinion/. Accessedon March 1, 2014.
Lapidus, Ira. (2002). *A history of Islamic societies*. Cambridge, UK: Cambridge Press.
Lari, Sayyed Mujtaba Musavi. (2011). *Western civilization through Muslim eyes*. F.J. Goulding (Trans.). Qom, Iran: Al-Hadi Press.

Laub, Zachary. (2014). "Egypt's Muslim Brotherhood." 15 January, 2014. Council of Foreign Relations backgrounders. http://www.cfr.org/egypt/egypts-muslim-brotherhood/p23991?cid=ppc-google-grantegypt_,uslim_brotherhood_backgrounder&gclid=CPKCtN-qm8UCFXDLtAodMgsAWg. Accessed on April 29, 2015.

Leaman, Oliver. (2015). "Introduction" in Oliver Leaman (Ed.), *The encyclopedia of Islamic philosophy* (reprint edition) (pp. xi–xvi). London, UK: Bloomsbury.

Leaman, Oliver. (1996). Ghazali and the Ash`arites. *Asian Philosophy, 6* (1), 17–27.

Lessa, Iara. (2006). Discursive struggles within social welfare: restaging teen motherhood. *The British Journal of Social Work, 36* (2), 283–298.

Lewis, A. (2011). Profile: Tunisia's Ennahda party. 25, October, 2011. *BBC News*. http://www.bbc.co.uk/news/world-africa-15442859. Accessed on May 2, 2014.

Liddell, Henry, Robert Scott, Henry S. Jones, and Roderick Mackenzie. (1996). *A Greek-English lexicon* (9th edition). New York: Oxford Press.

Liebesny, Herbert. (1975). *The law of the Near and Middle East readings, cases, and materials*. Albany, NY: State University of New York Press.

Liow, Joseph Chinyong. (2009). *Piety and politics: Islamism in contemporary Malaysia*. New York: Oxford Press.

Lipset, Seymour. (1959). Some social requisites of democracy: economic development and political legitimacy. *The American Political Science Review, 53* (1), 69–105.

Little, Donald. (1975). Did Ibn Taymiyyah have a screw loose? *Studia Islamica, 41*, 93–111.

Lo, Ching Wing and Chee Seng Leow. (2014). Islamic banking in Malaysia: a sustainable Growth of the Consumer Market. *International Journal of Trade, Economics and Finance, 5* (6), 526–529.

Locke, John. (1982). *The second treatise of civil government*, Richard Cox (Ed.), Wheeling, IL: Harlan Davidson.

Lovejoy, Arthur. (1964). *The great chain of being: a study of the history of an idea.* Cambridge, MA: Harvard Press.

Lucas, Scott C. (2006). "Sunni theological schools," in Joseph Meri (Ed.), *Medieval Islamic civilization: an encyclopedia* (Vol. 1) (p. 809). New York: Routledge.

Lutz, Donald S. (1980). *Popular consent and popular control: Whig political theory in the early state constitutions*. Baton Rouge, LA: Louisiana State University Press.

Maddy-Weitzman, Bruce. (2014). A turning point? The Arab Spring and the Amazigh movement. *Ethnic and Racial Studies, 38* (14), 2499–2515.

Mahathir. (2008). *The Malay Dilemma*. Singapore: Martin Cavdendish.

Mahathir. (1991). "Malaysian: this way forward (Vision 2020) (pp. 1–12)." http://unpan1.un.org/intradoc/groups/public/documents/apcity/unpan003223.pdf. Accessed on December 20, 2016.

Mahdi, Muhsin. (2001). *Al-Farabi and the foundation of Islamic political philosophy*. Chicago: University of Chicago Press.

Makdisi, George. (1962). Ash'ari and the Asharites and Islamic history I. *Studia Islamica, 17*, 37–80.

March, Andrew. (2015). Political Islam: theory. *Annual Review of Political Science, 18*, 103–123.

March, Andrew. (2013). Genealogies of sovereignty in Islamic political theology. *Social Research: An International Quarterly, 80* (1), 293–320.

Marcotte, Roxanne D. (2010). "Muslim women's scholarship and the new gender jihad," in Z. Kassam (Ed.), *Women in Islam* (pp. 131–162). Denver: Praeger Publishers.

Martin, Vanessa. (2007). *Creating an Islamic state: Khomeini and the making of a new Iran*. New York: St Martin's Press.

Marx, Karl. (1977). *A contribution to the critique of political economy*. Moscow: Progress Publishers.

Matvievskaya, Galina. (1987). The theory of quadratic irrationals in medieval oriental mathematics. *Annals of the New York Academy of Sciences, 500*, 253–277.

Maududi, Abul Ala. (2009). "The Islamic law," in R. Euben and M. Zaman (Eds.), *Princeton readings in Islamist thought*. Princeton, NJ: Princeton University Press.

Maududi, Abul Ala. (1960). *Islamic law and constitution*. Khurshid Ahmad (Ed.). Lahore, Pakistan: Islamic Publications.

Mavani, Hamid. (2013). *Religious authority and political thought in twelver Shi'ism: from Ali to post-Khomeini*. New York: Routledge.

Mekay, Emad. (2013). Exclusive: US bankrolled anti-Morsi activists. 10 July, 2013. *Al Jazeera*. http://www.aljazeera.com/indepth/features/2013/07/2013710113522489801.html. Accessed on September 13, 2015.

Melchert, Christopher. (2004). Ahmad Ibn Hanibal and the Qur'an. *Journal of Qur'anic Studies, 6* (2), 22–34.

Menocal, Maria Rosa. (2002). *The ornament of the world: how Muslims, Jews, and Christians created a culture of tolerance in medieval Spain*. New York: Little, Brown, and Company

Mernissi, Fatima. (1991). *The veil and the male elite: a feminist interpretation of women's rights in Islam*. Mary Jo Lakeland (Trans.). New York: Perseus Publishing.

Midlarsky, Manus. (1998). Democracy and Islam: implications for civilizational conflict and the democratic Peace. *International Studies Quarterly, 42* (3), 485–511.

Miller Jr., Fred. (2007). "*Aristotelian* statecraft and modern politics," in Len Goodman and Robert Talisse (Eds.), *Aristotle's Politics Today* (pp. 13–32). Albany, NY: SUNY Press.

Mills, C. Wright. (2000). *The Power Elite*. New York: Oxford Press.

Milne, Rober S., and Diane K. Mauzy. (1999). *Malaysian politics under Mahathir*. London, UK: Routledge.

Milner, Helen. (2006). The digital divide: the role of political institutions in technology diffusion. *Comparative Political Studies, 39* (2), 176–199.

Minault, Gail. (1982). *The khilafat movement: religious symbolism and political mobilization in India*. New York: Columbia University Press.

Mir, Mustansir. (1986). *Coherence in the Quran: A Study of Islahi's Concept of Nazm in Tadabbur-i-Quran*. Plainfield, IN: American Trust Publication.

Mitchell, Richard. (1993). *The society of the Muslim brothers*. New York: Oxford Press.

Moe, Terry. (1984). The new economics of organization. *American Journal of Political Science, 28* (4), 739–777.

Moghadam, Valentine. (1991). The reproduction of gender inequality in Muslim societies: a case study of Iran in the 1980's. *World Development, 19* (10), 1335–1349.

Mohamed, Yasien. (2006). "Fate" in Oliver Leaman (Ed.), *The Qur'an: an encyclopedia* (pp. 203–207). London: Routledge.

Mok, Opalyn. (2014). Islam not a religion but way of life, says Kuwaiti writer. 25 February, 2014. *The Malaymail Online*. http://www.themalaymailonline.com/malaysia/article/islam-not-a-religion-but-way-of-life-says-kuwaiti-writer#sthash.LBRy8RUC.dpuf. Accessed on July 26, 2015.

Montazeri, Ayatollah Hussein-Ali. (2000). *Democracy and constitution* (pp. 1–41). Ayatollah Montazeri Official Website. http://www.amontazeri.com/farsi/fl.asp. Accessed on May 1, 2015.

Morsi, Mohammed. (2012). Statement of H.E. Dr. Mohammed Morsi President of the Arab Republic of Egypt before the 67th General Assembly of the United Nations. 26 September, 2012. http://gadebate.un.org/sites/default/files/gastatements/67/EG_en.pdf. Accessed on December 19, 2014.

Mosca, Gaetano. (1939). *The ruling class (elementi di scienza politica)*. Arthur Livingston (Ed.). New York: McGraw Hill.

Montazeri, Ayatollah Hussein-Ali. (2000). *Democracy and constitution* (pp. 1–41). Ayatollah Montazeri Official Website. http://www.amontazeri.com/farsi/fl.asp. Accessed on May 1, 2015.

Mosca, Gaetano. (1939). *The ruling class (elementi di scienza politica)*. Arthur Livingston (Ed.). New York: McGraw Hill.

Mubarakpuri, Safi-ur-Rahman. (Ed.). (2003). *Tafsir ibn Kathir (Abridged)*. *Volume 6*. Brooklyn, NY: Dar-us-Salaam Publishers.

Mubarakpuri, Safi-ur-Rahman. (2002). *The sealed nectar: biography of the noble Prophet*. Brooklyn, NY: Dar-us-Salaam Publishers.

Mueller, Hannes. (2009). Patronage or meritocracy: political institutions and bureaucratic efficiency. Spanish National Research Council. Unpublished

Musnad Ahmad Ibn Hanbal (3 Vols.). (2012). Compiled by Ahmad Ibn Hanbal. Translated by Nassirudin al-Khattab. Houston, TX: Dar-us-Salaam Publishers.

Mutahhari, Mortaza. (2009). "The human status of women in the Qur'an," in R. Euben, M. Zaman (Eds.), *Princeton readings in Islamist thought* (pp. 254–274). Princeton, NJ: Princeton University Press.

Muzaffar, Chandra. (2002). *Rights, religion and reform: enhancing human dignity through spiritual and moral transformation*. New York: Routledge.

Nadwi, Abul Hasan A.H. (2005). *Shaikh-ul-Islam Ibn Taimiyah life and achievements*. London: UK Islamic Academy.

Najjar, Fauzi. (2004). Ibn Rushd (Averroes) and the Egyptian enlightenment movement. *British Journal of Middle Eastern Studies, 31* (2), 195–213.

Nasr, Sayeed Hossein. (2010). *Islam in the modern world*. New York: Harper One Publishers.

Nasr, Vali. (2010). *The rise of Islamic capitalism: why the new Muslim middle class is key to defeating extremism*. New York: Free Press.

Nasr, Vali. (1996). *Mawdudi and the making of Islamic revivalism*. New York: Oxford University Press.

Nasution, Harun. (1997). "*Kaum Mu'tazilah dan pandangan rasionalanya* (The Mu'tazila and rational philosophy)," in Mark Woodward, Richard Martin, and Dwi Atmaja (Trans.), *Defenders of reason in Islam: Mu'tazilism from medieval school to modern symbol* (pp 180–193). London: Oneworld Publications.

Nawas, John A. (1996). The *Miḥna* of 218 A. H. /833 A. D. revisited: an empirical study. *Journal of the American Oriental Society, 116* (4), 698–708.

Niskanen, William. (1975). Bureaucrats and politicians. *Journal of Law and Economics, 18*, 617–643.

Nobelprize.org. (2015). "The Nobel Peace Prize for 2015." https://www.nobelprize.org/nobel_prizes/peace/laureates/2015/press.html. Accessed on October 30, 2016.

Noor, Farish. (2009). "Reformist Muslim thinkers in Malaysia: engaging with power to uplift the *Umma?*" in Shireen Hunter (Ed.) *Reformist Voices in Islam: Mediating Islam and Modernity* (pp. 208–226). New York: Routledge.

Norhashimah, Mohammed Yasin. (1996). *Islamisation/Malaynisation: a study on the role of Islamic law in the economic development of Malaysia: 1969–1993*. Kuala Lumpur, Malaysia: A. S. Noordeen.

North, Douglass. (2005). *Understanding the process of economic change*. Princeton, NJ: Princeton University Press.

North, Douglass. (1990). *Institutions, institutional change, and economic performance*. Cambridge, UK: Cambridge University Press.
Öberg, Magnus and Erik Melander. (2010). On the effect of quality of governance, as compared to, e.g., democracy, on civil war Ooutbreak. Paper presented at the annual meeting of the American Political Science Association, Washington DC, August 31–September 3.
Oğurlu, Yücel. (2014). 'E-government portal' and e-government services in Turkey. *Epiphany Journal of Transdisciplinary Studies, 7*(2), 17–26.
Olcott, William. (2004). *Star lore: myths, legends, and facts*. Mineola, NY: Courier Dover Publications.
Olimat, Mohammed. (2014). "Introduction: democratization, Arab Spring and Arab women," in Mohammed Olimat (Ed.), *Arab Spring and Arab women: challenges and opportunities* (pp. 1–16). New York: Routledge International Handbooks.
Olsen, Johan. (2005). Maybe it's Time to Rediscover Bureaucracy. *Journal of Public Administration and Theory, 16*, 1–24.
Olson, Mancur (2002). *The logic of collective action*. Harvard Press: Cambridge, MA.
Oprisko, Robert and Caplan, Josh. (2014). Beyond the cake model: critical intersectionality and the relative advantage of disadvantage. *Epiphany: Journal of Transdisciplinary Studies, 7*(2), 35–54.
O'Sullivan, Feargus. (2015). Why Istanbul is building the largest monorail network in Europe? 4 February, 2015. *CityLab*. http://www.citylab.com/commute/2015/02/istanbul-monorail/385162/. Accessed on February 18, 2015.
Otto, Jan M. (2008). *Sharia and national law in Muslim countries: tensions and opportunities for Dutch and EU foreign policy*. Amsterdam, Netherlands: Amsterdam University Press.
Özkan, Mehmet. (2014). *Turkey's involvement in Somalia: assessment of a statebuilding in Progress*. Istanbul, Turkey: SETA Publications, 1–66.
Özkan, Mehmet. (2013). Turkey, Islamic politics, and the 'Turkish model,' *Strategic Analysis, 37*(5), 534–538.
Ozzano, Luca. (2013). The many faces of the political God: a typology of religiously oriented parties. *Democratization, 20*, 807–830.
Paldam, Martin. (2009). "The macro perspective on generalized trust," in G. Svendsen and G. Svendsen (Eds.), *Handbook of social capital: the troika of sociology, Political Science and Economics* (pp. 354–375). Cheltenham, UK: Edward Elgar.
Paldam, Martin and Gundlach, Erich. (2008). Two views on institutions and development: the grand transition vs the primacy of institutions. *Kyklos, 61*(1), 65–100.

Pew Research Center: *Forum on Religious & Public Life*. (2011). The Future of the World's Global Muslim Population: Projections from 2010-2030. Project Directed by Brian Grim and Mehtab Kerim. January 2011. http://www.pewforum.org/files/2011/01/FutureGlobalMuslimPopulation-WebPDF-Feb10.pdf. Accessed on March 4, 2014.

Pew Research Center: *Forum on Religious & Public Life*. (2013). The world's Muslims: religion, politics and society. Project directed by James Bell. 30 April, 2013. http://www.pewforum.org/files/2013/04/worlds-muslims-religion-politics-society-full-report.pdf. Accessed on February 1, 2014.

Plato. (1961). *The collected dialogues of Plato including the letters*. Edith Hamilton and Huntington Cairns (Eds.). New York: Pantheon Books.

Plotinus. (1930). *The Enneads*. Stephen MacKenna (Trans.). London: Medici Society.

Popper, Karl. (1959). *The logic of scientific discovery*. New York: Basic Books.

Pryor, Fredric. (2007). Are Muslim countries less democratic? *Middle East Quarterly, XIV*, 53–58.

Przeworski, Adam and Fernando Limongi. (1997). Modernization: theories and facts. *World Politics, 49* (2), 155–183.

Puddington, Arch. (2011). Freedom in the world 2011: the authoritarian challenge to democracy. Published by Freedom House. http://www.freedomhouse.org/images/File/fiw/FIW_2011_Booklet.pdf. Accessed on July 8, 2014.

Purdie-Vaughns, Valerie, and Richard Eibach. (2008). Intersectional invisibility: the distinctive advantages and disadvantages of multiple subordinate-group identities. *Sex Roles, 59* (1), 377–391.

Putnam, Robert. (2001). *Bowling alone: the collapse and revival of American community*. New York: Simon & Schuster.

Qaradawi, Yusuf. (2001). *The lawful and the prohibited in Islam* (2nd Edition). K. al-Hilbawi, M. Siddiqi, and S. Shukri (Trans.). Cairo, Egypt: Al Falah Foundation for Translation.

Qur'ān. *The meaning of the glorious Qur'an*. (2001). Mohammed Pickthall (Trans.). New York: Alavi Foundation.

Qutb, Seyyid. (2007). *Milestones*. Damascus, Syria: Kazi Publishers.

Rafiabadi, Hamid Naseem. (2009). *The intellectual legacy of Ibn Taymiyyah*. New Dehli, India: Sarup Book Publishers.

Rahman, Fazlur. (1982). *Islam and modernity: transformation of an intellectual tradition*. Chicago: University of Chicago Press.

Ramadan, Hisham. (2006). *Understanding Islamic law: from classical to contemporary*. New York: Altamira Press.

Ramadan, Tariq. (2009). *In the footsteps of the Prophet: lessons from the life of Mohammed*. New York: Oxford Press.

Ramadan, Tariq. (2006). "*Ijtihad* and *maslaha*: foundations of governance," in Muqtedar Khan (Ed.), *Islamic Democratic Discourse* (pp. 3–20). Lanham, MD: Lexington Books.

Ramage, Douglas. (1995). *Politics in Indonesia: democracy, Islam, and the ideology of tolerance.* New York: Routledge.

Rauch, James and Peter Evans. (2000). Bureaucratic structure and bureaucratic performance in less developed countries. *Journal of Public Economics, 75,* 49–71.

Rawls, John. (1999). *A theory of justice* (2nd Edition). Cambridge, MA: Belknap Press.

Reporters Without Borders. (2014). Contribution to universal periodic review United Nations Human Rights Council, second cycle – 21st session – Jan-Feb 2015. "Written contribution by Reporters Without Borders on freedom information in TURKEY June 2014." http://fr.rsf.org/IMG/pdf/turkey_upr_en-2.pdf. Accessed on February 9, 2015.

Rescher, Nicholas. (1963). Al-Farabi on logical tradition. *Journal of the History of Ideas, 24*(1), 127–132.

Riley, Patrick. (1986). *The general will before Rousseau: the transformation of the divine into the civic.* Princeton, NJ:Princeton University Press.

Riyadh-us-Saliheen. (2 Vols.) (1999). Compiled by Abu Zakariya Nawawi. Muhammad Amin and Abu Usamah Al-Arabi bin Razduq (Trans.). New York: Dar-us-Salam Publications.

Rorty, Richard. (1989). *Contingency, irony, and solidarity.* Cambridge, UK: Cambridge University Press.

Ross, Michael. (2001). Does oil hinder democracy? *World Politics, 53,* 325–361.

Rothstein, Bo. (2011). *The quality of government: corruption, social trust, and inequality in international perspective.* Chicago: University of Chicago Press.

Rousseau, Jean-Jacques. (1987). On the Social Contract. *The Basic Political Writings.* Peter Gay (Ed.). Indianapolis, IN: Hackett Publishing.

Roy, Oliver. (2012). The transformation of the Arab world. *Journal of Democracy, 23*(3), 5–18.

Roy, Oliver. (2004). *Globalized Islam: The Search for a New Ummah.* New York: Columbia University Press.

Royce, Josiah. (2005). *The basic writings of Josiah Royce* (2 Vols.) John McDermott (Eds.).New York: Fordham Press.

Rubin, Barry. (ed.). (2010). *The Muslim Brotherhood: the organizational policies of a global Islamist movement.* New York: Palgrave.

Rutland, Peter. (1993). *The politics of economic stagnation in the Soviet Union: the role of local party organs in economic management.* Cambridge, UK: Cambridge University Press.

Rutland, Peter. (1985). *The myth of the plan: Lessons from the Soviet planning experience.* London, UK: Hutchinson and Co. Ltd.

Ṣaḥīḥ al-Bukhārī (Vols. 9). (2002). Compiled by Muhammed bin Ismail Bukhari. M. Matraji and F. A. Z. Matraji (Eds.). New Delhi, India: Islamic Book Services.
Said, Edward. (1978). *Orientalism.* New York: Random House Publishers.
Safi, Omid. (2010). "Between 'ijtihad of the presupposition' and gender equality: cross-pollination between progressive Islam and Iranian reform," in Carl Ernst (ed.), *Rethinking Islamic studies: from orientalism to cosmopolitanism* (pp. 72–96). Columbia, SC: University of South Carolina Press.
Sakwa, Richard. (1998). *Soviet politics: in perspective* (2nd edition). New York: Routledge.
Sallaabee, Mohammed. (2007). *The biography of Abu Bakr as-Siddique.* Faisal Shafeeq (Trans.). Riyadh, Saudi Arabia: Dar-us-Salaam Publishers.
Salvatore, Armando. (2013). New media, the 'Arab Spring,' and the metamorphosis of the public sphere: beyond western assumptions of collective agency and democratic politics. *Constellations, 20* (2), 217–228.
Sandel, Michael. (1998). *Liberalism and the limits of justice,* Cambridge, UK: Cambridge University Press.
Sandnes, Karl O. (2004). Belly and body in the pauline epistles. Cambridge, UK: Cambridge University Press.
Sardar, Ziauddin. (2003). "Rethinking Islam," in *Islam, postmodernism and other futures: a Ziauddin Sardar reader* (pp. 27–34). Sohail Inayatullah and Gail Boxwell (Eds). London: Pluto Press.
Scherman, Nossom (Ed). (1994). "An overview: Torah—written and oral," in *The Chumash: the Stone edition.* Brooklyn: Mesorah Publications Ltd.
Schleifer, Abdullah. (2013). The problems of Islamist politics in Egypt. 10 April, 2013. *Al Arabiya English.* http://english.alarabiya.net/en/views/2013/04/10/The-problems-of-Islamist-politics-in-Egypt.html. Accessed on September 15, 2014.
Schmar-Dobler, Elizabeth. (2003). Reading on the internet: the link between literacy and Technology. *Journal of Adolescent & Adult Literacy, 47* (1), 80–85.
Schnose, Viktoryia. (2015). Who is in charge here? legislators, bureaucrats, and the policy making process. *Party Politics,* 1–22. DOI: 10.1177/1354068815597896.
Schumpeter, Joseph. (1942). *Capitalism, socialism and democracy.* New York: Harper.
Sedghi, Hamideh. (2007). *Women and politics in Iran: veiling, unveiling, and reveling.* Cambridge, UK: Cambridge University Press.
Sextus Empiricus. (2000). *Outlines of scepticism.* Julia Annas and John Barnes (Eds.). Cambridge, UK: Cambridge University Press.
Shadid, Anthony and David Kirkpatrick. (2011). In Arab World, Bin Laden's Legacy is Confused. May 2, 2011. *New York Times.* http://www.nytimes.

com/2011/05/03/world/middleeast/03arab.html. Accessed on December 14, 2016.
Shah, M. (2006). "Later developments," in Joseph Meri (Ed.), *Medieval Islamic civilization:an encyclopedia* (Vol. 1) (p. 640). New York: Routledge.
Shah, Zulfiqar. (2012). *Anthropomorphic depictions of God: the concept of God in Judaic, Christian and Islamic traditions—representing the unrepresentable.* Herndon, VA: International Institute of Islamic Thought (IIIT).
Shamsul, Amri B. (2001). "The redefinition of politics and the transformation of Malaysian pluralism," in Robert Hefner (ed.), *The politics of multiculturalism: pluralism and citizenship in Malaysia, Singapore, and Indonesia* (pp. 204–226). Honolulu: University of Hawaii Press.
Shanks, Michael. (1992). *Experiencing the past: on the character of archaeology.* London: Routledge Press.
Sikimic, Simona. (2011). Activist highlights women's rights in Islam. 16 June, 2011. *The Daily Star.* http://www.dailystar.com.lb/News/Local-News/2011/Jun-16/Activist-highlights-womens-rights-in-Islam.ashx#ixzz1PSKdmW4L. Accessed on June 14, 2014.
Sisk, Timothy. (1994). *Islam and democracy: religion, politics, and power in the Middle East.* Washington, D.C.: United States Institute of Peace.
Soage, Ana and J.F. Franganillo. (2010). "The Muslim brothers in Egypt," in B. Rubin (Ed.), *The Muslim Brotherhood: The Organization and Policies of a Global Islamist Movement* (pp. 39–56). New York: Palgrave.
Sondrol, Paul. (2009). Totalitarian and authoritarian dictators: a comparison of Fidel Castro and Alfredo Stroessner. *Journal of Latin American Studies, 23*, 599–620.
Souli, Sarah. (2016). Why Tunisia's top Islamist party rebranded itself. May 2016. *Al Monitor.* http://www.al-monitor.com/pulse/originals/2016/05/tunisia-ennahda-islamist-party-rebranding-congress.html. Accessed on October 19, 2016.
Spellberg, Denise A. (1994). *Politics, gender, and the Islamic past: the legacy of Aisha bint Abi Bakr.* New York: Columbia University Press.
Stefanczak, Karolina, and Eileen Connolly. (2015). Gender and political representation in the de facto states of the Caucasus: women and parliamentary elections in Abkhazia. *Caucasus Survey, 3* (3), 1–11.
Stepan, Alfred and Graeme Robertson. (2004). Arab, not Muslim exceptionalism. *Journal of Democracy, 15* (4), 140–146.
Stiglitz, Joseph E. (2006). *Making globalization work.* New York: W.W. Norton & Company.
Stowasser, Barbara. (1994). *Women in the Qur'an: traditions and interpretations.* New York: Oxford Press.
Sunan Ibn Mājah. (5 Vols.). (2007). Compiled by Ibn Majah al Qazwini. Hafiz Abu Tahir Zubair 'AliZa'i (Ed.) and Nasiruddin al-Khattab (Trans.). Houston, TX: Darussalaam Publishers.

Sunan Abī Dāwūd (5 Vols.). (2008). Compiled by Abu Dawud. Hafiz Abu Tahir Zubair 'Ali Za'I (Ed.) and Nasiruddin al-Khattab (Trans.). Houston, TX: Darussalaam Publishers.

Sunan an-Nasā'ī (6 Vols.). (2007). Compiled by Ahmad an-Nasa'i. Translated by Nasiruddin al-Khattab. Houston, TX: Dar-us-Salaam Press.

Svolik, Milan. (2009). Power sharing and leadership dynamics in authoritarian regimes. *American Journal of Political Science,* 53, 477–494.

Tabatabae'i, Muhammad Husayn. (1975). *Shi'ite Islam.* Seyyed Hossein Nasr (Trans. and Ed.). Albany, NY: SUNY Press.

Tamimi, Azzam. (2001). *Rachid Ghannouchi: a democrat within Islamism.* New York: Oxford Press.

Tampio, Nicholas. (2014). "Pluralism in the Ethical Commonwealth," in Gordon E. Michalson (Ed.), Kant's Religion within the Boundaries of Mere Reason: A Critical Guide (pp. 175–192). New York: Cambridge University Press.

Targ, Harry. (2013). "Transitional Steps to a Socialist Future: Part 1, the Vietnam Case," The Labor and Working-Class Studies Project, Working Class Studies Association. Madison College. Madison, Wisconsin. 12–15 June, 2013.

Taşkin, Yuskel. (2013). Hegemonizing conservative democracy and the problems of democratization in Turkey: conservatism without democrats? Turkish Studies, 14 (2), 292–310.

Tönnies, Ferdinand. (2010). *Community and civil society.* J. Harris (Ed.) and M. Hollis (Trans.). Cambridge, UK: Cambridge Press.

Taylor, Charles. (1991). "Language and society," in Axel Honneth and Hans Joas (Eds.), *Communicative Action* (pp. 23–35). Cambridge, MA: MIT Press.

Taylor, Charles. (1992). Sources of the self, Cambridge, MA: Harvard University Press.

Taylor, Richard C. (2012). "Averroes on the Sharī'ah of the philosophers," in Richard C. Taylor and Irfan A. Omar (Eds.), *The Judeo-Christian-Islamic heritage: philosophical & theological perspectives* (pp. 283–304). Milwaukee, WI: Marquette University Press.

Taylor, Richard C. (2009). Ibn Rushd/Averroes and Islamic rationalism. *Medieval Encounters,* 15, 225–235.

Taylor, Thomas (Trans.). (1994). *Collected Writings of Plotinus.* Somerset, UK: Prometheus Trust.

T.C. Dişişeri Baklanliği (Turkish Ministry of Foreign Affairs) official website. (2015a). "Foreign Minister Davutoğlu, "EU membership has been our strategic goal for almost 50 years and will continue to be." http://www.mfa.gov.tr/foreign-minister-davutoglu-_eu-membership-has-been-our-strategic-goal-for-almost-50-years-and-will-continue-to-be.en.mfa. Accessed on February 8, 2015.

T.C. Dişişeri Baklanliği (Turkish Ministry of Foreign Affairs) official website. (2015b). "Relations between Turkey and Bosnia and Herzegovina." http://

www.mfa.gov.tr/relations-between-turkey-and-bosnia-and-herzegovina. en.mfa. Accessed on February 9, 2015.

T.C. Dişişeri Baklanliği (Turkish Ministry of Foreign Affairs) official website. (2015c). "Foreign Minister Davutoğlu "We will stand by the Syrian people until they live with honor in all around Syria." http://www.mfa.gov.tr/foreign-minister-davutoglu-we-will-stand-by-the-syrian-people-until-they-live-with-honor-in-all-around-syria.en.mfa. Accessed on February 18, 2015.

Tillich, Paul. (1957). *Dynamics of faith*. New York: Harper Row.

Tilly, Charles. (1985). "War making and state making as organized crime," in P. Evans, D. Rueschemeyer, and T. Skocpol (Eds.), *Bringing the state back in* (pp. 169–191). Cambridge, UK: Cambridge University Press.

Tocqueville, Alexis. (2003). *Democracy in America*. Isaac Kramnick (Trans.). New York: Penguin Classics.

Tocqueville, Alexis. (1852). "The art & science of politics." Unpublished address given to the *Séances et Travaux de l'Académie de Sciences Morales et Politiques*.

Today's Zaman. (2015a). Turkish police check newspaper over Charlie Hebdo cartoons. 14 January, 2015. http://www.todayszaman.com/national_turkish-police-check-newspaper-over-charlie-hebdo-cartoons_369741.html. Accessed online: 9 February, 2015.

Today's Zaman. (2015b). Turkish court rules to block web pages featuring Charlie Hebdo cover. 14 January, 2015. http://www.todayszaman.com/_turkish-court-rules-to-block-web-pages-featuring-charlie-hebdo-cover_369784.html. Accessed on February 9, 2015.

Tombuş, H. Ertuğ. (2013). Reluctant democratization: the case of the Justice and Development Party in Turkey. *Constellations, 20* (2), 312–327.

Tonso, Karen L. (1996). The impact of cultural norms on women. *Journal of Engineering Education, 85* (3), 217–225.

Tunisian Constitution of 2014. *Constituteproject.org*, Translated into English by UNDP and reviewed by International IDEA. https://www.constituteproject.org/constitution/Tunisia_2014.pdf. Accessed on July 15, 2015.

Ulfelder, Jay. (2007). Natural resource wealth and the survival of autocracy. *Comparative Political Studies, 40*, 995–1018.

UNESCO (2014). International Literacy Data. http://www.uis.unesco.org/literacy/Pages/literacy-data-release-2014.aspx. Accessed on July 24, 2015.

UNHCR UN Refugee Agency. (2015). Kobani refugees encouraged to move into Turkey's newest and largest camp. 16 February, 2015. http://www.unhcr.org/54e1efe39.html. Accessed on February 18, 2015.

UNICEF .(2010). Report on World Countries: Education Statistics. http://www.unicef.org/search/search.php?q=Educationstatistics&type=Main. Accessed on June 23, 2011.

United Nations Population Division. (2008). World Population Prospects: 2008 Revision Population Database. http://www.un.org/esa/population/. Accessed on April 4, 2013.

U.S. Constitution, art. II, § 2.

Üşenmez, Özgür. (2007). Backlash: a neo-Gramscian approach to the rise of political Islam in Turkey. PhD. Dissertation. City University of New York-Graduate Center.

Veenendaal, Wouter. (2015). *Politics and democracy in microstates*. New York: Routledge.

Voll, John. (1997). "Sultans, saints, and presidents: the Islamic community and the state in North Africa," in J. Entilis, et al. (Eds.), *Islam, democracy, and the state in North Africa* (pp. 1–17). Bloomington, IN: Indiana University Press.

Voll, John. (1975). *Muḥammad Ḥayyā al-Sindī and Muḥammad ibn Abd al-Wahhab:* an analysis of an intellectual group in eighteenth-century Madīna. *Bulletin of Oriental and African Studies, 38*, 32–39.

Waardenburg, Jean Jacques. (2002). *Islam: historical, social, and political perspectives*. Berlin: Walter de Gruyter.

Wain, Barry. (2010). *Malaysian maverick: Mahathir Mohamad in turbulent times*. New York: Palgrave.

Waldron, Jeremy. (2002). *God, Locke, and equality: Christian foundations in Locke's political thought*. Cambridge, UK: Cambridge Press.

Wallsten, Scott. (2005). Regulation and internet use in developing countries. *Economic Development and Cultural Change, 53*, 501–523.

Waterbury, John. (1997). "From social contracts to extraction contracts," in J. Entilis, et al. (Eds.), *Islam, democracy, and the state in North Africa* (pp. 141–176). Bloomington, IN: Indiana University Press.

Watt, John. (1995). From Themistius to al-Farabi: Platonic political philosophy and Aristotle's rhetoric in the East. *Rhetorica: A Journal of the History of Rhetoric, 13*(1), 17–41.

Webb, William. (1971). "Who was James Allen?" in *As a man thinketh: James Allen's greatest inspirational essays*. W. Franklin and W. Webb (Eds.), Kansas City, MO. Hallmark Crown Editions.

Weber, Max. (2001). *The Protestant ethic and the spirit of capitalism* (2nd Edition). New York: Routledge Classics.

Weber, Max. (1964). *The theory of social and economic organization*. New York: The Free Press.

Weiss, Bernard G. (1998). *The spirit of Islamic law*. Athens, Georgia: University of Georgia Press.

Weiss, Dieter. (1995). Ibn Khaldun on economic transformation. *International Journal of Middle East Studies, 27*(1), 29–37.

Woodward, Mark, Richard Martin and Dwi Atmaja. (1997). *Defenders of reason in Islam: Muʻtazilism from medieval school to modern symbol.* New York: Oxford Press.

Yasin, Khalid. (2006). *The purpose of life lectures.* Produced and recorded by 1-Islam Productions. http://www.1islam.net. Accessed on August 8, 2015.

Yezdani, İpek. (2011). 'Shari'a in Egypt is enough for us,' Muslim Brotherhood leader says. 23, May 2011. *Hürriyet Daily News.* http://www.hurriyetdailynews.com/default.aspx?pageid=438&n=8220shari8217a-law-in-egypt-is-enough-for-us8221-tells-a-muslim-brotherhood-leader-2011-05-23. Accessed on July 12, 2015.

Yilmaz, İhsan. (2013). "Kemalo-Islamism in full force. 23 October, 2013. *Today's Zaman.* http://www.todayszaman.com/columnist/i-hsan-yilmaz/kemalo-islamism-in-full-speed_329588.html. Accessed on February 27, 2016.

Youssef, Adham. (2015). "Giza schools burns alleged Islamist books," 14 April, 2015. *Daily News Egypt.* http://www.dailynewsegypt.com/2015/04/14/giza-school-burns-alleged-islamist-books/#dnePhoto/0/. Accessed on April 15, 2015.

Yusuf, Hamza. (2013). "Islamic state and Shari'a law are fantasies" [Lecture]. Part of the Deen Intensive Foundation Lecture Series: 2013 Videos and Resources, *Introduction to Logic.* https://www.youtube.com/watch?v=qraC3-VPi94. Accessed on February 19, 2015

Zakaria, Fareed. (2013). Egypt must reach out to the Islamists it is now jailing. *Time, 182* (4). http://content.time.com/time/magazine/article/0,9171,2147277,00.html. Accessed on November 7, 2016.

Zaman, Asad. (2015). "Crisis in Islamic economics: diagnosis and prescriptions," in H. A. El-Karanshawy, et al. (Eds.), *Islamic economic: Theory, policy and social justice* (pp.1–11). Doha, Qatar: Bloomsbury Qatar Foundation.

Zaman, Asad. (2013). *Islamic economics: A survey of the literature.* Islamabad, Pakistan: IRI Press.

Žižek, Slavoj, (2014). *Absolute recoil: towards a foundation of a new dialectical materialism.* London: Verso.

Index

A

'Abbāsid Dynasty, 47
Abdul Fattah al-Sisi, 237
Abu Bakr as-Saddiq, 120
Abū l-Ḥasan al-Ashʿarī, 38
Abu Ishaq al-Shatibi, 133
Abul ala Maududi, 7, 87
Accountability, 17, 43, 107, 147, 151, 157, 196, 198, 202
Adalet ve Kalkınma Partisi (AKP), 212
Administrative policy, 143
'aḥādīṯh, 20, 21, 38, 40, 41, 60, 61, 124–126
Ahmad al-Qalqashandi, 143
Ahmed ibn Ḥanbal, 36, 61
Ahmet Davutoğlu, 212
AKP-Kurdish relations, 225, 226
Al-ʿadl al-Ilāhī, 36
Alexis de Tocqueville, 93, 111
Al-Fārābī, 23, 31–33, 43–48, 50, 52, 91, 95
Al-fard, 83, 84
Al-Ghazālī, 23, 50, 51, 54, 65, 84
Ali Allawi, 18, 81
Alija Izetbegović, 7, 74, 98
Al-Ma'mun, 36
Al maṣlaḥa, 194, 201
Almoravid Dynasty, 47, 49
Al-qaḍā' wa al-qadr, 35
Al-Shabāb, 2
Al-shūrā, 153, 154
Al-Ṭabari, 174, 178
Al-wahn, 291
Al-wasaṭiyyah, 193, 194
Ancient Greek Thought, 21, 23, 46, 119
Andrew March, 2, 202
Anthony Downs, 9, 143
'aqīdah, 40, 41
ʿaql, 38, 39
2011 Arab Revolutions, 16, 117
Aristotle, 43, 47, 49, 79, 88, 91–95, 99, 105, 115, 119, 161, 162
Ashʿarī, 36, 38, 39, 42, 54
Atharī, 36, 40–42, 54, 81, 120
Authoritarianism, 5, 14, 119, 142, 175, 179, 276
Ayatollah Hussein-Ali Montazeri, 111
Ayatollah Khomeini, 7, 8, 65, 78, 114, 121, 199

B

Baghdad, 31, 32, 34, 36, 46, 52–54, 62, 143
Balkans, the, 213, 216, 217
Bāṭin, 41
Bay'ah, 36
Bid'ah, 20, 59
Bo Rothstein, 96, 138
Bosnia and Herzegovina, 43, 217
Bureaucracy, 23, 137, 143–148, 150, 151, 153, 185, 271

C

Censored press, 223
Charles Tilly, 85, 260
Civil Society, 5, 14, 18, 73, 142, 157, 158, 233, 259, 273, 275
Cold War, the, 16, 88, 194
Colonialism, 65, 71, 148, 180, 185, 265
Communication, 18, 19, 117, 148, 149, 151, 182, 183, 257, 290
Communicative action, 182, 183
Constitution, 6, 10, 53, 76, 79–81, 87, 91, 92, 97, 99, 122, 157, 162, 202, 235, 242, 243, 258, 259, 264, 267, 276
Corruption, 10, 20, 96, 120, 123, 141, 143, 145, 148, 151, 154, 155, 160, 162, 176, 199, 200, 252, 273, 276, 291
Critical theory, 54

D

Damascus, 55, 57–59, 251
Dar-al-Islam, 79
Democracy, 9–15, 23, 74, 88, 89, 115, 117, 131, 137, 138, 142, 153, 155, 156, 158, 160, 162, 178, 182, 185, 189, 218, 220, 221, 238, 254, 260, 261, 266, 276
Digital Era Governance (DEG), 151, 152
Diplomacy, 212
Discourse, 2–4, 6, 7, 12–14, 17, 20–22, 33, 35, 36, 38, 42, 43, 46, 47, 54, 58, 59, 61, 64, 65, 76, 82, 86, 91, 98, 106, 107, 113, 115, 116, 129, 137, 160, 176, 182–184, 202, 204, 212, 221, 224, 252, 253, 255, 262, 265, 273, 275, 286, 288–290
Douglass North, 117, 192
Dunyā, 287

E

Ebu Su'ud Efendi, 170
Economic development, 138–141, 190, 269
Economic justice, 9, 23, 189, 191, 197, 201, 202, 252, 289
Economics, 72, 117, 139, 191, 193, 194, 196, 197, 201
Edict of Gülhane, 146
Education, 16, 34, 72, 127, 170, 178, 180–182, 184, 203, 215, 233, 238, 239, 261
E-governance, 220
Egypt, 231–234, 236, 238, 240, 242–244, 258, 260, 261
Elections, 75, 138, 141, 153, 155, 158, 159, 219, 220, 222, 231, 233, 236, 241, 242, 244, 254, 256–258, 290
Electoral/Civil Rights, 15, 138–142, 155, 233, 235, 253, 255, 258
Enlightenment, 11, 13, 15, 21, 31, 75–77, 83, 86, 87, 162, 197, 281, 282, 285, 288
Ennahda, 129, 249, 250, 255–258, 261, 262
Ernesto Laclau, 4
Essences, 48, 56

Eva Bellin, 142
Extremism, 10, 17, 19, 219, 234, 239, 240

F
Fairness and justice, 12
Falāsifah, 50, 56
Faqīh, 8, 116, 122, 170
Fatima Mernissi, 173
Feminism, 185
Fetullah Gülen, 218, 224
Fitnah, 55, 78, 79, 120
Fiṭrah, 78
Fred Dallmayr, 13
Freedom and Justice Party (FJP), 233, 234
Free will, 35, 36, 39, 41, 77, 84, 86, 283, 284

G
Gaetano Mosca, 121
Gemeinschaft, 79
Gender equality, 175, 176, 178, 179, 218, 258
Gesellschaft, 79, 80
Globalization, 183, 212
Grand Transition Theories, 140
Great Chain of Being, 34, 35
Greek metaphysics, 51

H
Habib Bourguiba, 249, 254, 260
Hajj, 79
Halkların Demokratik Partisi (HDP), 219
Hamza Yusuf, 7
Ḥarām, 201
Harun Nasution, 43, 65
Hasan al Banna, 7
Hegemony, 4, 213, 269
Hijrah, 36, 80

Ḥudūd, 124, 125, 130

I
Ibn Qayyim al Jawziyyah, 120
Ibn Rushd, 23, 31, 33, 47–52, 64, 251
Ibn Sīnā, 31, 33, 34, 50
Ibn Taymiyyah, 32, 41, 49, 52, 55–59, 65, 78, 79
Ideology, 4, 5, 14, 117, 195, 255, 266, 267, 288
Ifrāṭ, 193
Ijmāʿ, 129, 147
Ijtihād, 20, 61, 62, 161
Ikhtīyār, 35
ʿImān, 40
Immanuel Kant, 83
Income inequality, 190
Individual morality, 5, 288
Indonesia, 6, 89, 140, 266, 267
Inequality, 72, 96, 179, 189, 196, 275
Institutional development, 138, 140, 142
Institutions, 138–143, 146, 153, 154, 158, 183, 202, 243, 245, 252, 285, 288, 290
1960 Internal Security Act (ISA), 273
International Islamic University of Malaysia (IIUM), 271
Intersectionality, 184
1979 Iranian Revolution, 8, 117, 176, 252
ISIS, 214, 215, 218, 225, 256
Islamic banking and insurance, 271
Islamic civilization, 18, 20, 43, 53, 54, 62
Islamic Golden Age, 32, 46, 47
Islamic governance, 6, 7, 81, 83, 84, 147, 156, 201, 203, 231, 270
Islamic governed state, 3, 5, 8, 9, 33, 48, 71, 73–75, 88, 92,

95, 105–107, 114, 115, 118,
120, 126, 128, 130, 131, 137,
138, 141, 142, 153–155, 157,
158, 161–163, 169, 171, 175,
176, 189, 191, 193, 197, 200,
202–204, 211, 218, 226, 236,
241, 243, 265, 268, 273, 274,
281, 285, 286, 288
Islamic Neo-Platonism, 43
Islamic Political Philosophy, 7
Islamism, 6, 244, 251, 274
Islamization, 270–273, 275
Istikhlaf, 287

J
Jahm ibn Ṣafwān, 36
Jamal al-Din al-Afghani, 52
James Allen, 281
Jean-Jacques Rousseau, 85
Jesus Christ, 57
Jihād, 117
John Esposito, 15, 88, 273
John Locke, 77, 78
John Voll, 1, 13, 244
Josiah Royce, 284
Jürgen Habermas, 182
Justice, 5, 12, 13, 38, 39, 81, 86, 88, 97, 106, 112, 117, 120, 125, 161, 191, 196, 201, 252, 270, 273

K
Kalām, 35, 41
Kasb, 39
Kemalism, 221, 266
Khadija al-Kūbra, 175
Khaled Abou El Fadl, 11, 60, 128
Khalīfah, 107
Khawārij, 42, 56, 58
Khilāfa, 94, 131, 287

Komiteh, 5
Kufr, 42, 62

L
Laws, 11, 12, 44, 60, 73, 79, 84, 87, 97, 116, 119, 123, 125, 127, 129, 130, 144, 156, 171, 234, 270, 274, 280
Leadership, 10, 18, 45, 53, 92, 96, 105–107, 115, 118, 123, 131, 143, 176, 197, 235, 237, 253, 285
Lebanon, 88, 141, 289
Legal rights, 118, 170
Legitimacy, 18, 39, 115, 126, 138, 154, 176, 195, 237, 242, 243, 253
Liberal democracy, 11, 15, 17, 75, 76, 138, 139, 155
Liberalism, 17, 72, 76, 80, 83, 84, 99, 138, 281
Liberty, 19, 21, 78, 80, 82
Literacy, 177, 181, 182
Literalism, 20, 42
Logic, 34, 38, 39, 41, 46, 49–51, 56, 65, 112
Love, 282, 283, 286, 291
Luca Ozzano, 255

M
Madhab, 41, 52, 61
Mahathir bin Mohammed, 268
Malaysia, 6, 23, 140, 265–276
Malek Bennabi, 253
Malik, 10, 107, 174, 196
M.A. Muqtedar Khan, 163
Manṣūr al-Ḥallāj, 57
Manus Midlarsky, 87
Maqāṣid, 61
Martin Buber, 283

INDEX 329

Maṣlaḥa, 61
Māturīdī, 36, 40–42
Max Weber, 9, 144, 244
Mecca, 63, 87
Medina Charter, the, 80
Meritocracy, 153
Michel Foucault, 3
Miḥnah, 36
Modernity, 13, 17, 19, 129, 218, 245, 288
Modernization, 97, 146, 148, 149, 178, 179, 181, 269, 274, 289
Mohammad ibn 'Abd al-Wahhāb, 32, 52, 59, 60, 62, 63, 239
Mohammed ibn Salih al-Uthaymeen, 1
Mohammed Iqbal, 2
Mohammed Morsi, 231, 234, 236, 239
Mongol and Tatar invasions, 55
Muslim Brotherhood, 129, 214, 231–234, 236, 238, 239, 243, 244, 256, 258
Muṭawwi'īn, 5
Mu'tazilah, 36, 38, 42, 56, 65, 81, 84, 283

N
Nader Hashemi, 14, 17, 75
Nasiruddin al-Albani, 178, 287
National Dialogue Quarter, 259
Negative liberty, 21, 22
Neo-Ottomanism, 213
New public management (NPM), 150
Niqab, 177, 178

O
Obedience, 50, 78, 121
Occasionalism, 43, 50
OIC Member States, 158, 184, 234
Ontology, 47

Oppression, 122, 180, 215, 239, 290
Orthodoxy and Orthopraxy, 20
Ottoman Empire, 130

P
Pancasila, 266, 267
Parti Islam Se-Malaysia, 272
Paul Kubicek, 218
Peripateticism, 33, 34
Pertubuhan Kebangsaan Melayu Bersatu, 269
Plato, 21, 22, 31, 34, 44, 105, 107, 111, 113, 122
Plotinus, 22, 23, 95, 122
Political parties, 6, 76, 203, 233, 243, 255, 267, 275
Polyarchy, 155
Popular sovereignty, 86
Positive liberty, 22
Postcolonial societies, 180
Power, 4, 6, 15, 22, 36, 39, 54, 55, 63, 74, 76, 86, 93, 111, 115, 117–119, 143, 152, 158, 175, 180, 211, 213, 217, 221, 225, 233, 240, 243, 245, 254, 255, 260, 265, 273, 276, 282, 288, 290
Power relations, 5, 213
Pragmatism, 249, 254, 258
Private property, 77, 80, 84, 195
Prophet Muhammad, 19, 80
Public administration, 9, 137, 144–147, 150–152, 161, 175, 275

Q
Qānūn, 130, 147
Quality of governance (QOG), 8, 151
Qur'ān, 2, 11, 12, 16, 35, 36, 38, 39, 41, 44, 45, 50, 55, 56, 60, 61, 76, 78, 79, 82, 87, 93, 97, 111,

113, 116, 124, 128, 142, 145, 154, 161, 169–171, 173, 177, 197, 285–287, 291
Qur'āniyyūn, 21

R
Rachid al-Ghannouchi, 73, 162, 191, 250
Recep Tayyip Erdoğan, 211
Reformers, 15, 60, 88, 290
Rentier-States, 260
Revelation, 11, 36, 40, 43, 79, 82, 87, 113, 185, 202, 273, 285
Reza Aslan, 122, 170
Ribā, 200, 271, 274
Richard Falk, 212, 226
Richard Rorty, 290
Robert Dahl, 9, 155

S
Saudi Arabia, 6, 20, 52, 63, 149, 159, 177, 243, 249, 260
Sayyid Qutb, 74
Secularism, 11, 14, 17, 75, 222, 224, 244
Self-discipline, 281, 282
Seymour Lipset, 9, 260
Seyyed Hossein Nasr, 22
Sharīʿah, 3, 8, 12, 71–73, 87–89, 116, 118, 122, 123, 125–131, 139, 147, 156, 157, 161, 234, 244, 271, 285, 286
Sherri Berman, 142, 157
Shīʿah, 2, 10, 38, 41, 65, 78, 115, 122, 131, 253, 289
Shirk, 57, 62
Social contract, 11, 76, 77, 80–82, 85–88
Social justice, 8, 13, 197, 252, 266, 269, 275

Social media, 18, 117–119
Soft power, 212
Steven Fish, 179
Ṣūfī, 41, 57
Sunnah, 12, 16, 44, 45, 61, 111, 128, 142, 147, 154, 161, 201–203
Sunni, 2, 10, 32, 40, 41, 52, 56, 61, 62, 78, 115, 126, 127, 253, 289
Syed Mohammed Naquib al-Attas, 78

T
Tafrīṭ, 193
Tafsīr, 171, 172
Taqlīd, 49, 50, 62
Taqwā, 40, 254
Tawḥīd, 122
Taʾwīl, 41
Technology, 18, 19, 148, 149
Theology, 20, 32, 34–36, 38, 40, 42, 54, 61
Thomas Jefferson, 162
Trade, 147, 193, 199, 216, 226, 259
Tunisia, 1, 6, 14, 23, 97, 98, 117, 129, 142, 155, 157, 249, 250, 252–260, 262
2014 Tunisian constitution, 259
Turkey, 6, 21, 23, 179, 195, 211–222, 224–226, 242, 243, 255, 266, 271, 276, 289

U
ʿUlamāʾ, 38, 62, 273
Ummah, 2, 73, 94, 125, 291
Ummatan wasaṭan, 194
ʿurf, 88, 129, 130, 147

V
Velāyat-e faqīh, 8, 114, 122

Violence, 7, 17, 58, 78, 118, 142, 144, 179, 240, 249, 254, 256, 258, 260, 268
Virtue, 21, 35, 95, 98, 106, 107, 114, 162, 197, 251
Vision 2020, 270

W

Wael Hallaq, 17, 56, 71, 83, 288
West, the, 10, 14–16, 18, 19, 22, 34, 47, 71, 74, 76, 81, 83, 84, 98, 118, 137, 147, 160, 177, 180, 182, 186, 212, 214, 234, 262, 286, 288

Women, 71, 122, 125, 169–173, 175–185, 191, 202, 238, 240, 245
Women's rights, 9, 23, 177, 184, 185, 261, 286

Z

Ẓāhir, 41
Zakāt, 79, 197, 286
Zero Problems with Neighbours policy, 214
Ziauddin Sardar, 4

The manufacturer's authorised representative in the EU is Springer Nature Customer Service Centre GmbH, Europaplatz 3, 69115 Heidelberg, Germany. If you have any concerns regarding our products, please contact ProductSafety@springernature.com

Printed and bound by CPI Group (UK) Ltd, Croydon, CR0 4YY
23/03/2026
02076736-0014